HIGHER

COMPUTING SCIENCE

Jane Paterson &
John Walsh

HODDER GIBSON
AN HACHETTE UK COMPANY

Publisher's note: Course assessment specifications for national courses may be updated from time to time. We make every effort to update books as soon as possible when this happens, but – especially if you're using an old copy of this book – it's always worth checking with your teacher or lecturer whether there have been any alterations since this book was printed. Alternatively, check the SQA website (www.sqa.org.uk) for current course assessment specifications. We also make every effort to ensure accuracy of content, but if you discover any mistakes, please let us know as soon as possible.

The Publishers would like to thank the following for permission to reproduce copyright material.

Photo credits

Images reproduced by permission of: **p.43** © Stefan Szeider, used under a CC-BY-SA 4.0 licence; **p.265** Newscast/Getty Images; **p.295** © Carlos Jones, used under a CC BY 4.0 licence; **p.302** *t* SamJonah/Alamy Stock Photo, *tr* Iconic Cornwall/Alamy Stock Photo, *b* PhotoEdit/Alamy Stock Photo; **p.303** bl Jeffrey Blackler/Alamy Stock Photo, *br* dpa picture alliance/Alamy Stock Photo; **p.305** Dawson Images/Alamy Stock Photo; **p.307** Finbarr Webster/Alamy Stock Photo.

Dilbert cartoons on pp. 3, 7, 78, 255, 323 used by permission of ANDREWS MCMEEL SYNDICATION. All rights reserved.

Acknowledgements

To Craig and Laura.

To Helen, Peter John, Mary, Sarah, Siobhan, Cecilia, Orla, Poppy, Michelle and Erin.

Every effort has been made to trace all copyright holders, but if any have been inadvertently overlooked, the Publishers will be pleased to make the necessary arrangements at the first opportunity.

Although every effort has been made to ensure that website addresses are correct at time of going to press, Hodder Education cannot be held responsible for the content of any website mentioned in this book. It is sometimes possible to find a relocated web page by typing in the address of the home page for a website in the URL window of your browser.

Hachette UK's policy is to use papers that are natural, renewable and recyclable products and made from wood grown in well-managed forests and other controlled sources. The logging and manufacturing processes are expected to conform to the environmental regulations of the country of origin.

Orders: please contact Hachette UK Distribution, Hely Hutchinson Centre, Milton Road, Didcot, Oxfordshire, OX11 7HH. Telephone: +44 (0)1235 827827. Email education@hachette.co.uk
Lines are open from 9 a.m. to 5 p.m., Monday to Friday. You can also order through our website: www.hoddereducation.co.uk.

ISBN: 978 1 5104 8381 1

© Jane Paterson and John Walsh 2021

First published in 2021 by

Hodder Gibson, an imprint of Hodder Education
An Hachette UK Company
211 St Vincent Street
Glasgow, G2 5QY

www.hoddereducation.co.uk

Impression number   5 4 3 2 1

Year   2025 2024 2023 2022 2021

Cover photo ©phonlamaiphoto - stock.adobe.com

Illustrations by Integra Software Services Pvt. Ltd., Pondicherry, India

Typeset by Integra Software Services Pvt. Ltd., Pondicherry, India

Printed in Italy

A catalogue record for this title is available from the British Library.

We are an approved supplier on the Scotland Excel framework.

Schools can find us on their procurement system as: Hodder & Stoughton Limited t/a Hodder Gibson.

Contents

Answers available online at https://www.hoddergibson.co.uk

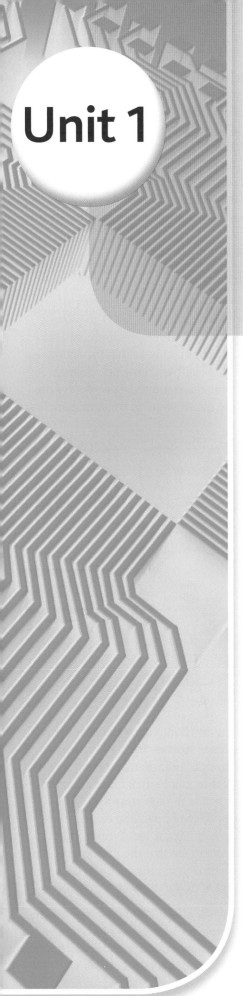

Unit 1

Software design and development

Chapter 1 Development methodologies

This chapter looks at and compares two different software development methodologies.

The following topics are covered:

- Describe and compare the development methodologies:
  - iterative development process.
  - agile methodologies.

Development methodologies

When creating new programs or applications (apps), software developers follow a development methodology to design the software from start to finish.

The first of these is the iterative development process.

The iterative development process

The iterative development process is better known as the Waterfall development methodology, Waterfall life-cycle or Waterfall model and follows a traditional, linear approach which consists of seven stages as shown in Figure 1.1 on the next page. This sequence of steps, beginning with analysis, is known as the software development process. It is iterative in nature, meaning that steps can be revisited at any point in the life-cycle of the development process (multiple times if necessary) if new information becomes available and changes need to be made or errors discovered.

Looking at and understanding a problem is called 'analysis'. In the Waterfall model, the software developers need to know up front and in detail exactly what the client wants the software to do. The design phase involves working out a detailed series of steps to solve the problem. Once a solution to a problem has been worked out, it needs to be turned into instructions for the computer (a program). This is implementation. The program must then be tested to make sure that it does not contain any mistakes which would prevent it from working properly. A description of what each part of the program does, i.e. documentation, should also be included. Evaluation is the process which measures how well the solution fulfils the original requirements. Maintenance involves changing the program, often quite some time after it has been written.

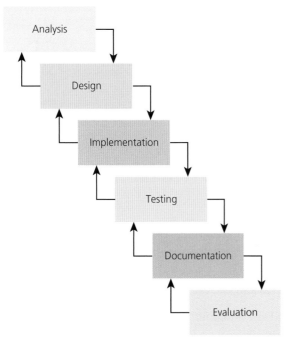

Figure 1.1 An iterative development process (the Waterfall model)

Documentation is needed at each stage of the iterative development process.

- Analysis: the documentation at this stage consists of the **software specification**. This is important because it is the basis of all of the remaining stages of the software development process. It is usually a legally binding document (see Chapter 2 for more information).
- Design: the documentation consists of the description of the program design in an appropriate design notation and the design of the user interface. This description is important because it is the 'bridge' between the software specification and the code.
- Implementation: the documentation at this stage is the program listing(s), complete with internal commentary. This is important because it explains the purpose of each part of the code, and therefore eases the process of maintenance.
- Testing: the documentation at this stage includes the test plan and the results of testing. This is important because it demonstrates whether or not the program does what it was designed to do.
- Documentation: this stage has the technical guide and the user guide. These are important because they explain how to install and operate the software.
- Evaluation: the acceptance test report, the results of evaluation against suitable criteria. This is important because it means that the program has been written

to the satisfaction of the client and therefore the software company can be paid for their work.

- Maintenance: documentation at this stage is a log of changes made to the program code, together with the date and the new version number of the program. This is important because it will be updated constantly throughout the life of the software in order to inform programmers about earlier changes that have been made. Maintenance is beyond the scope of Higher Computing Science but is included here for completeness.

Agile methodologies

Agile methodologies belong to a wider category of rapid application development methodologies. The process of designing a program using Agile development is to produce working software quickly so that the client can test it and then give feedback, at which point it can be altered and refined as required. It works on the principal of delivering the software in small increments instead of all at once.

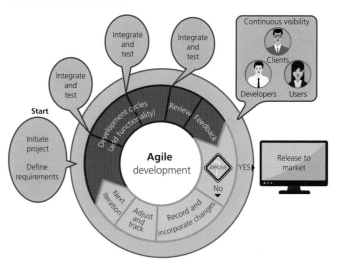

Figure 1.2 Agile methodology

Each project is broken down into what the client needs, otherwise known as **'user stories'**. Each of these user stories is part of the overall Agile plan and encourages the software developers to talk to their clients about what they would like to see in their software. The plan should include an idea of how long each of these stories will take to develop. These are prioritised in conjunction with the client (so that the important requirements are delivered first) and included in the plan for the development of the software.

Teams will normally work in short **'sprints'** to produce working prototypes which can be tested by the client. A sprint is a short, fixed time period (typically two weeks) during which planning, analysis, design, implementation and testing are completed. At the end of the sprint, the prototype is ready to be tested by the client (acceptance testing). The client will then be able to give regular feedback and alterations can be made when required. The plan itself can be updated when and where required.

Figure 1.3 User stories

Often by the time the project comes to an end, all the client's requirements may not have been built, and there will be one of two outcomes. Either the client may opt for software which has fewer features or the software development team may ask for more money to complete the software as originally required.

The development of software using Agile methodology is a constant process of analysis, design, implementation and testing. This means it is iterative as each of the stages will be visited multiple times as the software is refined. When what can be delivered differs from was originally requested, Agile allows plans to be changed. This is known as 'adaptive planning'.

Agile methodology vs. Waterfall model

The Waterfall model is an older approach to developing software and is based on the idea that each of the phases of the development life-cycle are discrete parts which should be completed in turn. It gives both client and developer a clear path as to how each project should progress.

The main emphasis of Agile development is speed. Project goals are determined quickly and all phases are iterated continuously rather than individually, so that the software is developed and adapted quickly as shown in Figure 1.4.

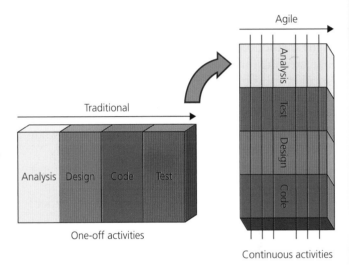

Figure 1.4 Agile methodology vs. Waterfall model

Advantages of the Waterfall model

The Waterfall model is best suited to larger projects and large teams of developers with a long lead time. As the client is usually less involved during development, they need to know exactly what they want at the start of the process because it forms part of the legally binding agreement. Due to its tendency to focus on quality of software over speed of development, the software is tested more fully and the software produced tends to have less bugs. Projects that follow the Waterfall model are generally finished on time and within the set budget. Milestones set at the start of the project give both developer and client an easy way to track its progress.

Disadvantages of the Waterfall model

The linear setup of the Waterfall model is its main failing as there can be no deviation from the plan once it has commenced. Because requirements are only sought at the start of the project, clients are not continuously involved. So, if a client does not have a clear idea about what the software should do and their needs change over the course of the project, there is a strong possibility that the software delivered will not then meet their requirements.

Once the software has reached the testing phase, changes can be difficult to make. If changes then do need to be made, this can take more time and will cost more money.

To try to mitigate this, client feedback can be built in to the phases of the life-cycle so that changes can be made.

Advantages of Agile methodology

Agile methodology is best suited to smaller projects, like creating (or frequently updating) apps, with smaller teams of developers. The client is involved at all stages of the development of the software and feedback is sought constantly. This means that the software developed is more likely to be exactly what the client wants even if they were not completely certain of the requirements at the start of the project. It also allows the client an element of flexibility in that, if they change their minds or would like other features included, adding them does not present too

much of a challenge to the developers. Because of the constant iterative nature of Agile methodology, improvements to the software can be incorporated after each cycle.

The main focus of Agile development is to deliver software at speed, which makes it perfect for projects which are required quickly.

Disadvantages of Agile methodology

At the start of the Agile process, there tends not to be a legally binding agreement due to the changing nature of client's requirements. It is also not suited to large projects and large teams. The client needs to be prepared to spend a large amount of time being involved with the project as their involvement is required throughout.

Strict sprint deadlines can be a huge disadvantage and can result in a project not being completed. Either the customer pays more for the project to be completed, or they simply have to accept what has been developed, however much reduced in scope. The frequent updates can be difficult to track and need strict control over the version numbers given to each iteration or update.

CHECK YOUR LEARNING
Now answer questions 1–10 below

QUESTIONS

1 State what is meant by the term 'iteration'.
2 State why a development stage might need to be revisited.
3 Describe each stage in the software development life-cycle.
   a) Analysis
   b) Design
   c) Implementation
   d) Testing
   e) Documentation
   f) Evaluation
4 State the category of methodologies to which Agile belongs.
5 Describe what is meant by the term 'user story'.
6 How does the developer prioritise the order in which to develop the user stories?
7 Describe how working prototypes are produced by the developers.
8 a) Describe a situation where a client's requirements may not have been met.

b) What two options may the client have if the requirements have not been met?
9 State what is meant by 'adaptive planning'.
10 Complete the table of iterative (Waterfall method) vs. Agile methodology. The first line has been completed for you.

Iterative	Agile
Suited to large software projects	Suited to small software projects

KEY POINTS

- Two types of development methodologies are iterative (Waterfall) and Agile.
- The Waterfall model follows a traditional, linear approach.
- The iterative methodology means that steps can be revisited at any point in the life-cycle.
- Analysis is looking at and understanding a problem.
- Design is working out a series of steps to solve a problem.
- Implementation is turning a design into a computer program.
- Testing makes sure that a computer program does not contain any mistakes.
- Documentation is a description of what each part of the program does.
- Evaluation ensures that the software fulfils the original software specification.
- Agile methodologies belong to a wider category of rapid application development methodologies.
- Agile works on the principal of delivering the software in small increments instead of all at once.
- Each project is broken down into user stories.
- User stories are prioritised by the client and developer, so that the important requirements are delivered first.
- Teams work in short sprints to produce working prototypes which are tested by the client.
- A sprint is a short, fixed time period typically lasting two weeks.
- The development of software using Agile methodology is a constant process of analysis, design, implementation and testing.
- Adaptive planning allows the requirements to be changed on request.
- Iterative is best suited to large projects which require a large team of developers.
- Analysis in the iterative process produces a legally binding contract.
- Software produced using an iterative method is usually high quality and bug free.
- Iterative projects tend to finish on time and within budget.
- The client has limited involvement during the entire iterative process.
- Changes can become more difficult and expensive as the project progresses in iterative projects.
- Agile is best suited to small software projects and requires a small team of developers.
- There is no legally binding contract in the Agile process.
- The client is involved throughout the Agile process.
- Changes can be easily made as the Agile process progresses.
- Agile projects can run over time, are not always completed and can cost more money to finish.
- Version control is important to keep track of updates.

Chapter 2 Analysis

This chapter considers how to analyse a problem to help create the software specification.

The following topics are covered:

- Identify the:
  - purpose
  - scope
  - boundaries and functional requirements of a problem that relates to the design and implementation at this level, in terms of:
    - inputs
    - processes
    - outputs.

Analysis

Analysis first of all involves reading and understanding a problem. If you are set a problem in class, you should read the problem several times and think about it carefully. It often helps to write out the problem in your own words. Sometimes the problem contains parts which are not very clear, and you will have to make some assumptions about what you think is meant by these parts of the problem.

Eventually you will get to the stage where you will be able to create a precise software specification. The software specification should contain what the software is supposed to do but does not indicate how this is to be achieved.

It is very important that the software specification is correct, since mistakes at this stage can be very costly to put right later on in the software development process. The software specification is a clear unambiguous statement of the problem and forms the basis of a legal contract.

Here is an example of what could happen if a software specification is not correct:

A farmer, as can be seen in commissioned a software company to write a database program to store details of his herd of cattle. The maximum size was to be 1000 records. Cow number 1000 had a calf. The farmer entered the new calf's details into the program and the program crashed. Who was to blame? Was it the software company for not anticipating that the herd of cattle would increase in size or was it the farmer's fault for agreeing to the maximum size of 1000 records? In any case, if the program matched the software specification correctly, then the software company would still be entitled to be paid for their work.

Figure 2.1 The software specification forms the basis of a legal contract between the client and the software company

Figure 2.2 Numbers

The analysis phase can be broken down into a series of discrete sections.

Purpose

The purpose of the problem is stating what the software should do once completed. The detail for this is written in the scope, boundaries and functional requirements.

Scope

The scope should state clearly and concisely what the software must do, i.e. specific project goals. It should also state the start and end dates, cost, deliverables (including but not limited to, the design of the software, the software itself, results of testing and the test plan), milestones and deadlines. A milestone is a completed step in a software development project. It means that developers know what work is due and by which date.

If the project is poorly managed and changes are constantly made, then **scope creep** can occur. This usually happens if the scope is not properly defined or documented. It is also known as 'requirement creep', 'function creep' or 'kitchen sink syndrome'.

The scope should also define the boundaries of the software.

Figure 2.3 Scope creep

Boundaries

Boundaries help to clarify what the software should and should *not* do. They should also state any assumptions that are being made about what the client requires.

WORKED EXAMPLE

Consider the following simple problem outline:

Average problem: Write a program which calculates and displays the average of a set of numbers.

This could hardly be described as a precise software specification. If you, as a programmer, were given this task you would need to ask some questions before you could begin to design a solution.

Questions you may ask about the Average problem:

- How many numbers are in the set?
- What is the maximum value of a number?
- Are numbers to be whole numbers (integers) or numbers with a fractional part (real numbers)?
- To how many significant figures should the average value be displayed?
- How are numbers to be obtained as input to the program (i.e should the program ask the user to enter each number every time the program is run)?

- Are any of the numbers entered to be stored after the program is complete?
- What output device(s) are to be used (i.e. display on screen or hard copy to printer)?

If there is no one available to ask for clarification of a problem, then you should examine the problem carefully and write down some assumptions.

For the Average problem, these assumptions might be:

- The maximum amount of numbers is 10.
- The minimum value of a number is 1.
- The maximum value of a number is 100.
- All the numbers are whole numbers, apart from the average, which has to be displayed correct to two decimal places.

Putting these assumptions together with the original Average problem, would give a more precise description of the scope and boundaries.

Functional requirements

The functional requirements describe how the software should function or perform. They involve identifying the problem **inputs**, the **process**(es) and the problem **outputs**. The best way to do this is to create a table with the three headings: Input, Process and Output and use the information given in the problem as shown in Table 2.1.

Input	Process	Output
A maximum of 10 numbers (integers), within a range of 0 to 100.	Calculate the average (sum the numbers and divide the total by the amount of numbers).	Display the average value (a real number, correct to two decimal places).

Table 2.1 Example table for the Average problem

CHECK YOUR LEARNING

Now answer questions 1–3 below

QUESTIONS

1 Why does the software specification have the status of a legal contract?
2 Give an example of what could happen if the software specification was not correct.
3 Analyse the following problem outlines and produce a precise software specification by reporting on:
   • the purpose of the software.
   • scope and boundaries of the software.
   • functional requirements of the software.
   You should ensure that you include any assumptions that need to be made and identify the problem inputs, process(es) and outputs as part of the functional requirements.
   a) Write a program which will ask the user for two numbers and give their sum (+), product (*) and quotient (/).
   b) Write a program which will take in a word of up to 15 letters and display it on the screen backwards.
   c) Write a program which will only allow the user to enter words consisting of five letters and display them on the screen.
   d) Write a program which will calculate how fast a cyclist is travelling if you input their time taken to travel 100 metres.
   e) Write a program which will accept a temperature in degrees Celsius and output the temperature in either degrees Fahrenheit or degrees Kelvin as required by the user. (Kelvin = Celsius + 273.15; deg F = 9/5 Celsius + 32)
   f) Write a program which will capitalise the first character of a word entered by the user (i.e. john to John).
   g) Write a program which will calculate the length of one side of a right-angled triangle if the lengths of the other two sides is input (Pythagoras).
   h) Write a program which will change a student's percentage test mark into a letter grade (A–E).
   i) Write a program which will calculate the area of a triangle if you enter its base and height. (area = 1/2 base × height)
   j) Write a program which will take in a message and display it on the centre of the screen.

KEY POINTS

- Analysis involves reading and understanding a problem.
- The purpose of the problem is what the software should do once completed.
- The software specification should contain what the software is supposed to do but does not indicate how this is to be achieved.
- The scope should state clearly and concisely what the software must do.
- Boundaries help to clarify what the software should and should *not* do.
- Boundaries should also state any assumptions that are being made about what the client requires.

- The functional requirements describe how the software should function or perform.
- The functional requirements should define inputs, processes and outputs to the program.
- Inputs should clearly state what data must be provided for the program to function.
- Processes should determine what has to be done with the data entered.
- Outputs should show the results of the program when it is run.

Chapter 3 Design

This chapter considers how to turn the software specification created at the analysis stage into a design for a program.

The following topics are covered:

- Identify the data types and structures required for a problem that relates to the implementation at this level.
- Read and understand designs of solutions to problems at this level, using the following design techniques:
  - pseudocode
  - structure diagrams.
- Exemplify and implement efficient design solutions to a problem, using a recognised design technique, showing:
  - top-level design
  - the data flow
  - refinements.
- Describe, exemplify and implement user-interface design, in terms of input and output, using a wireframe.

Simple data types and structures

When designing the solution to a problem, the data types and structures to be used in the solution should be identified so that the software developer knows the type of data each variable will store.

The data types stored by a program may be a number, a character, a string, a date, an array, a sound sample, a video clip or indeed, any kind of data. Some high-level languages, such as C++, allow programmers to specify their own data types; these are called user-defined data types.

Some of the more important data types are listed below:

- **Alphanumeric data**: may include letters, digits and punctuation. It includes both the character and string data types. **Character data** is a single character represented by the character set code, e.g. ASCII (American Standard Code for Information Interchange). **String data** is a list of characters, e.g. a word in a sentence.
- **Numeric data**: may consist of **real data** or **integer data**. Real or float data includes *all* numbers, both whole and fractional. Integer data is a subset of real data which includes only whole numbers, either positive or negative.
- **Date data**: is data in a form representing a valid date, e.g. 29/2/2020 is valid date data, 30/2/2020 is not.
- **Boolean** or **logical data**: may only have two values, *true* or *false*. Boolean data is used in a program's control structures.
- **Sample data**: consists of digitally recorded **sound data** (e.g. MP3) and **video data** (e.g. a video clip MPEG). These are complex data types which contain enough data to allow a subprogram or application to reproduce the original data.

One factor which may influence a programmer's choice of software development environment is the range of data types available. For example, C++ has at least six different numeric data types, whereas some versions of the BASIC language may only have the two numeric data types described above.

Data structures include arrays, records and arrays of records. More detailed information on data structures can be found in Chapter 4.

WORKED EXAMPLE 1

Take the Average problem we discussed in Chapter 2 and Table 2.1 from the Functional Requirements. We would need to consider which data types and structures would be suitable for storing the data in this problem.

We know from the input part of the functional requirements that 10 numbers are required. If we assume that those 10 numbers are whole numbers, then we could say that the data type for input is integer.

A running total would be required total the numbers and since the input is an integer so too must be the total.

Output for the program is a little easier as it would always be a real (float) number unless the output is a multiple of 10.

Data types and structures

number, total: integer

average: real (float)

Designing the solution to a problem

Once you have a precise software specification, then you can begin to design your solution to the problem.

In a normal problem-solving situation, you should always ask these questions:

- Is writing a program the best way to solve this problem?
- Can it be solved more easily another way?

Returning to the Average problem again, if the average is to be found for only *one* set of numbers, i.e. as a one-off, then it would probably be much more efficient to use a calculator and work out the average that way, rather than entering the numbers into a computer. However, if you have to work out many different averages for lots of sets of numbers, then it would be worthwhile using a computer software solution.

If you decide to use a computer to solve the problem, then you should begin by looking at the highest level of software you have available.

For instance, would it be possible to solve this problem using a general-purpose application package such as a spreadsheet or a database rather than by writing a program in a high-level language?

How could you use a spreadsheet to solve the *Average Problem*?

Answer: create a new spreadsheet document; enter the set of numbers into a column or a row and enter the formula =AVERAGE(cell range) into an unused cell.

However, in this unit on software design and development, you are concerned with producing a computer solution to a problem using some kind of programming language. Your approach to problem solving should therefore take account of this.

Program **design** is the process of planning the solution. The design of the program is very important for its success. Time spent at this stage is very worthwhile and can reduce the chance of errors appearing later on in the solution.

Consider the many home improvement, DIY and gardening make-over programs which appear on television. Their success appears magical as a team of 'experts' descends on a person's home and completes the conversion in two or three days. Despite how casual it may appear, all these transformations are planned out to the last detail. The 'experts' have all visited the homes weeks, if not months, in advance, and have gone away and drawn up detailed plans for the conversion.

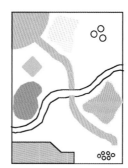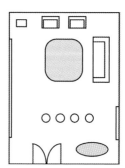

Figure 3.1 Garden plans and room plans

It is just the same with programming: the more time you spend thinking about and planning the design of the program, the less time you will spend wondering why your program does not work as it should.

Modular design

Modular design is a method of organising a large computer program into self-contained parts called **modules**, which can be developed simultaneously by different programmers or programming teams. Modules are specially constructed so that they can be designed, coded and maintained independently of one another. Some modules may be linked to other modules and some may be separate programs. **Top-down design** and **bottom-up design** are both forms of modular design.

Top-down design

Top-down design involves looking at the whole problem (top) and breaking it down into smaller, easier to solve, sub-problems. Each sub-problem may be further sub-divided into smaller and simpler sub-problems (modules). This process of breaking down sub-problems into yet smaller steps is called **stepwise refinement**. Eventually the stage is reached where each sub-problem can no longer be broken down and the refinement process comes to a halt.

At this point each small step can be translated into a single line of program code.

When stepwise refinement is complete, then you have created an **algorithm**, which is a sequence of instructions that can be used to solve a problem.

Figure 3.2 Breaking down a problem ...

Bottom-up design

The bottom-up method of designing a solution to a problem begins with the lowest levels of detail and works upwards to the highest level of the idea. It seems strange to think that it is sensible to work towards something without really knowing what that something is before you begin. However, using a bottom-up design approach means writing modules or procedures first. This approach is sometimes called '**prototyping**', where you construct a procedure separately before joining it together with the rest of a program.

Design techniques

The way of representing the program design or algorithm is called the **design technique** (or **design notation**). The programmer has a choice of design techniques. Common design techniques include drawing a **flow chart**, a **structure diagram** or writing **pseudocode**. Some design techniques use graphical objects such as icons to represent the design of a program. However, in Higher Computing Science, we look only at pseudocode and structure diagrams.

Pseudocode

Pseudocode is the name given to the language used to define problems and sub-problems before they are changed into code in a high-level computer language. Pseudocode uses ordinary English terms rather than the special keywords used in high-level languages. Pseudocode is therefore language independent.

Here is some pseudocode showing part of the design of one possible solution to the Average problem. This pseudocode shows the top-level design with stepwise refinements.

Algorithm

```
1 initialise
2 take in numbers
3 calculate average value
4 display average value

Refine sub-problem 2:

2.1 loop REPEAT
2.2   add one to counter
2.3   ask user for a number
2.4   take in a number
2.5 UNTIL counter equals amount required

Refine sub-problem 2.4:

2.4.1 loop REPEAT
2.4.2   get number from user
2.4.3   IF number is outwith range THEN
        display error message
2.4.4 UNTIL number is within range
```

Pseudocode is very useful when you are programming in languages like LiveCode or Python, because it fits in neatly with the structure of the code. The main steps in the algorithm relate directly to (in fact, become) the main program, the refinements of each sub-problem become the code in the procedures. (See Chapter 6 for more examples of pseudocode.)

WORKED EXAMPLE 2

Implementation

Suppose that your chosen software development environment is a high-level programming language such as Python. Let's look at how you might choose to implement part of the solution to the Average problem in Python.

Design (Pseudocode)

```
2.1 loop WHILE not equal to amount
    required
2.2   add one to counter
2.3   ask user for a number between 1
      and 100
2.4   take in a number between
      1 and 100
```

Python (actual program code)

```
def takeInNumbers():
    while counter != amount_required:
        counter= counter+1
        print('Please enter a number
        between 1 and 100')
        number=checkInput(number)
```

Pseudocode is useful for representing the design of the types of problem that you are likely to face in this unit.

In a more complex professional programming situation, or in a much larger project, structure diagrams may be more appropriate.

Structure diagrams

Structure diagrams use linked boxes to represent the different sub-problems within a program. The boxes in a structure diagram are organised to show the level or hierarchy of each sub-problem within the solution. In general, structure diagrams follow a left to right sequence.

Table 3.1 shows the function of each symbol in a structure diagram.

Symbol	Name	Description
	Process	This represents an action to be taken, a function to run, or a process to be carried out, e.g. a calculation.
or	Loop	The loop symbol indicates that a process has to be repeated either a fixed number of times or until a condition is met.

Symbol	Name	Description
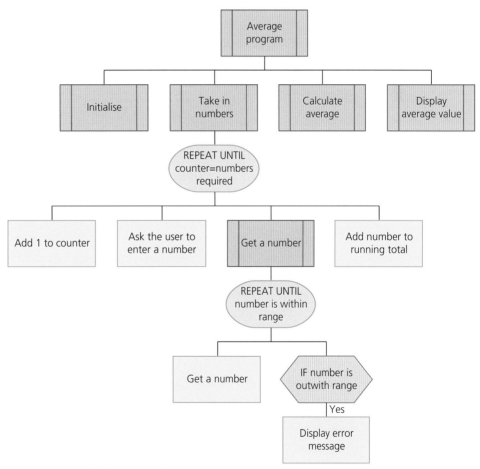	Pre-defined process	This symbol describes a process that contains a series of steps. It is most commonly used to indicate a sub-process or subroutine but could also indicate a pre-defined function like the random number function.
	Selection	This symbol shows that there may be different outcomes depending on user input or the result of an earlier process.

Table 3.1 Structure diagram symbols

Figure 3.3 shows one possible design for the Average problem from Chapter 2.

Figure 3.3 Structure diagram

Data flow

Giving some indication of the **flow of data** between modules of your program is important. Some design techniques allow data flow to be shown clearly. Pseudocode uses the terms in:, out: and in-out: to represent the flow of data used in subprograms. For Higher, we will only use in: and out:. Structure diagrams use up and down arrows to indicate data flow into and out of subprograms.

Describing the data flow

Pseudocode

It is necessary to describe the data flow in the design in order to work out how the data should be passed between the main program and any subprograms and between the subprograms themselves.

Consider the following algorithm and refinement, which describe a solution to the problem:

Count the number of five letter words in a list.

Top level

Algorithm	Data flow

```
1 initialise                              (out: noFiveLetterWords)
2 take in list of words and count number  (in: noFiveLetterWords; out:
  of five letter words                    noFiveLetterWords)
3 display result                          (in: noFiveLetterWords)
```

Refinement

```
1.1 set number of five letter words to zero
2.1 loop REPEAT
2.2   take in a word
2.3   IF the word has five letters THEN add one to the
      number of five letter words
2.4 UNTIL the word "stop" is entered
3.1 display number of words with five letters
```

The data being passed in the above example is the variable **noFiveLetterWords**, which, at the end of the program, will contain the value representing the number of words found to have five letters.

Remember: 'in' and 'out' when referring to data flow within a program are between procedures; they do not correspond to program inputs and outputs.

Structure diagrams

The structure diagram in Figure 3.3 below shows a solution to the same problem. Notice how the in and out data flow is indicated. Data flowing into a procedure or function is indicated with an upward facing arrow. Data flowing out of a procedure or function is indicated with a downward facing arrow.

Top level

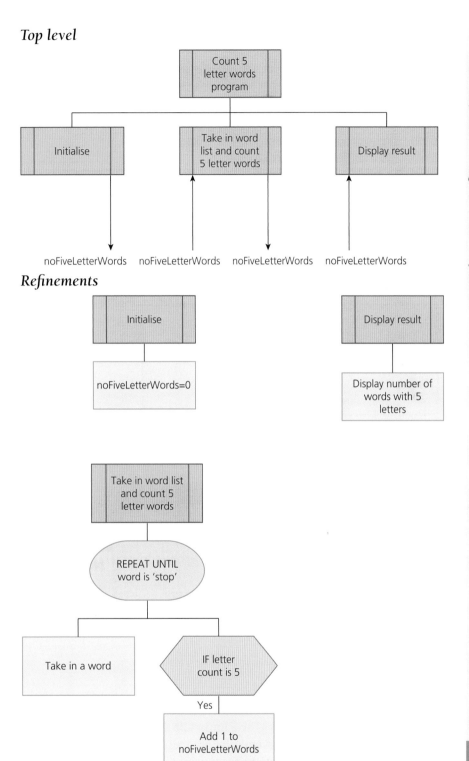

Figure 3.4 Top-level design with refinements and data flow

When indicating data flow for arrays, empty brackets should be included after the name of the array in both pseudocode and structure diagrams.

WORKED EXAMPLE 3

Consider the following problem for both design techniques.

Find all the qualifying bakers in a baking contest. Each baker can score a maximum of 70 marks. Bakers must score over 70% to qualify.

Data types and structures required

- bakerName – array of type string
- score – array of type integer
- percent – array of type real (float)

Example of arrays in pseudocode

1 Get baker's name and score (out: bakerName(), score())
2 Calculate and store percentage (in:score(); out:percent())
3 Search for and display qualifiers (in:bakerName(), percent())

Arrays in structure diagram

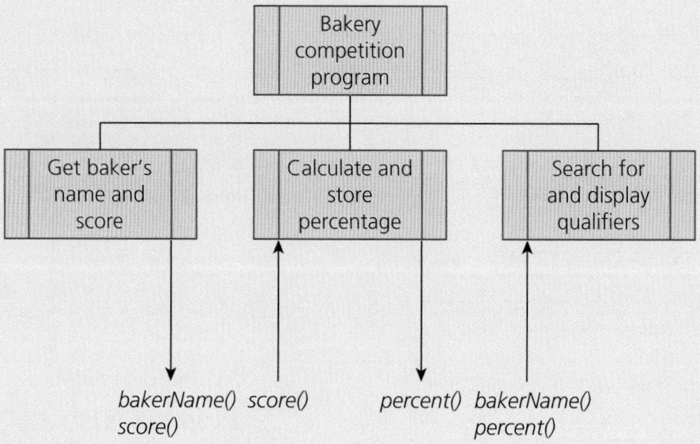

Figure 3.5 Data flow – arrays

Data flow in tables

In tabular format, the data flow for the baking competition would look like that shown in Table 3.2.

Step	IN/OUT	Data flow
1	IN	
	OUT	bakerName[], score[]
2	IN	score[]
	OUT	percent[]
3	IN	bakerName[], percent[]
	OUT	

Table 3.2 Data flow

NOTE

An array has a square bracket when data flow is written in this way.

User-interface design

When designing the program, it is also important to design how the user will interact with the program. To do this, either a hand- or computer-drawn wireframe should be created to show how this will happen. In programming, a wireframe is a diagram or sketch of the input and output screens. The wireframe design for programs is designed in a similar fashion to that of a wireframe for a website and should contain placeholders where data is to be input and output. The wireframe should also include prompts and labels next to where data is to be displayed and any buttons that may be required.

This is especially useful for Agile methodologies and is important as it allows the client to see how they will interact with the program. It means that any changes can be made at this early stage before the software is prototyped.

Figure 3.6 shows a simple example of a wireframe for the Average program.

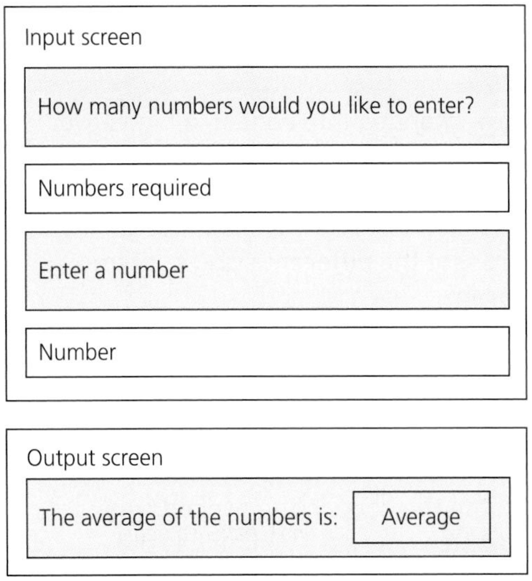

Input screen

How many numbers would you like to enter?

Numbers required

Enter a number

Number

Output screen

The average of the numbers is: | Average

Figure 3.6 Wireframe example

QUESTIONS

1 State two forms of modular design.
2 Which modular design begins with writing modules or procedures?
3 Name and describe one design technique with which you are familiar.
4 Why is pseudocode said to be language independent?
5 Name one graphical design technique and draw a diagram of it.
6 What terms does pseudocode use to indicate the flow of data between program modules?
7 Why is it helpful to describe the data flow in a program alongside your chosen design technique?
8 Design solutions to the following problems using the technique indicated next to the problem. Your solution should include data types and structures, data flow at the top level and refinements as appropriate.
   a) Structure diagram: Design a program which will ask the user for two whole numbers between 1 and 10 inclusive and give their sum (+), product (*) and quotient (/).
   b) Pseudocode: Design a program which will accept a temperature in degrees Celsius and output the temperature in either degrees Fahrenheit or degrees Kelvin as required by the user. (Kelvin = Celsius + 273.15; deg F = 9/5 Celsius + 32).
   c) Structure diagram: Design a program which will ask for and store 10 song names and their chart positions and will then display only the top five song names and positions. Chart positions should be validated to be between 1 and 10.
   d) Pseudocode: Design a program which will read 100 holiday destinations from a file and the number of visitors per year. The output

should display the number of destinations whose visitor numbers are in excess of 10,000 per year (counting occurrences algorithm, see Chapter 6).
9 Design algorithms for the following problem outlines using either pseudocode or structure diagrams, showing data types and structures, data flow and refinements as appropriate.
   a) Take in a first name and a second name and display them.
   b) Calculate the area of a circle given the radius as input (πr^2).
   c) Take in ten test marks and calculate the average mark.
   d) Take in a sentence and display it 50 times.
   e) Take in a name and ask the user how many times the name is to be displayed and then display the name.
   f) Take in five names using a loop with a terminating value.
   g) A pass or fail algorithm for up to 20 pupils' marks.
   h) Input validation for months 1–12 with a suitable message.
   i) A quiz with 10 questions and a score at the end.
   j) Calculate the result of doubling a number 10 times. The number should start at 1.
   k) The number of weeds on a football pitch doubles every month. If there are 200 weeds today, how many weeds will there be in a year?
   l) You have a bank account with £100 in it. How much money will you have in ten years if the annual interest is 5%?
10 Design a suitable user interface for one of the problems in question 9.

KEY POINTS

- Program design is the process of planning the solution.
- The data types stored by a program may be a number, a character, a string, a date, a file, an array, a sound sample, a video clip or indeed, any kind of data.
  - Numeric data may consist of real type data or integer type data.
  - Real type data includes ALL numbers, both whole and fractional.
  - Integer type data is a subset of real type data which includes only whole numbers, either positive or negative.
  - Boolean or Logical data may only have two values, *true* or *false*. Boolean data is used in a program's control structures.
- Data structures include arrays, records and arrays of records.
- The way of representing the program design or algorithm is called the design notation.
- Pseudocode is the name given to the language used to define problems and sub-problems before they are changed into code in a high-level computer language.
- Pseudocode fits neatly with the structure of the code.
- Structure diagrams, like flow charts, use linked boxes to represent the different sub-problems within a program.
- The boxes in a structure diagram are organised to show the level of each sub-problem within the solution.
- The main steps in the algorithm become the main program and the refinements of each sub-problem become the code in the procedures.
- Data flow indicates how data will be passed between sub-problems in a program.
- Data flow in pseudocode is shown by using the words in: and out: with the associated variable.
- Data flow in a structure diagram is indicated using arrows.
- A wireframe is a diagram or sketch used to represent the appearance and function of the input and output screens within a program.

Chapter 4 Implementation (data types and structures)

This chapter describes the basic data types and structures used for programming in any language.

The following topics are covered:

- Describe, exemplify and implement appropriately the following structures:
  - parallel 1D arrays
  - records
  - arrays of records.

Data types and structures

Variables

Data is stored in a computer's memory in storage locations. Each storage location in the computer's memory has a unique address. A variable is the name that a programmer uses to identify a storage location. (This is much more convenient than using a memory address; compare 'number' with 90987325.) By using a variable name, a programmer can store, retrieve and handle data without knowing what the data will be. Variable names, procedure and function names are sometimes also called identifiers, because they are used to identify that particular item. (See Chapter 5 for more information on procedures and functions.)

Simple data types

Simple data types stored by a program may be a number (real [or float] and integer), a character, a string, a date, a Boolean value, a sound sample, a video clip or indeed, any kind of data. (See Chapter 3 for more information on simple data types.)

Structured data types

Structured data types include (1D) arrays, parallel 1D arrays, records and arrays of records.

1D arrays

A set of data items *of the same type* grouped together using a single variable name is called an **array**. Each part of an array is called an **element**. Each element in an array is identified by the **variable name** and a **subscript** (**element number** or **index**).

An array of names might look like this:

```
name (1) – John
name (2) – Helen
name (3) – Peter
name (4) – Mary
```

This array has four parts. Element number 3 of this array is the name 'Peter'. Arrays which have one number as their subscript are called **one-dimensional (1D) arrays**. Arrays may have more than one dimension, and, in that case, would have a separate subscript number for each dimension, e.g. point (x,y) would refer to a two-dimensional array of points. When programming using arrays, it is necessary to declare the name of the array and its size at the start of the program, so that the computer may set aside the correct amount of memory space for the array. For example, this declaration sets aside space for an array called 'apples' with a size of 15 in Python, LiveCode and C:

```
apples=[0]*15
local arrayApples
int apples [15];
```

Arrays are a particularly useful way of storing data as each individual element can be easily referred to using the subscript. As we will see in Chapter 5, they are easier to parameter pass than multiple, individual variables.

When a number of separate 1D arrays are used to store a set of related data using the same element number or index, these are known as **parallel one-dimensional arrays**.

If we need to store individual pieces of data on one person such as forename, surname, age and height there are two possible ways to do this. Either as individual parallel 1D arrays or as an array of records.

An example of such data could be:

Forename   Alison {string}

Surname   Burns {string}

Age   55 {integer}

Height   1.62 {float/real}

Student   false {Boolean}

Parallel 1D arrays

Each individual array will store one type of data and should be declared individually so that there are four parallel arrays.

Setting up four parallel arrays to store four elements of data in SQA Reference Language would look like the this:

```
DECLARE forename AS ARRAY OF STRING
INITIALLY [] *4

DECLARE surname AS ARRAY OF STRING
INITIALLY [] *4

DECLARE age AS ARRAY OF INTEGER
INITIALLY [] *4

DECLARE height AS ARRAY OF REAL
INITIALLY [] *4

DECLARE student AS ARRAY OF BOOLEAN
INITIALLY [] *4
```

And then, storing the information above would look like this:

```
SET forename[0] TO "Alison"

SET surname[0] TO "Burns"

SET age[0] TO 55

SET height[0] TO 1.62

SET student[0] TO false
```

More realistically, we would need to store more data than this to make the arrays viable, because one person's data could simply be stored in four variables.

Table 4.1 shows four sets of data to be stored in the four parallel arrays. As you can see, the same index can be used to view the information stored at the same point in each array.

index	0	1	2	3
forename	Alison	Michael	Campbell	Andrew
surname	Campbell	Burns	Macdonald	Francis
age	55	52	20	18
height	1.62	2.00	1.97	1.98
student	false	false	true	false

Table 4.1 Personal information

This would be stored as follows:

```
SET forename TO ["Alison","Michael","Camp
bell","Andrew"]

SET surname TO ["Campbell", "Burns","
Macdonald "," Francis "]

SET age TO [55,52,20,18]

SET height TO [1.62,2.00,1.97,1.98]

SET student TO [False, False, True, False]
```

Using arrays in Python and LiveCode

Python

Python does not have an array type but instead makes use of lists. However, for ease of reference, in this book, we will refer to these as arrays rather than lists.

Structured data can be stored in different ways in Python. Your teacher will show you the method they would prefer you to use.

```
forename=[""]*4
surname=[""]*4
age=[0]*4
height=[0.0]*4
student=[False]*4
```

> **NOTE**
>
> You can find out more about using lists in Python here: www.digitalocean.com/community/tutorials/understanding-lists-in-python-3

LiveCode

LiveCode has an array type but it is declared in the same way as any normal variable.

```
local arrayForename, arraySurname
local arrayAge
local arrayHeight
local arrayStudent
```

Some languages like LiveCode require that the array be initialised before it is used, that is, the contents set to zero or empty.

```
repeat with counter=0 to 3
        put "" into arrayForename[counter]
        put "" into arraySurname[counter]
        put 0 into arrayAge[counter]
        put 0.0 into arrayHeight[counter]
        put false into arrayStudent[counter]
end repeat
```

Writing to and reading from the arrays involves using a counter as the array index, which will allow the array to be traversed. Traversing the array is where we access each element in the array using the subscript, in this case the loop counter, so that the contents can be checked or used as part of a comparison or calculation.

Python

```
for counter in range(0,4):
        print("Enter your forename")
        forename[counter]=input()
        print("Enter your surname")
        surname[counter]=input()
        print(forename[counter],"enter your age")
        age[counter]=int(input())
        print(forename[counter],"enter your height")
        height[counter]=float(input())
        print("Are you a
        student",forename[counter],"?")
        answer=input()
        if answer=="y" or answer=="Y":
                student[counter]=True
...
for counter in range(0,4):
        if student[counter]:
                print(forename[counter],
                surname[counter],"is", age
                [counter], "years of age and
                is",height[counter], "metres in height and
                is a student")
```

LiveCode

```
repeat with counter = 0 to 3
        ask "Enter your forename"
        if the result=cancel then exit to top
        put it into arrayForename[counter]
        ask "Enter your surname"
        if the result=cancel then exit to top
        put it into arraySurname[counter]
        ask arrayForename[counter] && "enter your
        age"
        if the result=cancel then exit to top
        put it into arrayAge[counter]
        ask arrayForename[counter] && "enter your
        height"
```

```
        if the result=cancel then exit to top

        put it into arrayHeight[counter]

        ask "Are you a student"&&arrayForename
        [counter] &&"?"

        if the result=cancel then exit to top

        put it into ans

        if ans="y" or ans="y" then

                put true into arrayStudent[counter]

        end if

end repeat

...

repeat with counter = 0 to 3

        if arrayStudent[counter] then

        put arrayForename[counter] && arraySurname
        [counter] &&"is" && arrayAge[counter] &&
        "years of age and is" && arrayHeight[counter]
        && "metres in height and is a student" &
        return after field "output"

        end if

end repeat
```

Here is an example of an algorithm which makes use of parallel arrays for data storage:

```
*algorithm to read names and marks into
two arrays*

1 set array counter to zero
2 set aside space for ten pupils' names
  in the array name []
3 set aside space for ten pupils' marks
  in the array mark []
4 loop REPEAT
5     add one to array counter
6     READ value into name array [counter]
7     READ value into mark array [counter]
8 UNTIL end of data is reached
```

NOTE

On the above algorithm

'End of data' is a useful feature, present in some high-level languages. When there is no more data to be read, 'end of data' is set to true, causing the loop to stop. 'End of file' is a similar feature. If you know in advance the number of data items to be read, a terminating condition such as 'counter equals ten'

may be used. If the data contains a terminating value, such as −1, then 'mark equals −1' may be used as the terminating condition for the loop.

Records

An alternative to storing related data in parallel arrays is a record structure. This means that all the related data can be stored together regardless of data type. This is the same principal as storing records in a database.

Using SQA Reference Language, it is relatively straightforward to set up a record structure with the same attributes as that stored in the parallel arrays. For example:

```
RECORD personalDetails IS {STRING
forename, STRING surname, INTEGER age,
REAL height}
```

To store *one* piece of data on *one* person, a suitable variable would have to be declared. For example:

```
DECLARE person INITIALLY personalDetails
```

This will declare one empty record in which we can store one individual piece of data. We can now give a value to this record.

```
SET person TO {forename= "Alison",
surname= "Campbell", age=55, height=1.62}
```

Python

Python does not contain the data structure for a record but one way this can be set up is using **class**. For example:

```
class personalDetails:
        forename:str ="""
        surname:str ="""
        age:int=0
        height:float=0.0
        student:bool=False
```

NOTE

Python has several different approaches to records, including dictionaries, and it may also depend on the version being used. Your teacher will show you the way they would like you to program a record.

LiveCode

LiveCode does not contain the data structure for a record but one way this can be set up is by creating an array with a keyed (by word) index. For example:

```
local personalRecordDetails

...

put "" into personalRecordDetails[0]["forename"]

put "" into personalRecordDetails[0]["surname"]

put 0 into personalRecordDetails[0]["age"]

put 0.0 into personalRecordDetails[0]["height"]

put false into personalRecordDetails[0]["student"]
```

Arrays of records

Obviously, it would make no sense to only declare one record and only store one piece of data. To allow us to store more than one piece of data, we make use of arrays. However, this time we declare an array of records. Using an array of records makes it possible to access a complete record's worth of data with a single reference.

Table 4.2 below shows the data that our array of records will store.

Array of personalDetails					
index	forename	surname	age	height	student
1	Alison	Campbell	55	1.62	false
2	Michael	Burns	52	2.00	false
3	Campbell	Macdonald	20	1.97	true
4	Andrew	Francis	18	1.98	false

Table 4.2 Personal data

```
class personalDetails():
    forename:str=""
    surname:str=""
    age:int=0
    height:float=0.0
    student:bool=False
def initialise():
    arrayPerson=[personalDetails() for x in range(4)]
    return arrayPerson
```

You should notice that an array of records looks like a database and is the programming equivalent of one.

Using SQA Reference Language, an array of records can store four elements, which can be represented as follows:

```
DECLARE arrayPerson AS ARRAY OF
personalDetails INITIALLY []*4

DECLARE arrayPerson [10] AS ARRAY OF
personalDetails

DECLARE arrayPerson [0..9] AS ARRAY OF
personalDetails
```

To assign the data in Table 4.1 to each record in the array, we could use the following:

```
SET arrayPerson[0] TO {forename="Alison",
surname= "Campbell", age=55, height=1.62}

SET arrayPerson[1] TO {forename=
"Michael", surname= "Burns", age=52,
height=2.00}

SET arrayPerson[2] TO {forename=
"Campbell", surname= "Macdonald",
age=20, height=1.97}

SET arrayPerson[3] TO {forename=
"Andrew", surname= "Francis", age=18,
height=1.98}
```

Python

In Python, we make use of the class already declared earlier in the program (**personalDetails**) and set up an array of that class (**arrayPerson**). Entering data is done by referring to the array of records as required throughout the program.

23

```
def getData():
    for counter in range(0,4):
        print("Enter your forename")
        arrayPerson[counter].forename=input()
        print("Enter your surname")
        arrayPerson[counter].surname=input()
        print(arrayPerson[counter].forename,"enter your age")
        arrayPerson[counter].age=int(input())
        print(arrayPerson[counter].forename,"enter your height")
        arrayPerson[counter].height=float(input())
        answer=input()
        if answer=="y" or answer=="Y":
            arrayPerson[counter].student=True
    return arrayPerson
def displayData():
    for counter in range(0,4):
        if arrayPerson[counter].student:
            print(arrayPerson[counter].forename, arrayPerson[counter].surname,"is",
            arrayPerson[counter].age,"years of age and is",arrayPerson[counter].height,"metres
            in height and is a student")
#Main program
arrayPerson=initialise()
arrayPerson=getData()
displayData()
```

LiveCode

In LiveCode, we make use of the array **local personalRecordDetails** declared earlier in the program. It can then be used as an array of records, first initialising it with the keyed index in **on initialise** and then later using it to store data as if it were an array of records (**on getData**).

```
on mouseUp
    put empty into field "output"
    local personalRecordDetails
    initialise
    getData personalRecordDetails
    displayData personalRecordDetails
end mouseUp
on initialise
    local counter
    put 0 into counter
```

```
        repeat with counter = 0 to 3
                put "" into personalRecordDetails[counter]["forename"]
                put "" into personalRecordDetails[counter]["surname"]
                put 0 into personalRecordDetails[counter]["age"]
                put 0.0 into personalRecordDetails[counter]["height"]
                put false into personalRecordDetails[counter]["student"]
        end repeat
end initialise
on getData @personalRecordDetails
        local counter
        put 0 into counter
        repeat with counter = 0 to 3
                ask "Enter your forename"
                if the result=cancel then exit to top
                put it into personalRecordDetails[counter]["forename"]
                ask "Enter your surname"
                if the result=cancel then exit to top
                put it into personalRecordDetails[counter]["surname"]
                ask personalRecordDetails[counter]["forename"] && "enter your age"
                if the result=cancel then exit to top
                put it into personalRecordDetails[counter]["age"]
                ask personalRecordDetails[counter]["forename"] && "enter your height"
                if the result=cancel then exit to top
                put it into personalRecordDetails[counter]["height"]
                ask "Are you a student"&&personalRecordDetails[counter]["forename"]&"?"
                if the result=cancel then exit to top
                put it into ans
                if ans="y" or ans="Y" then
                        put true into personalRecordDetails[counter]["student"]
                end if
        end repeat
end getData
on displayData @personalRecordDetails
        local counter
        put 0 into counter
        repeat with counter = 0 to 3
                if personalRecordDetails[counter]["student"] then
```

```
        put personalRecordDetails[counter]["forename"] && personalRecordDetails[counter]
        ["surname"] && "is" &&personalRecordDetails[counter]["age"] && "years of age and is"
        && personalRecordDetails[counter]["height"] && "metres in height and is a student"&
        return after field "output"

            end if

        end repeat

    end displayData
```

QUESTIONS

1 a) State what is meant by the term 'variable'.
  b) State five simple data types.
2 Which structured data type uses elements and subscripts?
3 State one advantage of using an array rather than unique variable names when programming.
4 Globally, solar energy production has increased in recent years. The data on each region in the world, its code, the year and solar generation in TWh (terawatt hours) has been recorded in a csv file since 1965 and currently stores 5092 items of data. Part of the file is shown below.

   Kuwait, KWT, 2018, 0.088143148

   Philippines, PHL, 2005, 0.001517

   United Kingdom, GBR, 2009, 0.020000206

The data is to be stored in parallel 1D arrays.

Using either SQA Reference Language or a programming language of your choice, declare parallel 1D arrays that can store the data for the 5092 items of data.

5 There are currently 270 weather stations located all around the British Isles that record data every day about current weather situations. A sample of some of the data recorded is shown below.

Weather data	Sample data
Location	Machrihanish
Windspeed (mph)	48
Temperature (°C)	11.5
Rainfall (mm)	13
Hours of sunshine	2

Using either SQA Reference Language or a programming language of your choice define:
a) a suitable record data structure for the data above.
b) the variable which can store the details of the 270 readings. Your answer should use the record data structure created in part a).

KEY POINTS

● A variable is the name that a programmer uses to identify a storage location.
● Simple data types may be a number (real (or float) and integer), a character, a string, a date, a Boolean value, a sound sample or a video clip.
● Structured data types include (1D) arrays, parallel 1D arrays, records and arrays of records.
● Arrays which have one number as their subscript are called one-dimensional arrays.
● Each part of an array is called an element.

● Each element in an array is identified by the variable name and a subscript.
● Parallel 1D arrays store a set of related data using the same element number or index.
● A record structure stores all related data together regardless of data type.
● Using an array of records makes it possible to access a complete record's worth of data with a single reference.

Chapter 5 Implementation (computational constructs)

This chapter describes a wide range of the computational constructs required for programming in any language.

The following topics are covered:

- Describe, exemplify and implement the appropriate constructs in a procedural high-level (textual) language:
  - subprograms/routines, defined by their name and arguments (inputs and outputs):
    - procedures
    - functions
  - parameter passing (formal and actual)
  - the scope of local and global variables
  - pre-defined functions (with parameters):
    - to create substrings
    - to convert from character to ASCII and vice versa
    - to convert floating-point numbers to integers
    - modulus
  - file handling:
    - sequential CSV and txt files (open, create, read, write, close).
- Read and explain code that makes use of the above constructs.

Computational contstructs

Modularity

Modularity means that when a program is designed and written, it is divided into smaller sections called **subprograms** or **subroutines**. Subprograms may be called in any order in a program and they may be reused many times over. Each subprogram performs a particular task within the program. Subprograms may be written at the same time as the rest of the program or they may be prewritten. Prewritten subprograms are known as **library modules**.

High-level procedural languages use two types of modules or subprograms. These are **procedures** and **functions**.

Procedures

Before a procedure may be used in a program, it must be defined. Defining a procedure gives it a name, and also allows the programmer to state which data the procedure requires to have sent to it from the program. Data is passed to a procedure using **parameters** (see page 29 in this chapter). When a procedure receives data, it carries out an operation using the data and makes results available to the program. These results may simply be displayed on screen from within the procedure, or they may be passed back out of the procedure to another procedure, again using parameters. A procedure is said to produce an effect.

Python

In Python, procedures use the keyword **def**.

Procedure definitions are at the top of the program.

```
def sum (numberOne, numberTwo):
    total= numberOne + numberTwo        #note formal parameters print(total)
```

Procedure calls are at the bottom of the program (after the definitions).

```
sum (firstNumber, secondNumber)        #note actual parameters
```

LiveCode

In LiveCode, procedures use the keywords **on** and **end** to start and finish the procedure definition.

Procedure calls are at the top of the program.

```
getNum numberOne, numberTwo

sumNum numberOne, numberTwo,
total        //note actual parameters
```

Procedure definitions are at the bottom of the program (after the calls).

```
on getNum @numberOne, @numberTwo
    ask "Enter your first number"
    if the result=cancel then exit to top
    put it into numberOne
    ask"Enter your second number"
    if the result=cancel then exit to top
```

```
    put it into numberTwo
end getNum
on sumNum firstNumber, secondNumber, @total
//note formal parameters
    put 0 into total
    put firstNumber+secondNumber into total
end sumNum
```

Functions

A **function** is similar to a procedure but returns one or more values to a program. Like a procedure, a function must be defined and given a name before it can be used in a program. The name of the function is used to represent a variable containing the value to be returned.

Python

In Python, functions also use the keyword **def**.

Function definition

```
def areaOfCircle(radius):               #note the parameter in a
    area = math.pi * radius * radius    #function is sometimes
    return area                         #called the argument
```

Function call

```
area= areaOfCircle (number)
```

DID YOU KNOW

Python has a number of external modules that can be imported to increase the functionality of the language. The 'math' module allows Python programs to use mathematical functions.

LiveCode

In LiveCode, functions use the keywords **function** and **end** to start and finish the function.

Function call

```
put areaOfCircle(radius) into area
```

Function definition

```
function areaOfCircle radius
        put 6 into radius
        put pi*radius*radius into area
        return area
end areaOfCircle
```

Parameters

The movement of data (or the data flow) between subprograms is implemented using parameters. Data structures (such as variables, arrays, records, lists and classes) which are passed into subprograms are known as **in** parameters. Variables which are passed out of subprograms are known as **out** parameters.

A parameter is information about a data item being supplied to a subprogram (function or procedure) when it is called into use. When the subprogram is used, the calling program must pass parameters to it. This is called **parameter passing**. Parameter passing relates directly to the data flow explained in Chapter 3 (see page 13). So, when the data flow on the top-level design is shown as **in:** it is an in parameter and when it is shown as **out:** , it is an out parameter.

Let's take as an example a validation procedure which checks that a number is within a certain range. The procedure is called 'validate' and the variable we wish to pass to this procedure is 'test', which has a value input by the user.

```
begin program
ask for test mark
take in test mark       This is the calling program
validate (test)    (or main program)
end program
begin procedure validate (number)
     loop WHILE number is outwith range
     prompt to re-enter number     This is the subprogram
     take in the number        (procedure)
     end loop
end procedure
```

Actual and formal parameters

The parameter test contains the value that is being passed into the procedure validate – the parameter test is called the **actual parameter**. *Number* is the name of the parameter which is used in the procedure definition, so number is called the **formal parameter**.

Remember: parameters which are passed into a procedure (or function) when it is called from any other part of the program are called the actual parameters.

Parameters used in the procedure or function are the formal parameters.

When writing programming code, the parameters must be written in both the calling program and the subprogram in lists that are known as **arguments**. Care must be taken when listing the arguments to make sure that they are in the same order in the subprogram call and the subprogram itself. If they are in the wrong order, then the wrong values will be passed to the arguments in the subprogram.

WORKED EXAMPLE 1

Python

```
def initialise():
        test=0
        minimum=1
        maximum=10
return test, minimum, maximum
def askForMark(minm,maxm):
        print("Enter a number between",minm,"and",maxm,"to check")
def getMark(fnum):
        fnum=int(input())
        return fnum
def validate(fnum,minm,maxm):
        while fnum<minm or fnum>maxm:
                print("Number is out of range")
                print("Please re-enter between", minm,"and", maxm)
                fnum=int(input())
        return fnum
def inRange(fnum):
        print("The number",fnum,"is within range")
#Main program
test, minimum, maximum=initialise()
askForMark(minimum,maximum)
test=getMark(test)
test=validate(test,minimum,maximum)
inRange(test)test=0
```

> fnum, minm and maxm are formal parameters as they are listed as arguments in the declaration of the procedure and functions

> test, minimum and maximum are actual parameters as they are listed as arguments in the procedure and function calls

WORKED EXAMPLE 2

LiveCode

```
on mouseUp
        put empty into field "output"
        initialise
        askForMark test, minimum, maximum
        put validate(test,minimum,maximum) into test
        inRange test
end mouseUp
```

> test, minimum and maximum are actual parameters as they are listed as arguments in the procedure and function calls

```
on initialise
      local test
      local minimum, maximum
      put 0 into test
end initialise
on askForMark @fnum @minm, @maxm
      put 1 into minm
      put 10 into maxm
      put 0 into fnum
      ask "Enter a number between"&&minm&&"and"&&maxm&&"to check"
      if the result = cancel then exit to top
      put it into fnum
end askForMark
function validate fnum, minm, maxm
      repeat until fnum>=minm and fnum<=maxm and fnum is an integer
            put "Number is out of range" &return after field "output"
            ask "Please re-enter between"&&minm&&"and"&&maxm
            if the result =cancel then exit to top
            put it into fnum
      end repeat
      return fnum
end validate
on inRange fnum
      put "The number"&&fnum&&"is within range" &return after field "output"
end inRange
```

> fnum, minm and maxm
> are formal parameters
> as they are listed
> as arguments in
> the declaration of
> the procedure and
> functions

Local and global variables

Two types of variables are **global variables** and **local variables**. Global variables may be used anywhere in a program, but local variables are defined only for use in one part of a program (a subprogram – normally a function or a procedure). Local variables only come into existence when that procedure is entered and the data that they contain is lost when the processing of that procedure is complete. Using local variables reduces the unplanned effects of the same variable name being used in another part of the program and accidentally being changed. Global variables should only be used for data that needs to be shared between different procedures within a program, because they are accessible to any part of the whole program. It is good practice to declare global variables at the start of a program. Look further on in this chapter for the implementation of an algorithm which shows the difference between local and global variables. The algorithm for this example is not shown here because looking at the algorithm on its own is not particularly helpful. In order to understand this

NOTE

It is not necessary to give the parameters different names in the arguments in the calling program and the subprogram. This means that any of these subprograms can be reused when required, with no change, in another program.

31

properly, you need to look at the implementation and the sample output. The sample output shows that the values of the local variables (**sum** and **product**) within the calculate procedure have no effect on the values of the global variables (also called **sum** and **product**) outside the calculate procedure, i.e. throughout the rest of the program.

Scope of variables

The **scope** of a variable is the range of statements for which a variable is valid. So, the scope of a local variable is the subprogram it is used in. This means that in a large programming project, where a number of programmers are writing separate subprograms, there is no need to be concerned about using different (or similar) local variable names, since they cannot have any effect outside their scope.

User-defined functions

The function **areaOfCircle** described earlier in this chapter, is known as a **user-defined function**. A user-defined function is a function which is created within a program rather than being already present or pre-defined as part of the normal syntax of a programming language.

WORKED EXAMPLE 3

A pre-defined function

The **sqrt** function returns the square root of a number.

Python

```
import math
number=4
root=(math.sqrt(number))
print(root)
The square root of 4 is 2.0
```

LiveCode

```
on mouseUp
    put empty into field "output"
    local sqnum
    local root
    put 4 into sqnum
    put sqrt(sqnum) into root
    put root &return after field "output"
end mouseUp
```

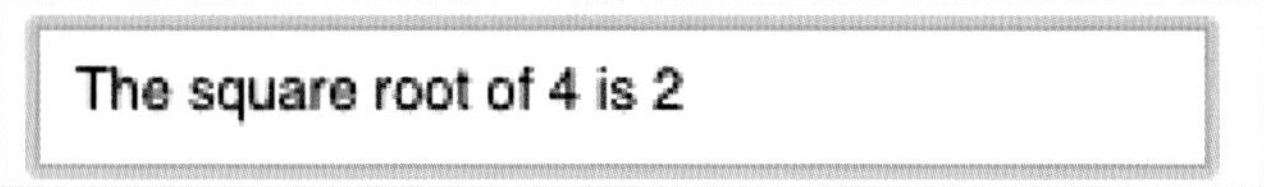

```
The square root of 4 is 2
```

Figure 5.1 LiveCode square root output

We will take a look at four pre-defined functions with parameters using both Python and LiveCode languages:

- String operations – create substrings
- Convert from character to ASCII and ASCII to character
- Convert floating-point numbers to integers
- Modulus

> **NOTE**
>
> In this book the terms procedures/subroutines/subprograms and modules are interchangeable.

String operations

String operations can process string data. A string is a list of characters, i.e. a letter, a number or a symbol. String operations include joining strings, known as **concatenation**, and selecting parts of strings, known as **substrings**. Individual characters can also be converted into ASCII and ASCII characters can be converted into individual characters. Strings can also be thought of as a list of characters.

Creating substrings

Python

In Python, a string is recognised as anything that is between either single or double quotation marks, i.e. ' ' or " ".

WORKED EXAMPLES 4 AND 5

Display substrings

```
word="Saint Matthew's Academy"
print(word[0])          #display first character
print(word[0:1])        #display first character
print(word[0:3])        #display first three characters
print(word[:3])         #display first three characters
print(word[-3:])        #display last three characters
print(word[3:])         #display all but the first three characters
print(word[:-3])        #display all  but the last three characters
```

Create a username

```
import random           #random is an imported module
forename="Lucy"
surname="Locket"
number=random.randint(1,100)
num = str(number)
userName=forename[0:4]+surname[0:5]+num     #this is a combination of substrings and concatenation.
print(userName)
print (len(userName))    # produces the length of the string stored in userName
```

NOTE

Further reading and some practical exercises may be on found LiveCode's website: https://livecode.com/docs/9-5-0/core-concepts/processing-text-and-data/

LiveCode

In LiveCode, a string is recognised as anything that is between double quotation marks, i.e. " " and also as any part of an external text file.

In LiveCode, the pre-defined functions **char**, **word**, **line** and **item** are used. These are known as 'chunk expressions'. A chunk allows the programmer to specify a portion of text and also allows it to be edited. For the purposes of these notes we will only consider **char**.

WORKED EXAMPLES 6 AND 7

Examples of substring operations: char

```
on mouseUp
        put empty into field "output"
        local origWord
        put "Saint Matthew's Academy" into origWord
        put( char 1 of origWord) into newWord1           //display first character
        put newWord1 &return after field "output"
        put( char 1 to 3 of origWord) into newWord2       //display first three characters
        put newWord2 &return after field "output"
        put( char -3 to -1 of origWord) into newWord3     //display last three characters
        put newWord3 &return after field "output"
        put( char 4 to -1 of origWord) into newWord4      //display all but the first three characters
        put newWord4 &return after field "output"
        put( char 1 to -4 of origWord) into newWord5      //display all but the last three characters
        put newWord5 &return after field "output"
end mouseUp
```

Create a username

```
on mouseUp
        put empty into field "output"
        local forename, surname
        local rnum
        local username
        put "Lucy" into forename
        put "Locket" into surname
        put random(100) into rnum
        put (char 1 to 4 of forename) & (char 1 to 5 of surname) &rnum into username
        put username &return after field "output"
        put the length of username &return after field "output"
end mouseUp
```

Convert from character to ASCII and ASCII to character

Take in a character and convert it to its ASCII equivalent and vice versa.

Python

Python makes use of the pre-defined functions **ord( )** and **chr( )** to convert from a character to ASCII and ASCII to a character. **chr( )** will convert ASCII characters in the range 0 to 255. Both **ord( )** and **chr( )** require a parameter in the brackets.

```
asciiNumber=ord(character)
character=chr(asciiNumber)
```

For example:

```
asciiNumber=ord("q")    #produces the output 113
character=chr(63)        #produces the output ?
```

LiveCode

The pre-defined functions **charToNum( )** and **numToChar( )** are used to convert characters into their corresponding ASCII code and vice versa. **numToChar( )** converts in the ASCII range 0 to 255. Both of these pre-defined functions will require a parameter to be supplied in the brackets.

```
put charToNum("Character") into field "ASCII"
put numToChar(it) into field "Character"
```

For example:

```
put charToNum("q") into field "ASCII"
put numToChar(63) into field "Character"
```

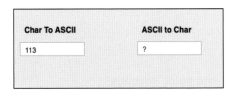

Figure 5.2 LiveCode ASCII to character and vice versa

Some other string operations include:

- changing strings to numbers and numbers to strings.
- changing case: 'j' to 'J' and vice versa.
- removing blank spaces from a string.

> **NOTE**
> Some languages may not contain specific keywords for all of these operations.

Convert floating-point numbers to integers

Remove the decimal part from a number and store it as an integer.

Python

Python uses the pre-defined function **int( )** to convert from floating point numbers to integer numbers by removing the decimal portion, for example:

```
num1=126.357
num2=1387.964

print(int(num1))        #produces the output 126
print(int(num2))        #produces the output 1387
```

It is also possible and sometimes more desirable to round to the nearest whole number, in which case, the pre-defined function **round( )** should be used.

```
print(round(num1))      #produces the output 126
print(round(num2))      #produces the output 1388
```

LiveCode

The pre-defined function **trunc** displays only the integer part of a number and removes the decimal part. The code shown below gives two examples to produce the integer part.

```
on mouseUp
    local num1, num2
    local integer1, integer2
    put empty into field "intNo"
    put 126.357 into num1
    put 1387.964 into num2
    //assigns the integer value straight to the
       output window
    put the trunc of num1 &return after field "intNo"
    put the trunc of num2 &return after field "intNo"
    //assigns the integer value to a variable
    put trunc(num1) into integer1
    put trunc(num2) into integer2
    put integer1 &return after field "intNo"
    put integer2 &return after field "intNo"
end mouseUp
```

As with Python, it is sometimes desirable to round to the nearest whole number and again the pre-defined function **round** should be used.

```
on mouseUp
    local num1, num2
    local round1, round2
    put empty into field "roundNo"
    put 126.357 into num1
    put 1387.964 into num2
    //assigns the rounded value straight to the
    output window
    put the round of num1 &return after field
    "roundNo"
    put the round of num2 &return after field
    "roundNo"
    //assigns the integer value to a variable
    put round(num1) into round1
    put round(num2) into round2
    put round1 &return after field "roundNo"
    put round2 &return after field "roundNo"
end mouseUp
```

Notice the difference in output between trunc and round shown in Figure 5.4.

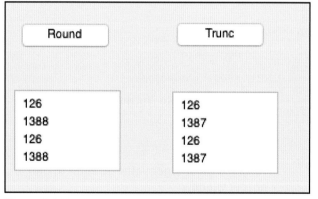

Figure 5.3 LiveCode **trunc** and **round** pre-defined functions

Modulus

The modulus of a number is the remainder after integer division; that is, the number left over when one number is divided by another. For completeness, functions for both the modulus (the remainder) and quotient (the integer part or quotient) have been included in both languages.

Python

In Python the % symbol is used to produce the modulus. The // symbol is used to produce the quotient. The function **divmod** produces both in one operation.

```
seconds=150%60
# evaluates the remainder as 30
minutes=150//60
# evaluates the quotient as 2
seconds=150
quotient,remainder=divmod(seconds,60)
print(quotient,remainder)
#displays both quotient and remainder as 2  30
```

LiveCode

In LiveCode, the pre-defined function **mod** is used to produce the modulus. The **div** function is used to produce the quotient.

```
put 150 mod 60 into seconds
// evaluates the remainder as 30
put 150 div 60 into hours
// evaluates the quotient as 2
```

Div

```
on mouseUp
    put empty into field "hours"
    local hours
    put 0 into hours
    put 150 div 60 into hours
    put hours &return after field "hours"
end mouseUp
```

Mod

```
on mouseUp
    put empty into field "seconds"
    local seconds
    put 0 into seconds
    put 150 mod 60 into seconds
    put secondz &return after field "seconds"
end mouseUp
```

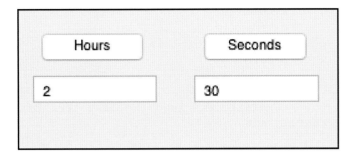

Figure 5.4 LiveCode **div** and **mod** pre-defined functions

File handling

Files are created by programs and are used to store data permanently on backing storage. It is useful for programs to be able to access these external files especially where they contain a large amount of data which would otherwise have to be input manually. This data can be accessed using file-handling techniques. These techniques involve being able to open the file, read the data contained in the file into the appropriate data structure, edit or process the data where required and lastly write the new data to the file. New files can be created and also deleted from within a program.

At Higher you need to be able to open, create, read, write and close both **txt** and CSV files. Txt files contain only plain, unformatted text. A **Comma Separated Variable (CSV)** file is a type of text file that separates the values using a comma.

Python

There are a number of different operations that can be performed on both txt and CSV files in Python.

To access both txt and CSV files the keyword **open( )** should be used. open( ) is used with two parameters: **open(filename, mode)**. When open( ) is used to open a file, then it must be closed using **file.close( )**. The default value for mode is **r** and does not have to be explicitly stated if the file is being read.

It is also possible to use the keywords **with open( )**. This automatically closes the file after use and does not need

to be closed. The default value for mode is also **r** and as with open( ), does *not* have to be explicitly stated.

There are several methods (modes) for opening files as shown in Table 5.1.

Mode	Definition
r	Read: the default value and opens the file for reading.
a	Append: opens the file and adds new data to the end.
w	Write: opens the file for writing and will create one where one does not exist.
x	Create: creates a new file but will generate an error if one already exists.

Table 5.1 Methods for opening files in Python

We will look only at the read and write modes for txt and CSV files.

txt files
Open a txt file for reading

```
file=open("textfile.txt","r") {or
file=open ("textfile.txt")}

print(file.read())

file.close()
```

```
with open("textfile.txt","r")]: as file or
{with open("textfile.txt") as file:}

        print(file.read())
```

Open a txt file for writing

```
file=open("textfile.txt","w")

file.write(text)

file.close()
```

```
with open("textfile.txt","w") as file:

        file.write(text)
```

CSV files

To read from a CSV file, the CSV module should first be imported into Python.

Open a CSV file for reading

```
import csv
file = open("csvfile.csv", "r") {or file=open("csvfile.csv")}
reader = csv.reader(file, delimiter=',', quotechar=',',
quoting=csv.QUOTE_MINIMAL)
for row in reader:
        print(row)
file.close()


with open("csvfile.csv") as file:
        reader = csv.reader(file,
        delimiter=',', quotechar=',',
        quoting=csv.QUOTE_MINIMAL)
        for row in reader:
                print(row)
```

Open a CSV file for writing

```
file = open("csvfile.csv", 'w')
with file:
        writer = csv.writer(file)
        writer.writerows(data)


with open("csvfile.csv", "w") as file:
        with file:
                writer = csv.writer(file)
                writer.writerows(data)
```

These are only samples of how this can be done in Python as there are multiple ways in which this can be programmed. Your teacher will show you the method they wish you to use when programming.

LiveCode

As with Python, there are a number of operations that can be performed on external files in LiveCode. The first task is to set up where the file has to be read from. Assuming that the file is stored in the same folder as the program (or stack), the following code is used to determine the path to the file using the filename of the stack.

Open a txt file

```
put the fileName of this stack into
theFilePath
set itemDel to "/"
put "textfile.txt" into the last item of
theFilePath
```

Open a CSV file

```
put the fileName of this stack into
theFilePath
set itemDel to "/"
put "csvfile.csv" into the last item of
theFilePath
```

This code will store the file in a temporary variable to store the path and filename. The temporary variable in this code snippet is called **theFilePath**.

To open both txt and CSV files for reading, the keyword **open** should be used. open is used with the temporary variable and the keyword **read**. When open has been used to open a file, then it must be closed using **close**. The default value for mode is read and does *not* have to be explicitly stated if the file is being read.

A delimiter is set and used to split the data, either tab or comma depending on how the data is to be stored or is currently stored in the file.

When reading from an external file, the length of the file does not need to be known in advance as the end of file marker **EOF** can be used.

In summary, there are several file operations as shown in Table 5.2.

Mode	Definition
read	The default value and opens the file for reading.
write	Opens the file for writing and will create one where one does not exist.
append	Opens the file and adds new data to the end.
close	Closes file after being read into a temporary variable.
eof	End of file marker.

Table 5.2 File operations in LiveCode

We will look only at the read and write modes for txt and CSV files.

a) Write the programming code using substrings to assign the value 'inbla55' to the variable **passwordOne**.

b) State the password generated by the following string variables using your answer from part a).

```
DECLARE firstOne INITIALLY "corbett"

DECLARE secondOne INITIALLY
"gooseberry"

DECLARE thirdOne INITIALLY "912883"
```

9 Using a programming language of your choice, write the programming code to convert the following:
a) character to ASCII: H
b) ASCII to character: 121

10 Using a programming language of your choice, write a program to calculate the volume of a sphere. The output should show the answer:
a) rounded to the nearest whole number.
b) as an integer.

11 A chocolate shop uses trays to mould their chocolates. Each tray holds 24 chocolates. A chocolatier would like to be able to enter the number of chocolates they intend to make, then find out how many full trays will be required and how many chocolates are left over on the last tray.
Using a programming language of your choice, write the code that will be required to find out how many chocolates would be on the last tray.

12 A survey of how people have been travelling to work has been done over the last year and the results of this information are to be written to a new txt file called transportSurvey. The mode of transport and how many times in one year each form of transport has been used will be written to the file.
Some simple, sample data is shown in the table below.

Mode of transport	Number of times used
Car	250
Bus	100
Rail	120
Plane	25

Using a programming language of your choice, write the programming code to open, create and write to the new file and then close the file.

13 A team of data scientists have been studying the changes in female height worldwide over 100 years from 1896 to 1996. They have a very large CSV file containing 21,008 items of data called *changesInFemaleHeight* that has to be read into a program to be analysed. The file stores the country, the country's code, the year and the mean height. The data from the file should be read into parallel arrays to be analysed.
Using a programming language of your choice, write the programming code to open, read from and close the file.

14 The Official Online Download Company (OOD Co.) produce a weekly chart of the top 100 songs streamed in Scotland. The data is stored in txt format and is analysed by the company using a program. OOD Co. then produce the number one download for that week.

Line 10	RECORD songData IS {STRING artist, STRING trackName, INTEGER trackLength, INTEGER timesPlayed}
Line 11	DECLARE songs AS ARRAY OF songData INITIALLY[]*100
Line 12	SET song[0] TO {artist= "Catherine Hedge", trackName= "Jogging up that Lane", trackLength=245, timesPlayed=256909}
Line 13	SET song[1] TO {artist= "Exodus", trackName="We can Tango", trackLength=290, timesPlayed=234141}
Line 14	SET song[2] TO {artist="Charity Shop Woman", trackName= "Miniature", trackLength=229, timesPlayed=125000}
Line 15	SET song[3] TO {artist="Knee", trackName="Your Happy Deckhands", trackLengthsecs=360, timesPlayed=232555}
Line 16	SET song[4] TO {artist="And Party", trackName="Worst Week", trackLengthsecs=240, timesPlayed=923145
Line 17	SEND song[3].trackName TO DISPLAY

41

a) Explain the purpose of lines 10 and 11.
b) State the output from line 17.
c) Some new code is added to the program in lines 60 to 63. The variable position will store the most streamed song in any week.

d) The way in which the data is to be stored in the program is to be changed to parallel 1D arrays. Using a programming language of your choice, declare parallel 1D arrays that can store the data for the top 100 songs.

```
Line 60    DECLARE minutes INITIALLY 0
Line 61    DECLARE seconds INITIALLY 0
Line 62    SET minutes TO songs[position].
           trackLengthsecs /60
Line 63    SET seconds TO songs[position].
           trackLengthsecs mod 60
```

Explain the purpose of lines 62 and 63.

KEY POINTS

- Modularity means that when a program is designed and written, it is divided into smaller sections called subprograms or subroutines.
- High-level procedural languages use two types of modules or subprograms. These are procedures and functions.
- A procedure is said to produce an effect; a function returns one or more values to a program.
- The movement of data (or the data flow) between subprograms is implemented using parameters.
- A parameter is information about a data item being supplied to a subprogram.
- When a subprogram is used, the calling program must pass parameters to it. This is parameter passing.
- Data structures (such as variables) which are only passed into subprograms are known as 'in' parameters.
- Variables which are passed into a subprogram and are changed or updated are referred to as 'out' parameters.
- Parameters which are passed into a procedure (or function) when it is called from any other part of the program are actual parameters.
- Parameters used in the procedure or function are the formal parameters.

- Parameters written in both the calling program and the subprogram in lists are known as arguments.
- Arguments must be in the same order in both subprogram call and subprogram.
- Two types of variables are global variables and local variables.
- Global variables may be used anywhere in a program, but local variables are defined only for use in one part of a program (a subprogram).
- The scope of a variable is the range of statements for which a variable is valid.
- A user-defined function is a function which is created within a program rather than being already present or pre-defined as part of a programming language.
- A pre-defined function is part of the normal syntax of a programming language.
- String operations include joining strings, known as concatenation, and selecting parts of strings, known as substrings.
- Modulus is the remainder after integer division.
- Files are created by programs and are used to store data permanently on backing storage.
- File operations include open, create, read, write and close.

Chapter 6 Implementation (algorithm specification)

This chapter looks at the design and implementation for four standard algorithms.

The following topics are covered:

- Describe, exemplify and implement the following standard algorithms using 1D arrays or arrays of records:
  - linear search
  - count occurrences
  - find minimum and maximum.

Algorithms

An **algorithm** is a sequence of instructions that can be used to solve a problem.

In this chapter the following standard algorithms are described and implemented:

1 input validation
2 linear search
3 count occurrences
4 find minimum and maximum (finding min/max).

In some cases, more than one algorithm is described within each category. The algorithms that you need to know about are shown in **bold type**. The input validation algorithm is National 5 level content. It is included here for completeness.

"I can't find an efficient algorithm, but neither can all these famous people."
Figure 6.1 Efficient algorithm

1 Input validation

Input validation is the process of checking that the input is acceptable or within a certain range. Some form of validation is required when checking user input to a program. For example, valid dates in the year 2030 could range from 1/1/2030 to 31/12/2030. Ages of pupils in the fifth year at school might have a range of 15 to 17 years. A well-written program should validate all user input.

There are a variety of possible input validation algorithms:

```
this is sometimes called
a validation loop (note
the structured listing)
```

```
1.1    loop — REPEAT
1.2           ask user for data input
1.3           take in the data
1.4    end loop — UNTIL data is within
       range
```

This is not very user-friendly, since it does not give any indication to the user of what might be wrong with any rejected input. The user may think that they are entering a list of data rather than being repeatedly asked to re-enter an invalid item. Adding an IF statement makes this algorithm more useful.

```
1.1    loop — REPEAT
1.2           ask user for data input
1.3           take in the data
1.4           IF data is outwith range
              THEN display error message
1.5    end loop — UNTIL data is within
       range
```

Or, alternatively, enter the data first, and if the user correctly inputs the valid data on the first occasion, the validation loop need not be entered at all:

```
1.1    ask user for data input
1.2    take in the data
1.3    loop WHILE data input is outwith
       range
1.4           prompt to re-enter data
1.5           take in the data
1.6    end loop
```

Some software development environments, such as high-level languages, may automatically provide some form of input validation. For instance, entering a string (text value) into a program designed to accept a numeric input will sometimes provide the user with a re-entry prompt because of a variable type error.

```
Please enter a number
? w
Bad value.
? 1.2
```

In other languages, it will cause the program to halt execution altogether.

```
Please enter a number
w
Traceback (most recent call last):
File "/Volumes/Programs/ inputval.py",
line 2, in <module>
      number=int(input())
ValueError: invalid literal for int()
with base 10: 'w'
```

2 Linear search

A linear search algorithm is used to find an item of data (the target value) in a list.

This algorithm reports if the item has been found and its location. However, it does not tell the user if the target value is not in the list, nor does it find more than one occurrence of the target value in a list (see the count occurrences algorithm below).

```
2.1    ask user for target value
2.2    take in target value
2.3    loop — FOR each item in the list
2.4           IF current item = target
              value THEN
2.5                  display found message
2.6                  display item and its
                     location in the list
2.7           END IF
2.8    end loop — NEXT item
```

The following algorithm may be used in order to tell the user that the target value is not in the list if the search is unsuccessful. A Boolean variable called **found** is set to FALSE at the start of the search and is only set to TRUE if the target value is found.

```
2.1    set the value of found to be FALSE
2.2    ask user for target value
2.3    take in target value
2.4    loop — FOR each item in the list
2.5            IF current item = target value THEN
2.6                    set the value of found to be TRUE
2.7                    note the location of the target in the list
2.8            END IF
2.9    end loop — NEXT item
2.10   IF found is TRUE THEN
2.11           display found message
2.12           display item and its location in the list
2.13   ELSE
2.14           display item not found message
2.15   END IF
```

This algorithm will perform a linear search on an array of records.

```
2.1    set the value of found to FALSE
2.2    ask user for the target value
2.3    take in the target value
2.4    loop — FOR number of records in array
2.5            IF array[loop].item = target value THEN
2.6                    set the value of found to be TRUE
2.7                    note the location of the target in the list
2.8            END IF
2.9    end loop — NEXT item
2.10   IF found is TRUE THEN
2.11           display found message
2.12           display item and its location in the list
2.13   ELSE
2.14           display item not found message
2.15   END IF
```

All of the above linear search algorithms will work on a list in any order. If the list is sorted in, say, descending order, then it becomes possible to stop the search as soon as the current item being examined is smaller than the target item.

For example, when searching the ordered list: 99, 88, 65, 54, 32, 23 for the target value 90, you can stop searching once the value 88 is reached, since 90 is larger than 88.

In a short list like this, such an algorithm would not be of much benefit, but if a long list containing, say, 10,000 items was being searched then it would reduce the average search time.

The following linear search algorithm takes advantage of such an ordered list. It uses an additional variable called **exit** which is set to FALSE at the start of the search and is only set to TRUE when the current item being examined is smaller than the target item.

```
2.1   set the value of found to be FALSE

2.2   set the value of exit to be FALSE

2.3   start at first item in list

2.4   ask user for target value

2.5   take in target value

2.6   loop — WHILE (found is FALSE) AND (end of list not reached) AND (exit is FALSE)

2.7      CASE current item OF

2.8         WHEN = target value

2.9            set the value of found to be TRUE

2.10           note the location of the target in the list

2.11           display item and its location in the list

2.12        WHEN < target value

2.13           set the value of exit to be TRUE

2.14           display item not found message

2.15        WHEN > target value

2.16           move to next location in list

2.17     END CASE

2.18 end loop — END WHILE
```

If you know in advance that the list you are searching is sorted in order, then it is much more efficient to use a different algorithm called a binary search. The binary search algorithm is more efficient than the linear search algorithm because it usually requires fewer comparisons to find an item in a list. However, the binary search algorithm is outwith the scope of this unit on software development.

3 Counting occurrences

A counting occurrences algorithm will count how many times a value appears in a list. Compare this algorithm with the first linear search algorithm above.

```
3.1   set the number of times item found (hits) to zero
3.2   ask user for the target value
3.3   take in the target value
3.4   loop — FOR each item in the list
3.5       IF current item = target value THEN
3.6           add 1 to number of hits
3.7       END IF
3.8   end loop — NEXT item
3.9   display number of times item found (hits)
```

This algorithm will count occurrences in an array of records.

```
3.1   set the number of times item found (hits) to zero
3.2   ask user for the target value
3.3   take in the target value
3.5   loop — FOR number of records in array
3.6       IF array[loop].item = target value THEN
3.7           add 1 to number of hits
3.8   end loop — NEXT item
3.9   display number of times item found (hits)
```

4 Finding maximum and minimum

The maximum value is the highest value in a list. Here is one possible method of finding the maximum value. Note that it will only work correctly if the maximum value in the list is greater than or equal to zero.

> **NOTE**
>
> In some languages the loop may execute [number of records in array-1] times. (see above)

```
4.1   set the maximum value to be zero
4.2   loop — REPEAT
4.3       IF the current item is greater than the maximum value THEN
4.4           set the maximum value to be equal to the current item
4.5       END IF
4.6   end loop — UNTIL end of data has been reached
4.7   display maximum value
```

A better method is to set the maximum value to the first item in the list, like this:

```
4.1   set the maximum value to be equal to the first item
4.2   loop — FOR each item in the list
4.3       IF the current item is greater than the maximum value THEN
4.4           set the maximum value to be equal to the current item
4.5       END IF
4.6   end loop — NEXT item
4.7   display maximum value
```

This algorithm will find the maximum item in an array of records.

```
4.1   set maximum =array[0].item
4.2   set position to 0
4.3   loop — FOR number of records in array
4.4       IF array[loop].item > array[maximum].item THEN
4.5           set maximum index to loop
4.6           set position to loop
4.7       END IF
4.8   end loop — NEXT item
```

The minimum value is the smallest value in a list. This algorithm will find the minimum value in a list:

```
4.1   set the minimum value to be equal to the first item
4.2   loop — FOR each item in the list
4.3       IF the current item is less than the minimum value THEN
4.4           set the minimum value to be equal to the current item
4.5       END IF
4.6   end loop — NEXT item
4.7   display minimum value
```

Algorithms for finding the maximum and minimum value in a list are useful when sorting a list of items into order. However, the sort algorithm is outwith the scope of this unit on software development.

Implementation of standard algorithms

Each of the algorithms is implemented in Python and LiveCode. Note that no implementation for finding the minimum value is given, since it is very similar to finding the maximum. You should implement this algorithm in your chosen software development environment. See the questions at the end of this chapter.

Python implementations

NOTE

These solutions are provided for guidance only as there are many other ways to implement these algorithms in Python and LiveCode. Your teacher will guide you to the method they would like you to use to implement each algorithm.

Input validation

```
def checkValue():
        print("Enter a number in the range 1 to 10")
        value=int(input())
        while value<1 or value>10:
                print("The number you have entered is outwith the range 1 to 10. Please re-enter")
                value=int(input())
        return value
#Main Program
value=checkValue()
```

SAMPLE OUTPUT

```
Enter a number in the range 1 to 10

111

The number you have entered is outwith the range 1 to 10. Please re-enter

-1

The number you have entered is outwith the range 1 to 10. Please re-enter

0

The number you have entered is outwith the range 1 to 10. Please re-enter

1
```

Linear search

Fixed loop

This version of the program will find all occurrences of the search item in a list.

Search for a number in a list

```
def initialise(numbers):
        numbers=[45,65,23,67,88,90,1,67,6,22,78,31,99,28,84,54,71,16,49,11]
        return numbers
def getValue(targetNumber):
        print("Enter the value you wish to search for")
        targetNumber=int(input())
        return targetNumber
def search(targetNumber, numbers):
        found=False
        for counter in range(0,20):
                if numbers[counter]==targetNumber:
                        print(targetNumber,"was found at position", counter+1)
```

```
                        found=True
        if found==False:
                        print("Sorry, no matches found")
#Main Program
numbers=[0]*20
targetNumber=0
numbers= initialise(numbers)
targetNumber=getValue(targetNumber)
search(targetNumber, numbers)
```

```
SAMPLE OUTPUT
Enter the value you wish to search for
22
22 was found at position 10
Enter the value you wish to search for
4
Sorry, no matches found
Enter the value you wish to search for
67
67 was found at position 4
67 was found at position 8
```

Search for a name in a list

```
def initialise(names):
        names=["Anna","Ben","Carrie","Dennis","Eden","Frank","Gillian","Harry","Isla","Jordyn","Karis",
        "Larry", "Michaella","Norman","Olive","Ben"]
        return names
def getValue(targetName):
        print("Enter the name you would like to search for")
        targetName=input()
        return targetName
def search(targetName, names):
        found=False
        for counter in range(0,16):
                if names[counter]==targetName:
                        print(targetName,"was found at position",counter+1)
                        found=True
        if found==False:
                        print("Sorry, no matches found")
```

```
#Main Program
names=[""]*16
targetName=""
names= initialise(names)
targetName= getValue(targetName)
search(targetName, names)
```

SAMPLE OUTPUT

```
Enter the name you would like to search for
Isla
Isla was found at position 9
Enter the name you would like to search for
John
Sorry, no matches found
Enter the name you would like to search for
Ben
Ben was found at position 2
Ben was found at position 16
```

Conditional loop

This version of the program will find the first occurrence of the search item in a list.

Search for a number in a list

```python
def initialise(numbers):
        numbers=[45,65,23,67,88,90,1,67,6,22,78,31,99,28,84,54,71,16,49,11]
        return numbers
def getValue(targetNumber):
        print("Enter the value you wish to search for")
        targetNumber=int(input())
        return targetNumber
def search(targetNumber, numbers):
        found=False
        counter=0
        while found==False and counter!=20:
                if numbers[counter]==targetNumber:
                        found=True
                counter=counter+1
        if found==True:
                print(targetNumber,"was found at position",counter)
```

```
        else:
                print("Sorry, no matches found")
#Main Program
numbers=[0]*20
targetNumber=0
numbers= initialise(numbers)
targetNumber=getValue(targetNumber)
search(targetNumber, numbers)
```

SAMPLE OUTPUT

```
Enter the value you wish to search for
22
22 was found at position 10
4
Sorry, no matches found
67
67 was found at position 4
```

Notice that the conditional loop halts execution as soon as the first value 67
is found in the list, so it will never find the second value.

Search for a name in a list

```
def initialise(names):
        names=["Anna", "Ben", "Carrie", "Dennis", "Eden", "Frank", "Gillian", "Harry", "Isla", "Jordyn",
        "Karis", "Larry", "Michaella", "Norman", "Olive", "Ben"]
        return names
def getValue(targetName):
        print("Enter the name you would like to search for")
        targetName=input()
        return targetName
def search(targetName, names):
        found=False
        counter=0
        while found==False and counter!=16:
                if names[counter]==targetName:
                        found=True
                counter=counter+1
        if found==True:
                print(targetName,"was found at position",counter)
```

```
        else:
                print("Sorry, no matches found")
#Main Program
names=[""]*16
targetName=""
names=initialise(names)
targetName=getValue(targetName)
search(targetName, names)
```

SAMPLE OUTPUT

```
Enter the name you would like to search for
Isla
Isla was found at position 9
Enter the name you would like to search for
John
Sorry, no matches found
Enter the name you would like to search for
Ben
Ben was found at position 2
```

Again, notice that the conditional loop halts execution as soon as the first Ben is found in the list, so it will never find the second Ben.

External file

This version of the program will find all occurrences of the search item in an external file on Classic cars (classicCars.txt).

Search for the year 1953 in the external file

```
class carData():
        make:str
        model:str
        year:int
        cost:int
def readFile():
        cars = [carData() for x in range(50)]
        counter=0
        with open('classicCars.txt','r') as readfile:
                line = readfile.readline().rstrip('\n')
                while line:
                        items = line.split(",")
                        cars[counter].make = items[0]
                        cars[counter].model = items[1]
```

```
                            cars[counter].year = int(items[2])
                            cars[counter].cost=int(items[3])
                            line = readfile.readline().rstrip('\n')
                            counter += 1
                return cars
    def getYear(year):
                print("Enter the year you would like to search in")
                year=int(input())
                return year
    def search():
                found=False
                position=0
                for counter in range (len(cars)):
                            if cars[counter].year==year:
                            position=counter
                            print("The",cars[counter].make,cars[counter].model,"was found at position",position+1)
                            found=True
                if found==False:
                            print("Sorry, no matches found")
    #Main Program
    year=0
    cars = readFile()
    year=getYear(year)
    search()
```

```
SAMPLE OUTPUT
Enter the year you would like to search in
1953
The Jaguar XK 120SE Roadster was found at position 15
The Morris Minor Saloon was found at position 46
```

Counting occurrences

Fixed loop

Count the number of occurrences of a name in a list.

```
def initialise(names):
        names=["Anna", "Ben", "Carrie", "Dennis", "Eden", "Frank", "Gillian", "Harry", "Isla", "Jordyn",
        "Karis", "Larry", "Michaella", "Norman", "Olive", "Ben"]
        return names
def getValue(targetName):
```

```
        print("Enter the name you would like to search for")
        targetName=input()
        return targetName
def count(hits):
        for counter in range(0,16):
                if names[counter]==targetName:
                        hits=hits+1
        return hits
def displayHits(hits):
                print(targetName,"was found",hits,"times")
#main
names=[""]*16
hits=0
targetName=""
names=initialise(names)
targetName=getValue(targetName)
hits =count(hits)
displayHits(hits)
```

SAMPLE OUTPUT

```
Enter the name you would like to search for
Ben
Ben was found 2 times
```

External file

This version of the program will count all occurrences of the search item in an external file on Classic cars (classicCars.txt).

Search for the make 'Morris' in the external file

```
class carData():
        make:str
        model:str
        year:int
        cost:int
def readFile():
        cars = [carData() for x in range(50)]
        counter=0
        with open('classicCars.txt','r') as readfile:
                line = readfile.readline().rstrip('\n')
```

```
            while line:
                    items = line.split(",")
                    cars[counter].make = items[0]
                    cars[counter].model = items[1]
                    cars[counter].year = int(items[2])
                    cars[counter].cost=int(items[3])
                    line = readfile.readline().rstrip('\n')
                    counter += 1
        return cars
def getMake(make):
        print("Enter the make of car you would like to search for")
        make=input()
        return make
def count(hits):
        for counter in range (len(cars)):
                if cars[counter].make==make:
                        hits+=1
        return hits
def displayHits():
        print("The",make,"was found",hits,"times")
#Main Program
hits=0
make=""
cars = readFile()
make=getMake(make)
hits=count(hits)
displayHits()
```

Finding the maximum

Display the largest number in a list.

```
def initialise(numbers):
        numbers=[45,65,23,67,88,90,1,67,6,22,78,31,99,28,84,54,71,16,49,11]
        return numbers
```

```
def findMax(numbers):
        maxNo=numbers[0]
        for counter in range(len(numbers)):
                if numbers[counter]>maxNo:
                        maxNo=numbers[counter]
        return maxNo
def displaymaxNo(maxNo):
        print("The largest number in the list is",maxNo)
#main
numbers=[0]*20
numbers=initialise(numbers)
maxNo=findmaxNo(numbers)
displaymaxNo(maxNo)
```

SAMPLE OUTPUT

```
The largest number in the list is 99
```

External file – Finding the minimum

This version of the program will display the cheapest car in an external file
on Classic cars (classicCars.txt).

```
class carData():
        make:str
        model:str
        year:int
        cost:int
def readFile():
        cars = [carData() for x in range(50)]
        counter=0
        with open("classicCars.csv") as csvDataFile:
                csvReader = csv.reader(csvDataFile)
                for row in csvReader:
                        cars[counter].make=row[0]
                        cars[counter].model=row[1]
                        cars[counter].year=int(row[2])
                        cars[counter].cost=int(row[3])
                        counter += 1
        return cars
```

```
def findCheapest(cars):
        cheapest = cars[0].cost
        position=0
        for counter in range (1,50):
                if cars[counter].cost < cheapest:
                        cheapest = cars[counter].cost
                        position=counter
        return cheapest, position
def displayCheapest(position,cheapest):
        print("The cheapest classic car is a",cars[position].make, cars[position].model,"at £",cheapest)
#Main Program
import csv
cars = readFile()
cheapest,position = findCheapest(cars)
displayCheapest(position,cheapest)
```

> **SAMPLE OUTPUT**
>
> ```
> The cheapest classic car is a Hillman Minx at £2000
> ```

LiveCode implementations

These solutions are provided for guidance only. Your teacher will guide you
to the method they would like you to use to implement each algorithm.

Input validation

```
on mouseUp
        local userValue
        initialise
        put checkValue(userValue) into userValue
end mouseUp
on initialise
        put empty into field "output"
        put 0 into userValue
end initialise
function checkValue userValue
        ask "Enter a number in the range 1 to 10"
        if the result =cancel then exit to top
        put it into userValue
        repeat until userValue>=1 and userValue<=10 and userValue is an integer
```

```
        ask "The number you have entered is not an integer or is outwith the range 1 to 10.
        Please re-enter"

        if the result =cancel then exit to top

        put it into userValue

    end repeat

    return userValue

end checkValue
```

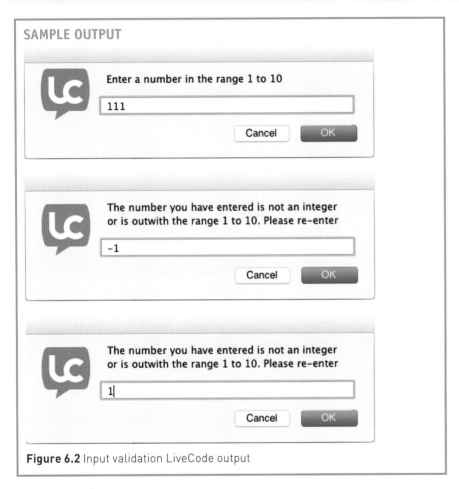

SAMPLE OUTPUT

Enter a number in the range 1 to 10

111

Cancel   OK

The number you have entered is not an integer
or is outwith the range 1 to 10. Please re-enter

-1

Cancel   OK

The number you have entered is not an integer
or is outwith the range 1 to 10. Please re-enter

1|

Cancel   OK

Figure 6.2 Input validation LiveCode output

Linear search

Fixed loop

This version of the program will find all occurrences of the search item in a list.

> **NOTE**
>
> **on initialise** contains an array of integers. This integer array will be used for all subsequent LiveCode programs in on initialise where an integer array is used but will not be explicitly stated in each program

Search for a number in a list

```
on mouseUp
        local arrayNumbers
        put empty into field output
        local targetNumber
        initialise arrayNumbers
        getValue targetNumber
        search targetNumber, arrayNumbers
end mouseUp
on initialise @arrayNumbers
        put 0 into targetNumber
        put 45 into arrayNumbers[0]
        put 65 into arrayNumbers[1]
        put 23 into arrayNumbers[2]
        put 67 into arrayNumbers[3]
        put 88 into arrayNumbers[4]
        put 90 into arrayNumbers[5]
        put 1 into arrayNumbers[6]
        put 67 into arrayNumbers[7]
        put 6 into arrayNumbers[8]
        put 22 into arrayNumbers[9]
        put 78 into arrayNumbers[10]
        put 31 into arrayNumbers[11]
        put 99 into arrayNumbers[12]
        put 28 into arrayNumbers[13]
        put 84 into arrayNumbers[14]
        put 54 into arrayNumbers[15]
        put 71 into arrayNumbers[16]
        put 16 into arrayNumbers[17]
        put 49 into arrayNumbers[18]
        put 11 into arrayNumbers[19]
end initialise
on getValue @targetNumber
        ask"Enter the value you wish to search for"
        if the result=cancel then exit to top
        put it into targetNumber
end getValue
```

```
on search targetNumber, @arrayNumbers
    local found
    local counter
    put false into found
    repeat with counter = 0 to 19
        if targetNumber=arrayNumbers[counter] then
            put targetNumber & " was found at position " &counter+1 &return after field "output"
            put true into found
        end if
    end repeat
    if found=false then
        put "Sorry, no matches found" & return after field "output"
    end if
end search
```

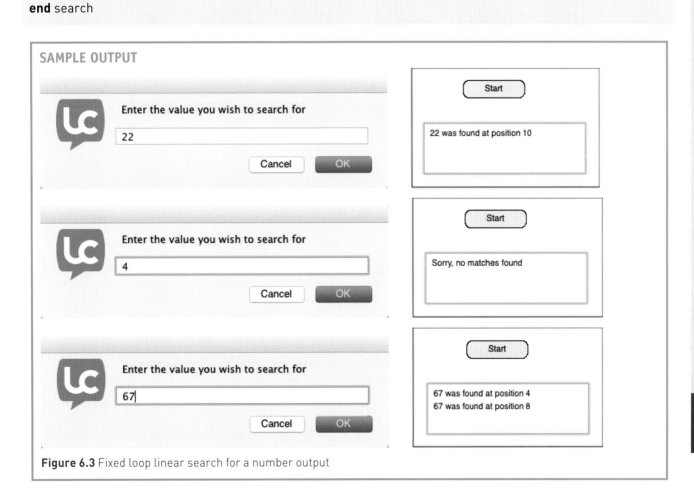

SAMPLE OUTPUT

Figure 6.3 Fixed loop linear search for a number output

> **NOTE**
>
> **on initialise** contains an array of string.
>
> This string array will be used for all subsequent LiveCode programs in on initialise where a string array is to be used but will not be explicitly stated in each program.

Search for a name in a list

```
on mouseUp
        local arrayNames
        put empty into field output
        local targetName
        initialise arrayNames
        getValue targetName
        search targetName, arrayNames
end mouseUp
on initialise @arrayNames
        put "" into targetName
        put "Anna" into arrayNames[0]
        put "Ben" into arrayNames[1]
        put "Carrie" into arrayNames[2]
        put "Dennis" into arrayNames[3]
        put "Eden" into arrayNames[4]
        put "Frank" into arrayNames[5]
        put "Gillian" into arrayNames[6]
        put "Harry" into arrayNames[7]
        put "Isla" into arrayNames[8]
        put "Jordyn" into arrayNames[9]
        put "Karis" into arrayNames[10]
        put "Larry" into arrayNames[11]
        put "Michaella" into arrayNames[12]
        put "Norman" into arrayNames[13]
        put "Olive" into arrayNames[14]
        put "Ben" into arrayNames[15]
end initialise
on getValue @targetName
        ask"Enter the name you would like to search for"
        if the result=cancel then exit to top
        put it into targetName
```

```
end getValue
on search targetName, @arrayNames
        local found
        local counter
        put false into found
        repeat with counter = 0 to 15
                if targetName=arrayNames[counter] then
                        put targetName & " was found at position " &counter+1 &return after field "output"
                        put true into found
                end if
        end repeat
        if found=false then
                put "Sorry, no matches found" & return after field "output"
        end if
end search
```

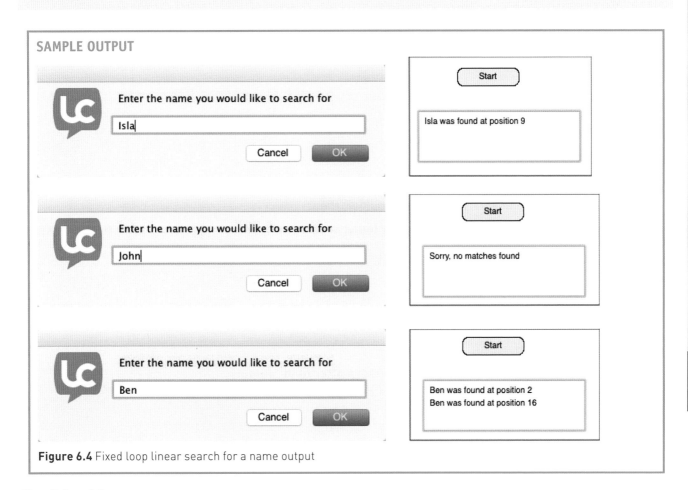

SAMPLE OUTPUT

Figure 6.4 Fixed loop linear search for a name output

Conditional loop

This version of the program will find the first occurrence of the search item in a list.

Search for a number in a list

```
on mouseUp
        local arrayNumbers
        put empty into field output
        local targetNumber
        initialise arrayNumbers
        getValue targetNumber
        search targetNumber, arrayNumbers
end mouseUp
on initialise @arrayNumbers
```

The array of integers can be found in the fixed loop program on page 61.

```
end initialise
on getValue @targetNumber
        ask"Enter the value you wish to search for"
        if the result=cancel then exit to top
        put it into targetNumber
end getValue
on search targetNumber, @arrayNumbers
        local found
        local counter
        put false into found
        put 0 into counter
        repeat until counter=20 or found=true
                if targetNumber=arrayNumbers[counter] then
                        put targetNumber & " was found at position " &counter+1 &return after field "output"
                        put true into found
                end if
                put counter+1 into counter
        end repeat
        if found=false then
                put "Sorry, no matches found" & return after field "output"
        end if
end search
```

SAMPLE OUTPUT

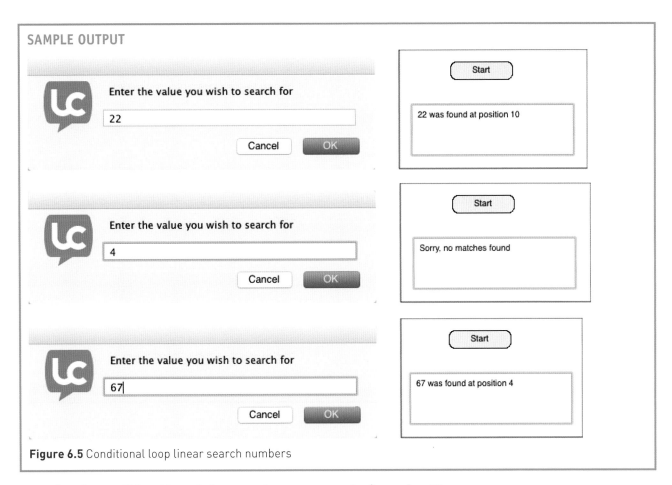

Figure 6.5 Conditional loop linear search numbers

Notice that the conditional loop halts execution as soon as the first value 67 is found in the list, so it will never find the second value.

Search for a name in a list

```
on mouseUp
        local arrayNames
        put empty into field output
        local targetName
        initialise arrayNames
        getValue targetName
        search targetName, arrayNames
end mouseUp
on initialise @arrayNames
```

The array of string can be found in the fixed loop program on page 61.

```
end initialise
on getValue @targetName
        ask"Enter the name you would like to search for"
        if the result=cancel then exit to top
        put it into targetName
end getValue
```

```
on search @targetName, @arrayNames
    local found
    local counter
    put false into found
    repeat until counter=16 or found=true
        if targetName=arrayNames[counter] then
            put targetName & " was found at position " &counter+1 &return after field "output"
            put true into found
        end if
        put counter+1 into counter
    end repeat
    if found=false then
        put "Sorry, no matches found" & return into field "output"
    end if
end search
```

Figure 6.6 Conditional loop linear search names

Again, notice that the conditional loop halts execution as soon as the first Ben is found in the list, so it will never find the second Ben.

External file

This version of the program will find all occurrences of the search item in an external file on Classic cars (classicCars.txt).

Search for the year 1953 in the external file

```
on mouseUp
        local arrayRecordCars
        put empty into field "output"
        initialise
        readFile arrayRecordCars
        getYear year
        search arrayRecordCars, year
end mouseUp
on initialise
        local year
        put 0 into year
        local counter
        local hits
        repeat with counter = 0 to 49
                put "" into arrayRecordCars[counter]["make"]
                put "" into arrayRecordCars[counter]["make"]
                put 0 into arrayRecordCars[counter]["year"]
                put 0 into arrayRecordCars[counter]["cost"]
        end repeat
end initialise
on readFile @arrayRecordCars
        local counter
        local theFilePath
        put 0 into counter
        put the fileName of this stack into theFilePath
        set itemDel to "/"
        put "classicCars.txt" into the last item of theFilePath
        open file theFilePath for read
        read from file theFilePath until eof
        put it into theData
        close file theFilePath
        set itemDel to comma
        repeat for each line theLine in theData
                put item 1 of theLine into arrayRecordCars[counter]["make"]
                put item 2 of theLine into arrayRecordCars[counter]["model"]
```

```
            put item 3 of theLine into arrayRecordCars[counter]["year"]
            put item 4 of theLine into arrayRecordCars[counter]["cost"]
            add 1 to counter
        end repeat
end readFile
on getYear @year
        ask "Enter the year you would like to search for"
        if the result=cancel then exit to top
        put it into year
end getYear
on search @arrayRecordCars,year
        local found
        local counter
        put false into found
        repeat with counter = 0 to 49
            if arrayRecordCars[counter]["year"] = year then
                put counter into position
                put "The" && arrayRecordCars[counter]["make"] && arrayRecordCars[counter]
                ["model"] &&"was found at position" && position+1 & return after field "output"
                put true into found
            end if
        end repeat
        if found = false then
            put "Sorry, no matches found" &return after field "output"
        end if
end search
```

SAMPLE OUTPUT

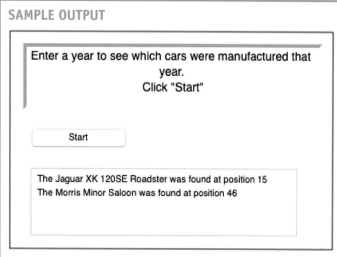

Figure 6.7 Linear search - external file

Counting occurrences

Fixed loop

Count the number of occurrences of a name in a list.

```
on mouseUp
        local arrayNames
        put empty into field output
        local hits
        initialise arrayNames
        getValue targetName
        count targetName,hits, arrayNames
        displayHits targetName, hits
end mouseUp
on initialise @arrayNames
end initialise
on getValue @targetName
        ask"Enter the name you would like to search for"
        if the result=cancel then exit to top
        put it into targetName
end getValue
on count targetName,@hits, @arrayNames
        local counter
        put 0 into hits
        repeat with counter = 0 to 15
                if targetName=arrayNames[counter] then
                        put hits+1 into hits
                end if
        end repeat
end count
on displayHits targetName, hits
        put targetName&" was found " &hits& " times" after field "output"
end displayHits
```

Enter the name you would like to search for

Ben

Cancel   OK

Start

Ben was found 2 times

Figure 6.8 Counting occurrences

External file

This version of the program will count all occurrences of the search item in an external file on Classic cars (classicCars.txt).

Search for the make 'Morris' in the external file

```
on mouseUp
        local arrayRecordCars
        put empty into field "output"
        initialise
        readFile arrayRecordCars
        getMake make
        count arrayRecordCars,hits,make
        displayHits make, hits
end mouseUp
on initialise
        local make
        put "" into make
        local counter
        local hits
        repeat with counter = 0 to 49
                put "" into arrayRecordCars[counter]["make"]
                put "" into arrayRecordCars[counter]["make"]
                put 0 into arrayRecordCars[counter]["year"]
                put 0 into arrayRecordCars[counter]["cost"]
        end repeat
end initialise
```

```
on readFile @arrayRecordCars
        local counter
        local theFilePath
        put 0 into counter
        put the fileName of this stack into theFilePath
        set itemDel to "/"
        put "classicCars.txt" into the last item of theFilePath
        open file theFilePath for read
        read from file theFilePath until eof
        put it into theData
        close file theFilePath
        set itemDel to comma
        repeat for each line theLine in theData
                put item 1 of theLine into arrayRecordCars[counter]["make"]
                put item 2 of theLine into arrayRecordCars[counter]["model"]
                put item 3 of theLine into arrayRecordCars[counter]["year"]
                put item 4 of theLine into arrayRecordCars[counter]["cost"]
                add 1 to counter
        end repeat
end readFile
on getMake @make
        ask "Enter the make of car you would like to search for"
        if the result=cancel then exit to top
        put it into make
end getMake
on count @arrayRecordCars,@hits,make
        local counter
        put 0 into hits
        repeat with counter = 0 to 49
                if arrayRecordCars[counter]["make"] = make then
                        put hits+1 into hits
                end if
        end repeat
end count
on displayHits make, hits
        put make&" was found " &hits& " times" & return after field "output"
end displayHits
```

Enter the make of car you would like to search for

Morris

Cancel   OK

Count the number of each make of car.
Click "Start"

Start

Morris was found 5 times

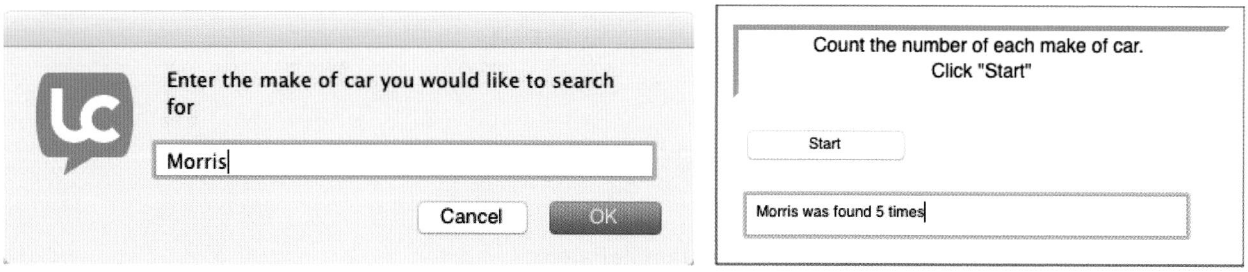

Figure 6.9 Counting occurrences – external file

Finding the maximum

Display the largest number in a list.

```
on mouseUp
        local arrayNumbers
        put empty into field output
        initialise arrayNumbers
        findMax maxNo, arrayNumbers
        displayMax maxNo
end mouseUp
on initialise @arrayNumbers
```

The array of integer can be found in the fixed loop program on page 59.

```
end initialise
on findMax @maxNo,@arrayNumbers
        local counter
        put arrayNumbers[0] into maxNo
        repeat with counter = 1 to 19
                if arrayNumbers[counter]>maxNo then
                        put arrayNumbers[counter] into maxNo
                end if
        end repeat
end findMax
on displayMax maxNo
        put "The largest number in the list is " &maxNo &return after field "output"
end displayMax
```

SAMPLE OUTPUT

> Start

The largest number in the list is 99

Figure 6.10 Finding the maximum in a list

External file – finding the minimum

This version of the program will display the cheapest car in an external file on Classic cars (classicCars.txt).

```
on mouseUp
        local arrayRecordCars
        put empty into field "output"
        initialise
        readFile arrayRecordCars
        findCheapest position,cheapest, arrayRecordCars
        displayCheapest position,cheapest, arrayRecordCars
end mouseUp
on initialise
        local position, cheapest
        local counter
        repeat with counter = 0 to 49
                put "" into arrayRecordCars[counter]["make"]
                put "" into arrayRecordCars[counter]["make"]
                put 0 into arrayRecordCars[counter]["year"]
                put 0 into arrayRecordCars[counter]["cost"]
        end repeat
end initialise
on readFile @arrayRecordCars
        local counter
        local theFilePath
        put 0 into counter
        put the fileName of this stack into theFilePath
        set itemDel to "/"
        put "classicCars.csv" into the last item of theFilePath
        open file theFilePath for read
```

```
        read from file theFilePath until eof
        put it into theData
        close file theFilePath
        set itemDel to comma
        repeat for each line theLine in theData
                put item 1 of theLine into arrayRecordCars[counter]["make"]
                put item 2 of theLine into arrayRecordCars[counter]["model"]
                put item 3 of theLine into arrayRecordCars[counter]["year"]
                put item 4 of theLine into arrayRecordCars[counter]["cost"]
                add 1 to counter
        end repeat
end readFile
on findCheapest @position,@cheapest, @arrayRecordCars
        local counter
        put 0 into counter
        put 0 into position
        put 0 into cheapest
        put arrayRecordCars[counter]["cost"] into cheapest
        repeat with counter = 1 to 49
                if arrayRecordCars[counter]["cost"] < cheapest then
                        put arrayRecordCars[counter]["cost"] into cheapest
                        put counter into position
                end if
        end repeat
end findCheapest
on displayCheapest position,cheapest, @arrayRecordCars
        put "The cheapest classic car is a " & arrayRecordCars[position]["make"] &" "&
        arrayRecordCars[position]["model"] &" at £"&cheapest &return after field "output"
end displayCheapest
```

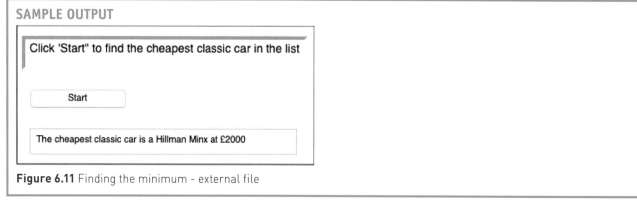

SAMPLE OUTPUT

Click 'Start' to find the cheapest classic car in the list

Start

The cheapest classic car is a Hillman Minx at £2000

Figure 6.11 Finding the minimum - external file

CHECK YOUR LEARNING

Now answer questions 1–13 below

QUESTIONS

1 At which stage in the software development process is an algorithm produced?

2 Which algorithm would you use to:
   a check program input?
   b find an item in a list?
   c count how many times an item appears in a list?
   d find the highest and lowest values in a list?

3 a Which design notation is used to represent the algorithms in this chapter?
   b Suggest why this design notation was chosen.
   c Choose one of the algorithms from this chapter and show how it would be represented using a structure diagram design notation. Look back at Chapter 3 for examples of structure diagrams.

4 Which algorithm described in this chapter would be likely to appear in a robust program?

5 Look at both the linear search and the count occurrences algorithms on pages 44–47. State one difference and one similarity between these two algorithms.

6 Look at the linear search algorithms on page 44. What advantage is provided by using an ordered list?

7 Why does the input validation algorithm use a conditional (REPEAT/WHILE) rather than an unconditional (FOR) loop structure?

8 Write a new algorithm which finds *both* the minimum and maximum values in a list.

9 Look back at the algorithms described in this chapter whose implementations are *not* shown. Choose one of these algorithms and implement it in your chosen software development environment.

10 The data used in the linear search program on page 44 ranges from 1 to 100. Change the linear search algorithm by adding input validation.

11 The finding maximum implementation is shown on page 47. Implement the finding minimum algorithm.

12 In both the finding maximum and finding minimum algorithms, why is it not a good idea to set the maximum or minimum to zero at the start?

13 The 10th annual Europa Canticum song competition has just taken place. The competition has singing acts from 44 European countries. Each act is given a score out of 100 based on its performance on the night by a panel of 10 judges. A file stores data about each country for each year the country took part. A sample of this data is shown below.

Act name	The Cannae Scot
Song name	Just bella bella
Country	Scotland
Year	2015
Total score	86

a) This data is to be stored in a record data structure. Using a programming language with which you are familiar, define a suitable data structure for this sample data.

b) This file contains data about 44 countries from each of the 10 years the competition has taken place. Define the variable which would be able to store this data using the data structure from part a).

c) Design an algorithm which will find the country with the highest score over the 10 years.

d) Design an algorithm which will show how many times 0 points has been scored.

KEY POINTS

- Input validation is used to check that data input is within a certain (acceptable) range.
- Linear search is used to find an item of data (the target value) in a list.
- Counting occurrences is used to count how many times a value appears in a list.
- Finding maximum and minimum is used to find the maximum and minimum values in a list.

Chapter 7 Testing

This chapter looks at how programs are tested, the types of errors and tools used to debug a program.

The following topics are covered:

- Describe, exemplify and implement a comprehensive final test plan to show that the functional requirements are met.
- Identify syntax, execution and logic errors at this level.
- Describe and exemplify debugging techniques:
  - dry runs
  - trace tables/tools
  - breakpoints
  - watchpoints.

What is testing?

To make sure that your program actually solves the problem it is supposed to (i.e. meets the software specification) you have to **test** it. Testing a program means that you have to run it to see whether or not it behaves as expected.

Testing should be both systematic and comprehensive. **Systematic testing** means that your testing, should follow a plan and not just be haphazard. To properly carry out systematic testing, it is necessary to develop a **test plan**.

A test plan should outline what you are trying to test and how you are going to do it, for example:

- What program (or module) is being tested.
- What the program (or module) should do.
- List suitable **test data** which can be input into the program.
- Expected results or desired outcomes from the test data.

Comprehensive testing means that you should test your programs as thoroughly and completely as you can ensuring that they meet the functional requirements. It would be ideal if it was possible to test *every* part of a program with all kinds of test data. This is called **exhaustive testing** and it is discussed in greater detail later on in this chapter. Unfortunately, exhaustive testing is not *always* possible, because that would mean testing every single line in the program and every possible program pathway. What is a program pathway?

Look at the following example of a program pathway:

```
<program line 1>

<program line 2>

<program line 3>
```

This is a **sequence**, and it represents a single program pathway. However, it is usual for programs to have many different pathways. Which pathway is taken depends upon the result of **selection**, which is based on a **control structure** (such as IF…THEN) together with at least one condition.

For instance:

```
IF number = target THEN

     pathway 1

ELSE

     pathway 2

END IF
```

This represents two separate pathways, one for *number = target* and another for *number <> target*. This is fine for small programs, but most programs have many possible pathways. Some people think that testing can *never* ensure that a program is totally correct, because it is impossible to test all the program pathways. However, any programs that you will be asked to write will be relatively short and should not have too many pathways for you to test, so you should be able to ensure that your programs are free from error.

> **NOTE**
> For Higher, you only need to know about comprehensive testing.

Test data

One method of testing a program is to use a set of data, called test data. It would take far too long to test a program for all possible sets of test data, so you have to choose a representative set of data. If the program works correctly for the test data, then you can be reasonably certain that the program will work for other similar data. There are three different types of test data: **normal**, **extreme** and **exceptional**.

The best way to use test data is to calculate what the answer will be if your program works properly, *before* you run the program. Then, run the program with the test data. If the results from the program match the answers you got from your manual calculation, the program is probably correct.

Another way of testing a program is to get someone else to do it for you. By the time you've finished writing your program, you're usually so familiar with the program code you've written, that you can't see any mistakes. Someone else looking at it might be able to spot mistakes that you've missed.

Let's look at a problem which will help you to understand what is meant by normal, extreme and exceptional test data.

Remember the assumptions for the Average problem. The maximum amount of numbers is 10. The maximum value of a number is 100. All the numbers are whole numbers, apart from the average, which has to be displayed correct to two decimal places.

Suppose you have written a program which solves this problem and you are getting ready to test your program. Here are some examples of test data:

Normal: the program should accept this data	Expected output
45,86,93,4,23,67,43	Average = 51.57
90,10,78,89,54,34,17,66,98	Average = 59.56

Table 7.1 Normal test data for the Average problem

Normal data is data which is within the limits that your program should be able to deal with.

Extreme data is data which is at the ends of the acceptable range of data – on the limit(s) or boundaries of the problem. Extreme data may also be called limit or boundary data.

Extreme: the program should accept this data	Expected output
1,100,0	Average = 33.67
1,100	Average = 50.50
100,100	Average = 100.00
1,1	Average = 1.00
0,0	Average = 0.00
1	Average = 1.00
0	Average = 0.00

Table 7.2 Extreme test data for the Average problem

Exceptional data is data which is invalid. A well-written program should be able to detect any exceptional data, warn the user of the error, and give them another chance to enter the data. Sometimes it is possible to reduce the chance of error messages caused by invalid data appearing in your program. A well-written program should validate all user input.

Exceptional: the program should reject this data	Possible error message
–1	Out of range, please enter a whole number between 0 and 100
101	Out of range, please enter a whole number between 0 and 100
0.2	Not a whole number, please enter a whole number between 0 and 100
number	Not a number, please enter a whole number between 0 and 100

Table 7.3 Exceptional test data for the Average problem

Figure 7.1 Anecdotal testing

Test table

When testing the data to be input, it helps to set up a test table as shown in Tables 7.4 and 7.5. You should ensure that you create a test table whenever you have a program that needs to be tested.

Data	Type of test	Expected	Actual
45,86,93,4,23,67,43	Normal	Accepted	
45,86,93,4,23,67,43	Normal	Accepted	
1,100,0	Extreme	Accepted	
1,100	Extreme	Accepted	
–1	Exceptional	Out of range, please enter a whole number between 0 and 100	
101	Exceptional	Out of range, please enter a whole number between 0 and 100	
0.2	Exceptional	Not a whole number, please enter a whole number between 0 and 100	
number	Exceptional	Not a number, please enter a whole number between 0 and 100	

Table 7.4 Testing input validation using the test data for the Average problem

Data	Expected	Actual
45,86,93,4,23,67,43	51.57	
90,10,78,89,54,34,17,66,98	59.56	
1,100,0	33.67	
1,100	50.50	
100,100	100.00	
1,1	1.00	
0,0	0.00	
1	1.00	
0	0.00	

Table 7.5 Testing calculations using the test data for the Average problem

The *Expected* column shows what the program should output when the test data is input. The *Actual* column shows what was actually output when the test data was input. Any differences should be noted in the test report (see later in this chapter), the program corrected and then retested to check that it now produces the correct output. This continues until the program operates as requested in the functional requirements.

Other types of testing

Exhaustive testing

Suppose that you have written a program to solve the Average problem (see Chapter 2) and have tested it with the above test data. Your program passes all the tests and appears to work properly. Can you then say that you have *fully tested* your program? No, because you have not tested *all* the possible sets of numbers that the program is designed to handle.

How many different sets of numbers would you need to test?

Let's work it out:

Total range of numbers 0 to 100, a total of 101 numbers

Quantity of numbers, 1 to 10

That makes a total of 70,484,500,000,000,000,000 possible different sets of numbers!

You can see that even for a relatively simple (some would say trivial) problem, like the Average problem, it is practically impossible to test all of the possible sets of numbers.

Suppose you decided to try and test all the possible sets of numbers and let's say it takes you one minute to run the program, enter the numbers, and record the output: that would be a total of 70,484,500,000,000,000,000 minutes … that makes 1,174,741,666,666,666,500 hours or 134,102,929,984,779 years. In fact, if you worked it all out (I did!), it would take you 134,102,930 million years to enter and test all the different sets of numbers you could possibly have with this program. Obviously, it is unrealistic to expect anyone to try and carry out exhaustive testing. How could you speed up the testing process? (Answer – use a computer to test the program.)

Most commercial programs are so large and complicated that it is impossible to test them and be sure that you've got rid of all the errors. Consider the following example:

> On June 4, 1996, the maiden flight of the European Ariane 5 launcher crashed about 40 seconds after takeoff. Media reports indicated that the amount lost was half a billion dollars – uninsured. The subsequent enquiry concluded that the explosion was the result of a software error – possibly the costliest in history (at least in dollar terms, since earlier cases have caused loss of life).

One report on the incident recommended more software testing, but:

testing can be used to show the presence of errors but never to prove their absence

and, the only fully 'realistic' test was to launch the rocket. However, the launch was not really intended as a $500 million test of the software!

Some software companies have exploited the need for exhaustive testing by producing special test software which will test applications and identify parts of the code which have not been tested. One such program is Unicom's TeamBLUE™ software PurifyPlus™ which is designed to test programs written in VisualC/ C++, Visual Basic and Java. I wonder who tests the PurifyPlus software …

However, it is possible to write programs that are correct if you follow the software development process carefully, paying particular attention to the analysis and design stages. Remember the iterative nature of the software development process described earlier in this unit. You will certainly have to go through some stages of the software development process more than once before your program is correct.

Depending on the problem you've been asked to solve, you might be given a set of test data to use, or you might have to make up your own. If you have to make up your own test data, you should try to choose a set of test data which includes normal, extreme and exceptional data. If your program doesn't produce the results you expect, you'll have to check through each line of the code. Sometimes it is useful to put extra statements into your program which will print out the values of certain variables at different stages of the run. This is called **printing a snapshot of selected variables**. It can help you find out exactly where the program may be going wrong. **Breakpoints** and **watchpoints** (see later in this chapter) can also be set to view values of variables.

Field testing

Software companies whose programs are used on many types of computer system face a major challenge to ensure that their programs will work correctly under all circumstances. It is impossible for the software company to replicate all the different possible types of hardware set-up or operating system software that the user may have. In this case, the company is largely dependent on the user for error reporting; the user is in fact the program tester as well.

Field testing means allowing users (i.e. people other than the programmer who wrote the program) to test the program. When you are field testing a program, you should keep a careful record of how the software behaves on your computer. If the program crashes, then the conditions which caused the crash should be noted, and the programmer informed, so that the error can be corrected.

In a field-testing situation, a software company will send out different versions of a program for testing. The **alpha test version** is usually distributed within the company and is not released to outsiders. The **beta test version** is given to selected outsiders or is put on general release with users acknowledging the fact that they do not have a finished product. This **beta testing** stage is also known as **acceptance testing**. Software companies often persuade a wide range of users to become beta testers by distributing free copies of software at this stage of its development. In some cases, beta testers who do a good job of thoroughly testing the software may be given a free copy of the final version as a reward for their hard work.

Test reports may be produced at various points during the testing process. A test report summarises the results of testing. In commercial and professional programming situations, an **acceptance test report** often forms a contractual document within which acceptance of software is agreed between the programmer and the client for whom the software has been written.

Independent test group

Specialised companies known as **independent test groups** have been set up in order to test software. These groups of people are not associated with the software company or the programmers who wrote the software and so can be relied upon to provide an unbiased opinion. An independent test group may carry out the following sequence of operations while testing software:

- examine the source code, object code, test plan and results of testing already carried out by the software developer.
- document additional tests to be carried out if appropriate.
- retest the software, repeating all the original tests and performing any additional tests.
- document any errors found and communicate these to the software developer for correction.

- receive corrected code from the developer.
- repeat all tests on the corrected code.

This sequence of operations will be repeated (iteration) until all test results are acceptable, or it is decided that any remaining problems do not require to be fixed.

Cost of faulty software

A recent report from software testing company Tricentis, *Software Fail Watch: 5th Edition*, recorded that software failures had impacted 3.7 billion people, 314 companies and had cost an estimated $1.7 trillion in assets. That's about £1.4 trillion and by their own estimation, doesn't cover every piece of software with defects!

In 2020, the UK government spent £12 million on a centralised contact tracing smartphone app for COVID-19 which was beset with problems, not least of which was the issue of data privacy. The UK government finally opted in favour of an already working decentralised model developed by Apple™ and Google. At the time of writing, development work on this app was still ongoing with the app and the Google/Apple framework.

CHECK YOUR LEARNING

Now answer questions 1–8 (on page 85)

Error reporting

Error reporting is the communication and explanation of errors in the software to the user. Most computers attempt to indicate the likely source of an error in a piece of software by producing error messages.

Debugging

Debugging is the process of finding and correcting the errors in your program. Program errors have been called 'bugs' since the early days of computing, because the failure of one of the first computers in 1945 was caused by a dead moth being caught in the electrical components. The first stage of debugging is to find the part of the program which is causing the error; the second stage is to fix it.

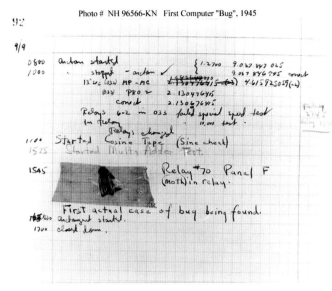

Photo # NH 96566-KN First Computer "Bug", 1945

Figure 7.2 The first ever computer bug

Errors are a regular feature of programming. In this chapter, we will look at syntax, execution and logic errors as well as system errors and compilation errors.

Syntax and compilation errors

A **compilation error** is an error which is detected during the process of compilation (or translation) of the program into the object code before it is run. Compilation errors are usually **syntax errors**.

Linking errors may occur when a compiled program is linked to a subroutine or module library. For example, if the required module is not present in the library or you have made a mistake in the parameter block.

> **NOTE**
>
> Linking errors are included for completeness and are not required for Higher Computing Science.

Syntax errors occur when the syntax, or rules of the programming language are broken.

A **statement syntax error** is misspelling a keyword, like typing *rpint* instead of *print* or *reapeat* instead of *repeat*.

A **program** or **structure syntax error** happens when you have made a mistake in the structure of your program, such as incorrect use of a control structure. This type of syntax error may be detected by examining or proofreading a structured listing (see Figure 7.6).

Example of incorrect use of a control structure:

```
FOR counter FROM 1 TO 10 DO
    FOR time FROM 1 TO 7 DO
        SEND times & counter TO DISPLAY
    END FOR
```

Can you spot the mistake?

If you are using a compiled language, you will find that it reports both types of syntax errors only when the program is compiled. An interpreted language usually reports statement syntax errors when the line containing the mistake is entered.

Execution (run-time) errors

Execution or run-time errors are errors which show up during program execution. **Overflow**, **rounding** and **truncation** are types of error which are caused by a limited amount of memory either in the computer (e.g. a fixed amount of space to store numbers) or decided by the programmer (e.g. a DIM statement). **Division by zero** is another typical run-time error.

Overflow errors

Overflow is a general term which describes what happens when something becomes too large to be processed accurately. For example, the result of a calculation may become too large to be stored in the space the computer has for numbers. The farmer and cattle problem in Chapter 2 is an example of an overflow error. An overflow error will normally cause a program to crash if it is allowed to occur. The error which caused the loss of the Ariane space rocket, described earlier in this chapter, was an example of an overflow error. The program tried to put a 64-bit number into a memory location capable of holding only 16 bits.

Rounding errors

Rounding happens when a number is reduced to a given number of decimal places, for instance 3.89 may be rounded up to 3.9. A rounding error is an error caused by rounding (+0.01) in this case.

Truncation errors

Truncation means shortening a number to a given number of decimal places. If the number 3.89 in the example above was truncated to one decimal place it would become 3.8. The truncation error would amount to -0.09 in this case.

Division by zero errors

Division by zero may be caused by incorrect validation of an input variable or a result of a calculation. Division by zero will normally cause a program to crash if it is allowed to occur.

Logic errors

Logic errors are mistakes in the design of the program. Logic errors only show up when you run the program and you can spot them because the program does not do what it is supposed to do, for instance, it produces the wrong results.

Example of a logic error in part of a program written in the LiveCode language:

```
on mouseUp
    local counter
    put 0 into counter
    repeat until counter = 0
        put counter+1 into counter
    end repeat
end mouseUp
```

Can you explain what will happen when this part of the program is run?

System errors

A **system error** occurs when the computer system (rather than just the program that you are working on) stops working properly. Windows™ users will no doubt be familiar with the so-called 'blue screen of death'.

Figure 7.3 Windows 10 critical process died

Detecting errors

Your chosen software development environment may have built-in features to help the programmer check for bugs which cause errors. These may be part of a separate debugger program or may exist as a feature within the programming language. Using **dry runs**, **trace facilities**, **breakpoints** and **watchpoints** are all methods of detecting errors.

Debugging techniques

Dry run or hand testing

Hand testing is the process of going through the program code manually either on paper or on screen, in order to find mistakes (usually logic errors). Proofreading is one method of hand testing and it is made easier using a structured listing.

Trace table

A dry run usually involves the use of a **trace table**. It is usually carried out on a small part of a program (such as a procedure) at one time. To start with, you make a list of all the variables in the part of the program you are going to examine. This is the trace table and, as you go through the program, it allows you to write down how the values of the variables change at each line, for example:

	counter	times	total	average
Line 250	25	2	5760	230.40
Line 260	45	3	13098	453.78

and so on …

By comparing the values of the variables calculated in the program and the values which you have calculated yourself, you should be able to spot where the program is going wrong.

Trace tools

Many programming languages have **trace tools**, which allow the programmer to follow the path through the program at the same time as it is being run.

A trace tool allows the user to go through the program one line at a time. This is called **single stepping**.

Breakpoints

Another useful facility provided by some programming languages is the ability to set breakpoints or temporary halts in your program. While the program is paused in this way, it is possible to examine the values of the program's variables. These are particularly useful when you are trying to locate logic errors in your programming code.

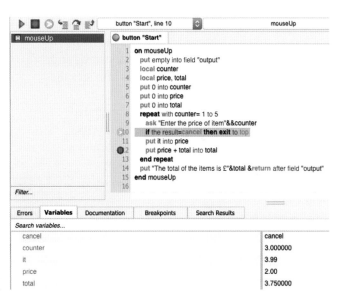

```
1  total=0
2  price=0
3  for items in range(0,5):
4      print("Enter the price of item",items+1)
5      price=float(input())
6      total=total+price
7      breakpoint()
8  print("the total of the items is £",total)
9
10 #Enter the prices £1.75,£2.00,£3.99,£1.58 and £0.59
11 #Expected output £9.91
12
```

```
2.0
(Pdb) continue
Enter the price of item 3
3.99
> /Volumes/Mrs Paterson/Higher te
er book/debug.py(3)<module>()
-> for items in range(0,5):
(Pdb) +items
2
(Pdb) +total
7.74
(Pdb) +price
3.99
(Pdb) continue
Enter the price of item 4
1.58
> /Volumes/Mrs Paterson/Higher te
er book/debug.py(3)<module>()
-> for items in range(0,5):
(Pdb) +items
3
(Pdb) +total
9.32
(Pdb) +price
1.58
(Pdb) continue
Enter the price of item 5
0.59
> /Volumes/Mrs Paterson/Higher te
er book/debug.py(3)<module>()
-> for items in range(0,5):
(Pdb) +items
4
(Pdb) +total
9.91
(Pdb) +price
0.59
(Pdb) continue
the total of the items is £ 9.91
>>>
```

Figure 7.4 Breakpoints in Python and LiveCode

Watchpoints

A watchpoint is used for following the value of one particular variable (as opposed to breakpoints which allows you to examine all the variables' contents). This pauses execution when a particular value is reached or if a value is changed in a variable, e.g. False to True.

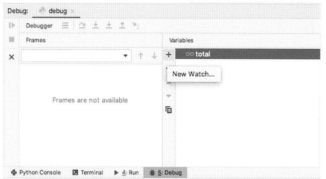

Figure 7.5 Watchpoints in PyCharm™ IDE (Python environment)

Structured listing

A program listing is a printout or hard copy of the program code. A structured listing is a program listing which uses indentations (formatting) to show some of the structure of the program. Program structures such as the beginning and end of procedures, control structures such as loops and decisions are usually all indented in a structured listing. See later in this chapter for a definition of a structured listing.

In addition to this, a structured listing may also highlight language keywords and variable names in some way. One form of highlighting keywords and variable names is to put the keywords into specific coloured lettering and the variable names into camel case letters (e.g. namePerson). Many integrated development environments (IDEs), for instance JetBrains® PyCharm™ or Codewarrior™ and also LiveCode and the Python IDE, use different colours in their structured listings.

Indenting program structures in this way has two main advantages.

1. You can see at a glance where each of the program control structures begins and ends. This makes it easy to understand the structure of each part of the program.
2. You are more likely to be able to spot mistakes in the program when you examine a structured listing as opposed to one which is unstructured. The indentations which form the control structures move to the right at the start of each control structure and return to the same relative position at the end of the control structure. The highlighting of keywords and variables also helps you to spot mistakes, since you can see at a glance if the keywords and variables have been entered correctly.

```
1 def initialise(numbers):
2     numbers=[45,65,23,67,88,90,1,67,6,22,78,31,99,28,84,54,71,16,49,11]
3     return numbers
4
5 def getValue(targetNumber):
6     print("Enter the value you wish to search for")
7     targetNumber=int(input())
8     return targetNumber
9
10 def search(targetNumber, numbers):
11     found=False
12     for counter in range(0,20):
13         if numbers[counter]==targetNumber:
14             print(targetNumber,"was found at position",counter+1)
15             found=True
16     if found==False:
17         print("Sorry, no matches found")
18
19 #main
20 numbers=[0]*20
21 targetNumber=0
22 numbers=initialise(numbers)
23 targetNumber=getValue(targetNumber)
24 search(targetNumber, numbers)
```

```
22     put "Harry" into arrayNames[7]
23     put "Isla" into arrayNames[8]
24     put "Jordyn" into arrayNames[9]
25     put "Karis" into arrayNames[10]
26     put "Larry" into arrayNames[11]
27     put "Michaella" into arrayNames[12]
28     put "Norman" into arrayNames[13]
29     put "Olive" into arrayNames[14]
30     put "Ben" into arrayNames[15]
31 end initialise
32
33 on getValue @targetName
34     ask"Enter the name you would like to search for"
35     if the result=cancel then exit to top
36     put it into targetName
37 end getValue
38
39 on count targetName,@hits, @arrayNames
40     local counter
41     repeat with counter = 0 to 15
42         if targetName=arrayNames[counter] then
43             put hits+1 into hits
44         end if
45     end repeat
46 end count
47
48 on displayHits targetName, hits
49     put targetName&" was found " &hits& " times" after field "output"
50 end displayHits
```

```
8     def initialise():
9         arrayPerson=[personalDetails() for x in range(4)]
10        return arrayPerson
11
12    def getData():
13        for counter in range(0,4):
14            print("Enter your forename")
15            arrayPerson[counter].forename=input()
16            print("Enter your surname")
17            arrayPerson[counter].surname=input()
18            print(arrayPerson[counter].forename,"enter your age")
19            arrayPerson[counter].age=int(input())
20            print(arrayPerson[counter].forename,"enter your height")
21            arrayPerson[counter].height=float(input())
22            print("Are you a student",arrayPerson[counter].forename,"?")
23            answer=input()
24            if answer=="y" or answer=="Y":
25                arrayPerson[counter].student=True
26        return arrayPerson
27
28    def displayData():
29        for counter in range(0,4):
30            if arrayPerson[counter].student:
31                print(arrayPerson[counter].forename, arrayPerson[counter].surname,"is
32
33
34    arrayPerson=initialise()
35    arrayPerson=getData()
36    displayData()
```

Figure 7.6 Structured listings (Python IDE, LiveCode, PyCharm EDU)

CHECK YOUR LEARNING

Now answer questions 9–17 on page 85

QUESTIONS

1 What is the purpose of test data?
2 What is the purpose of a test plan?
3 State two items that should be considered in a test plan.
4 Name three types of test data.
5 Look back at the questions on problem analysis in Chapter 2 page 8. Choose one of the problems dealing with numerical data and one of the problems dealing with textual data. Create a set of test data for each of the two problems you have chosen.
6 What is exhaustive testing?
7 Why can it be true to say that 'you can never ensure that a program is totally correct'?
8 State two events that form part of the sequence of operations that an independent test group would carry out.
9 What is debugging?
10 What is:
a) a syntax error?
b) a linking error?
c) an execution error?
11 a) How can a logic error be detected in a program?
b) Give an example of either a piece of program code or an algorithm which contains a logical error.
12 Give one example of a statement syntax error and one of a structure syntax error.
13 Describe one situation where an error would be generated from the operating system during the execution of a program.
14 What is a dry run or hand testing?
15 WatchTV is a company who analyse the viewing figures for all television programmes on all channels. Part of the program produces the most watched television programme in that particular week.
The section of code that produces the most watched programme is shown below.
The program uses this function to produce the most watched programme.

Line 1	FUNCTION mostWatched (ARRAY OF REAL figure) RETURNS REAL
Line 2	DECLARE highest INITIALLY figure[0]
Line 3	DECLARE position INITIALLY 0
Line 4	FOR counter FROM 1 TO 8 DO
Line 5	IF highest > figure[counter] THEN

Line 6	SET highest TO figure[counter]
Line 7	SET position TO counter
Line 8	END IF
Line 9	END FOR
Line 10	RETURN position
Line 11	END FUNCTION

The function is called in this part of the main program on Line 56.

Line 51	DECLARE top INITIALLY 0
Line 52	DECLARE tvProgs AS ARRAY OF STRING INITIALLY []*10
Line 53	DECLARE viewersMillion AS ARRAY OF REAL INITIALLY []*10
Line 54	SET tvProgs TO ["The News at Teatime","Westside","Brampton General", "The 20-20 Show", "Watch the Telly", "Endmoordale", "Dig up your Garden", "The Fixit Place", "The Great British Travel Show", "Breakaway Street"]
Line 55	SET viewersMillion TO [5.173, 4.795, 3.584, 3.809, 4.949, 5.408, 3.687, 5.404, 6.038, 7.097]
Line 56	SET top TO mostWatched(viewersMillion)
Line 57	SEND tvProgs[top] & "was the most watched TV programme" TO DISPLAY

When the program is tested, errors are found in the function.
a) Copy and complete the following trace table and identify the errors in the function

Line No	highest	position	counter	highest > figure[counter]?
2	5.173			
3		0		
4			1	

b) Identify the lines of code that are incorrect and rewrite the corrected lines of the program.
c) State the type of error identified.
16 a) What is a structured listing?
b) Explain one way in which a structured listing can aid the programmer.
17 What features does your chosen software development environment contain which can help you to find errors in your programs?

KEY POINTS

- Systematic testing involves using a test plan.
- Comprehensive testing means that all programs should be tested as thoroughly as possible.
- Test data is a set of data used to make sure a program actually solves the problem it is supposed to (i.e. meets the software specification).
- Test data should include normal, extreme and exceptional data.
- Normal data is data which is within the limits that your program should be able to deal with.
- Extreme data is data which is at the ends of the acceptable range of data, on the limit(s) or boundaries of the problem.
- Exceptional data is data which is invalid.
- Exhaustive testing is testing all the possible sets of data that the program is designed to handle.
- Field testing means allowing users to test the program.
- An independent test group is not associated with the software company or the programmers who wrote the software and so can be relied upon to provide an unbiased opinion.
- Error reporting is the communication and explanation of errors in the software to the user.
- Debugging is the process of finding and correcting the errors in a program.
- Syntax errors occur when the syntax, or rules of the programming language, are broken.

- Execution errors are errors which show up during program execution.
- Logic errors are mistakes in the design of the program.
- Dry runs, trace facilities, breakpoints and watchpoints are all methods of detecting errors.
- A dry run or hand testing is the process of going through the program code manually either on paper or on screen, in order to find mistakes, usually logic errors.
- A trace table is used to list all the variables in a program and then manually track all the variables as the program executes.
- A trace tool allows the user to go through the program one line at a time (also known as single stepping).
- Breakpoints or temporary halts in a program allow the programmer to examine the values of the program's variables.
- Watchpoints are used to follow the value of one particular variable and pause execution when a particular value is reached or if a value is changed in a variable.
- Structured listing is a program listing which uses indentations (formatting) to show some of the structure of the program.

Chapter 8 Evaluation

This chapter considers how to evaluate the solution to a problem.

The following topics are covered:

- Describe, identify and exemplify the evaluation of a solution in terms of:
  - fitness for purpose
  - efficient use of coding constructs
  - usability
  - maintainability
  - robustness.

Evaluation

Evaluation involves reviewing the solution against suitable criteria. The criteria against which you should evaluate software are **fitness for purpose**, **efficient use of code constructs**, **usability**, **maintainability** and **robustness**.

Fitness for purpose

Does your solution solve the original problem from the analysis stage?

Does the program that you have written meet the software specification and functional requirements? You should carefully examine the software specification. Identify and account for any differences between what your program does and what is stated in the specification.

You should also consider the test data results at this point. While creating the test data, you calculated what the expected results should be. Do the actual results of testing match the expected results?

Efficient use of code constructs

Does your software require excessive resources in order to run properly?

In general terms, efficiency means that your program should not require excessive resources in order to run, such as a large quantity of free memory or a great deal of backing storage space. Some application programs require hundreds of megabytes of backing storage space in order to install them on your computer system. Because of this, such programs usually offer a range of installation options – a full or complete installation, customised or a minimal installation. The minimal installation is useful if your computer system has a limited amount of free backing storage space. The customised installation option allows the user to choose which parts of the software are installed.

When looking at the efficiency of your program, you should also consider your choice of coding constructs. Efficiency means that although you may have a program which is fit for purpose, it does not necessarily mean that it has been coded in the most efficient way possible.

When you are checking whether your program is efficient, you should look at:

- choice of data types or structures
- type of loop: fixed or conditional

- selection statements (use of nested IF)
- arrays versus individual variable assignment
- modularity: reuse and parameter passing.

Data types and structures

The choice of the correct data type for storing data is important because different data types have different storage requirements. For example, the number 4 could, in theory, only require 3 bits as a binary number but if stored as a standard ASCII string would require 7 bits, or even 16 bits if stored as Unicode.

Type of loop

Certain situations may call for a fixed loop to run on a set number of occasions. However, this would not be practical if, for example, a search was required to find the first match and the fixed loop continued to run through all iterations regardless. In this case, a conditional loop would be preferable because it would find the first occurrence of that value. In certain cases, a conditional loop may not need to be executed at all if the condition is at the start of the loop.

Selection statements

Python

Original (multiple IF statements)	else IF statements	Nested IF statements

if guess==randNum:
    print("You guessed my number!")
if abs(guess-randNum)==1:
    print("Extremely hot!")
if abs(guess-randNum)==2:
    print("You are warm")
if abs(guess-randNum)==3:
    print("You are lukewarm")
if abs(guess-randNum)==4:
    print("You are cold")
if abs(guess-randNum)>=5:
    print("Absolutely freezing!")
	if guess==randNum:
	    print("You guessed my number!")
	elif abs(guess-randNum)==1:
	    print("Extremely hot!")
	elif abs(guess-randNum)==2:
	    print("You are warm")
	elif abs(guess-randNum)==3:
	    print("You are lukewarm")
	elif abs(guess-randNum)==4:
	    print("You are cold")
	else:
	    print("Absolutely freezing!")
		if guess==randNum:
		    print("You guessed my number!")
		else:
		    if abs(guess-randNum)==1:
		        print("Extremely hot!")
		    else:
		        if abs(guess-randNum)==2:
		            print("You are warm")
		        else:
		            if abs(guess-randNum)==3:
		                print("You are lukewarm")
		            else:
		                if abs(guess-randNum)==4:
		                    print("You are cold")
		                else:
		                    print("Absolutely freezing!")

> **NOTE**
>
> The **abs** function returns the value of a number and is always positive.

LiveCode

Original (multiple IF statements)	else IF statements	Nested IF statements

Original (multiple IF statements):

```
if abs(guess-randNum)=1 then
    put "Extremely hot!" &return after field "output"
end if
if abs(guess-randNum)=2 then
    put "You are warm" &return after field "output"
end if
if abs(guess-randNum)=3 then
    put "You are lukewarm" &return after field "output"
end if
if abs(guess-randNum)=4 then
    put "You are cold" &return after field "output"
end if
if abs(guess-randNum)>=5 then
    put "Absolutely freezing!" &return after field "output"
end if
```

else IF statements:

```
if guess=randNum then
    put "You guessed my number!" &return after field "output"
else if abs(guess-randNum)=1 then
    put "Extremely hot!" &return after field "output"
else if abs(guess-randNum)=2 then
    put "You are warm" &return after field "output"
else if abs(guess-randNum)=3 then
    put "You are lukewarm" &return after field "output"
else if abs(guess-randNum)=4 then
    put "You are cold" &return after field "output"
else
    put "Absolutely freezing!" &return after field "output"
end if
```

Nested IF statements:

```
if guess=randNum then
    put "You guessed my number!" &return after field "output"
else
    if abs(guess-randNum)=1 then
        put "Extremely hot!" &return after field "output"
    else
        if abs(guess-randNum)=2 then
            put "You are warm" &return after field "output"
        else
            if abs(guess-randNum)=3 then
                put "You are lukewarm" &return after field "output"
            else
                if abs(guess-randNum)=4 then
                    put "You are cold" &return after field "output"
                else
                    if abs(guess-randNum)>=5 then
                        put "Absolutely freezing!" &return after field "output"
                    end if
                end if
            end if
        end if
    end if
end if
```

In the original columns in the tables below in both languages, *all* of the IF statements would be executed, even if the first one is the correct one as they are all individual statements. However, in the amended code, which contain the ELSE IF (ELIF) structure and nested IF statements, the first statement is always executed. If this is found to be a match, then the rest are not executed.

Arrays versus individual variable assignment

Python

Multiple input statements	Array/list
```def getData(): print("Enter the name of item 1") item1=input() print("Enter the name of item 2") item2=input() print("Enter the name of item 3") item3=input() print("Enter the name of item 4") item4=input() print("Enter the name of item 5") item5=input() return item1, item2, item3, item4, item5 def displayData(): print(item1) print(item2) print(item3) print(item4) print(item5) #Main program item1, item2, item3, item4, item5=getData() displayData()```	```def getData(): for counter in range (0,5): print("Enter the name of item", counter+1) item[counter]=input() return item def displayData(): for counter in range(0,5): print(item[counter]) #Main program item=[""]*5 item=getData() displayData()```

LiveCode

Multiple input statements	Array
```global item1, item2, item3, item4, item5 on mouseUp getData displayData end mouseUp```	```global arrayItem on mouseUp initialise getData displayData end mouseUp```

Multiple input statements	Array
| ```
on getData
        ask "Enter the name of item 1"
        if the result=cancel then exit to top
        put it into item1
        ask "Enter the name of item 2"
        if the result=cancel then exit to top
        put it into item2
        ask "Enter the name of item 3"
        if the result=cancel then exit to top
        put it into item3
        ask "Enter the name of item 4"
        if the result=cancel then exit to top
        put it into item4
        ask "Enter the name of item 5"
        if the result=cancel then exit to top
        put it into item5
end getData
on displayData
        put item1 &return after field "output"
        put item2 &return after field "output"
        put item3 &return after field "output"
        put item4 &return after field "output"
        put item5 &return after field "output"
end displayData
``` | ```
on initialise
        repeat with counter = 0 to 4
        put "" into arrayItem[counter]
        end repeat
end initialise
on getData
        repeat with counter = 0 to 4
        ask "Enter the name of item" &&counter+1
        if the result=cancel then exit to top
        put it into arrayItem[counter]
        end repeat
end getData
on displayData
        repeat with counter = 0 to 4
        put arrayItem[counter] &return after field "output"
        end repeat
end displayData
``` |

Use of an array (or list) allows for more compact code, easier manipulation of data in a module and movement of data around a program when parameter passing. However, there are situations where it may not be necessary to use an array and you should think carefully about what works best in your program.

Modularity

Does your program make use of procedures and functions?

Modularity means that frequently used pieces of code (modules or subprograms) only require to be written once but may be reused many times over in the same program. Prewritten modules taken from another program have already been tested and are therefore less likely to contain errors. Modularity also allows use of actual and formal parameters so that there is no requirement to change any of the variables contained in the module being reused (see Chapter 5).

Usability

Does your program provide a clear user interface?

How usable a program is, depends a great deal on the **user interface**, i.e. the means of communication between the user and the computer, also called the **human computer interface** (HCI).

When evaluating the user interface in your solution, you should consider the *nature of the HCI, help screens, instruction screens, visual appeal, screen layout and prompts for the user*.

The nature of the human computer interface

Speech is the most common form of communication between people and voice recognition is now widely available between people and computers. A variety of user interfaces are currently employed on computer systems. These include the graphical user interface (GUI), menu selection interface, forms dialogue interface and voice user interface.

The most common graphical user interface is the WIMP (Window Icon Menu Pointer) environment. A menu selection interface is one in which the computer displays a list of options from which the user may choose. In a forms dialogue interface, the computer outputs separate prompt and response fields for a number of options and the user may complete a number of fields before moving on. Forms dialogue interfaces are common methods of collecting personal data from the user, for instance, completing a response frame on a web page in order to purchase goods. A voice user interface (VUI) uses speech recognition technology to allow the user to interact with a device using voice commands. Amazon Alexa™ and Apple Siri® are two examples of devices which use VUI.

Help screens and instruction screens

No matter how experienced a computer user may be, help is usually required when an unfamiliar program is encountered. If possible, your program should allow the user to access help or instructions from any point within the software.

It is becoming more common for commercial programs, especially application packages, to include **context-sensitive** help. A context-sensitive help system will always be aware of what the user is currently doing and will respond appropriately when help is sought. For instance, supposing you are using a presentation package and you insert a new image, then call upon the help facility. The help system will assume that you want help on inserting an image and an appropriate screen will be displayed.

Visual appeal and screen layout

If you want your program to be attractive to users, then you should pay careful attention to its visual appeal. This is particularly important if your program is designed to be used by young children, who will be attracted to a colourful, eye-catching display.

Users always prefer a neat, uncluttered screen layout to one where the screen which is too 'busy'. The screen layout should make it obvious to the user what is happening in the program, with clear areas for input and output operations as required.

Prompts for the user

A prompt is a character or message displayed on a screen to indicate that the user is expected to do something, such as input data into the system or confirm a selected operation. The prompts in your programs should be clear and give some indication to the user regarding the nature of the expected response, for example:

Please enter a number …

is NOT a very helpful prompt!

Please enter a whole number in the range 1 to 100 and press <Enter> …

is much more helpful.

In addition, prompts should give some visible (or audible) feedback to the user that the response has been received correctly. This is particularly important if the required response is a mouse click on an area of the screen.

Maintainability

How easy is it to correct and/or update your program in future?

Maintainability is the term used to describe how easy it is to update a program some time after it has been delivered. One factor that helps program maintenance is **readability**. Readability means that the design and the code in your programs should be easily understandable by other people. Using modularity, meaningful variable names, structured listings and internal documentation all aid readability.

Robustness

Is your program able to cope with errors during execution without failing? For example, any errors in input, such as numbers outwith the range required, should be reported to the user during input validation. A clear prompt to re-enter data in the correct range should then be issued. Exceptional data should not crash the program. File access should also be considered to ensure that the correct data is being read and input to the program. You cannot assume that the data being read from the external file is necessarily in the right order or of the right data type for your program.

An example of this in use in the real world would be if a peripheral, such as a printer, jams or runs out of paper or ink, then this should not cause the computer program to fail. In this example, a robust program will begin by asking the user whether or not a printer is actually connected, and if so, testing the printer to check that it is working properly before sending a print job to it. If there is a problem, the user should be advised to take appropriate action and the program should continue working instead of crashing.

CHECK YOUR LEARNING

Now answer questions 1–5 (on page 93)

QUESTIONS

1 What is an evaluation?
2 List three questions that the programmer should ask at the evaluation stage in the software development process.
3 What is program maintenance?
4 Why is efficiency a desirable characteristic of software?
5 LJC Inc. are a clothing company who specialise in fancy dress costumes. They give discounts to their customers depending on the number of costumes hired. The maximum number of costumes that can be hired is ten. The discounts are as follows.
   • one hire: 0% discount
   • two hires: 5% discount
   • three hires: 10% discount
   • four hires: 15% discount
   • five or more hires: 20% discount
   Two modules from the program are shown below. The first module asks for input from the user and the second module is an algorithm to work out the discount for each hire.

```
FUNCTION getHires(INTEGER hires)
RETURNS INTEGER

    SET hires TO 0

    SEND "Enter how many costumes are
    being hired" TO DISPLAY

    RECEIVE hires FROM KEYBOARD

    RETURN hires

END FUNCTION
```

```
FUNCTION calculateDiscount(INTEGER
hires, REAL discount) RETURNS REAL

    IF hires = 1 THEN

        SET discount TO 0

    END IF

    IF hires = 2 THEN

        SET discount TO 0.05

    END IF

    IF hires = 3 THEN

        SET discount TO 0.1

    END IF

    IF hires = 4 THEN

        SET discount TO 0.15

    END IF

    IF hires = 5 THEN

        SET discount TO 0.2

    END IF

    RETURN discount

END FUNCTION
```

At the evaluation stage, it has been discovered that there are issues with both modules. One module is not robust and the other has been found to be inefficient. Using either a design technique or programming language of your choice, rewrite the modules to make them more:
a) robust.   b) efficient.

KEY POINTS

● Fitness for purpose is when the solution solves the original problem.
● Efficiency is when the software does not require excessive resources in order to run.
● Modularity means that frequently used pieces of code (modules or subprograms) only require to be written once but may be reused many times over in the same program.
● Usability depends on the user interface and looks at the nature of the HCI, help screens, instruction screens, visual appeal, screen layout and prompts for the user.
● Maintainability is how easy it is to correct or update the software in future.
● Reliability is how well software operates without stopping due to design faults.
● Robustness is the ability of software to cope with errors during execution without failing.

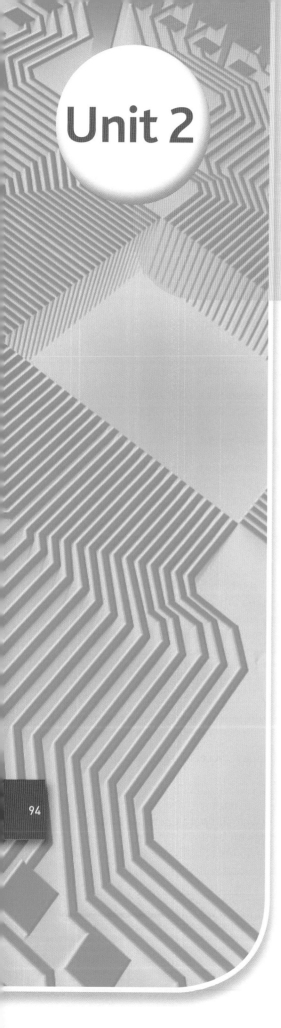

Unit 2

Database design and development

Chapter 9 Database analysis

> This chapter looks at analysing the requirements of a database solution.
>
> The following topics are covered:
>
> - identify the end-user and functional requirements of a database problem that relates to the implementation at this level.

Who is the end-user?

The end-user is the person, people or business that is going to be using the database.

What are the end-user requirements?

This is a planning document that details what the client wants to be able to do with the completed database. It involves the database developer identifying, gathering, communicating and documenting what the client requires. End-user requirements should include details of tasks that the client would like to be able to perform using the database.

It is essential that the end-user requirements are correct. This should involve both the client and the database development team. It may take several meetings until both sides agree. This will ensure that there is clarity about what is required before work can begin on the database.

If the end-user requirements are incorrect or incomplete, then there are likely to be major problems at some point in the development process. These can include having to add new requirements not in the original document, misunderstanding what was in the original document or specifying unnecessary elements that are not likely to be used.

What are functional requirements?

The functional requirements are used to describe what the database system will do in order to achieve the end user requirements. The functional requirements should contain the types of operations the database needs to be able to perform, including simple and complex queries and calculations. It should also contain the type of data that is to be entered and stored, what should happen to the data and the way in which the data should be displayed on the screen. Functional requirements should include tables, fields and keys.

Just like the end-user requirements, it is vital that this document is an accurate reflection of what is required.

Remember, the end-user requirements reflect what types of actions the **user** would like the database to be able to do. The functional requirements detail the type of queries the **database** should perform.

Both of these documents form part of a larger document known as a Requirements Specification. This is a legally binding document and usually forms the basis of a contract between client and developer. It allows the developer and client to clearly see how the database is to be designed and what types of features are to be implemented in the database. Once the database has been developed, revisiting the requirements specification will allow reflection on the database that has been created. In other words, its fitness-for-purpose will be evaluated against what was originally requested in the Requirements Specification document.

The database design and development chapters will follow the development of a database for the Red Tiles Estate Agents.

WORKED EXAMPLE

Red Tiles Estate Agents

Red Tiles Estate Agents want to create a relational database to store details of all their branches, agents, clients and houses for sale. The database will allow administrators, managers and agents to view details of all their clients and the houses for sale. The information the database has to store could be categorised as follows:

- Client (used to store details of Red Tiles' customers)
- House (used to store details about each house that is for sale)
- Agent (used to store details on each estate agent in a branch)
- Branch (used to store information about each branch of Red Tiles)

Each of these categories then becomes an entity in the design of a database. You can read more about entities in Chapter 10.

Database developers have been given the task of creating the relational database to fulfil Red Tiles' demands. At the analysis stage, the database developers must ensure that they gain a clear picture of what tasks Red Tiles and its employees would like the database to be able to perform.

Using information-gathering techniques such as interviewing, observing and issuing questionnaires, the database development team have a well-defined list of the tasks their clients at Red Tiles would like to be able to perform. What follows is a selection of these tasks gathered from their findings.

- As manager of my branch I need to be able to calculate how much commission each agent is due per month. Commission is paid at 2% per sale.
- I also need to work out how much commission to charge our clients, based on the sale price of their property. Client commission is 3% per sale.
- As managing director, I would like to see how many properties every branch has sold from most to least.
- I would also like to be able to see the annual commission made by each agent in each branch.
- My clients like to know the average property sales price in a given town.
- It would be helpful to be able to find out the highest and lowest price of available properties in the database.
- I want to be able to show different property types available in a specified town within a set price range. For example, many older people want to buy bungalows.
- I need to know how many properties of a given type have been sold in, for example, June 2020.
- People looking for properties often want a set number of bedrooms. I'd like to be able to show them, for example, those with three bedrooms.
- Some people would like to have one feature but not necessarily another. For example, someone may want an ensuite but no conservatory.
- We all need to be able to add new property details to the database for new clients.
- Incidentally, clients do not always live in the property that is being sold.

This list of requests is now translated into a more formal list of end-user requirements and subsequently functional requirements.

End-user requirements

Estate agency staff should be able to perform a range of queries. The searches they would like to be able to perform are to find:

1 properties with a specified number of bedrooms
2 full details of a specific type of property for sale in a town within a certain price range
3 specific features required in a property

The managing director should be able to sort the search results in order of the branch which has sold the most properties.

Staff and managers should be able to perform the following calculations:

1 amount of commission to pay to each agent per month
2 amount of commission each client should pay on house sales
3 amount of annual commission made by agents per branch
4 number of properties sold by each branch
5 average property sales price in each town
6 highest and lowest prices of available properties
7 total the number of properties of a particular type sold in any given month.

Staff would also like to be able to add new clients to the database.

Functional requirements

This relational database will have four tables: Agent, Branch, Client and Property.

Agent	Branch	Client	Property
AgentNo	BranchCode	ClientCode	PropertyID
BranchCode	Address	ClientName	AgentNo
AgentName	Town	Address	ClientCode
Email	Postcode	Town	Address
	TelNo	Postcode	Town
	WebAddress	TelNo	Postcode
		clientEmail	FirstListed
			DateSold
			AskingPrice
			SoldPrice
			Sold
			Description

The database should be able to perform the following queries.

1 a simple query to search on the number of bedrooms
2 a complex query to search in a given town and property type within a set price range
3 a complex query to search for specific details required in a property
4 a query to sort search results on the total properties sold per branch
5 a query to calculate agent commission per month
6 a query to calculate the annual agent commission made per branch
7 a query to calculate client commission on houses sold
8 a query to display the average property price in each town
9 a query to show the maximum and minimum price of unsold properties
10 a query to display the total number of properties of a given type sold in a specified month
11 a query to add new client details.

CHECK YOUR LEARNING

Now answer questions 1–5 on page 96–97.

QUESTIONS

1 What information does the end-user requirements document contain?
2 What information does the functional requirements document contain?
3 Flyball is a racing competition for relay teams of at least four dogs who run over a series of low obstacles to catch a ball and run back to their owner. The relay team that can complete the course the fastest is the winner.

Figure 9.1 Flyball racing

The UK Flyball Racing Association (UKFA) wants to create a database to store details of members and their racing dogs. The database will allow administrators and members to view details of divisions, awards and teams for each dog.

The UKFA require details of dogs, owners, teams, divisions and awards to be stored so that the database can be queried.

Once a dog starts racing with a team, it must be registered with the UKFA and owners must supply the name and breed of dog. The team must make sure that they register with the UKFA so that they are allowed to race in competitions.

The records the UKFA keep about each team include the date on which the team was registered, the division in which they race as well as the team captain. They also keep track of seed times for each team from competitions and the type of dogs running (either Open or Multi-breed). Each team is then issued with a seed ranking depending on the type of dog and which division they are part of.

Five separate categories (entities) will be required:

- Owner (used to store details of the owners of racing dogs)
- Dog (used to store details of each racing dog)
- Division (used to store details of which region a team belongs to)
- Team (used to store details about each team including seed times)
- Award (used to store awards given to dogs)

A partial analysis of inputs for the OWNER, DIVISION and AWARD entities is shown below. Complete the missing information for the TEAM and DOG tables.

OWNER	TEAM	DIVISION	DOG	AWARD
OwnerNumber		DivisionCode		AwardNumber
Forename		Division		Award
Surname		Type		Tournament
Address		Area		Date
Town				UKFANumber
PhoneNumber				

4 TeeVeeFi is an online TV and film streaming service. It provides users with simple access to all their favourite TV programmes from mainstream TV and the latest film releases as well as their own brand programmes and documentaries. TeeVeeFi keep records of all their customers, an account which stores the package they have bought and what they watch including the date on which they joined.

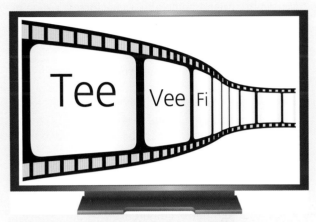

Figure 9.2 TeeVeeFi Logo

Customers can choose from one of the following five packages each of which is a set price per month. Each package allows a set number of users per account to be able to view the programmes and films. Cheaper packages allow for fewer users up to a maximum of five for the most expensive package.

- White: TeeVeeFi's own programmes + one user
- Black: As the White package plus Classic TV programmes + two users
- Blue: As the Black package plus Classic films + three users
- Red: As the Blue package plus Films/TV programmes (six months after initial broadcast/release) + four users
- Gold: As the Red package plus new Film/TV programme releases + five users

When setting up the initial account users must state how they intend to pay for the service, either standing order, direct debit or credit/debit card. TeeVeeFi must advise customers on which date they will be billed and monies owed will either be taken off directly from their bank account or the customer must log in to their account to pay. They also need to be able to identify late or non-payers of bills. TeeVeeFi's customers must be able to look for TV programmes and films to stream that fit certain criteria such as the runtime, type (TV programme or film) or the genre such as a documentary or comedy. Depending on the type of package paid for, the customers can have extra users added. Customers and their users can watch multiple TV programmes and films. Data stored about who watches which type of broadcast allows TeeVeeFi to send customers information on other available programmes and films they may wish to view. Database developers have interviewed TeeVeeFi's staff and management to identify the tasks they require the database to be able to do. What follows is a small selection of the end-user requirements.

Management should be able to perform a range of searches including those to show:

- the most popular tv programmes and films in order of popularity
- the number of customers who are on a specific contract
- the amount to pay on each customer's bill.

Staff should be able to add new:

- customers as they subscribe to the service
- users to a customer's account.

Staff should be able to sort any search results where required and amongst others, should be able to calculate:

- the total number of customers who pay by direct debit.

Use the end-user requirements above to determine the functional requirements for TeeVeeFi.

5 Seudair is a small chain of ten jewellery shops across the north-west and islands of Scotland. They mainly specialise in Celtic jewellery but also sell other types of jewellery in their shops.

Seudair

Figure 9.3 Seudair jewellers

Your team of database developers has been employed by the owner of the shops to create a relational database to store information about the jewellery sold in the shops. Your team has elicited a number of responses from the owner, shop managers and staff.

- We need to store details of every item of jewellery that we sell and details about each.
- Customers are often working to a budget, so I need to be able to find available jewellery from our designers within a given price range sorted from cheapest to dearest.
- As the owner, I would like to be able to view the most and least popular gemstones.
- I would also like to be able to view the total number of items sold of each particular type.
- Is it possible to view how much each shop has sold from each manufacturer?
- Some customers only like jewellery made from certain precious metals. It would be helpful to be able to find which manufacturers make, for example, rings made of white gold.
- Each shop has to provide information every month on each jewellery type and a total of what has been sold.
- Sales staff usually provide a hand-written receipt including the date, each item purchased, its cost and the total amount due. We would like to produce this electronically.

Use the responses in the list above from the owner, managers and staff to determine the
a) end-user requirements.
b) functional requirements.

KEY POINTS

- An end-user is the person, people or business that is going to be using the database.
- End-user requirements are the tasks users expect to be able to do using the database.
- Database developers must identify, gather, communicate and document what the user will require.
- The end-user requirements document must also contain queries the user would like to be able to perform.
- Functional requirements describe what the database will do.
- The functional requirements document should contain the types of operations the database should be able to perform, including simple and complex queries and calculations.
- It is essential that both the end-user and functional requirements are correct to avoid problems later on in the development process.
- The end-user and functional requirements form part of the larger requirements specification document.
- These requirements documents will contain specific details about both the design of the database and what it is required to do.
- The requirements specification document is used to assess the fitness-for-purpose of the database during the evaluation stage.

Chapter 10 Database design

This chapter looks at the design of a database.

The following topics are covered:

- describe and exemplify entity-relationship diagrams with three or more entities, indicating:
  - entity name
  - attributes
  - name of relationship
  - cardinality of relationship (one-to-one, one-to-many, many-to-many).
- describe and exemplify an instance using an entity-occurrence diagram.
- describe and exemplify a compound key.
- describe and exemplify a data dictionary with three or more entities:
  - entity name
  - attribute name
  - primary and foreign key
  - attribute type:
    - text
    - number
    - date
    - time
    - Boolean
  - attribute size
  - validation:
    - presence check
    - restricted choice
    - field length
    - range.
- exemplify a design of a solution to a query:
  - tables and queries
  - fields
  - search criteria
  - sort order
  - calculations (with aliases)
  - grouping
  - using the result of a previous query.

NOTE

Aliases and *Using the result of a previous query* do not appear in the arrangements discretely but designing queries to perform these operations is part of the Higher course.

Relational databases

A **database** is a structured collection of similar information, which can be queried. A program that is used for organising data on a computer system is called a database package or database management system.

A **relational database** is one that is made up of entities, attributes and relationships to link the entities.

What is an entity?

An entity is a person, place, thing, event or concept of interest to the business or organisation about which data is to be stored. For example, in a school, possible entities might be Student, Teacher, Class and Subject. When implemented in a relational database this information is stored in a table. A table contains data about a single entity.

Entities are made up of attributes which describe how the information will be represented.

For easy reference, entity names are normally written in capital letters although this is not strictly necessary.

clientCode	clientName	address	town	postcode	telNo
000016	**Rory Redwing**	**2 Moonstone Terrace**	**Portussie**	**PT1 5TZ**	**01572 427033**
000018	Raymond Rook	7 Moonstone Mews	Friarso	LL3 3DB	01622 876261
000061	Consolata Crossbill	7 Peridot Walk	Axelbridge	AX1 2JM	01692 630829
000099	Jackson Jay	9 Mother of Pearl Park	Invertrose	PT3 6HY	01545 675297
000106	Abdullah Auk	19 Rhodonite Way	Farkirk	PT5 9VG	01599 120357

Table 10.1 Extract from the CLIENT table for the Red Tiles Estate Agency

What is an attribute?

An entity is described by its attributes. Each attribute is a characteristic of the entity. For example, attributes of the Student entity would include studentID, firstname, surname and dateOfBirth. Attributes become fields when we talk about the relations or table in a relational database. So, when an attribute is implemented in a database it is normally known as a field.

For example, from the CLIENT table in the Red Tiles Estate Agency (Table 10.1) the attributes would be:

```
CLIENT(clientCode, clientName, address,
town, postcode, telNo)
```

Primary and foreign keys

An attribute or combination of attributes that uniquely identifies one, and only one, entity occurrence is called a primary key.

A primary key must have a unique value as it is used to identify a single instance or row of data in a table.

For example, in the CLIENT table for the Red Tiles Estate Agency, an entity instance or row would look like the extracted row in Table 10.2.

000016	Rory Redwing	2 Moonstone Terrace	Portussie	PT1 5TZ	01572 427033

Table 10.2 Extract from the CLIENT table for the Red Tiles Estate Agency

with 000106 being the primary key used to uniquely identify the client Abdullah Auk.

Any field, once implemented in a database, which is used as a primary key must always contain a value; that is, it cannot be empty (or null).

A foreign key is a field in an entity which links to the primary key in a related entity.

A primary key is usually shown with an underline to differentiate between it and other attributes in an entity. An asterisk * is used to indicate a foreign key.

Relationships

Establishing a relationship creates a link between the primary key in one entity and the foreign key in another entity. Once implemented, this relationship may then be used to find all of the information contained in both related entities.

At Higher level you should be able to work with three or more linked entities.

Database modelling

When designing a database, database developers model the system they are creating before any work on implementation takes place. They make use of a variety of techniques to help create the model including:

● entity occurrence diagrams
● entity relationship diagrams
● data dictionaries.

Each of these allows the developer to see clearly how each entity relates to another entity and how the data should be stored. This means that when implementation commences, there is a clear understanding of how the current system works and how the new system should work once complete.

Entity occurrence diagrams

The first step in working out the relationship between entities in a database is to see how specific occurrences of data relate to one another within the current system. An entity occurrence (EO) diagram shows the relationship between entities using the occurrences within each entity.

A specific example of an entity is called an instance or entity occurrence. For example, John Smith, Mary McLeod and Omar Shaheed are all entity occurrences found in the Student entity; English, Computing and Chemistry are all entity occurrences within the Subject entity.

The diagram, once created, refers to how these occurrences are related to one another between two or more entities.

To draw the diagram, the database developers must have some sample data to work with so that the relationship can be illustrated.

An entity occurrence diagram requires primary keys from each of the entities. This means that the database developer must identify a primary key for each of the samples of data provided.

Once primary keys have been identified in the data supplied, each of the values should be written down so that the entity occurrence diagram can be created, and relationships identified.

There are three types of relationships:

● one-to-one (1:1)
● one-to-many (1:M)
● many-to-many (M:N).

These are otherwise known as the cardinality of the relationship.

Figure 10.1 shows what a one-to-one relationship would look like in an entity occurrence diagram using the data below. Notice that a single line is drawn between each instance in the entity and that each entity is a large, labelled oval. The oval shape is not a necessity, but it does help to show the distinction between one entity and another. What is required however, is that a line is drawn between related entity occurrences in order that the relationship between each entity is clearly identified.

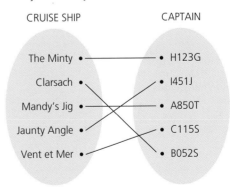

Figure 10.1 One-to-one entity occurrence diagram

This shows that there is a one-to-one relationship between a cruise ship and its captain. This also means that a captain can only be in charge of one cruise ship.

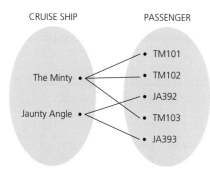

Figure 10.2 One-to-many entity occurrence diagram

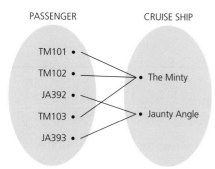

Figure 10.3 Many-to-one entity occurrence diagram

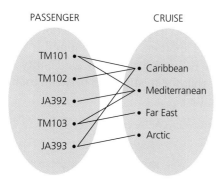

Figure 10.4 Many-to-many entity occurrence diagram

Figure 10.2 shows what a one-to-many relationship would look in an entity occurrence diagram using the data below. Note how the line is drawn from one instance in one entity to multiple instances in the other.

This shows that a cruise ship has many passengers. It also shows that one passenger may be on board only one ship.

It can be drawn either way to indicate the relationship as can be seen in Figure 10.3.

Figure 10.4 shows what a many-to-many relationship would look in an entity occurrence diagram. Note how the line is drawn from multiple instances in one entity to multiple instances in the other.

This shows that many passengers can go on many cruises. It also shows that many cruises can be taken by many passengers.

In the Red Tiles Estate Agents example, we need to use existing data supplied by the company to work out the relationship between each of the entities. The tables in Table 10.3 contains instances of data from each of the entities. This will allow us to construct an entity occurrence diagram and work out the relationship between each of the entities.

BRANCH				
branchCode	address	town	postcode	telNo
RTD100	8 Linen Cross	Dunallan	AX2 5RN	01988 765321
RTF101ç	5 Cotton Street	Farfour	PT15 2LY	01534 234566
RTF102	31 Wool Avenue	Farfour	PT15 7QQ	01534 233457
RTF104	1 Silk Way	Friarso	LL3 4CJ	01622 648753

AGENT			
agentNo	branchCode	agentName	email
0002	RTF104	Lawrence Lily	llily@redtilesestag.co.uk
0013	RTF101	Alexander Ace	aace@redtilesestag.co.uk
0016	RTF102	Harriet Heart	hheart@redtilesestag.co.uk
0030	RTD100	Vanessa Vanilla	vvanilla@redtilesestag.co.uk
0032	RTD100	Andrew Anise	aanise@redtilesestag.co.uk

PROPERTY					
propertyID	agentNo	clientCode	address	town	postcode
95	0002	000018	7 Moonstone Mews	Friarso	LL3 3DB
97	0016	000016	2 Moonstone Terrace	Portussie	PT1 5TZ
98	0016	000099	9 Mother of Pearl Park	Invertrose	PT3 6HY
107	0013	000106	12 Opal Row	Farfour	PT15 1BT
108	0013	000106	16 Opal Row	Farfour	PT15 1BT
109	0013	000106	3 Opal Row	Farfour	PT15 1BT
119	0030	000061	14 Peridot Place	Axelbridge	AX1 2JN
120	0032	000061	4 Peridot Walk	Axelbridge	AX1 2JM

CLIENT					
clientCode	clientName	address	town	postcode	telNo
000016	Rory Redwing	2 Moonstone Terrace	Portussie	PT1 5TZ	01572 427033
000018	Raymond Rook	7 Moonstone Mews	Friarso	LL3 3DB	01622 876261
000061	Consolata Crossbill	7 Peridot Walk	Axelbridge	AX1 2JM	01692 630829
000099	Jackson Jay	9 Mother of Pearl Park	Invertrose	PT3 6HY	01545 675297
000106	Abdullah Auk	19 Rhodonite Way	Farkirk	PT5 9VG	01599 120357

Table 10.3 Instances of data from Red Tiles Estate Agents

Figure 10.5 shows the relationship between each of the entities in the Red Tiles Estate Agents using instances from the supplied data in Table 10.3.

Figure 10.5 Entity occurrence diagram for Red Tiles Estate Agent

This means that the relationship between each of the entities identified at the analysis stage of the worked example can be clearly identified.

103

Entity relationship diagrams

Once the entity occurrence diagram is complete and entities and relationships have been identified, then an entity relationship (ER) diagram is drawn to show the how the database should be structured. It should include entities, their attributes, if necessary, the cardinality and the name of the relationship between each of the entities.

The convention is normally to write the name of each entity in capital letters and is usually written inside a rectangle. Attributes are added by drawing them as ovals and writing their name inside the oval. Primary keys should be underlined and foreign keys should be marked with an asterisk.

A straight line and a branching line or 'crow's foot' shown on the end of the line is used to indicate a relationship. The 'crow's foot' tells the designer which is the 'many' part of the relationship.

Establishing a relationship creates a link between the primary key in one table and the foreign key in another table. This relationship may then be used to find all of the information contained in both tables.

Using the estate agent example, we can look at the relationship between two of the entities: AGENT and PROPERTY.

Figure 10.6 Red Tiles Estate Agent one-to-many relationship

Figure 10.6 shows the one-to-many relationship between AGENT and PROPERTY. The description of the relationship can be read in two ways from left to right, where one agent is responsible for many clients, and from right to left, where each client can only be assigned to one agent.

Notice that the relationship is annotated with a description of how one entity relates to the other.

Remember from entity occurrence diagrams there are three types of relationships:

- one-to-one (1:1)
- one-to-many (1:M)
- many-to-many (M:N).

A one-to-one relationship exists between a country and its capital city or between a captain and a captain's licence.

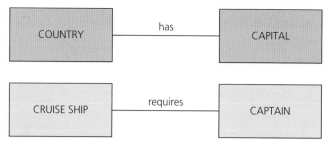

Figure 10.7 One-to-one relationship

Again, reading the relationships in Figure 10.7 in both directions, they can be read like this:

- Each country has one capital city.
- Each capital city is in one country.
- Each cruise ship requires one captain.
- Each captain is the captain of only one cruise ship.

A many-to-many relationship exists between passengers and cruises where many passengers can go on many cruises.

Figure 10.8 Many-to-many relationship

The relationships in Figure 10.8 can be read like this:

- Each passenger goes on many cruises.
- Each cruise can be gone on by many passengers.

Many-to-many relationships are generally best avoided where possible, as they are difficult to implement and search in a relational database.

A solution to this is to introduce another entity which will remove the repeating group(s) from both entities and allow one-to-many relationships to be created instead. This will contain a combination of data from both tables.

Figure 10.9 Removing repeating group(s)

The relationships now read:

- Each cruise can take many bookings.
- Each booking is for one cruise.

and

- Each passenger can make many bookings.
- Each booking is made by one passenger.

Entity relationship diagram

In Figures 10.10 and 10.11, the four entities are represented as a simple
ER diagram with no attributes and also with attributes shown.

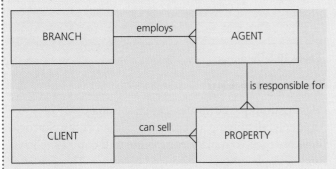

Figure 10.10 Red Tiles Estate Agent ER diagram

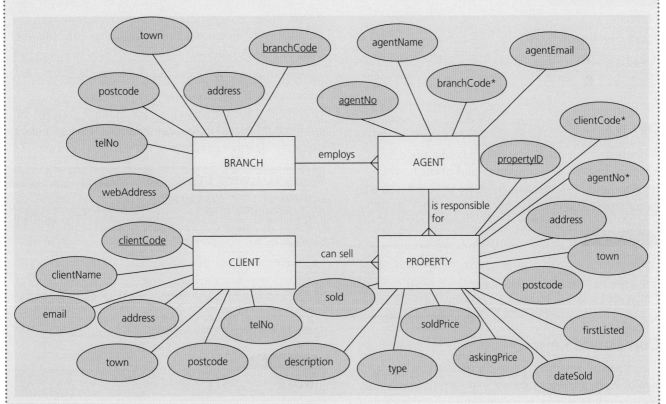

Figure 10.11 Red Tiles Estate Agent ER diagram with attributes

Notice for the ER diagram with attributes that primary and foreign
keys have been identified. You can read more about primary and
foreign keys on page 100.

105

**Now answer questions 1–8 (on pages 119–120) on entity
occurrence and relationship diagrams**

Identifying key fields

Identifying the primary key can frequently be quite tricky especially if there is no single attribute that can act as a unique identifier. In this case, there are three different solutions.

Composite or concatenated key

A composite key is where two or more attributes are used to provide a unique identifier for each entity occurrence in an entity where no one attribute can uniquely identify that occurrence. A composite key contains any combination of attributes in an entity which will help identify each occurrence uniquely. Table 10.4 shows an example of a composite key.

BOOKING
cruiseNo*
customerNo*
depDate*
arrDate
cost

Table 10.4 Composite key

A booked cruise cannot be uniquely identified by simply using the cruise number and needs both the depDate and customerNo attributes to be used as well to construct a composite key.

NOTE

You are not required to know about surrogate keys for Higher Computing Science.

Compound keys

A compound key is a type of composite key. Again, two or more attributes are used to identify each entity occurrence. However, in a compound key the attributes used to uniquely identify the occurrence must consist of foreign keys, i.e. they are primary keys in the other linked tables.

The combination of these two or more attributes should provide a unique identifier for each occurrence in the entity. Table 10.5 shows an example of a compound key in the BOOKING table. The compound key is made up using the attributes customerNo and cruiseNo, which are primary keys in the PASSENGER and CRUISE tables respectively, and which are foreign keys in the BOOKING table.

PASSENGER	BOOKING		CRUISE
customerNo	customerNo*		cruiseNo
forename	cruiseNo*		cruiseDest
surname	depDate		depPort
address	arrDate		arrPort
town	cost		
postcode			

Table 10.5 Compound key

Surrogate key

Having multiple attributes can be a clumsy way of uniquely identifying an occurrence in an entity. Surrogate keys are used to replace compound and composite keys with a single unique introduced identifier. This can often be, but is not restricted to, use of Autonumber.

Autonumber is a type of data used to generate an automatically incremented number in an attribute, e.g. 001, 002, 003, etc.

Table 10.6 shows an example of a surrogate key bookingRef. This removes the compound key of customerNo and cruiseNo from the example used for the compound key and introduces the bookingRef attribute to uniquely identify each instance of data.

PASSENGER	BOOKING		CRUISE
customerNo	bookingRef		cruiseNo
forename	customerNo*		cruiseDest
surname	cruiseNo*		depPort
address	depDate		arrPort
town	arrDate		
postcode	cost		

Table 10.6 Surrogate key bookingRef

NOTE

You are not required to know about surrogate keys for Higher Computing Science.

Entities and their attributes can also be written in the following format.

```
PASSENGER (customerNo, forename,
surname, address, town, postcode)

BOOKING (bookingRef, customerNo*,
cruiseNo*, depDate, arrDate, cost)

CRUISE (cruiseNo, cruiseDest, depPort,
arrPort)
```

Data dictionary

A **data dictionary** is a table which contains all the elements which need to be present in the database once it is implemented. A data dictionary, together with its associated entity relationship and entity occurrence diagrams, is known as a data model. A data model describes how a database should look and allows developers to check that their database design will work before it is implemented.

Entity	Attribute name	Key	Type	Size	Required	Validation
BRANCH	branchCode	PK	Text	6	Y	maxLength=6
	address		Text	30	Y	maxLength=30
	town		Text	30	Y	maxLength=30
	postcode		Text	8	Y	maxLength=8
	telNo		Text	12	Y	maxLength=12
	webAddress		Text	40	Y	maxLength=30
AGENT	agentNo	PK	Text	4	Y	maxLength=4
	agentName		Text	40	Y	maxLength=25
	agentEmail		Text	40	Y	maxLength=25
	branchCode	FK	Text	6	Y	maxLength=6, existing branchCode from BRANCH table
PROPERTY	propertyID	PK	Number		Y	>0
	address		Text	30	Y	maxLength=30
	town		Text	30	Y	maxLength=30
	postcode		Text	8	Y	maxLength=8
	firstListed		Date		Y	
	dateSold		Date		N	
	askingPrice		Number		Y	>0
	soldPrice		Number		N	>0
	sold		Boolean		Y	True or False
	type		Text	10	Y	Restricted choice: House, Flat, Apartment, Bungalow
	noOfBedrooms		Number		Y	Restricted choice:1,2,3,4,5
	description		Text	255	Y	maxLength=255
	agentNo	FK	Text	4	Y	maxLength=4, existing agentNo from AGENT table
	clientCode	FK	Text	6	Y	maxLength=6, existing clientCode from CLIENT table
CLIENT	clientCode	PK	Text	6	Y	maxLength=6
	clientName		Text	40	Y	maxLength=25
	address		Text	30	Y	maxLength=30
	town		Text	30	Y	maxLength=30
	postcode		Text	8	Y	maxLength=8
	telNo		Text	12	Y	maxLength=12
	email		Text	40	N	maxLength-25

Table 10.7 Data dictionary for Red Tiles Estate Agent

A data dictionary should include the entity name, attribute names, primary and foreign keys, attribute type, attribute size (text types only), required and any validation associated with the attributes.

Table 10.7 shows the data dictionary for all the entities in the estate agent example.

Each row in the data dictionary describes how each entity and attribute should be implemented in the database.

The Key column is used to indicate whether the attribute is a primary or foreign key.

The Type column is used to indicate the type of data associated with the attribute. Data types include text, number, date, time and Boolean.

- Text: used to hold letters, numbers and symbols.
- Number: A number type only stores numbers. These can be either real or integer types, e.g. 15.24 or 65.
- Date: Date types can only contain dates. When the field is created, you can decide how the date is to be displayed, for example 18/02/54 or 18 February 2054.
- Time: Time types can hold hours, minutes and seconds. Note that the time is held as a time of day rather than a time interval. For instance, 17:28:00 instead of 55 minutes.

The Size column indicates the maximum size associated with each text attribute. Text types should always have a maximum size assigned. The size can be further restricted by validation.

The Required column indicates whether or not an attribute has to have a value entered. Both primary and foreign keys must have an entry and cannot be left empty (or null).

The Validation column is a check to make sure that an item of data is sensible and allowable.

Validation checks

These include presence check, restricted choice, field length and range. Validation checks do not eliminate mistakes, but they make it difficult for incorrect data to get into the database.

Presence check

This checks to make sure that a field has not been left empty. This is shown in Table 10.7 in the Required column within the data dictionary.

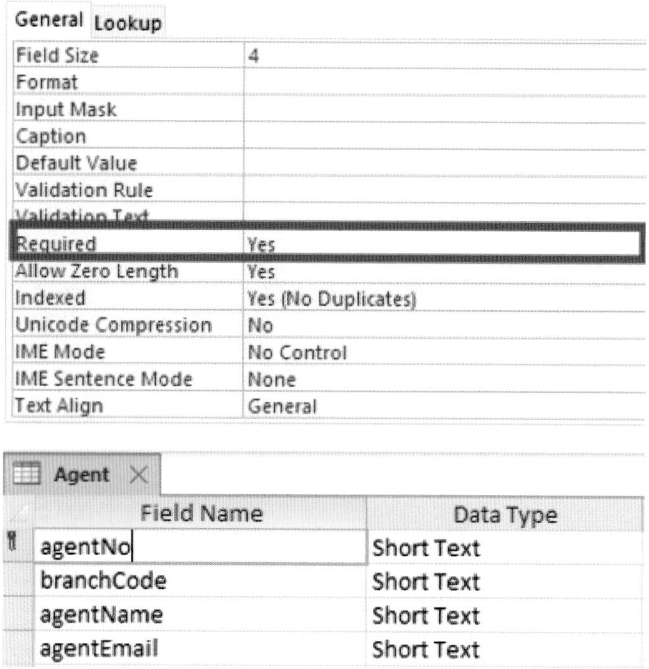

Figure 10.12 Presence check

Restricted choice

This gives users a list of options to choose from and so limits the input to pre-approved answers.

Figure 10.13 Restricted choice

Field length

This ensures the correct number of numbers or characters has been entered in a field. For example, UK postcodes are between six and eight characters long (including the space). 'KA21 5NT' would be allowed, but IV7HY would be rejected.

If the entry has more characters than will fit in the field, then an error message should appear. Limiting the size of a field also helps to reduce the amount of backing storage space required for the database file. A smaller file will be quicker to load and quicker to send over a network.

This is shown above in the Size column within the data dictionary and can also be included in the Validation column.

postcode		Short Text		
firstListed		Date/Time		
dateSold		Date/Time		
askingPrice		Number		
soldPrice		Number		
sold		Yes/No		
type		Short Text		
noOfBedrooms		Number		

General Lookup

Field Size	8
Format	
Input Mask	
Caption	
Default Value	
Validation Rule	Len([postcode])>=6 And Len([postcode])<=8 Or [postcode] Is Null
Validation Text	'The postcode must be between 6 and 8 characters and cannot be empty'
Required	Yes
Allow Zero Length	Yes

▾	town	▾	postcode	▾	firstListed	▾	dateSold	▾	askingPric
	Axelbridge		AX16B		01/09/2019				150000
	Axelbridge		AX1 6BF		01/08/2018		13/09/2018		152500
	Axelbridge		AX1 8NY		01/08/2018		25/09/2018		235000
	Axelbridge		AX1 8NY		22/07/2019				250000
	Thurdeen		AX3 4FV		03/08/2018		03/12/2018		175000
t	Thurdeen		AX3 4FV		26/10/2018		07/01/2019		180000
eet	Thurdeen		AX3 9XT		04/08/2018		26/11/2018		55000

Microsoft Access ✕

⚠ 'The postcode must be between 6 and 8 characters and cannot be empty'

OK   Help

Portussie	PT1 8XD	17/08/2018	31/10/2018	105000

Figure 10.14 Field length

Range

This keeps the data within given limits. A **range check** can be made on fields that contain numbers, like ages, money or dates, to check that the numbers are sensible. For example:

- an age of more than 120 or less than 0
- a total on a bill of £0.00
- a day of greater than 31 or less than 1
- a price greater than zero.

firstListed	Date/Time
dateSold	Date/Time
askingPrice	Number
soldPrice	Number
sold	Yes/No
type	Short Text
noOfBedrooms	Number
description	Short Text

General Lookup

Field Size	Double
Format	0
Decimal Places	Auto
Input Mask	
Caption	
Default Value	
Validation Rule	>0
Validation Text	'The price entered must be greater than zero'
Required	Yes
Indexed	No
Text Align	Left

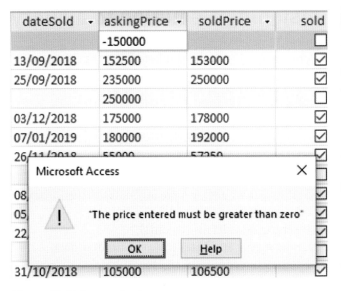

dateSold ▾	askingPrice ▾	soldPrice ▾	sold
	-150000		☐
13/09/2018	152500	153000	☑
25/09/2018	235000	250000	☑
	250000		☐
03/12/2018	175000	178000	☑
07/01/2019	180000	192000	☑
26/11/2018	55000	57250	☑
08/			☐
05/			☑
22/			☑
31/10/2018	105000	106500	☑

Microsoft Access ✕

⚠ 'The price entered must be greater than zero'

OK   Help

Figure 10.15 Range check

Data integrity

Data integrity is crucial to a database. If any of the values in the database are incorrect, then any information that is taken from that data will have no value. Rules have been created to prevent this from happening. These data integrity rules include entity integrity and referential integrity.

Entity integrity

Entity integrity exists if the table has a primary key which is unique and contains a value.

All four entities, BRANCH, AGENT, PROPERTY and CLIENT have unique primary keys and therefore conform to entity integrity. Having entity integrity guarantees that it is possible to access each row of a table by supplying the primary key value.

Referential integrity

Referential integrity is concerned with foreign keys and the links between the entities. Referential integrity ensures that a value in one table references an existing value in another table. A foreign key must have a matching record in its linked entity. This means that a foreign key must exist as a primary key in another entity.

CHECK YOUR LEARNING

Now answer questions 9–14 (on pages 121–122) on data dictionaries

109

Designing a solution to a query

A query in database can be used to carry out many different actions. Prior to implementing the query, database developers must design the queries that the database system must be is able to run.

A query in a database may involve some or a combination of the following actions.

- Searching the database returning results from one or more entities (tables).
- Sorting across one or more attributes (fields) from one or more entities (tables).
- Inserting new details (records).
- Updating the attributes (fields) with new data.
- Deleting a record from an entity (table).
- Calculations involving attributes (fields) and using aggregate functions (see Table 10.9).
- Grouping of data.

Relational operators are used to create conditions in queries.

Relational operators include:

- < less than
- <= less than or equal to
- = equal to
- > greater than
- >= greater than or equal to
- ≠ (or <> or !=) not equal to.

Logical operators are used to join conditions in a complex search:

- AND – both conditions must be met
- OR – one condition must be met.

To design these queries, the developer needs to state:

- which tables (entities) are to be used
- which fields (attributes) are required
- any search criteria and on which fields
- whether or not the data is to be sorted
- if appropriate, how the data is to be grouped
- calculations or aggregate functions required
- which fields should be displayed in the results
- whether or not an alias is to be used (see the paragraph on Aliases on page 116).

> **NOTE**
> Where two (or more) entities that are being referred to have attributes with the same name, dot notation must be used in the design of the query to indicate which entity the attribute has come from, e.g. team. name and owner.name.

Search and sort

We will use examples from the analysis of the Red Tiles Estate Agents to demonstrate how each query can be designed.

Simple search on one entity

One of the end-user requirements was to be able to search for properties with a specified number of bedrooms. Let's say the person who is house hunting would like to see the addresses and asking prices of all properties with three bedrooms.

One possible design for this query is shown in Table 10.8.

Field(s) and calculation(s)	address, town, postcode, askingPrice, noOfBedrooms
Table(s) and query	Property
Search criteria	noOfBedrooms = 3
Sort order	

Table 10.8 Design for simple search on one entity

Complex search on one entity

Another of the end-user requirements was to be able to search for properties in a specified town within a given price range. This query will display the details of all the bungalows in the database in Invertrose whose asking price is between £100,000 and £200,000.

Field(s) and calculation(s)	address, town, postcode, askingPrice, description
Table(s) and query	Property
Search criteria	town= "Invertrose" and type= "Bungalow" and askingPrice>100,000 and askingPrice<200,000
Sort order	

Table 10.9 Design for complex search on one entity

Simple search on two entities

This query is designed to display the names and email addresses of the agents that work in the Dumshiels branch of Red Tiles Estate Agents.

Field(s) and calculation(s)	Branch.town, Agent.agentName, Agent.agentEmail
Table(s) and query	Agent, Branch
Search criteria	town= "Dumshiels"
Sort order	

Table 10.10 Design for simple search on two entities

Complex search on two entities

A client would like to see the details of all the properties in Linkilbeg that are assigned to estate agent Robert Rose.

Field(s) and calculation(s)	Property.address, Property.town, Property.postcode, Property.askingPrice, Property.description
Table(s) and query	Agent, Property
Search criteria	Agent.agentName= "Robert Rose" and Property.town= "Linkilbeg"
Sort order	

Table 10.11 Design for complex search on two entities

Complex search on two entities using OR

A client would like to see the details of all available properties that have either three or four bedrooms on sale by estate agent Terry Thyme.

Field(s) and calculation(s)	Property.address, Property.town, Property.postcode, Property.noOfBedrooms, Property.askingPrice, Property.description
Table(s) and query	Agent, Property
Search criteria	(Property.noOfBedrooms=3 OR Property.noOfBedrooms=4) and Agent.agentName="Terry Thyme" and Property.sold=False
Sort order	

Table 10.12 Design for complex search using OR

Complex search on four entities

Red Tiles managing director would like a list of addresses of properties being sold by Gabriel Gannet that cost more than £180,000, the agents' names and branch addresses.

Field(s) and calculation(s)	Client.clientName, Property.address, Property.town, Property.postcode, Property.description, Property.askingPrice, Agent.agentName, Branch.address, Branch.town, Property.sold
Table(s) and query	Agent, Property, Branch, Client
Search criteria	Client.clientName= "Gabriel Gannet" and Property.askingPrice>180,000 and Property.sold=False
Sort order	

Table 10.13 Design for complex search on four entities

Queries using wildcards

Wildcards are used to replace one or more characters when querying a table for incomplete information contained somewhere in a longer string. Rather than using the existing logical operators =, <, >, <=, >= that are used in a normal query, the operator LIKE is used.

Different dialects of SQL use different characters to represent both single and multiple characters. Table 10.14 shows which characters are used by which dialect. These characters should also be used when designing your queries to search.

Dialect of SQL	None, one or more characters	One character only
Microsoft Access	*	?
MySQL and other dialects	%	_ (underscore)

Table 10.14 Wildcards in SQL

Table 10.15 shows examples of how and where wildcards can be used to return results using two dialects shown in Table 10.14 above.

Search criteria	Result
clientName LIKE "*catcher" clientName LIKE "%catcher"	Find all clients whose name ends with "catcher"
clientName LIKE "G*" clientName LIKE "G%"	Find all clients whose name starts with the letter "G"
address LIKE "*Citrine*" address LIKE "%Citrine%"	Find all houses in any road that contains "Citrine"
postcode LIKE "?T*" postcode LIKE "_T%"	Find all postcodes with second letter "T"
town LIKE "A*n" town LIKE "A%n"	Find all towns that start with "A" and end in "n"

Table 10.15 Examples of wildcards

WORKED EXAMPLE 2

Text replacement

A house hunter is looking for four bedroomed properties with a conservatory. The query should show the full address, asking price, sellers and descriptions of all these properties.

MS Access

Field(s) and calculation(s)	Client.clientName, Property. address, Property.town, Property.postcode, Property. askingPrice, Property. description
Table(s) and query	Client, Property
Search criteria	noOfBedrooms=4 and description LIKE "*conservatory*"
Sort order	

MySQL

Field(s) and calculation(s)	Property.address, Property. town, Property.postcode, Property.askingPrice, Client. clientName
Table(s) and query	Client, Property
Search criteria	noOfBedrooms =4 and description LIKE "%conservatory%"
Sort order	

WORKED EXAMPLE 3

Date replacement

A house hunter is looking for properties that went on sale in September 2019. The query should show the full address, date first listed, asking price and sellers of all these properties.

MS Access

Field(s) and calculation(s)	Client.clientName, Property.address, Property.town, Property.postcode, Property.firstListed, Property. askingPrice
Table(s) and query	Client, Property
Search criteria	Property.firstListed LIKE "??/09/2019"
Sort order	

MySQL

Field(s) and calculation(s)	Client.clientName Property.address, Property.town, Property.postcode, Property.firstListed, Property. askingPrice
Table(s) and query	Client, Property
Search criteria	Property.firstListed LIKE "_ _/09/2019"
Sort order	

WORKED EXAMPLE 4

Simple sort on one attribute in one entity

The managing director (MD) of Red Tiles would like to see a list of all sold properties in order of price from cheapest to dearest. The result of the query should show the full address and price of each property.

Field(s) and calculation(s)	address, town, postcode, soldPrice
Table(s) and query	Property
Search criteria	sold=True
Sort order	soldPrice ASC

WORKED EXAMPLE 5

Sort on two attributes in one entity (complex sort)

The MD of Red Tiles would like to see a list of all unsold properties in order of town from A to Z and then on price, with the most expensive property being displayed first. The result of the query should show the full address and price of each property.

Field(s) and calculation(s)	address, town, postcode, askingPrice
Table(s) and query	Property
Search criteria	sold=False
Sort order	town ASC, askingPrice DESC

NOTE

Boolean attributes should not be written with quotes.

WORKED EXAMPLE 6

Sort on two attributes in two entities (complex sort)

Finally, the MD of Red Tiles would like to see a list of all sold properties sorted alphabetically by branch code and then on sold price, starting with the least expensive. The result of the query should show the branch, full address and price of each property.

Field(s) and calculation(s)	Branch.branchCode, Property. address, Property.town, Property. postcode, Property.soldPrice
Table(s) and query	Property, Branch, Agent
Search criteria	Property.sold=True
Sort order	Branch.branchCode ASC, Property.soldPrice ASC

WORKED EXAMPLE 7

Insert a new record

Consolata Crossbill, client code 000061, has recently completed a renovation project and has a new house to put on the market.

Query type	INSERT (INTO)
Table	Property(propertyID, agentNo, clientCode, address, town, postcode, firstListed, askingPrice, sold, type, noOfBedrooms, description)
New/updated values	(172, "0030","000061", "20 Onyx Hill", "Thurdeen", "AX3 9YG", "19/08/2019", 85000, False, "House", 3, "3 bedrooms, 1 ensuite, 1 bathroom, kitchen, living room")
Criteria	

WORKED EXAMPLE 8

Update on fields using complex criteria

All property owned by Bjorn Buzzard is to be transferred from his current agent Ben Brown to Olivia Orange. Bjorn's clientCode is 000036, Ben Brown's agentNo is 0005 and Olivia Orange's agentNo is 0008.

Query type	UPDATE
Table	Property
New/updated values	agentNo="0008"
Criteria	agentNo="0005" and clientCode="000036"

WORKED EXAMPLE 9

Update on fields using wildcards

There has been a problem with the addresses in the PROPERTY table. They should have read Beryl Avenue but have incorrectly been entered as Beryl Road. All the addresses stored about Beryl Road have to be updated.

MS Access

Query type	UPDATE
Table	Property
New/updated values	address LIKE "*Beryl Avenue"
Criteria	address LIKE "*Beryl Road"

MySQL

Query type	UPDATE
Table	Property
New/updated values	address LIKE "%Beryl Avenue"
Criteria	address LIKE "%Beryl Road"

NOTE

This SQL code is outwith the scope of Higher

WORKED EXAMPLE 10

Update on multiple fields

Caroline Coot has moved to 12 Emerald End, Strathdonald. Her new postcode is ST1 2RD and her phone number is now 01258 315887. All the information stored about Caroline needs to be changed. Caroline's client code is 000056.

Query type	UPDATE
Table	Client
New/updated values	address = "12 Emerald End", town = "Strathdonald", postcode = "ST1 2RD", telNo = "01258 315887"
Criteria	clientCode="000056"

Calculations

SQL uses arithmetic expressions to calculate values. The calculation can contain attributes, arithmetic operators and both integer and real numbers.

WORKED EXAMPLE 11

Delete a record

Pushpa Pipit has removed the property at 21c Sunstone Flats, Linkilbeg as it has flooded and requires repair work. The propertyID is 147. This now has to be removed from the list of properties for sale.

Query type	DELETE (FROM)
Table	Property
New/updated values	
Criteria	propertyID= 147

WORKED EXAMPLE 12

Delete records using wildcards

All the Ironstone Apartments have been taken off the market and should be removed from the Property table.

MS Access

Query type	DELETE (FROM)
Table	Property
New/updated values	
Criteria	address LIKE "*Ironstone Apartments"

MySQL

Query type	DELETE (FROM)
Table	Property
New/updated values	
Criteria	address LIKE "%Ironstone Apartments"

CHECK YOUR LEARNING

Now answer questions 15–16

(on page 122) on design of basic queries

WORKED EXAMPLE 13

All properties that cost £250,000 or more and are not sold are to have their prices reduced by £5,000. The result of this query should display the client's name, full address of the property for sale and the new price starting with the cheapest.

Field(s) and calculation(s)	Client.clientName, Property.address, Property.town, Property.postcode, Property.askingPrice-5000
Table(s) and query	Client, Property
Search criteria	Property.askingPrice>=250,000 AND Property.sold=False
Sort order	Property.askingPrice ASC

This will not change the value in the entity but will simply change the displayed value. To reduce the amount in the entity an UPDATE query must be designed as follows.

Query type	UPDATE
Table	Property
New/updated values	askingPrice= askingPrice -5000
Criteria	askingPrice>=250,000 and sold=False

Aggregate functions

Aggregate functions are a collection of functions that are used to perform calculations on a set of values across multiple rows in a column. These calculations produce one single value as its output.

Table 10.16 shows the most commonly used aggregate functions.

COUNT()	Counts the number of rows in a column
SUM()	Sums/ adds all the values in a column
MIN()	Returns the lowest value in a column
MAX()	Returns the highest value in a column
AVG()	Calculates the average value across a set of values in a column

Table 10.16 Aggregate functions

COUNT ()

WORKED EXAMPLE 14

COUNT(*)

This will return the total number of records, including those with a null value, in a column. A null value means that there is nothing present in the column and it is empty.

An end-of-quarter report requires the total number of properties contained in the table that sold for £500,000 or more.

Field(s) and calculation(s)	Total number of properties=COUNT(*)
Table(s) and query	Property
Search criteria	soldPrice>=500,000
Sort order	

COUNT(attribute)

This will return the number of records or non-null values in a particular column. Non-null means that there is something present in the column and it is not empty.

The managing director would like to know the total number of bungalows that have been sold.

Field(s) and calculation(s)	Number of bungalows sold=COUNT(type)
Table(s) and query	Property
Search criteria	type = "Bungalow" and sold=True
Sort order	

WORKED EXAMPLE 15

SUM()

Harriet Heart's shop manager would like the total value of property she has sold. Her agent number is 0016.

Field(s) and calculation(s)	Total sold by Harriet Heart=SUM(soldPrice)
Table(s) and query	Property, Agent
Search criteria	Agent.agentNo= "0016"
Sort order	

Harriet earns 2% commission on her total sales. The design for the query above can be altered to include this calculation.

Field(s) and calculation(s)	Commission earned by Harriet Heart=SUM(soldPrice)*0.02
Table(s) and query	Property, Agent
Search criteria	Agent.agentNo= "0016"
Sort order	

MIN() and MAX()

MIN() will return the minimum value for all columns that contain non-null values. MAX() will return the maximum value for all columns that contain non-null values.

WORKED EXAMPLE 16

Red Tiles needs to be able to show the lowest and highest price of property that has been sold.

Field(s) and calculation(s)	Cheapest property=MIN(soldPrice), Dearest property=MAX(soldPrice)
Table(s) and query	Property
Search criteria	
Sort order	

This can be refined even more by looking at the lowest and highest price paid for an apartment.

Field(s) and calculation(s)	Cheapest apartment=MIN(soldPrice), Dearest apartment=MAX(soldPrice)
Table(s) and query	Property
Search criteria	type= "Apartment"
Sort order	

WORKED EXAMPLE 17

AVG()

Red Tiles includes the average price of property that year from the Property table in its annual report.

Field(s) and calculation(s)	Average property price=AVG(soldPrice)
Table(s) and query	Property
Search criteria	
Sort order	

ROUND

The result of this query may produce an average price with many places after the decimal point. To ensure that only two decimal places are displayed after the point the ROUND function may be used and the query design altered as follows.

Field(s) and calculation(s)	Average property price= ROUND(AVG(soldPrice),2)
Table(s) and query	Property
Search criteria	
Sort order	

WORKED EXAMPLE 18

Red Tiles has clients that sell many properties. A query has to be designed to produce the average price of property sold by Rafael Robin to the nearest whole pound.

Field(s) and calculation(s)	Average property price for Rafael Robin = ROUND(AVG(soldPrice),0)
Table(s) and query	Property
Search criteria	clientName= "Rafael Robin"
Sort order	

CHECK YOUR LEARNING

Now answer questions 17–19 (on pages 122–123) on aggregate functions

Aliases

In the previous tables you should have noticed different terms appearing in the *Field(s) and calculation(s)* part of the design. Often the attribute names are not helpful when displaying the data in a column, e.g. agentNo would be more readable if displayed as *Agent Number*. This is also true with calculations and aggregate functions, as you will find out in Chapter 11.

To overcome the problems with how data is to be displayed, **Aliases** are used. This assigns a temporary name which is only displayed in that query. In the design part, they are indicated as shown in the examples for each of the aggregate functions. In Chapter 11, you will see how these can be implemented in your queries.

Grouping data

Grouping data is used to group together rows that contain the same values and present the results for each of these 'summaries'.

Grouping is also commonly used with the aggregate functions COUNT, SUM, MIN, MAX, AVG to group the result into one single output rather than have multiple values for each query.

The order in which the query is designed is important, as this will determine the order in which the query is implemented. Grouping must appear *before* the Sort order in the design table.

WORKED EXAMPLE 19

In the user requirements, Red Tiles Estate Agents want to be able to run the queries shown below. Each of these queries would require the output to be grouped in different ways.

- The average property price in each town.
- The branch that has sold the most properties.
- The amount of commission to pay each agent per month.
- The amount of commission to be paid by each client.
- The amount of annual commission made by agents per branch.
- The total number of properties of a given type sold in a specified month.

The average property price in each town

Field(s) and calculation(s)	town, Average property price by town = ROUND(AVG(soldPrice),0)
Table(s) and query	Property
Search criteria	
Grouping	town
Sort order	

The branch that has sold the most properties

Field(s) and calculation(s)	Branch.branchCode, Properties sold = COUNT (*)
Table(s) and query	Property, Agent, Branch
Search criteria	Property.sold=True
Grouping	Branch.branchCode
Sort order	COUNT(*) DESC

The amount of commission to pay each agent in June 2019

Field(s) and calculation(s)	Agent.agentName, Commission June 2019= ROUND(SUM(Property.soldPrice*0.02),2)
Table(s) and query	Property, Agent
Search criteria	Property.sold=True AND Property.dateSold LIKE "??/06/2019"
Grouping	Agent.agentName
Sort order	

The amount of commission to be paid by each client

Field(s) and calculation(s)	Client.clientName, Commission to Pay= SUM(soldPrice*0.03)
Table(s) and query	Client, Property
Search criteria	Property.sold=True
Grouping	Client.clientName
Sort order	

The amount of annual commission made by agents per branch

Field(s) and calculation(s)	Branch.branchCode, Agent.agentName, Commission =ROUND(SUM(Property.soldPrice*0.02),2)
Table(s) and query	Property, Agent, Branch
Search criteria	Property.sold=True
Grouping	Branch.branchCode, Agent.agentName
Sort order	branch.branchCode ASC

The total number of properties of a given type sold in a specified month (June 2019)

Field(s) and calculation(s)	Branch.branchCode, Property.type, Number sold = COUNT (*)
Table(s) and query	Property, Agent, Branch
Search criteria	Property.sold=True AND Property.dateSold LIKE "??/06/2019"
Grouping	Branch.branchCode, Property.type
Sort order	

CHECK YOUR LEARNING

Now answer questions 20–22 (on page 123) on grouping and aliases

Using the result of a previous query

Sometimes it is not possible to design the query we need all in one operation. Often queries need to be split in order to produce a single value from one design part that can then be used in the second design part. This is also known as a nested query.

WORKED EXAMPLE 20

The managing director of Red Tiles Estate Agent would like to find the average commission earned by estate agents on each property sale in a particular month and then to display agents and property addresses which earned more commission on each property sale than the average from least to most.

To design this query, we have to think about it in two parts.

Firstly, the part where we need to produce a single value based on the average commission earned in one month.

If we use the month of May 2019 as our month and the estate agents earn 2% commission on each house's selling price, then the design of the query would look like this:

Query 1: Average agent commission

Field(s) and calculation(s)	Average commission = AVG (Property.soldPrice*0.02)
Table(s) and query	Property, Agent
Search criteria	Property.dateSold LIKE "??/05/2019"
Grouping	
Sort order	

Query 2: Display estate agents whose commission is more than the average

Field(s) and calculation(s)	Agent.agentName, Property.address, Property.town Commission = (soldPrice*0.02)
Table(s) and query	Agent, Property, [Average agent commission]
Search criteria	Commission > Average commission
Grouping	
Sort order	(soldPrice*0.02) ASC

WORKED EXAMPLE 21

A customer would like to know the price of the lowest priced available property in Axelbridge and which properties are available for this price sorted from the least to most expensive.

Query 1: Lowest priced property

Field(s) and calculation(s)	Lowest price = MIN (askingPrice)
Table(s) and query	Property
Search criteria	sold=False
Grouping	
Sort order	

Query 2: Properties available for minimum price

Field(s) and calculation(s)	address, town, postcode, askingPrice
Table(s) and query	Property, [Lowest priced property]
Search criteria	sold=False AND askingPrice=[Lowest Price]
Grouping	
Sort order	

CHECK YOUR LEARNING

Now answer questions 23–25 (on page 123) on using the result of a previous query

QUESTIONS

Entity occurrence and relationship diagrams

1 State what is meant by the term, 'entity' in a relational database.
2 State what is meant by the term 'attribute'.
3 a) State the techniques used to model a database.
   b) Why is a database model important?
4 State three types of relationship.
5 State the cardinality of these entity occurrence diagrams.

a)

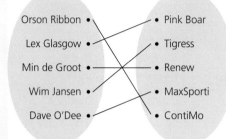

DRIVER   TEAM

b)

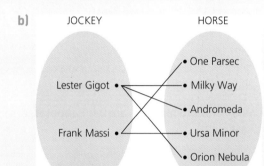

JOCKEY   HORSE

c)

SHOPPERS   SUPERMARKETS

Bert Summers • ── • Super Savers
Diane Decker • ── • Cheapco
Margo Copper • ── • Local Inc.
Dave Brymore • ── • Betterway
Les Aries •

6 What does the crow's foot in an entity relationship diagram indicate?
7 Using the Flyball for Dogs data provided in Table 10.17 below create the following:
   a) an entity occurrence diagram for the five entities
   b) an entity relationship diagram with an annotated relationship.

DIVISION			
divisionCode	division	type	area
SSC1	1	Senior	Scotland
JNE3	3	Junior	North-East

TEAM							
teamNumber	name	captain	seedRanking	seedtime (sec)	registrationDate	type	divisionCode
001	Carswell Flyers	Roger Clarke	4	18.45	17/05/1998	Open	SSC1
005	Furr Goodness Sake	Susan Crane	3	18.05	13/06/2013	Multi-breed	SSC1
012	The Growlers	Chris Danes	5	20.55	30/08/2015	Open	JNE3

OWNER					
ownerNumber	forename	surname	address	town	phoneNumber
AEF152	Roger	Clarke	6 Leven Road	Rowansville	07877 572547
XZQ395	Susan	Crane	8 Rannoch Avenue	Oakton	01987 574630
WHO167	Kitty	Kay	51 Ryan Road	Rowansville	01461 009761
TOT200	Rita	Jeanetta	15 Migdale Gate	Plumthorpe	07510 203040

DOG				
UKFANumber	name	breed	ownerNumber	teamNumber
0163A	Hamish	English Cocker Spaniel	AEF152	001
9283Y	Toggles	Whippet	AEF152	001
1135F	Pat	Border Collie/WSD	WHO167	001
2123S	Rex	Spanish Water Dog	XZQ395	005
3254G	Barney	Border Collie/WSD	TOT200	012

AWARD				
awardNumber	award	tournament	date	UKFANumber
1	Flyball Dog Intermediate	Birchham	01/04/2019	0163A
2	Flyball Dog Intermediate	Birchham	01/04/2019	9283Y
4	Flyball Dog Graduate	Yewfirth	13/07/2019	0163A
5	Flyball Dog Advanced	Yewfirth	13/07/2019	2123S
7	Flyball Dog Silver	Appledale	22/10/2019	0163A
10	Flyball Dog Gold	Boxbridge	03/01/2020	0163A
8	Flyball Dog Silver	Appledale	22/10/2019	2123S
3	Flyball Dog Graduate	Birchham	01/04/2019	3254G
9	Flyball Dog Gold	Appledale	22/10/2019	1135F

Table 10.17 Flyball for Dogs data

8 Using the Stromivar Athletics Club sample data
provided in Table 10.18 create the following:
  a) an entity occurrence diagram for the three
  entities.

  b) an entity relationship diagram with annotated
  relationships.

EVENT		
eventCode	type	name
TR100	Track	100m
FISP	Field	Shot Put
FIHA	Field	Hammer throw
TR1500	Track	1500m
TRH110	Track	110m Hurdles
TR200	Track	200m

ATHLETE					
athleteNo	forename	surname	address	town	postcode
SAC0096	Sammy	Cruikshank	3 Tower Flats	Stromivar	SV1 4QK
SAC0045	Tiffany	Paterson	21 Inverton Road	Stromivar	SV1 5BN
SAC0158	Sau Wai	Chin	12 The Grange	Achnafort	SV3 6XZ
SAC0055	Awais	Abbas	22 Manor Park Road	Bellatron	SV6 5UJ
SAC0017	David	Colins	51b Baker Street	Achnafort	SV3 6LV
SAC0125	Emma	MacDuff	11 Haggs Lane	Stromivar	SV1 8LU
SAC0056	John	Godfrey	15 The Lane	Bellatron	SV6 7RQ
SAC0259	Alex	Brady	12 The Grange	Achnafort	SV3 6XZ

ENTRY				
entryNo	athleteNo	eventCode	time	distanceMetres
1	SAC0045	TR100	00:00:11.52	
2	SAC0096	TRH110	00:00:13.65	
3	SAC0158	FISP		15.2
4	SAC0055	FIHA		67.54
5	SAC0017	TR1500	00:03:52.52	
6	SAC0045	TR200	00:00:24.65	
7	SAC0125	TR200	00:00:24.23	
8	SAC0125	TR100	00:00:12.02	
9	SAC0259	FIHA		62.21
10	SAC0056	FIHA		70.2

Table 10.18 Stromivar Athletics Club sample data

Data dictionaries

9 State what is meant by a compound key.
10 Name the elements that a data dictionary should contain to describe the data.
11 Copy and complete the data dictionary shown for the Account table for TeeVeeFi shown in Table 10.19. Sample data has been provided to indicate data types and any validation. Other details can be found on page 107 of Chapter 9.

Entity	Attribute Name	Key	Type	Size	Required	Validation	Sample data
ACCOUNT	customerID						100647888
	package						Gold
	costPerMonth						£45.98
	billingDate						1st of every month
	paymentType						Direct debit
	paymentDueDate						01/10/2020
	billPaid						N

Table 10.19 TeeVeeFi Accounts table data dictionary

12 Copy and complete the data dictionary shown for the Seudair jewellery chain shown in Table 10.20. Sample data has been provided to indicate data types and any validation.

Entity	Attribute Name	Key	Type	Size	Required	Validation	Sample data
MANUFACTURER	manufacturerID						Ace1648
	name						Acevers
	address						12 Parkhouse Avenue
	town						East Beaghill
	postcode						JW6 9XJ
	telNo						07955 346978
DESIGNER	designerID						GSB2147
	designerName						Jocelyn Jeffries
	speciality						Bracelet
	manufacturerID						Ace1648
JEWELLERY	itemCode						WR001

Entity	Attribute Name	Key	Type	Size	Required	Validation	Sample data
	itemType						Ring
	itemName						Engagement ring
	metalType						Gold
	gemStone						Diamond
	gemstoneShape						Teardrop
	price						£1345.00
	designerID						GSB2147
TRANSACTION	receiptNumber						46
	itemCode						WR001
	quantity						2
	dateSold						12/10/2020
RECEIPT	receiptNumber						46
	shopNumber						5
SHOP	shopNumber						5
	address						14 Appletree Lane
	town						High Bramley
	postcode						DC5 9HY
	telNo						07946 134311

Table 10.20 Seudair jewellery shop data dictionary

13 Using the data from Table 10.17 on pages 119–120, create the data dictionary for all of the Flyball entities.

14 Using the data from Table 10.18 on pages 120–121, create the data dictionary for all of the Stromivar Athletics Club entities.

Design of basic queries

Use the following template to design the queries that follow.

Field(s) and calculation(s)	
Table(s) and query	
Search criteria	
Sort order	

15 Use the data dictionary from the design for the Seudair database in Table 10.20 to design the queries below.
   a) Design a query to display the manufacturers whose designers make bracelets. The output should display manufacturers, designers and metal types.
   b) Design a query to display the name of the designer and price of each white gold wedding ring.
   c) A customer would like a list of engagement rings priced between £1850 and £2200. The output should display the designer name, metal type, gemstone, gemstone shape and price. It should be sorted in alphabetical order of metal type with the cheapest ring appearing first in the list.

16 Use the data dictionary from the design for the Flyball for Dogs database in question 13 to design queries to:
   a) display all the dogs and their owners in the Scottish division. The team name, owners and dogs' names should be displayed.
   b) update the address of Roger Clarke who has moved to 34 Leven Road, Rowansville.
   c) add a new award for the dog with UKFANumber 2123S. He earned his Flyball Dog Gold on January 22nd 2020 at the Figtreeton tournament. This will be the 12th award issued.
   d) remove Toggles the whippet as she has been retired from competition. Her UKFANumber is 9283Y.

17 Use the Flyball for Dogs data in Table 10.17 to design the following queries.
   a) Design a query to count the number of teams whose registration is before January 1st 2020.
   b) Design a query to display the fastest seed time.

18 Using the Seudair data dictionary in Table 10.20, design the following queries.
   a) Design a query to calculate the total amount for receipt number 5.
   b) Design a query to display the price of the most expensive piece of jewellery.

c) Design a query to count the number of necklaces designed by Harriet Henry.

d) Design a query to display the average price of gold wedding rings designed by Iain Ibbotsen.

19 The organisers of the Ravimorts Music Festival would like to store all of the information about the tickets, stage and musical acts in a relational database. The design for the attributes to be stored are shown below.

> TICKET {ticketNo, ticketType, quantity, price, stageName*}
>
> STAGE {stageName, location, underCover}
>
> ACT {actName, musicGenre, members, setLengthMins, startTime, day, stageName*}

Design a query to display the total number of tickets sold and the total amount of money made.

20 Using the design for the Ravimorts Music Festival database in question 19, design queries to display:
a) the number of acts appearing on each stage.
b) the total set length per stage starting with the longest.

21 Using the data dictionary for the Seudair database in Table 10.20, design queries to display:
a) the total of each gemstone sold sorted from most to least popular showing the gemstone type and quantity sold.

b) the total of each item type sold.
c) the sales from each manufacturer.

22 Using the design for the Flyball for Dogs database in Table 10.17, design queries to display:
a) the breeds of dog used in flyball racing sorted by the least to most popular.
b) the number of awards won by dogs from least to most.

Using the result of a previous query

23 Using the design for the Flyball for Dogs database in Table 10.17, design queries to display the team names and seed times of teams whose dogs run faster than the average seed time in ascending order.

24 Using the data dictionary for the Seudair database in Table 10.20, design queries to display:
a) the most expensive piece(s) of jewellery and the designer(s).
(Hint: you have already created the design for part of this query in question 18b.)
b) the number of pieces of jewellery that are more expensive than the average price of all the jewellery.
c) the name, designer and price of all engagement rings that are the same price as the cheapest engagement ring.

25 Using the design for the Ravimorts Music Festival database in question 19, design queries to display the acts whose set lengths are shorter than the average set length along with the stage on which they are appearing sorted from the longest set.

KEY POINTS

- A database is a structured collection of similar information which can be queried.
- A relational database is made up of entities, attributes and relationships to link the entities.
- An entity is an object about which information is modelled and stored.
- An entity is a person, place, thing, event or concept of interest to the business or organisation about which data is to be stored.
- A table contains data about a single entity.
- An entity is described by its attributes.
- An attribute is an individual data element in an entity.
- Each attribute is a characteristic of the entity.
- A database may have more than one entity.
- Key fields are used to link entities: they may be primary keys or foreign keys.
- An attribute or combination of attributes that uniquely identifies one, and only one, entity occurrence is called a primary key.
- A primary key must have a unique value as it is used to identify a single instance or occurrence of data.

- A primary key must contain an entry, it cannot be empty (or null).
- A foreign key is a field in an entity which links to the primary key in a related entity.
- Linking entities allows access to the information in all of the entities.
- A database which contains linked entities is called a relational database because linking the entities creates a relationship between them.
- Database developers model the system they are creating before any work on implementation takes place.
- A database model consists of:
  - entity occurrence diagrams
  - entity relationship diagrams
  - data dictionaries.
- A specific example of an entity is called an instance or entity occurrence.
- An entity occurrence diagram shows the relationship between entities using the occurrences within each entity.

- The cardinality of relationships are:
  - one-to-one
  - one-to-many
  - many-to-many.
- An entity relationship diagram shows the relationship between two or more entities.
- An entity relationship diagram should show entities, attributes and relationships between entities.
- A primary key is signified by underlining and a foreign key is signified by an asterisk in the entity-relationship diagram where attributes are included.
- A composite (or concatenated) key is where two or more attributes are used to provide a unique identifier for each entity occurrence in an entity where no one attribute can uniquely identify that occurrence.
- In a compound key, the attributes used to uniquely identify the occurrence must consist of foreign keys, i.e. they are primary keys in the other linked tables.
- Surrogate keys are used to replace compound and composite keys with a single unique introduced identifier.
- A data dictionary contains all the elements to be present in the database once implemented.
- Metadata is data about data.
- Each row in the data dictionary contains information on how each entity and attribute should be implemented in the database.
- The data dictionary contains columns of information on keys, data types, sizes, required and validation.
- The key column indicates whether the attribute is a primary or foreign key.
- The type column indicates the data type.
- Each attribute must have a data type.
- Data types include text, number, date, time and Boolean.
- A text type is used to hold letters, numbers and symbols.
- A numeric type only stores numbers.
- Date types can only contain dates.
- Time types can hold hours, minutes and seconds.
- A Boolean type contains only two values, for instance, true or false, yes or no.
- The size column shows the maximum number of characters associated with a text type.
- The required column shows whether or not an attribute must contain a value.
- Primary and foreign keys must always contain a value.

- Validation is a check to make sure that an item of data is sensible and allowable.
- Presence check checks to make sure that a field has not been left empty.
- Restricted choice gives users a list of options to choose from and so limits the input to pre-approved answers.
- Field length ensures the correct number of numbers or characters has been entered.
- Range check keeps the data within given limits.
- Data integrity rules include entity and referential integrity.
- Entity integrity is said to exist if a table has a primary key and contains a value.
- Referential integrity is said to exist if a foreign key has a matching primary key entry in a linked table.
- When designing a solution to a query, developers must include:
  - which tables (entities) are to be used
  - which fields (attributes) are required
  - search criteria
  - whether or not data is to be sorted
  - if appropriate, how the data is to be grouped
  - any calculations or aggregate functions that are required
  - which fields should be displayed in the results
  - whether or not an alias is to be used.
- Dot notation includes table and field names separated by a dot.
- SQL uses arithmetic expressions to calculate values.
- Calculations can contain attributes, arithmetic operators and both integer and real numbers.
- Aggregate functions are a collection of functions that are used to perform calculations on a set of values across multiple rows in column.
- Aggregate functions produce one single value as their output.
- COUNT(), SUM(), MIN(), MAX() and AVG() are all aggregate functions.
- An alias assigns a temporary name to attributes, calculations and aggregate functions which is only displayed in that query to make the result more readable to the user.
- Grouping data is used to group together rows that contain the same values.
- Grouping is also commonly used with the aggregate functions to group the result into one single output rather than have multiple values for each query.
- Grouping must appear before the sort order in the design table.
- A nested query can be used where the result of one query is required to run in another query.

Chapter 11 Database implementation

This chapter looks at the implementation of a database using MS Access and MySQL.

The following topics are covered:

- describe, exemplify and use SQL operations for pre-populated relational databases, with three or more linked tables.
- UPDATE, SELECT, DELETE, INSERT statements making use of:
  - wildcards
  - computed values, alias
  - aggregate functions (MIN, MAX, AVG, SUM, COUNT)
  - GROUP BY
  - ORDER BY
  - WHERE.
- read and explain code that makes use of the above SQL.

Implementation of basic queries

Remember from Chapter 10, that querying may involve some or a combination of the following actions.

- Searching the database returning results from two or more tables (simple or complex searches).
- Sorting across two or more fields from two or more tables (simple or complex sorts).
- Inserting new records.
- Updating the fields with new data.
- Deleting a record from a table.
- Calculations involving fields and use of aggregate functions.
- Grouping of data.

In addition, both relational and logical operators are required (see Chapter 10 page 110).

Each of the examples which follow will demonstrate the implementation of the queries that were designed in Chapter 10 as part of the Red Tiles Estate Agency relational database design.

WORKED EXAMPLE 1

Simple search on one table

This query will display the addresses and asking prices of all properties with three bedrooms.

```
SELECT address, town, postcode,
askingPrice, noOfBedrooms

FROM Property

WHERE noOfBedrooms = 3;
```

MS Access

address	town	postcode	askingPrice	noOfBedrooms
21 Agate Avenue	Axelbridge	AX1 6BF	150000	3
18 Amber Park	Fort Mags	AX4 6GH	75250	3
2 Amethyst Park	Portussie	PT1 8XD	99000	3
9 Amethyst Park	Portussie	PT1 8XD	105000	3
5a Amethyst Place	Stornavadie	PT8 7RT	245000	3
35 Ametrine Avenue	Stornavadie	PT8 3LA	225000	3
14 Ametrine Avenue	Stornavadie	PT8 3LA	240000	3
19 Ammolite Avenue	Farkirk	PT5 5XY	145000	3
5 Ammolite Cross	Farkirk	PT5 8ST	195000	3
3 Ammolite Cross	Farkirk	PT5 8ST	195000	3
22 Aquamarine Avenue	Invertrose	PT3 1QD	225000	3
3 Aquamarine Mews	Invertrose	PT3 3BN	235000	3
33 Beryl Road	Invertrose	PT3 6YB	154000	3
15 Beryl Road	Invertrose	PT3 6YB	155000	3

MySQL

address	town	postcode	askingPrice	noOfBedrooms
21 Agate Avenue	Axelbridge	AX1 6BF	150000	3
18 Amber Park	Fort Mags	AX4 6GH	75250	3
2 Amethyst Park	Portussie	PT1 8XD	99000	3
9 Amethyst Park	Portussie	PT1 8XD	105000	3
5a Amethyst Place	Stornavadie	PT8 7RT	245000	3
35 Ametrine Avenue	Stornavadie	PT8 3LA	225000	3
14 Ametrine Avenue	Stornavadie	PT8 3LA	240000	3
19 Ammolite Avenue	Farkirk	PT5 5XY	145000	3
5 Ammolite Cross	Farkirk	PT5 8ST	195000	3
3 Ammolite Cross	Farkirk	PT5 8ST	195000	3
22 Aquamarine Avenue	Invertrose	PT3 1QD	225000	3
3 Aquamarine Mews	Invertrose	PT3 3BN	235000	3
33 Beryl Road	Invertrose	PT3 6YB	154000	3
15 Beryl Road	Invertrose	PT3 6YB	155000	3

WORKED EXAMPLE 2

Complex search on one table

This query will display the details of all the bungalows in Invertrose with an asking price between £100,000 and £150,000.

```
SELECT address, town, postcode,
askingPrice, description

FROM Property

WHERE town= "Invertrose" AND type=
"Bungalow" AND askingPrice>100000 AND
askingPrice<200000
```

MS Access

address	town	postcode	askingPrice	description
12 Apatite Grove	Invertrose	PT3 5LP	195000	4 bedrooms, 1 ensuite, 1 bathroom, kitchen, living room, lounge, conservatory
33 Beryl Road	Invertrose	PT3 6YB	154000	3 bedrooms, 1 bathroom, kitchen, living room, conservatory
15 Beryl Road	Invertrose	PT3 6YB	155000	3 bedrooms, 1 bathroom, kitchen, living room, conservatory

MySQL

address	town	postcode	askingPrice	description
12 Apatite Grove	Invertrose	PT3 5LP	195000	4 bedrooms, 1 ensuite, 1 bathroom, kitchen, living room, lounge, conservatory
33 Beryl Road	Invertrose	PT3 6YB	154000	3 bedrooms, 1 bathroom, kitchen, living room, conservatory
15 Beryl Road	Invertrose	PT3 6YB	155000	3 bedrooms, 1 bathroom, kitchen, living room, conservatory

Equi-join

Both of the previous examples were simple searches from a single table. This means that it is quite clear which tables the fields belong to. However, where two or more tables are involved, there has to be some mechanism to allow the tables to read and match data from one another. This means that **equi-joins** will have to be implemented to allow the tables to extract the required data. An equi-join allows data from linked tables in the database to be queried. There must be a matching primary and foreign key in each table for this to be performed successfully. Equi-join uses the WHERE command and dot notation to test this match between the primary and foreign key in the tables concerned. Notice also that dot notation has been used to identify the tables and their associated fields.

Implementing this using two tables is a fairly simple process as shown in these examples.

WORKED EXAMPLE 3

Simple search on two tables

This query is designed to display the names and email addresses of the agents that work in the Dumshiels branch of Red Tiles Estate Agents.

```
SELECT Agent.agentName, Agent.agentEmail
FROM Agent, Branch
WHERE Agent.branchCode=Branch.
branchCode AND Branch.town= "Dumshiels"
```

MS Access

Simple search on two tables ✕		
agentName ▾	agentEmail ▾	town ▾
Ben Brown	bbrown@redtilesestag.co.uk	Dumshiels
Beatrice Black	bblack@redtilesestag.co.uk	Dumshiels
Gordon Green	ggreen@redtilesestag.co.uk	Dumshiels
Olivia Orange	oorange@redtilesestag.co.uk	Dumshiels
Ryan Red	rred@redtilesestag.co.uk	Dumshiels

MySQL

	agentName	agentEmail	town
▶	Ben Brown	bbrown@redtilesestag.co.uk	Dumshiels
	Beatrice Black	bblack@redtilesestag.co.uk	Dumshiels
	Gordon Green	ggreen@redtilesestag.co.uk	Dumshiels
	Olivia Orange	oorange@redtilesestag.co.uk	Dumshiels
	Ryan Red	rred@redtilesestag.co.uk	Dumshiels

WORKED EXAMPLE 4

Complex search on two tables

This query should display the details of all the properties in Linkilbeg that are assigned to estate agent Robert Rose.

```
SELECT Property.address, Property.town, Property.postcode, Property.askingPrice,
Property.description
FROM Agent, Property
WHERE Agent.agentNo=Property.agentNo AND Agent.agentName= "Robert Rose"
AND Property.town= "Linkilbeg"
```

MS Access

Complex search on two tables ✕				
address ▾	town ▾	postcode ▾	askingPrice ▾	description
14 Diamond Drive	Linkilbeg	LL7 3XZ	145000	3 bedrooms, 1 bathroom, kitchen, living room
41 Mother of Pearl Street	Linkilbeg	LL7 1PK	151250	3 bedrooms, 1 bathroom, kitchen, living room, conservatory

MySQL

	address	town	postcode	askingPrice	description
▶	14 Diamond Drive	Linkilbeg	LL7 3XZ	145000	3 bedrooms, 1 bathroom, kitchen, living room
	41 Mother of Pearl Street	Linkilbeg	LL7 1PK	151250	3 bedrooms, 1 bathroom, kitchen, living room, conservatory

WORKED EXAMPLE 5

Complex search on two tables using OR

This query will display all available properties that have either
3 or 4 bedrooms currently for sale by estate agent Terry Thyme.

```
SELECT Property.address, Property.town, Property.postcode, Property.noOfBedrooms,
Property.askingPrice, Property.sold

FROM Property, Agent

WHERE (Property.noOfBedrooms=3 OR Property.noOfBedrooms=4) AND Agent.
agentName="Terry Thyme" AND Property.agentNo=Agent.agentNo AND Property.sold=False
```

MS Access

address	town	postcode	noOfBedrooms	askingPrice	sold
14 Jade Lane	Auchabhainn	ST9 6VG	3	182000	☐
19 Pearl Close	East Stanbridge	ST18 3WD	4	145000	☐

MySQL

address	town	postcode	noOfBedrooms	askingPrice	sold
14 Jade Lane	Auchabhainn	ST9 6VG	3	182000	0
19 Pearl Close	East Stanbridge	ST18 3WD	4	145000	0

However, when using more than two tables in queries, it is sensible to draw
the entities and match the primary and foreign keys so that the tables
required in each query are simpler to identify and it is also easier to identify
the equi-joins. Figure 11.1 shows how this could be implemented for the
Red Tiles Estate Agency

Figure 11.1 Matching primary and foreign keys between entities

WORKED EXAMPLE 6

Complex search on four tables

This query should display a list of addresses of properties being sold by
Gabriel Gannet that cost more than £180,000, the agents' names and
branch addresses.

```
SELECT Client.clientName, Property.address, Property.town, Property.postcode,
Property.description, Property.askingPrice, Agent.agentName, Branch.address,
Branch.town, Property.sold

FROM Agent, Property, Branch, Client

WHERE Branch.branchCode=Agent.branchCode AND Agent.agentNo=Property.agentNo AND
Property.clientCode AND Client.clientCode AND Client.clientName= "Gabriel Gannet"
and Property.askingPrice>180000 AND Property.sold=False
```

MS Access

clientName	Property.address	Property.town	postcode	description	askingPrice	agentName	Branch.address	Branch.town	sold
Gabriel Gannet	5 Ammolite Cross	Farkirk	PT5 8ST	3 bedrooms, 1 ensuite, 1 bathroom, kitchen, living room, lounge, conservatory	195000	Desmond Diamond	31 Wool Avenue	Farfour	☐
Gabriel Gannet	3 Ammolite Cross	Farkirk	PT5 8ST	3 bedrooms, 1 ensuite, 1 bathroom, kitchen, living room, lounge, conservatory	195000	Harriet Heart	31 Wool Avenue	Farfour	☐
Gabriel Gannet	1a Ironstone Apartments	Farfour	PT15 3NJ	2 bedrooms, 1 ensuite, 1 bathroom, kitchen, living room	200000	Karis King	5 Cotton Street	Farfour	☐
Gabriel Gannet	5c Ironstone Apartments	Farfour	PT15 3NJ	3 bedrooms, 1 ensuite, 1 bathroom, kitchen, living room	250000	Karis King	5 Cotton Street	Farfour	☐
Gabriel Gannet	4b Ironstone Apartments	Farfour	PT15 3NJ	2 bedrooms, 1 ensuite, 1 bathroom, kitchen, living room	200000	Karis King	5 Cotton Street	Farfour	☐
Gabriel Gannet	12b Ironstone Apartments	Farfour	PT15 3NJ	3 bedrooms, 1 ensuite, 1 bathroom, kitchen, living room	255000	Karis King	5 Cotton Street	Farfour	☐

MySQL

clientName	address	town	postcode	description	askingPrice	agentName	address	town	sold
Gabriel Gannet	5 Ammolite Cross	Farkirk	PT5 8ST	3 bedrooms, 1 ensuite, 1 bathroom, kitchen, living room, lounge, conservatory	195000	Desmond Diamond	31 Wool Avenue	Farfour	0
Gabriel Gannet	3 Ammolite Cross	Farkirk	PT5 8ST	3 bedrooms, 1 ensuite, 1 bathroom, kitchen, living room, lounge, conservatory	195000	Harriet Heart	31 Wool Avenue	Farfour	0
Gabriel Gannet	1a Ironstone Apartments	Farfour	PT15 3NJ	2 bedrooms, 1 ensuite, 1 bathroom, kitchen, living room	200000	Karis King	5 Cotton Street	Farfour	0
Gabriel Gannet	5c Ironstone Apartments	Farfour	PT15 3NJ	3 bedrooms, 1 ensuite, 1 bathroom, kitchen, living room	250000	Karis King	5 Cotton Street	Farfour	0
Gabriel Gannet	4b Ironstone Apartments	Farfour	PT15 3NJ	2 bedrooms, 1 ensuite, 1 bathroom, kitchen, living room	200000	Karis King	5 Cotton Street	Farfour	0
Gabriel Gannet	12b Ironstone Apartments	Farfour	PT15 3NJ	3 bedrooms, 1 ensuite, 1 bathroom, kitchen, living room	255000	Karis King	5 Cotton Street	Farfour	0

Queries using wildcards

Remember from Chapter 10 that wildcards are used where incomplete
information is available for a query to be carried out. For more information
about wildcards and their operators see page 111.

WORKED EXAMPLE 7

Text replacement

This query should display the full address, asking price and sellers
of all properties which have four bedrooms and a conservatory.

MS Access

```
SELECT Client.clientName , Property.address, Property.town, Property.postcode,
Property.askingPrice, Property.description

FROM Client, Property

WHERE Property.clientCode = Client.clientCode AND noOfBedrooms=4 AND Property.
description LIKE "*conservatory*"
```

MySQL

```
SELECT Client.clientName , Property.address, Property.town, Property.postcode,
Property.askingPrice, Property.description

FROM Client, Property

WHERE Property.clientCode = Client.clientCode AND noOfBedrooms=4 AND Property.
description LIKE "%conservatory%"
```

clientName	address	town	postcode	askingPrice	description
Margaret Moorhen	4 Agate Avenue	Axelbridge	AX1 6BF	152500	3 bedrooms, 1 ensuite, 1 bathroom, kitchen, utilty room, living room, lounge, conservatory
Nancy Nightingale	15a Agate Circus	Axelbridge	AX1 8NY	235000	4 bedrooms, 2 ensuites, 1 bathroom, kitchen, utilty room, living room, lounge, conservatory
Oliver Osprey	3 Alexandrite Court	Thurdeen	AX3 4FV	175000	4 bedrooms, 1 ensuite, 1 bathroom, kitchen, living room, lounge, conservatory
Duncan Diver	10 Alexandrite Court	Thurdeen	AX3 4FV	180000	4 bedrooms, 1 ensuite, 1 bathroom, kitchen, living room, lounge, conservatory
Gordon Grouse	1 Ametrine Grove	Farkirk	PT5 5FK	500000	4 bedrooms, 2 ensuites, 1 bathroom, kitchen, utilty room, living room, lounge, conservatory
Frank Falcon	12 Apatite Grove	Invertrose	PT3 5LP	195000	4 bedrooms, 1 ensuite, 1 bathroom, kitchen, living room, lounge, conservatory
Gavin Godwit	2 Blue John View	Port Hamish	PT11 8SV	234000	4 bedrooms, 1 ensuite, 1 bathroom, kitchen, living room, lounge, conservatory
Bertie Bullfinch	1 Calcite Crescent	Gerryburgh	PT10 7GG	240000	4 bedrooms, 1 ensuite, 1 bathroom, kitchen, living room, lounge, conservatory
Bertie Bullfinch	7 Calcite Crescent	Gerryburgh	PT10 7GG	240000	4 bedrooms, 1 ensuite, 1 bathroom, kitchen, living room, lounge, conservatory
Bertie Bullfinch	4 Calcite Crescent	Gerryburgh	PT10 7GG	240000	4 bedrooms, 1 ensuite, 1 bathroom, kitchen, living room, lounge, conservatory
Shona Sheerwater	24 Chalcedony Avenue	Marymore	BV3 3NM	255000	4 bedrooms, 1 ensuite, 1 bathroom, kitchen, living room, lounge, conservatory
Caroline Coot	3 Druzy Court	Strathdonald	ST1 6HJ	189000	4 bedrooms, 1 bathroom, kitchen, living room, conservatory
Colin Cormorant	15 Emerald Crescent	Kirkinallen	ST6 3TT	230000	4 bedrooms, 1 ensuite, 1 bathroom, kitchen, living room, lounge, conservatory
Clarence Crow	1 Feldspar Meadow	Strathdonald	ST1 6DK	655000	4 bedrooms, 2 ensuites, 1 bathroom, kitchen, utilty room, living room, lounge, conservatory

WORKED EXAMPLE 8

Date replacement

This query should display the full address, date first listed, asking price and sellers of all the properties that went on sale in September 2019.

MS Access

```
SELECT Client.clientName, Property.address, Property.town, Property.postcode,
Property.firstListed, Property.askingPrice

FROM Client, Property

WHERE Property.clientCode = Client.clientCode AND Property.firstListed LIKE
"??/09/2019"
```

clientName	address	town	postcode	firstListed	askingPrice
Consolata Crossbill	21 Agate Avenue	Axelbridge	AX1 6BF	01/09/2019	150000
Gabriel Gannet	101 Beryl Street	Invertrose	PT3 5KP	02/09/2019	160000
Guy Guillemot	10 Chrysoberyl Lane	Kirkjohns	BV8 9BH	09/09/2019	230000
Ricardo Rhea	33 Malachite Street	Portacraig	BV5 3PQ	03/09/2019	99500
Ricardo Rhea	15 Obsidian Avenue	Portacraig	BV5 9SF	14/09/2019	113000
Chizzy Chough	2 Selenite View	East Stanbridge	ST18 4VC	17/09/2019	148000
Abdullah Auk	4 Stichtite Place	Farfour	PT15 2JY	22/09/2019	245000
Abdullah Auk	1 Stichtite Place	Farfour	PT15 2JY	18/09/2019	245000
Abdullah Auk	9 Stichtite Place	Farfour	PT15 2JY	24/09/2019	247000
Kwame Kittiwake	16 Topaz Terrace	Penkenneth	ST8 6EH	22/09/2019	125000
Kwame Kittiwake	10 Topaz Terrace	Penkenneth	ST8 6EH	22/09/2019	125000
Chizzy Chough	1 Tourmaline Way	East Stanbridge	ST18 2KP	28/09/2019	190000

MySQL

```
SELECT Client.clientName, Property.address, Property.town, Property.postcode,
Property.firstListed, Property.askingPrice

FROM Client, Property

WHERE Property.clientCode = Client.clientCode AND Property.firstListed LIKE
"2019-09-__"
```

clientName	address	town	postcode	firstListed	askingPrice
Consolata Crossbill	21 Agate Avenue	Axelbridge	AX1 6BF	2019-09-01	150000
Gabriel Gannet	101 Beryl Street	Invertrose	PT3 5KP	2019-09-02	160000
Guy Guillemot	10 Chrysoberyl Lane	Kirkjohns	BV8 9BH	2019-09-09	230000
Gabriel Gannet	12b Ironstone Apartments	Farfour	PT15 3NJ	2019-09-01	255000
Ricardo Rhea	33 Malachite Street	Portacraig	BV5 3PQ	2019-09-03	99500
Ricardo Rhea	15 Obsidian Avenue	Portacraig	BV5 9SF	2019-09-14	113000
Chizzy Chough	2 Selenite View	East Stanbridge	ST18 4VC	2019-09-17	148000
Abdullah Auk	4 Stichtite Place	Farfour	PT15 2JY	2019-09-22	245000
Abdullah Auk	1 Stichtite Place	Farfour	PT15 2JY	2019-09-18	250000
Abdullah Auk	9 Stichtite Place	Farfour	PT15 2JY	2019-09-24	247000
Kwame Kittiwake	16 Topaz Terrace	Penkenneth	ST8 6EH	2019-09-22	125000
Kwame Kittiwake	10 Topaz Terrace	Penkenneth	ST8 6EH	2019-09-22	125000
Chizzy Chough	1 Tourmaline Way	East Stanbridge	ST18 2KP	2019-09-28	190000

WORKED EXAMPLE 9

Simple sort on one field in one table

This query should display a list of all sold properties in order of price – cheapest to dearest. The result of the query should display the full address and price of each property.

```
SELECT address, town, postcode,
soldPrice
FROM Property
WHERE sold=True
ORDER BY soldPrice ASC
```

MS Access

Simple sort ✕

address	town	postcode	soldPrice
1 Tektite Yard	East Stanbridge	ST18 1JW	40000
4a Iolite Alley	South Pitinver	ST3 9DP	44550
9 Mother of Pearl Park	invertrose	PT3 6HY	46500
5 Lapis Lazuli Hill	Duncreige	DC1 4RD	55000
12 Ruby Passage	Portussie	PT1 5NJ	56000
4c Sapphire Close	Farfour	PT15 6GC	56500
771 Alexandrite Street	Thurdeen	AX3 9YT	57250
21 Amber Cross	Fort Mags	AX4 2QQ	65500
3 Amber Cross	Fort Mags	AX4 2QQ	66000
6c Verdite Villas	Dumshiells	DC3 8MA	72000
4f Verdite Villas	Dumshiells	DC3 8MA	72000
2a Verdite Villas	Dumshiells	DC3 8MA	72000
3d Verdite Villas	Dumshiells	DC3 8MA	72000
2a Sunstone Flats	Linkilbeg	LL7 3RW	75000
18 Amber Park	Fort Mags	AX4 6GH	75500
11a Opalite Court	invertrose	PT3 7EB	77500
5c Apatite Close	Invertrose	PT3 5NU	78250
17a Opalite Court	invertrose	PT3 7EB	78250

MySQL

address	town	postcode	soldPrice
1 Tektite Yard	East Stanbridge	ST18 1JW	40000
4a Iolite Alley	South Pitinver	ST3 9DP	44550
9 Mother of Pearl Park	invertrose	PT3 6HY	46500
5 Lapis Lazuli Hill	Duncreige	DC1 4RD	55000
12 Ruby Passage	Portussie	PT1 5NJ	56000
4c Sapphire Close	Farfour	PT15 6GC	56500
771 Alexandrite Street	Thurdeen	AX3 9YT	57250
21 Amber Cross	Fort Mags	AX4 2QQ	65500
3 Amber Cross	Fort Mags	AX4 2QQ	66000
3d Verdite Villas	Dumshiells	DC3 8MA	72000
2a Verdite Villas	Dumshiells	DC3 8MA	72000
4f Verdite Villas	Dumshiells	DC3 8MA	72000
6c Verdite Villas	Dumshiells	DC3 8MA	72000
2a Sunstone Flats	Linkilbeg	LL7 3RW	75000
18 Amber Park	Fort Mags	AX4 6GH	75500
11a Opalite Court	invertrose	PT3 7EB	77500

WORKED EXAMPLE 10

Sort on two fields in one table

This query should display a list of all unsold properties in order of town from A to Z and then on price with the most expensive property being displayed first. The result of the query should display the full address and price of each property.

```
SELECT address, town, postcode,
askingPrice
FROM Property
WHERE sold=False
ORDER BY town ASC, askingPrice DESC
```

MS Access

Sort on two fields one table ✕

address	town	postcode	askingPrice
16 Iolite Road	Aberkelvin	ST10 5LG	65500
6 Diamond Walk	Ardburgh	LL12 5YJ	215000
23 Chrysoberyl Street	Arnouston	BV2 3XZ	199000
14 Jade Lane	Auchabhainn	ST9 6VG	182000
1 Jade Lane	Auchabhainn	ST9 6VG	180500
19 Peridot Place	Axelbridge	AX1 2JN	295000
1c Agate Circus	Axelbridge	AX1 8NY	250000
14 Peridot Place	Axelbridge	AX1 2JN	220000
21 Agate Avenue	Axelbridge	AX1 6BF	150000
4 Peridot Walk	Axelbridge	AX1 2JM	90000
3 Cat's Eye Alley	Burryvale	BV1 4JD	56000
5 Pearl Place	Dalburgh	ST15 4FT	215000
19 Chrysoprase Lane	Dunallan	AX2 6UG	245000
1 Tourmaline Way	East Stanbridge	ST18 2KP	190000
2 Selenite View	East Stanbridge	ST18 4VC	148000
5 Selenite View	East Stanbridge	ST18 4VC	145000
19 Pearl Close	East Stanbridge	ST18 3WD	145000
3a Topaz Court	East Stanbridge	ST18 7DK	85000
12b Ironstone Apartments	Farfour	PT15 3NJ	255000
1 Stichtite Place	Farfour	PT15 2JY	250000
5c Ironstone Apartments	Farfour	PT15 3NJ	250000
9 Stichtite Place	Farfour	PT15 2JY	247000

MySQL

address	town	postcode	askingPrice
16 Iolite Road	Aberkelvin	ST10 5LG	65500
6 Diamond Walk	Ardburgh	LL12 5YJ	215000
23 Chrysoberyl Street	Arnouston	BV2 3XZ	199000
14 Jade Lane	Auchabhainn	ST9 6VG	182000
1 Jade Lane	Auchabhainn	ST9 6VG	180500
19 Peridot Place	Axelbridge	AX1 2JN	295000
1c Agate Circus	Axelbridge	AX1 8NY	250000
14 Peridot Place	Axelbridge	AX1 2JN	220000
21 Agate Avenue	Axelbridge	AX1 6BF	150000
4 Peridot Walk	Axelbridge	AX1 2JM	90000
3 Cat's Eye Alley	Burryvale	BV1 4JD	56000
5 Pearl Place	Dalburgh	ST15 4FT	215000
19 Chrysoprase Lane	Dunallan	AX2 6UG	245000
1 Tourmaline Way	East Stanbridge	ST18 2KP	190000
2 Selenite View	East Stanbridge	ST18 4VC	148000
5 Selenite View	East Stanbridge	ST18 4VC	145000
19 Pearl Close	East Stanbridge	ST18 3WD	145000
3a Topaz Court	East Stanbridge	ST18 7DK	85000
12b Ironstone Apartments	Farfour	PT15 3NJ	255000
1 Stichtite Place	Farfour	PT15 2JY	250000
5c Ironstone Apartments	Farfour	PT15 3NJ	250000
9 Stichtite Place	Farfour	PT15 2JY	247000

WORKED EXAMPLE 11

Sort on two fields in two tables

This query should display a list of all sold properties sorted alphabetically by branch and then on price starting with the least expensive. The result of the query should show the branch, full address and price of each property.

```
SELECT Branch.branchCode, Property.
address, Property.town, Property.
postcode, Property.soldPrice

FROM Property, Branch, Agent

WHERE Branch.branchCode=Agent.
branchCode AND Agent.agentNo=Property.
agentNo AND Property.sold=True

ORDER BY Branch.branchCode ASC,
Property.soldPrice ASC
```

NOTE

Even though the AGENT table is not used to display anything in the query, it is still required as there is no direct link between the PROPERTY and BRANCH tables. If this link were not established in the query, then it would display incorrectly. See Figure 11.1 to see how these relationships work.

MS Access

branchCode	address	town	postcode	soldPrice
RTD100	771 Alexandrite Street	Thurdeen	AX3 9YT	57250
RTD100	21 Amber Cross	Fort Mags	AX4 2QQ	65500
RTD100	3 Amber Cross	Fort Mags	AX4 2QQ	66000
RTD100	18 Amber Park	Fort Mags	AX4 6GH	75500
RTD100	31 Onyx Hill	Thurdeen	AX3 9YG	90000
RTD100	18 Onyx Hill	Thurdeen	AX3 9YG	91250
RTD100	9 Rose Quartz Walk	Fort Mags	AX4 5DR	122500
RTD100	4 Agate Avenue	Axelbridge	AX1 6BF	153000
RTD100	3 Alexandrite Court	Thurdeen	AX3 4FV	178000
RTD100	10 Alexandrite Court	Thurdeen	AX3 4FV	192000
RTD100	15a Agate Circus	Axelbridge	AX1 8NY	250000
RTD100	8 Chrysoprase End	Dunallan	AX2 6UH	360500
RTD107	5 Lapis Lazuli Hill	Duncreige	DC1 4RD	55000
RTD107	2a Verdite Villas	Dumshiells	DC3 8MA	72000
RTD107	4f Verdite Villas	Dumshiells	DC3 8MA	72000
RTD107	6c Verdite Villas	Dumshiells	DC3 8MA	72000
RTD107	3d Verdite Villas	Dumshiells	DC3 8MA	72000
RTD107	2 Lapis Lazuli Lane	Duncreige	DC1 4RE	132000
RTD107	82 Ruby Street	Dunmor	DC8 7SQ	132500
RTD107	4c Malachite Gardens	Inverrab	DC5 9KJ	132500
RTD107	14 Labradorite Street	Dunmor	DC8 7FJ	205000
RTD107	5 Labradorite Street	Dunmor	DC8 7FJ	210000
RTE105	1 Tektite Yard	East Stanbridge	ST18 1JW	40000
RTE105	4a Iolite Alley	South Ritinver	ST3 9DR	44550

MySQL

branchCode	address	town	postcode	soldPrice
RTD100	771 Alexandrite Street	Thurdeen	AX3 9YT	57250
RTD100	21 Amber Cross	Fort Mags	AX4 2QQ	65500
RTD100	3 Amber Cross	Fort Mags	AX4 2QQ	66000
RTD100	18 Amber Park	Fort Mags	AX4 6GH	75500
RTD100	31 Onyx Hill	Thurdeen	AX3 9YG	90000
RTD100	18 Onyx Hill	Thurdeen	AX3 9YG	91250
RTD100	9 Rose Quartz Walk	Fort Mags	AX4 5DR	122500
RTD100	4 Agate Avenue	Axelbridge	AX1 6BF	153000
RTD100	3 Alexandrite Court	Thurdeen	AX3 4FV	178000
RTD100	10 Alexandrite Court	Thurdeen	AX3 4FV	192000
RTD100	15a Agate Circus	Axelbridge	AX1 8NY	250000
RTD100	8 Chrysoprase End	Dunallan	AX2 6UH	360500
RTD107	5 Lapis Lazuli Hill	Duncreige	DC1 4RD	55000
RTD107	3d Verdite Villas	Dumshiells	DC3 8MA	72000
RTD107	2a Verdite Villas	Dumshiells	DC3 8MA	72000
RTD107	4f Verdite Villas	Dumshiells	DC3 8MA	72000
RTD107	6c Verdite Villas	Dumshiells	DC3 8MA	72000
RTD107	2 Lapis Lazuli Lane	Duncreige	DC1 4RE	132000
RTD107	4c Malachite Gardens	Inverrab	DC5 9KJ	132500
RTD107	82 Ruby Street	Dunmor	DC8 7SQ	132500
RTD107	14 Labradorite Street	Dunmor	DC8 7FJ	205000
RTD107	5 Labradorite Street	Dunmor	DC8 7FJ	210000
RTE105	1 Tektite Yard	East Stanbridge	ST18 1JW	40000

WORKED EXAMPLE 12

Insert a new record

NOTE

In MySQL the date is written as "2019-08-19"

This query will add the new property Consolata Crossbill has put on the market. Fieldnames and values must be in the same order.

```
INSERT INTO Property(propertyID, agentNo, clientCode, address, town, postcode,
firstListed, askingPrice, sold, type, noOfBedrooms, description)

VALUES(172, "0030", "000061", "20 Onyx Hill", "Thurdeen", "AX3 9YG",
"19/08/2019",85000,False, "House", 3, "3 bedrooms, 1 ensuite, 1 bathroom, kitchen,
living room")
```

MS Access

Property

propertyID	agentNo	clientCode	address	town	postcode	firstListed	dateSold	askingPrice
168	0005	000036	6c Verdite Villas	Dumshiells	DC3 8MA	11/12/2018	08/01/2019	72000
169	0025	000049	13 Zircon Drive	Gearastan	ST6 9NR	14/02/2019	27/02/2019	103000
170	0012	000066	15 Zircon Road	Farfour	PT15 3RQ	13/03/2019	01/04/2019	216000
171	0012	000001	26 Zircon Road	Farfour	PT15 3RQ	01/09/2018	17/10/2018	200000
172	0030	000061	20 Onyx Hill	Thurdeen	AX3 9YG	19/08/2019		85000

Property

soldPrice	sold	type	noOfBedrooms	description
72000	☑	Apartment	2	2 bedrooms, 1 bathroom, kitchen, living room
113000	☑	Bungalow	3	3 bedrooms, 1 bathroom, kitchen, living room, conservatory
220000	☑	House	3	3 bedrooms, 1 ensuite, 1 bathroom, kitchen, living room, lounge, conservatory
210000	☑	House	3	3 bedrooms, 1 ensuite, 1 bathroom, kitchen, living room, lounge, conservatory
	☐	House	3	3 bedrooms, 1 ensuite, 1 bathroom, kitchen, living room

MySQL

168	6c Verdite Villas	Dumshiells	DC3 8MA	2018-12-11	2019-01-08	72000
169	13 Zircon Drive	Gearastan	ST6 9NR	2019-02-14	2019-02-27	103000
170	15 Zircon Road	Farfour	PT15 3RQ	2019-03-13	2019-04-01	216000
171	26 Zircon Road	Farfour	PT15 3RQ	2018-09-01	2018-10-17	200000
172	20 Onyx Hill	Thurdeen	AX3 9YG	2019-08-19	NULL	85000

72000	1	Apartment	2	2 bedrooms, 1 bathroom, kitchen, living room		0005	000036
113000	1	Bungalow	3	3 bedrooms, 1 bathroom, kitchen, living room, conservatory		0025	000049
220000	1	House	3	3 bedrooms, 1 ensuite, 1 bathroom, kitchen, living room, lounge, conservatory		0012	000066
210000	1	House	3	3 bedrooms, 1 ensuite, 1 bathroom, kitchen, living room, lounge, conservatory		0012	000001
NULL	0	House	3	3 bedrooms, 1 ensuite, 1 bathroom, kitchen, living room		0030	000061

WORKED EXAMPLE 13

Update on fields using complex criteria

This query will update the Bjorn Buzzard's agentNo in the Property table.

```
UPDATE Property
SET agentNo= "0008"
WHERE agentNo = "0005" and clientCode = "000036"
```

MS Access

propertyID	agentNo	clientCode	address	town	postcode
102	0004	000103	9 Obsidian Walk	Friarso	LL3 2AL
165	0005	000036	3d Verdite Villas	Dumshiells	DC3 8MA
166	0005	000036	2a Verdite Villas	Dumshiells	DC3 8MA
167	0005	000036	4f Verdite Villas	Dumshiells	DC3 8MA
168	0005	000036	6c Verdite Villas	Dumshiells	DC3 8MA
91	0005	000092	4c Malachite Gardens	Inverrab	DC5 9KJ

propertyID	agentNo	clientCode	address	town	postcode
90	0008	000120	2 Lapis Lazuli Lane	Duncreige	DC1 4RE
165	0008	000036	3d Verdite Villas	Dumshiells	DC3 8MA
166	0008	000036	2a Verdite Villas	Dumshiells	DC3 8MA
167	0008	000036	4f Verdite Villas	Dumshiells	DC3 8MA
168	0008	000036	6c Verdite Villas	Dumshiells	DC3 8MA
89	0009	000090	5 Lapis Lazuli Hill	Duncreige	DC1 4RD

MySQL

propertyID	agentNo	clientCode	address	town	postcode
92	0005	000124	3d Malachite Gardens	Inverrab	DC6 9KJ
165	0005	000036	3d Verdite Villas	Dumshiells	DC3 8MA
166	0005	000036	2a Verdite Villas	Dumshiells	DC3 8MA
167	0005	000036	4f Verdite Villas	Dumshiells	DC3 8MA
168	0005	000036	6c Verdite Villas	Dumshiells	DC3 8MA
87	0006	000087	14 Labradorite Street	Dunmor	DC8 7FJ

propertyID	agentNo	clientCode	address	town	postcode
90	0008	000120	2 Lapis Lazuli Lane	Duncreige	DC1 4RE
165	0008	000036	3d Verdite Villas	Dumshiells	DC3 8MA
166	0008	000036	2a Verdite Villas	Dumshiells	DC3 8MA
167	0008	000036	4f Verdite Villas	Dumshiells	DC3 8MA
168	0008	000036	6c Verdite Villas	Dumshiells	DC3 8MA
89	0009	000090	5 Lapis Lazuli Hill	Duncreige	DC1 4RD

WORKED EXAMPLE 14

Update on fields using wildcards

This query will update all the addresses stored about Beryl Road to Beryl Avenue. Notice that the keyword REPLACE has to be used where part of a field's contents are required. This form of update using REPLACE with wildcards is outwith the scope of the Higher course.

MS Access

```
UPDATE Property

SET address=REPLACE(address,"Beryl
Road","Beryl Avenue")

WHERE address LIKE "*Beryl Road"
```

propertyID ▾	agentNo ▾	clientCode ▾	address ▾	town ▾
25	0016	000025	3 Aquamarine Mews	Invertrose
26	0014	000026	33 Beryl Road	Invertrose
27	0016	000041	15 Beryl Road	Invertrose
28	0014	000074	101 Beryl Street	Invertrose

propertyID ▾	agentNo ▾	clientCode ▾	address ▾	town ▾
25	0016	000025	3 Aquamarine Mews	Invertrose
26	0014	000026	33 Beryl Avenue	Invertrose
27	0016	000041	15 Beryl Avenue	Invertrose
28	0014	000074	101 Beryl Street	Invertrose

MySQL

```
UPDATE Property

SET address=REPLACE(address,"Beryl Road","Beryl Avenue")

WHERE address LIKE "%Beryl Road"
```

propertyID	address	town
25	3 Aquamarine Mews	Invertrose
26	33 Beryl Avenue	Invertrose
27	15 Beryl Avenue	Invertrose
28	101 Beryl Street	Invertrose

propertyID	address	town
25	3 Aquamarine Mews	Invertrose
26	33 Beryl Road	Invertrose
27	15 Beryl Road	Invertrose
28	101 Beryl Street	Invertrose

WORKED EXAMPLE 15

Update on multiple fields

This query will update the record for Caroline Coot to 12 Emerald End, Strathdonald, ST1 2RD, 01258 315887.

```
UPDATE Client
SET address = "12 Emerald End", town = "Strathdonald", postcode = "ST1 2RD",
telNo = "01258 315887"
WHERE clientName= "Caroline Coot"
```

MS Access

⊞	clientCode ▼	clientName ▼	address ▼	town ▼	postcode ▼	telNo ▼	email ▼
⊞	000055	Sumiko Scoter	6 Diamond Walk	Ardburgh	LL12 5YJ	01656 104566	scoter.sum0105888@woopwoop.net
⊞	000056	Caroline Coot	3 Druzy Court	Strathdonald	ST1 6HJ	01258 000123	carcoo@xgo.net
⊞	000057	Christopher Crossbill	1a Druzy Lane	Strathdonald	ST1 6HK	01258 676422	chriscross@qne.co.uk
⊞	000058	Colin Cormorant	15 Emerald Crescent	Kirkinallen	ST6 3TT	01263 987142	corcol34@supream.scot

⊞	clientCode ▼	clientName ▼	address ▼	town ▼	postcode ▼	telNo ▼	email ▼
⊞	000055	Sumiko Scoter	6 Diamond Walk	Ardburgh	LL12 5YJ	01656 104566	scoter.sum0105888@woopwoop.net
⊞	000056	Caroline Coot	12 Emerald Way	Strathdonald	ST1 2RD	01258 315887	carcoo@xgo.net
⊞	000057	Christopher Crossbill	1a Druzy Lane	Strathdonald	ST1 6HK	01258 676422	chriscross@qne.co.uk
⊞	000058	Colin Cormorant	15 Emerald Crescent	Kirkinallen	ST6 3TT	01263 987142	corcol34@supream.scot

MySQL

clientCode	clientName	address	town	postcode	telNo	email
000055	Sumiko Scoter	6 Diamond Walk	Ardburgh	LL12 5YJ	01656 104566	scoter.sum0105888@woopwoop.net
▶ 000056	Caroline Coot	3 Druzy Court	Strathdonald	ST1 6HJ	01258 000123	carcoo@xgo.net
000057	Christopher Crossbill	1a Druzy Lane	Strathdonald	ST1 6HK	01258 676422	chriscross@qne.co.uk
000058	Colin Cormorant	15 Emerald Crescent	Kirkinallen	ST6 3TT	01263 987142	corcol34@supream.scot

clientCode	clientName	address	town	postcode	telNo	email
000055	Sumiko Scoter	6 Diamond Walk	Ardburgh	LL12 5YJ	01656 104566	scoter.sum0105888@woopwoop.net
▶ 000056	Caroline Coot	12 Emerald End	Strathdonald	ST1 2RD	01258 315887	carcoo@xgo.net
000057	Christopher Crossbill	1a Druzy Lane	Strathdonald	ST1 6HK	01258 676422	chriscross@qne.co.uk
000058	Colin Cormorant	15 Emerald Crescent	Kirkinallen	ST6 3TT	01263 987142	corcol34@supream.scot

WORKED EXAMPLE 16

Delete a record

This query will remove all the details of property with propertyID 147 owned by Pushpa Pipit.

MS Access

```
DELETE *
FROM Property
WHERE propertyID=147
```

propertyID	agentNo	clientCode	address	town
143	0023	000069	16 Spinel Street	Aberkelvin
144	0010	000106	4 Stichtite Place	Farfour
145	0010	000106	1 Stichtite Place	Farfour
146	0010	000106	9 Stichtite Place	Farfour
147	0002	000110	21c Sunstone Flats	Linkilbeg
148	0002	000110	13d Sunstone Flats	Linkilbeg

propertyID	agentNo	clientCode	address	town
143	0023	000069	16 Spinel Street	Aberkelvin
144	0010	000106	4 Stichtite Place	Farfour
145	0010	000106	1 Stichtite Place	Farfour
146	0010	000106	9 Stichtite Place	Farfour
148	0002	000110	13d Sunstone Flats	Linkilbeg

MySQL

```
DELETE
FROM Property
WHERE propertyID=147
```

propertyID	address	town
143	16 Spinel Street	Aberkelvin
144	4 Stichtite Place	Farfour
145	1 Stichtite Place	Farfour
146	9 Stichtite Place	Farfour
147	21c Sunstone Flats	Linkilbeg
148	13d Sunstone Flats	Linkilbeg

propertyID	address	town
143	16 Spinel Street	Aberkelvin
144	4 Stichtite Place	Farfour
145	1 Stichtite Place	Farfour
146	9 Stichtite Place	Farfour
148	13d Sunstone Flats	Linkilbeg

WORKED EXAMPLE 17

Delete records using wildcards

This will delete all the Ironstone Apartments from the PROPERTY table.

MS Access

```
DELETE *
FROM Property
WHERE address LIKE "*Ironstone
Apartments"
```

propertyID	agentNo	clientCode	address	town
71	0024	000075	16 Iolite Road	Aberkelvin
72	0012	000074	1a Ironstone Apartments	Farfour
73	0012	000074	5c Ironstone Apartments	Farfour
74	0012	000074	4b Ironstone Apartments	Farfour
75	0012	000074	12b Ironstone Apartments	Farfour
76	0021	000076	5 Jade Lane	Auchabhainn

propertyID	agentNo	clientCode	address	town
71	0024	000075	16 Iolite Road	Aberkelvin
76	0021	000076	5 Jade Lane	Auchabhainn
77	0018	000125	1 Jade Lane	Auchabhainn

MySQL

```
DELETE
FROM Property
WHERE address LIKE "%Ironstone Apartments"
```

propertyID	address	town	postcode
71	16 Iolite Road	Aberkelvin	ST10 5LG
72	1a Ironstone Apartm...	Farfour	PT15 3NJ
73	5c Ironstone Apartm...	Farfour	PT15 3NJ
74	4b Ironstone Apartm...	Farfour	PT15 3NJ
75	12b Ironstone Apart...	Farfour	PT15 3NJ
76	5 Jade Lane	Auchabhainn	ST9 6VG

propertyID	address	town	postcode
71	16 Iolite Road	Aberkelvin	ST10 5LG
76	5 Jade Lane	Auchabhainn	ST9 6VG
77	1 Jade Lane	Auchabhainn	ST9 6VG
78	14 Jade Lane	Auchabhainn	ST9 6VG

Computed values

A SELECT query can also be used to calculate or compute an arithmetic expression. This allows you compute a new value created from other fields (columns) in your tables and display its result as part of the output from that query. These computed values can consist of fieldnames, numbers and arithmetic operators.

The result of the calculation appears as an added column in the output from the query wherever it occurs in the SELECT statement itself, i.e. it does not have to appear at the end of the selected fieldnames.

REMINDER

! Remember to take care when using UPDATE and DELETE queries as you cannot 'undo' the outcome if you accidentally update all or delete all.

CHECK YOUR LEARNING

Now answer questions 1–4 (on pages 153–154) on implementation of basic queries

WORKED EXAMPLE 18

SELECT query

This query will search for all properties that cost £250,000 or more and are not sold, and display the asking price reduced by £5000. The result of this query will display the client's name, full address of the property for sale and the new price starting with the cheapest.

```
SELECT Client.clientName, Property.
address, Property.town, Property.
postcode, Property.askingPrice-5000

FROM Client, Property

WHERE Property.clientCode=Client.
clientCode AND Property.
askingPrice>=250000 AND Property.
sold=False

ORDER BY Property.askingPrice ASC
```

MS Access

clientName	address	town	postcode	askingPrice
Abdullah Auk	1 Stichtite Place	Farfour	PT15 2JY	250000
Patricia Petrel	17 Chalcedony Avenue	Marymore	BV3 3NM	250000
Finn Fieldfare	1c Agate Circus	Axelbridge	AX1 8NY	250000
Shona Sheerwater	24 Chalcedony Avenue	Marymore	BV3 3NM	255000
Valerie Veery	19 Peridot Place	Axelbridge	AX1 2JN	295000

clientName	address	town	postcode	Expr1004
Abdullah Auk	1 Stichtite Place	Farfour	PT15 2JY	245000
Patricia Petrel	17 Chalcedony Avenue	Marymore	BV3 3NM	245000
Finn Fieldfare	1c Agate Circus	Axelbridge	AX1 8NY	245000
Shona Sheerwater	24 Chalcedony Avenue	Marymore	BV3 3NM	250000
Valerie Veery	19 Peridot Place	Axelbridge	AX1 2JN	290000

MySQL

clientName	address	town	postcode	askingPrice
Finn Fieldfare	1c Agate Circus	Axelbridge	AX1 8NY	250000
Patricia Petrel	17 Chalcedony Avenue	Marymore	BV3 3NM	250000
Abdullah Auk	1 Stichtite Place	Farfour	PT15 2JY	250000
Shona Sheerwater	24 Chalcedony Avenue	Marymore	BV3 3NM	255000
Valerie Veery	19 Peridot Place	Axelbridge	AX1 2JN	295000

clientName	address	town	postcode	Property.askingPrice-5000
Finn Fieldfare	1c Agate Circus	Axelbridge	AX1 8NY	245000
Patricia Petrel	17 Chalcedony Avenue	Marymore	BV3 3NM	245000
Abdullah Auk	1 Stichtite Place	Farfour	PT15 2JY	245000
Shona Sheerwater	24 Chalcedony Avenue	Marymore	BV3 3NM	250000
Valerie Veery	19 Peridot Place	Axelbridge	AX1 2JN	290000

Remember that this query will not actually reduce the property prices stored in the Property table.

NOTE

In MS Access and MySQL the fieldnames that contain calculations where the property price has been reduced appear as Expr1004 and Property.askingPrice-5000 instead of proper fieldnames. These are not very user-friendly and do not make for good readability, so an Alias will be used to replace them. Aliases are covered on page 116.

To reduce the property prices in the Property table, we must run an UPDATE query as follows.

```
UPDATE Property

SET Property.askingPrice= Property.
askingPrice-5000

WHERE Property.askingPrice>=250000 AND
Property.sold=False
```

MS Access

propertyID	agentNo	clientCode	address	town	postcode	firstListed	dateSold	askingPrice	soldPrice	sold
37	0026	000039	13 Chalcedony Avenue	Marymore	BV3 3NM	06/01/2019	10/05/2019	250000	254000	☑
38	0029	000040	17 Chalcedony Avenue	Marymore	BV3 3NM	10/01/2019		250000		☐
39	0029	000127	24 Chalcedony Avenue	Marymore	BV3 3NM	12/07/2019		255000		☐
40	0027	000121	6 Chrysoberyl Lane	Kirkjohns	BV8 9BH	25/06/2019		225000		☐
41	0026	000126	10 Chrysoberyl Lane	Kirkjohns	BV8 9BH	09/09/2019		230000		☐

propertyID	agentNo	clientCode	address	town	postcode	firstListed	dateSold	askingPrice	soldPrice	sold
37	0026	000039	13 Chalcedony Avenue	Marymore	BV3 3NM	06/01/2019	10/05/2019	250000	254000	☑
38	0029	000040	17 Chalcedony Avenue	Marymore	BV3 3NM	10/01/2019		245000		☐
39	0029	000127	24 Chalcedony Avenue	Marymore	BV3 3NM	12/07/2019		250000		☐
40	0027	000121	6 Chrysoberyl Lane	Kirkjohns	BV8 9BH	25/06/2019		225000		☐
41	0026	000126	10 Chrysoberyl Lane	Kirkjohns	BV8 9BH	09/09/2019		230000		☐

propertyID	address	town	postcode	firstListed	dateSold	askingPrice
37	13 Chalcedony Avenue	Marymore	BV3 3NM	2019-01-06	2019-05-10	250000
38	17 Chalcedony Avenue	Marymore	BV3 3NM	2019-01-10	NULL	245000
▶ 39	24 Chalcedony Avenue	Marymore	BV3 3NM	2019-07-12	NULL	250000
40	6 Chrysoberyl Lane	Kirkjohns	BV8 9BH	2019-06-25	NULL	225000
41	10 Chrysoberyl Lane	Kirkjohns	BV8 9BH	2019-09-09	NULL	230000

propertyID	address	town	postcode	firstListed	dateSold	askingPrice
37	13 Chalcedony Avenue	Marymore	BV3 3NM	2019-01-06	2019-05-10	250000
38	17 Chalcedony Avenue	Marymore	BV3 3NM	2019-01-10	NULL	250000
▶ 39	24 Chalcedony Avenue	Marymore	BV3 3NM	2019-07-12	NULL	255000
40	6 Chrysoberyl Lane	Kirkjohns	BV8 9BH	2019-06-25	NULL	225000
41	10 Chrysoberyl Lane	Kirkjohns	BV8 9BH	2019-09-09	NULL	230000

Aliases

To improve the output displayed from the query shown in Worked example 18 and to improve its readability, it would be appropriate to add an **alias** to the query so that the Expr1004 and Property.askingPrice-5000 field/column heading does not display. An alias assigns a temporary name which is only displayed in that query.

This is added to the query in the SELECT part of the statement using the word AS and the alias appears in square brackets after the field or expression it is to display in the output.

The general form for a query involving an alias is:

```
SELECT fieldName AS Alias

FROM Table
```

An alias that consists of two or more words separated by a space should be enclosed in either single or double quotation marks or square brackets for MS Access.

```
SELECT fieldName
AS "Alias Name"

FROM Table
```
Or
```
SELECT fieldName
AS [Alias Name]

FROM Table
```

Either an underscore or single quotes are used for MySQL.

```
SELECT fieldName AS 'Alias Name'

FROM Table
```

Or

```
SELECT fieldName AS Alias_Name

FROM Table
```

WORKED EXAMPLE 19

The original query can be written in one of the following forms.

MS Access

```
SELECT Client.clientName, Property.
address, Property.town, Property.
postcode, (Property.askingPrice-5000)
AS "Reduced Price"

FROM Client, Property

WHERE Property.clientCode=Client.
clientCode AND Property.
askingPrice>=250000 AND Property.
sold=False

ORDER BY Property.askingPrice ASC
```

Or

```
SELECT Client.clientName, Property.
address, Property.town, Property.
postcode, (Property.askingPrice-5000)
AS [Reduced Price]

FROM Client, Property

WHERE Property.clientCode=Client.
clientCode AND Property.
askingPrice>=250000 AND Property.
sold=False

ORDER BY Property.askingPrice ASC
```

And the output from the query alters as shown here.

clientName	address	town	postcode	Reduced Price
Abdullah Auk	1 Stichtite Place	Farfour	PT15 2JY	245000
Patricia Petrel	17 Chalcedony Avenue	Marymore	BV3 3NM	245000
Finn Fieldfare	1c Agate Circus	Axelbridge	AX1 8NY	245000
Shona Sheerwater	24 Chalcedony Avenue	Marymore	BV3 3NM	250000
Valerie Veery	19 Peridot Place	Axelbridge	AX1 2JN	290000

MySQL

```
SELECT Client.clientName, Property.
address, Property.town, Property.
postcode, (Property.askingPrice-5000)
AS 'Reduced Price'

FROM Client, Property

WHERE Property.clientCode=Client.
clientCode AND Property.
askingPrice>=250000 AND Property.
sold=False

ORDER BY Property.askingPrice ASC
```

Or

```
SELECT Client.clientName, Property.
address, Property.town, Property.
postcode, (Property.askingPrice-5000)
AS Reduced_Price

FROM Client, Property

WHERE Property.clientCode=Client.
clientCode AND Property.
askingPrice>=250000 AND Property.
sold=False

ORDER BY Property.askingPrice ASC
```

And the output from the query alters as shown here.

clientName	address	town	postcode	Reduced Price
Finn Fieldfare	1c Agate Circus	Axelbridge	AX1 8NY	245000
Patricia Petrel	17 Chalcedony Avenue	Marymore	BV3 3NM	245000
Abdullah Auk	1 Stichtite Place	Farfour	PT15 2JY	245000
Shona Sheerwater	24 Chalcedony Avenue	Marymore	BV3 3NM	250000
Valerie Veery	19 Peridot Place	Axelbridge	AX1 2JN	290000

The alias is normally only used to improve readability of the output of a query but cannot be used in other parts of the SQL statement. For example, it could not be used in the ORDER BY part of a SQL, as the computed statement to which it refers can only be used in this part. See page 140 to see some examples in SQL.

Rounding

Where the result of a calculation may produce more than the desired number of places after the decimal point, the ROUND function may be used.

WORKED EXAMPLE 20

To display the increase in the price of all unsold properties in the Property table under £100,000 by 1.25% and display clients' names and property addresses, the query would be written as follows.

MS Access

```
SELECT Client.clientName, Property.
address, Property.town, Property.
postcode, ROUND((Property.
askingPrice*1.0125),2)AS [New Price]

FROM Client, Property

WHERE Property.clientCode=Client.
clientCode AND Property.
askingPrice<100000 AND Property.
sold=False
```

This would produce the output as shown.

clientName	address	town	postcode	New Price
Consolata Crossbill	104 Alexandrite Street	Thurdeen	AX3 9YT	45562.5
Graham Goldfinch	2 Amethyst Park	Portussie	PT1 8XD	100237.5
Derek Dipper	4a Apatite Close	Invertrose	PT3 5NU	81000
Ricardo Rhea	3 Cat's Eye Alley	Burryvale	BV1 4JD	56700
Francis Fulmar	3b Iolite Alley	South Pitinver	ST3 9DP	45562.5
Grainne Garganey	16 Iolite Road	Aberkelvin	ST10 5LG	66318.75
Kwame Kittiwake	4 Jet Villas	Gearastan	ST6 8BZ	83531.25
Kwame Kittiwake	11 Jet Villas	Gearastan	ST6 8BZ	86568.75
Kwame Kittiwake	8 Jet Villas	Gearastan	ST6 8BZ	83531.25
Ricardo Rhea	33 Malachite Street	Portacraig	BV5 3PQ	100743.75
Consolata Crossbill	4 Peridot Walk	Axelbridge	AX1 2JM	91125
Pushpa Pipit	13d Sunstone Flats	Linkilbeg	LL7 3RW	75937.5
Chizzy Chough	3a Topaz Court	East Stanbridge	ST18 7DK	86062.5
Consolata Crossbill	20 Onyx Hill	Thurdeen	AX3 9YG	86062.5

MySQL

```
SELECT Client.clientName, Property.
address, Property.town, Property.
postcode, ROUND((Property.
askingPrice*1.0125),2)AS 'New Price'

FROM Client, Property

WHERE Property.clientCode=Client.
clientCode AND Property.
askingPrice<100000 AND Property.
sold=False
```

This will round all records which may have a value after the decimal point to two decimal places. However, it is unusual to have house prices advertised with places after the decimal point. To remove the decimal part the query can be altered like this.

MS Access

```
SELECT Client.clientName, Property.
address, Property.town, Property.
postcode, ROUND((Property.
askingPrice*1.0125),0)AS [New Price]

FROM Client, Property

WHERE Property.clientCode=Client.
clientCode AND Property.
askingPrice<100000 AND Property.
sold=False
```

This would produce the output as shown.

clientName	address	town	postcode	New Price
Consolata Crossbill	104 Alexandrite Street	Thurdeen	AX3 9YT	45562
Graham Goldfinch	2 Amethyst Park	Portussie	PT1 8XD	100238
Derek Dipper	4a Apatite Close	Invertrose	PT3 5NU	81000
Ricardo Rhea	3 Cat's Eye Alley	Burryvale	BV1 4JD	56700
Francis Fulmar	3b Iolite Alley	South Pitinver	ST3 9DP	45562
Grainne Garganey	16 Iolite Road	Aberkelvin	ST10 5LG	66319
Kwame Kittiwake	4 Jet Villas	Gearastan	ST6 8BZ	83531
Kwame Kittiwake	11 Jet Villas	Gearastan	ST6 8BZ	86569
Kwame Kittiwake	8 Jet Villas	Gearastan	ST6 8BZ	83531
Ricardo Rhea	33 Malachite Street	Portacraig	BV5 3PQ	100744
Consolata Crossbill	4 Peridot Walk	Axelbridge	AX1 2JM	91125
Pushpa Pipit	13d Sunstone Flats	Linkilbeg	LL7 3RW	75938
Chizzy Chough	3a Topaz Court	East Stanbridge	ST18 7DK	86062
Consolata Crossbill	20 Onyx Hill	Thurdeen	AX3 9YG	86062

MySQL

```
SELECT Client.clientName, Property.
address, Property.town, Property.
postcode, ROUND((Property.
askingPrice*1.0125),0)AS 'New Price'

FROM Client, Property

WHERE Property.clientCode=Client.
clientCode AND Property.
askingPrice<100000 AND Property.
sold=False
```

> **CHECK YOUR LEARNING**
>
> **Now answer questions 5–6 (on page 155) on implementation of computed values and aliases**

Aggregate functions

Remember from Chapter 10 that aggregate functions are a collection of functions that are used to perform calculations on a set of values across multiple rows in column. These calculations produce one single value as its output.

COUNT()

COUNT(*) will return the total number of records, including those with a null value, in a column. A null value means that there is nothing present in the column and it is empty.

WORKED EXAMPLE 21

This query will return the number of properties that sold for £500,000 or more contained in the Property table.

MS Access

```
SELECT COUNT(*) AS [Total number of
properties]
FROM Property
WHERE soldPrice>=500000
```

Total number of properties ▾
5

MySQL

```
SELECT COUNT(*) AS 'Total number of
properties'
FROM Property
WHERE soldPrice>=500000
```

Total number of properties
▶ 5

WORKED EXAMPLE 22

This query will show the total number of bungalows that have been sold.

MS Access

```
SELECT COUNT(Type) AS [Number of
bungalows sold]
FROM Property
WHERE type="Bungalow" AND sold=True
```

Number of bungalows sold ▾
36

MySQL

```
SELECT COUNT(Type) AS 'Number of
bungalows sold'
FROM Property
WHERE type="Bungalow" AND sold=True
```

Number of bungalows sold
▶ 36

SUM()

WORKED EXAMPLE 23

This query will display the total value of property sold by Harriet Heart, agent number 0016.

MS Access

```
SELECT SUM(Property.soldPrice) AS
[Total sold by Harriet Heart]

FROM Property, Agent

WHERE Property.agentNo = Agent.agentNo
AND Agent.agentNo= "0016"
```

Total sold by Harriet Heart ▾
1276500

MySQL

```
SELECT SUM(Property.soldPrice) AS
'Total sold by Harriet Heart'

FROM Property, Agent

WHERE Property.agentNo = Agent.agentNo
AND Agent.agentNo= "0016"
```

Total sold by Harriet Heart
▶ 1276500

WORKED EXAMPLE 24

This query will display the total commission earned by Harriet Heart (agent 0016) at a rate of 2% of her total sales.

MS Access

```
SELECT SUM(Property.soldPrice)*0.02 AS
[Commission earned by Harriet Heart]

FROM Property, Agent

WHERE Property.agentNo = Agent.agentNo
AND Agent.agentNo= "0016"
```

Commission earned by Harriet Heart ▾
25530

MySQL

```
SELECT SUM(Property.soldPrice)*0.02 AS
'Commission earned by Harriet Heart'

FROM Property, Agent

WHERE Property.agentNo = Agent.agentNo
AND Agent.agentNo= "0016"
```

Commission earned by Harriet Heart
▶ 25530.00

MIN() and MAX()

MIN() will return the minimum value for all columns that contain non-null values.
MAX() will return the maximum value for all columns that contain non-null values.

WORKED EXAMPLE 25

This query will show the lowest and highest price of all sold properties
in the Property table.

MS Access

```
SELECT MIN(soldPrice) AS [Cheapest
property], MAX(soldPrice) AS [Dearest
property]

FROM Property
```

Cheapest property ▾	Dearest property ▾
40000	750000

MySQL

```
SELECT MIN(soldPrice) AS 'Cheapest
property', MAX(soldPrice) AS 'Dearest
property'

FROM Property
```

Cheapest property	Dearest property
▸ 40000	750000

WORKED EXAMPLE 26

This query will show the lowest and highest price of apartments
that Red Tiles Estate Agents have sold that year.

MS Access

```
SELECT MIN(soldPrice) AS [Cheapest
apartment], MAX(soldPrice) AS
[Dearest apartment]

FROM Property

WHERE type= "Apartment"
```

Cheapest apartment ▾	Dearest apartment ▾
72000	230000

MySQL

```
SELECT MIN(soldPrice) AS 'Cheapest
apartment', MAX(soldPrice) AS 'Dearest
apartment'

FROM Property

WHERE type= "Apartment"
```

Cheapest apartment	Dearest apartment
▸ 72000	230000

AVG()

WORKED EXAMPLE 27

This query will show the average price of property from the Property table.

MS Access

```
SELECT AVG(soldPrice) AS [Average
property price]

FROM Property
```

Average property price ▾
186464.916666667

MySQL

```
SELECT AVG(soldPrice) AS 'Average
property price'

FROM Property
```

Average property price
▸ 186464.9167

Notice that the output has multiple decimal places. To combat this, we again use the ROUND function.

MS Access

```
SELECT ROUND(AVG(soldPrice),2) AS
[Average property price]

FROM Property
```

Average property price ▾
186464.92

MySQL

```
SELECT ROUND(AVG(soldPrice),2) AS
'Average property price'

FROM Property
```

Average property price
▶ 186464.92

WORKED EXAMPLE 29

This query will show the average price of property sold by Rafael Robin.

MS Access

```
SELECT ROUND(AVG(soldPrice),0) AS
[Average property price for Rafael
Robin]

FROM Client,Property

WHERE Client.clientCode=Property.
clientCode AND Client.clientName=
"Rafael Robin"
```

Average property price for Rafael Robin ▾
606667

MySQL

```
SELECT ROUND(AVG(soldPrice),0) AS
'Average property price for Rafael
Robin'

FROM Client,Property

WHERE Client.clientCode=Property.
clientCode AND Client.clientName=
"Rafael Robin"
```

Average property price for Rafael Robin
▶ 606667

CHECK YOUR LEARNING

Now answer questions 7–10 (on pages 155–158) on implementation of aggregate functions

Grouping data

Remember from Chapter 10, grouping data is used to group together rows that contain the same values and present the results for each of these 'summaries'. Grouping must appear **before** the Sort order in the SQL query.

As a general rule of thumb, any non-aggregated field that appears in the SELECT clause with an aggregate function must appear in the GROUP BY part of the SQL statement otherwise an error will occur in the SQL statement.

WORKED EXAMPLE 30

The average property price in each town

This query will display each town and the average price of property in that town.

MS Access

```
SELECT town, ROUND(AVG(soldPrice),0)
AS [Average property price by town]

FROM Property

GROUP BY town
```

MySQL

```
SELECT town, ROUND(AVG(soldPrice),0) AS
'Average property price by town'

FROM Property

GROUP BY town
```

town	Average property price by town
Aberkelvin	142000
Ardburgh	176000
Arnouston	173333
Auchabhainn	224286
Axelbridge	201500
Burryvale	129250
Dalburgh	131000
Dumshiells	72000
Dunallan	360500
Duncreige	93500
Dunmor	182500
East Stanbridge	190667
Farfour	307208
Farkirk	325250
Fort Mags	82375
Friarso	128188
Gearastan	113000
Gerryburgh	240000
Inverrab	132500
Invertrose	139908
Kilgavin	173083
Kirkinallen	169625
Kirkjohns	132250
Linkilbeg	125333
Lochlinton	157500

town	Average property price by town
Aberkelvin	142000
Ardburgh	176000
Arnouston	173333
Auchabhainn	224286
Axelbridge	201500
Burryvale	129250
Dalburgh	131000
Dumshiells	72000
Dunallan	360500
Duncreige	93500
Dunmor	182500
East Stanbridge	190667
Farfour	307208
Farkirk	325250
Fort Mags	82375
Friarso	128188
Gearastan	113000
Gerryburgh	240000
Inverrab	132500
Invertrose	139908
Kilgavin	173083
Kirkinallen	169625
Kirkjohns	132250
Linkilbeg	125333

WORKED EXAMPLE 31

The branch that has sold the most properties

This query will display the number of properties sold by each branch in order of most sold to least.

MS Access

```
SELECT Agent.branchCode, COUNT(*) AS
[Properties sold]

FROM Property, Agent, Branch

WHERE Agent.agentNo=Property.agentNo
AND Property.sold=True

GROUP BY Agent.branchCode

ORDER BY COUNT(*) DESC
```

branchCode	Properties sold
RTE105	25
RTF102	20
RTF101	18
RTP103	13
RTE106	12
RTD100	12
RTF104	10
RTD107	10

MySQL

```
SELECT Agent.branchCode, COUNT(*) AS
'Properties sold'

FROM Property, Agent

WHERE Agent.agentNo=Property.agentNo
AND Property.sold=True

GROUP BY Agent.branchCode

ORDER BY COUNT(*) DESC
```

branchCode	Properties sold
RTE105	25
RTF102	20
RTF101	18
RTP103	13
RTD100	12
RTE106	12
RTF104	10
RTD107	10

WORKED EXAMPLE 32

The amount of commission to pay each agent per month

MS Access

```
SELECT Agent.agentName,
ROUND(SUM(Property.soldPrice*0.02),2)
AS [Commission June 2019]

FROM Property, Agent

WHERE Agent.agentNo=Property.agentNo
AND Property.sold=True AND Property.
dateSold LIKE "??/06/2019"

GROUP BY Agent.agentName
```

agentName	Commission June 2019
Alison Almond	2450
Andrew Anise	7210
Beatrice Black	4100
Brian Basil	3700
Camilla Cinnamon	2640
Jeremy Jack	7160
Laura Lavender	3520
Lawrence Lily	6300
Nora Nutmeg	2300
Quintin Queen	2300
Russell Rosemary	13220
Ryan Red	1100
Selena Saffron	2950
Susan Spade	1120
Terry Thyme	22000

MySQL

```
SELECT Agent.agentName,
ROUND(SUM(Property.soldPrice*0.02),2)
AS 'Commission June 2019'

FROM Property, Agent

WHERE Agent.agentNo=Property.agentNo
AND Property.sold=True AND Property.
dateSold LIKE "2019-06-__"

GROUP BY Agent.agentName
```

agentName	Commission June 2019
Alison Almond	2450.00
Andrew Anise	7210.00
Beatrice Black	4100.00
Brian Basil	3700.00
Camilla Cinnamon	2640.00
Jeremy Jack	7160.00
Laura Lavender	3520.00
Lawrence Lily	6300.00
Nora Nutmeg	2300.00
Quintin Queen	2300.00
Russell Rosemary	13220.00
Ryan Red	1100.00
Selena Saffron	2950.00
Susan Spade	1120.00
Terry Thyme	22000.00

WORKED EXAMPLE 33

The amount of commission to be paid by each client

MS Access

```
SELECT Client.clientName,
SUM(soldPrice*0.03) AS [Commission to
Pay]

FROM Client, Property

WHERE Client.clientCode=Property.
clientCode AND Property.sold=True

GROUP BY Client.clientName
```

MySQL

```
SELECT Client.clientName,
SUM(soldPrice*0.03) AS 'Commission to
Pay'

FROM Client, Property

WHERE Client.clientCode=Property.
clientCode AND Property.sold=True

GROUP BY Client.clientName
```

clientName	Commission to Pay
Abdullah Auk	30900
Andrew Avocet	4755
Bashir Blackcap	4650
Bertie Bullfinch	21600
Bethany Brambling	1965
Bilal Bunting	5340
Bjorn Buzzard	8640
Cameron Crossbill	5160
Caroline Coot	5760
Catherine Curlew	5100
Chesney Chiffchaff	3390
Chizzy Chough	4230
Christopher Crossbill	2490

clientName	Commission to Pay
Abdullah Auk	30900.00
Andrew Avocet	4755.00
Bashir Blackcap	4650.00
Bertie Bullfinch	21600.00
Bethany Brambling	1965.00
Bilal Bunting	5340.00
Bjorn Buzzard	8640.00
Cameron Crossbill	5160.00
Caroline Coot	5760.00
Catherine Curlew	5100.00
Chesney Chiffchaff	3390.00
Chizzy Chough	4230.00
Christopher Crossbill	2490.00

WORKED EXAMPLE 34

The amount of annual commission made by agents per branch

```
SELECT Branch.branchCode, Agent.agentName, ROUND(SUM(Property.soldPrice*0.02),2) AS
Commission

FROM Property, Agent, Branch

WHERE Agent.agentNo=Property.agentNo AND Branch.branchCode=Agent.branchCode AND
Property.sold=True

GROUP BY Branch.branchCode, Agent.agentName

ORDER BY branch.branchCode ASC
```

branchCode	agentName	Commission
RTD100	Alison Almond	5510
RTD100	Andrew Anise	10040
RTD100	Leonard Lemon	8110
RTD100	Lesley Lime	7400
RTD100	Vanessa Vanilla	2970
RTD107	Beatrice Black	6750
RTD107	Ben Brown	8410
RTD107	Gordon Green	4200
RTD107	Olivia Orange	2640
RTD107	Ryan Red	1100
RTE105	Brian Basil	16700
RTE105	Russell Rosemary	28511
RTE105	Sandra Sage	29840
RTE105	Terry Thyme	31930
RTE106	David Dill	15260
RTE106	Gemma Garlic	4840
RTE106	Pamela Pepper	10130
RTE106	Petra Parsley	10170
RTF101	Alexander Ace	21730
RTF101	Jeremy Jack	17160
RTF101	Karis King	13600
RTF101	Quintin Queen	22950
RTF102	Carrie Club	8300
RTF102	Desmond Diamond	48669.8

branchCode	agentName	Commission
RTD100	Alison Almond	5510.00
RTD100	Andrew Anise	10040.00
RTD100	Leonard Lemon	8110.00
RTD100	Lesley Lime	7400.00
RTD100	Vanessa Vanilla	2970.00
RTD107	Beatrice Black	6750.00
RTD107	Ben Brown	8410.00
RTD107	Gordon Green	4200.00
RTD107	Olivia Orange	2640.00
RTD107	Ryan Red	1100.00
RTE105	Brian Basil	16700.00
RTE105	Russell Rosemary	28511.00
RTE105	Sandra Sage	29840.00
RTE105	Terry Thyme	31930.00
RTE106	David Dill	15260.00
RTE106	Gemma Garlic	4840.00
RTE106	Pamela Pepper	10130.00
RTE106	Petra Parsley	10170.00
RTF101	Alexander Ace	21730.00
RTF101	Jeremy Jack	17160.00
RTF101	Karis King	13600.00
RTF101	Quintin Queen	22950.00
RTF102	Carrie Club	8300.00
RTF102	Desmond Diamond	48669.80

WORKED EXAMPLE 35

The total number of properties of a given type sold in June 2019

MS Access

```
SELECT Branch.branchCode, Property.
type, COUNT(*) AS [Number sold]

FROM Property, Agent, Branch

WHERE Agent.agentNo=Property.agentNo
AND Branch.branchCode=Agent.branchCode
AND Property.sold=True AND Property.
dateSold LIKE "??/06/2019"

GROUP BY Branch.branchCode, Property.
type
```

MySQL

```
SELECT Branch.branchCode, Property.
type, COUNT(*) AS 'Number sold'

FROM Property, Agent, Branch

WHERE Agent.agentNo=Property.agentNo
AND Branch.branchCode=Agent.branchCode
AND Property.sold=True AND Property.
dateSold LIKE "2019-06-__"

GROUP BY Branch.branchCode, Property.
type
```

branchCode	type	Number sold
RTD100	Bungalow	1
RTD100	House	1
RTD107	Flat	1
RTD107	House	1
RTE105	Bungalow	3
RTE105	House	2
RTF101	Apartment	1
RTF101	House	2
RTF102	Flat	1
RTF104	House	3
RTP103	House	3

branchCode	type	Number sold
RTD100	Bungalow	1
RTF104	House	3
RTF101	Apartment	1
RTE105	Bungalow	3
RTE105	House	2
RTD107	House	1
RTD107	Flat	1
RTP103	House	3
RTF101	House	2
RTD100	House	1
RTF102	Flat	1

Using the result of a query in another query

As we saw in Chapter 10, queries often need to be split in order to produce a single value from one SQL query that can then be used in the second design part. Although in MS Access the queries may be saved and run separately, in MySQL this is not possible. This means that the first query is a **sub-query** in the main query. This is also known as a **nested query**.

CHECK YOUR LEARNING

Now answer questions 11–15 (on pages 159–160) on implementation of grouping queries

WORKED EXAMPLE 36

The managing director of Red Tiles Estate Agent would like to find the average commission earned by estate agents on each property sale in a particular month and then to display all those who have earned more commission on a property sale than the average from least to most.

MS Access

Query 1: Average agent commission

```
SELECT ROUND(AVG(Property.
soldPrice*0.02),0) AS [Average
commission]

FROM Agent, Property

WHERE Agent.agentNo=Property.agentNo
AND Property.dateSold LIKE "??/05/2019"
```

Average commission ▾
3481

Query 2: Display estate agents whose commission is more than the average

```
SELECT Agent.agentName, Property.
address, Property.town,
(soldPrice*0.02) AS Commission

FROM Agent, Property, [Average agent
commission]

WHERE Agent.agentNo=Property.agentNo
AND (soldPrice*0.02) > [Average
commission]

ORDER BY soldPrice*0.02 ASC
```

agentName ▾	address	▾	town	▾	Commission ▾
Russell Rosemary	17 Jade Lane		Auchabhainn		3520
Laura Lavender	67 Super Seven Road		Ardburgh		3520
Lesley Lime	3 Alexandrite Court		Thurdeen		3560
Jeremy Jack	1a Coral Mews		Farfour		3560
Jeremy Jack	23 Quartz Bank		Port Hamish		3600
Pamela Pepper	27 Quartz Terrace		Penkenneth		3610
Brian Basil	5 Jade Lane		Auchabhainn		3700
David Dill	7 Tourmaline Way		East Stanbridge		3760
Terry Thyme	22 Tourmaline Way		East Stanbridge		3800
Sandra Sage	3 Druzy Court		Strathdonald		3840
Lesley Lime	10 Alexandrite Court		Thurdeen		3840
Desmond Diamond	12 Apatite Grove		Invertrose		3970
Nora Nutmeg	31 Chrysoberyl Street		Arnouston		3980
Beatrice Black	14 Labradorite Street		Dunmor		4100
Karis King	26 Zircon Road		Farfour		4200
Gordon Green	5 Labradorite Street		Dunmor		4200
Karis King	15 Zircon Road		Farfour		4400
Sandra Sage	5 Turquoise Gate		South Pitinver		4400
Sandra Sage	3 Jasper Hill		Auchabhainn		4500
Sandra Sage	6 Jasper Hill		Auchabhainn		4500
Harriet Heart	3 Aquamarine Mews		Invertrose		4600
Desmond Diamond	22 Aquamarine Avenue		Invertrose		4619.8
Petra Parsley	15 Emerald Crescent		Kirkinallen		4680
Sandra Sage	19 Jasper Hill		Auchabhainn		4700
Quintin Queen	7 Calcite Crescent		Gerryburgh		4800
Jeremy Jack	1 Calcite Crescent		Gerryburgh		4800
Quintin Queen	4 Calcite Crescent		Gerryburgh		4800
Sandra Sage	8 Jasper Hill		Auchabhainn		4900
Quintin Queen	35 Ametrine Avenue		Stornavadie		4910
Karis King	2 Blue John View		Port Hamish		5000

MySQL

```
SELECT Agent.agentName, Property.
address, Property.town, (Property.
soldPrice*0.02) AS Commission

FROM Agent, Property

WHERE Agent.agentNo=Property.agentNo
AND (soldPrice*0.02) > (SELECT
ROUND(AVG(Property.soldPrice*0.02))

FROM Agent, Property

WHERE Agent.
agentNo=Property.agentNo
AND Property.dateSold
LIKE "2019-05-__")

ORDER BY Property.
soldPrice*0.02 ASC
```

The sub-query highlighted here

agentName	address	town	Commission
▶ Laura Lavender	67 Super Seven Road	Ardburgh	3520.00
Russell Rosemary	17 Jade Lane	Auchabhainn	3520.00
Lesley Lime	3 Alexandrite Court	Thurdeen	3560.00
Jeremy Jack	1a Coral Mews	Farfour	3560.00
Jeremy Jack	23 Quartz Bank	Port Hamish	3600.00
Pamela Pepper	27 Quartz Terrace	Penkenneth	3610.00
Brian Basil	5 Jade Lane	Auchabhainn	3700.00
David Dill	7 Tourmaline Way	East Stanbridge	3760.00
Terry Thyme	22 Tourmaline Way	East Stanbridge	3800.00
Lesley Lime	10 Alexandrite Court	Thurdeen	3840.00
Sandra Sage	3 Druzy Court	Strathdonald	3840.00
Desmond Diamond	12 Apatite Grove	Invertrose	3970.00
Nora Nutmeg	31 Chrysoberyl Street	Arnouston	3980.00
Beatrice Black	14 Labradorite Street	Dunmor	4100.00
Gordon Green	5 Labradorite Street	Dunmor	4200.00
Karis King	26 Zircon Road	Farfour	4200.00
Sandra Sage	5 Turquoise Gate	South Pitinver	4400.00
Karis King	15 Zircon Road	Farfour	4400.00
Sandra Sage	3 Jasper Hill	Auchabhainn	4500.00
Sandra Sage	6 Jasper Hill	Auchabhainn	4500.00
Harriet Heart	3 Aquamarine Mews	Invertrose	4600.00
Desmond Diamond	22 Aquamarine Avenue	Invertrose	4619.80
Petra Parsley	15 Emerald Crescent	Kirkinallen	4680.00
Sandra Sage	19 Jasper Hill	Auchabhainn	4700.00

WORKED EXAMPLE 37

A customer would like to know the price of the lowest priced available property and which properties are available for this price.

MS Access

Query 1: Lowest priced property

```
SELECT MIN(askingPrice) AS [Lowest price]

FROM Property

WHERE sold=False
```

Lowest Price ▾
45000

Query 2: Properties available for minimum price

```
SELECT address, town, postcode,
askingPrice

FROM Property, [Lowest priced property]

WHERE sold=False AND
askingPrice=[Lowest Price]
```

address	town	postcode	askingPrice
104 Alexandrite Street	Thurdeen	AX3 9YT	45000
3b Iolite Alley	South Pitinver	ST3 9DP	45000

MySQL

```
SELECT address, town, postcode,
askingPrice

FROM Property

WHERE sold=False AND askingPrice=
(SELECT MIN(askingPrice)

FROM Property

WHERE sold=False)
```

The sub-query highlighted here

address	town	postcode	askingPrice
▶ 104 Alexandrite Street	Thurdeen	AX3 9YT	45000
3b Iolite Alley	South Pitinver	ST3 9DP	45000

CHECK YOUR LEARNING

Now answer questions 16–19 (on pages 160–161) on implementation of using the result of a previous query

QUESTIONS

Basic queries

1

MANUFACTURER	DESIGNER	JEWELLERY	TRANSACTION	RECEIPT	SHOP
manufacturerID	designerID	itemCode	receiptNumber*	receiptNumber	shopNumber
name	designerName	itemType	itemCode*	shopNumber*	address
address	speciality	itemName	quantity		town
town	manufacturerID*	metalType	date		postcode
postcode		gemStone			telNo
telNo		gemstoneShape			
		price			
		designerID*			
		receiptNumber*			

Table 11.1 Seudair database structure

Use the database structure in Table 11.1 and the query designs below to create SQL queries to display:

a) the manufacturers whose designers make bracelets.

Field(s) and calculation(s)	Manufacturer.name, Designer.designerName, Jewellery.metalType
Table(s) and query	Manufacturer, Designer, Jewellery
Search criteria	Jewellery.itemType = "bracelet"
Sort order	

b) the name of the designer and price of each white gold wedding ring.

Field(s) and calculation(s)	designerName, price
Table(s) and query	Designer, Jewellery
Search criteria	metalType = "white gold" AND itemName = "wedding ring"
Sort order	

c) a list of engagement rings priced between £1850 and £2200. The output should display the designer name, metal type, gemstone, gemstone shape and price. It should be sorted in alphabetical order of metal type with the cheapest ring appearing first in the list.

Field(s) and calculation(s)	designerName, metalType, gemstone, gemstoneShape, price
Table(s) and query	Designer, Jewellery
Search criteria	itemName = "engagement ring" AND price>1850 AND price<2200
Sort order	metalType ASC, price ASC

2 Read the following SQL queries and explain what will be displayed when they are executed.

a)
```
SELECT itemType, gemStone
FROM Jewellery
WHERE gemstone = "Emerald"
```

b)
```
SELECT address, town, postcode, telNo
FROM Shop
WHERE town = "Strathbannon"
```

c)
```
SELECT Manufacturer.name, Designer.designerName
FROM Manufacturer, Designer, Jewellery
WHERE Manufacturer.manufacturerID=
Designer.manufacturerID
AND speciality="necklace"
```

3 Use the database structure in Table 11.2 and the query designs below to create SQL queries.

DIVISION	TEAM	DOG	OWNER	AWARD
divisionCode	teamNumber	UKFANumber	ownerNumber	awardNumber
division	name	name	forename	award
type	captain	breed	surname	tournament
area	seedRanking	ownerNumber*	address	date
	seedTime(sec)	teamNumber*	town	UKFANumber*
	registrationDate		phoneNumber	
	type			
	divisionCode*			

Table 11.2 Flyball for Dogs database structure

a) Display all the dogs and their owners in the Scottish division. The team name, owners and dogs' names should be displayed.

Field(s) and calculation(s)	team.name, owner.forename, owner.surname, dog.name
Table(s) and query	Division, Team, Owner, Dog
Search criteria	Division.divisionCode= "SSC1"
Sort order	

b) Update the address of Roger Clarke who has moved to 34 Leven Road, Rowansville.

Query Type	UPDATE
Table	Owner
New/updated values	address = "34 Leven Road", town = "Rowansville"
Criteria	forename = "Roger" AND surname= "Clarke"

c) Add a new award for the dog with UKFANumber 2123S. He earned his Flyball Dog Gold on 22nd January 2020 at the Figtreeton tournament. This will be the twelfth award issued.

Query Type	INSERT (INTO)
Table	Award
New/updated values	(12, "Flyball Dog Gold", "Figtreeton", #22/01/2020#, "2123S")
Criteria	

d) Remove Toggles the whippet as she has been retired from competition. Her UKFANumber is 9283Y.

Query Type	DELETE (FROM)
Table	Dog
New/updated values	
Criteria	UKFANumber = "9283Y"

4 Read the following SQL queries and explain what will happen when they are executed.

a)
```
SELECT Owner.forename, Owner.
surname, Dog.dogName

FROM Dog, Owner

WHERE Dog.ownerNumber=Owner.
owerNumber AND Owner.town=
"Cherrybrook"
```

b)
```
SELECT Team.teamName, Dog.dogName

FROM Dog, Owner, Team

WHERE Dog.ownerNumber=Owner.
owerNumber AND

Team.teamNumber=Dog.teamNumber
AND Owner.surname=

"Crane" AND Team.teamName= "Furr
Goodness Sake"
```

c)
```
INSERT INTO Team

VALUES ("013", "Fluff and Nonsense",
"Eric Smith",5,23.55, "11/11/2020",
"Open","SMI3")
```

d)
```
UPDATE Team

SET captain= "Rita Jeanetta"

WHERE captain= "Chris Danes" AND
teamName="The Growlers"
```

d)
```
DELETE FROM Dog

WHERE UKFANumber="1031K"
```

Implementation of computed values and aliases

5 Using the query design below and the database structure in Table 11.1, create SQL queries to display:

a) an increase of 10% in the price of all rings. The query should display the designer name, item name and new price.

Field(s) and calculation(s)	designerName, itemName, New price = price*1.1
Table(s) and query	Designer, Jewellery
Search criteria	itemType = "ring"
Sort order	

b) the sale price on all necklaces that have been reduced by 25%. The query should display the item name, metal type and sale price.

Field(s) and calculation(s)	itemName, metalType, Sale price = price*0.75
Table(s) and query	Jewellery
Search criteria	itemType = "necklace"
Sort order	

6 State what happens when this query is executed on the Seudair database.

```
SELECT Jewellery.itemName, Designer.
designerName, (Jewellery.price*0.85)
AS [New price(£)]

FROM Designer,Jewellery

WHERE Designer.designerID=Jewellery.
designerID AND Designer.
designerName= "Harriet Henry"
```

Implementation of aggregate functions

7 Using the query design below and the Flyball for Dogs database structure in Table 11.2, create SQL queries to:

a) count the number of teams whose registration is before 1 January 2000.

Field(s) and calculation(s)	Teams registered before Jan 1st 2000 = COUNT(*)
Table(s) and query	Team
Search criteria	registrationDate < #01/01/2000#
Sort order	

b) display the fastest seed time.

Field(s) and calculation(s)	Fastest seed time = MIN(seedtime)
Table(s) and query	Team
Search criteria	
Sort order	

FLYBALL FOR DOGS

DIVISION			
divisionCode	division	type	area
SSC1	1	Senior	Scotland
SNW2	2	Senior	North-West
SMI3	3	Senior	Midlands
JSE1	1	Junior	South-East
JSC2	2	Junior	Scotland
JNE3	3	Junior	North-East

TEAM							
teamNumber	name	captain	seedRanking	seedTime	registrationDate	type	divisionCode
001	Carswell Flyers	Roger Clarke	4	18.45	1998-05-17	Open	SSC1
002	Canis Racers	Alice Whitaker	5	21.32	2001-08-22	Multi-breed	SNW2
003	Furball Runners	Thomas Walsh	6	22.01	1996-01-05	Multi-breed	SNW2
004	Speedy Paws	George Firth	2	17.40	2010-11-08	Multi-breed	JNE3
005	Furr Goodness Sake	Susan Crane	3	18.05	2013-06-13	Open	SMI3
006	Bark 'n' Run	Nell Smith	1	17.25	2009-07-21	Open	SSC1
007	Sparks	Des Tring	1	17.05	1996-03-13	Multi-breed	JSE1
008	Hairy Barkers	Ellie Mac	6	22.63	2000-10-19	Open	JSE1

teamNumber	name	captain	seedRanking	seedTime	registrationDate	type	divisionCode
009	Ball Chasers	Mo Dixon	4	19.25	1999-01-06	Open	SMI3
010	Aston Jumpers	Lesley McNicol	3	18.16	2001-04-04	Multi-breed	JSC2
011	Loch Fyne Leapers	Craig Anderson	2	17.42	2002-06-21	Open	SSC1
012	The Growlers	Chris Danes	5	20.55	2015-08-30	Open	JNE3

DOG

UKFANumber	name	breed	ownerNumber	teamNumber
0163A	Hamish	English Cocker Spaniel	AEF152	001
8256L	Oscar	Border Collie/WSD	GDO891	001
7701Z	Lady	Cross-Breed	GDO891	001
9283Y	Toggles	Whippet	AEF152	001
1135F	Pat	Border Collie/WSD	WHO167	001
2212Q	Rose	Cross-Breed	TCM983	001
3256N	Tara	Manchester Terrier	KLF518	005
9716Y	Murphy	Golden Retriever	XZQ395	005
8312W	Patch	Cross-Breed	TLF196	005
6291T	Heather	English Cocker Spaniel	LAL291	005
2123S	Rex	Spanish Water Dog	XZQ395	005
3199A	Harvey	Whippet	FOC696	005
7905B	Bracken	Border Collie/WSD	XZQ395	005
2163E	Eric	English Cocker Spaniel	LFM424	012
3254G	Barney	Border Collie/WSD	TOT200	012
8516X	Dave	Whippet	STS808	012
7732T	Matty	Cross-Breed	TFE101	012
5864J	Lily	Border Collie/WSD	TOT200	012
1031K	Belle	Cross-Breed	WFM003	012
3236Q	Fern	Springer Spaniel	BRD226	010
5721V	Teddy	Jack Russell Terrier	QUE299	010
1311M	Bailey	Cross-Breed	HFS204	010
8378N	Gixxer	Golden Retriever	TSC015	010
4468R	Lillou	Cross-Breed	RST213	010
7152W	Gypsy	Border Collie/WSD	QUE299	010
2239E	Xenie	Staffordshire Bull Terrier	RST213	010

AWARD

awardNumber	award	tournament	date	UKFANumber
1	Flyball Dog	Birchham	2019-04-01	0163A
2	Flyball Intermediate	Birchham	2019-04-01	9283Y
4	Flyball Graduate	Yewfirth	2019-07-13	0163A
5	Flyball Advanced	Yewfirth	2019-07-13	2123S

awardNumber	award	tournament	date	UKFANumber
7	Flyball Silver	Appledale	2019-10-22	0163A
10	Fylball Gold	Boxbridge	2020-01-03	0163A
8	Flyball Silver	Appledale	2019-10-22	2123S
6	Flyball Graduate	Yewfirth	2019-07-13	8378N
3	Flyball Graduate	Birchham	2019-04-01	3254G
11	Flyball Advanced	Boxbridge	2020-01-03	3236Q
9	Fylball Gold	Appledale	2019-10-22	1135F

OWNER

ownerNumber	forename	surname	address	town	phoneNumber
AEF152	Roger	Clarke	6 Leven Road	Rowansville	07877 572547
XZQ395	Susan	Crane	8 Rannoch Avenue	Oakton	01987 574630
BRD226	Lesley	McNicol	13A Morar Place	Elmleigh	07814 139186
LFM424	Chris	Davies	101 Ness Street	Ashtown	01562 702666
KLF518	Tony	Sciutto	12 Etive Road	Hazelbridge	07426 668415
STS808	Nancy	McGill	17 Tay Crescent	Ashtown	01562 315981
QUE299	Elizabeth	O'Dowd	5 Maree Road	Elmleigh	07013 356122
WHO167	Kitty	Kay	51 Ryan Road	Rowansville	01461 009761
GDO891	Terry	O'Neil	22 Gairloch Street	Cherrybrook	07546 887140
TCM983	Mary	Scott	5 Insh Way	Cherrybrook	01781 272159
TLF196	Linda	Smith	12A Killingate	Willowby	01231 295922
LAL291	Ida	Stewart	14A Killingate	Willowby	01231 776543
FOC696	Linda	Campbell	34 Migdale Way	Oakton	07543 980777
TFE101	Laura	Stenhouse	89 Martnaham Bar Lane	Peartreewick	07978 352666
TOT200	Rita	Jeanetta	15 Migdale Gate	Plumthorpe	07510 203040
WFM003	Ron	Honeyman	89 Martnaham Bar Lane	Peartreewick	01515 980443
HFS204	Eric	Inglis	21 Garry Street	Glenalder	01234 675743
TSC015	Willie	Johnson	18 Lowes Lane	Beechburgh	07654 123098
RST213	Angela	Inglis	21 Garry Street	Glenalder	01234 675743
SWM010	Susan	Inglis	21 Garry Street	Glenalder	01234 675743

Table 11.3 Flyball for Dogs sample data

8 Answer the following questions using the Flyball for Dogs sample data from Table 11.3.
 a) State:
  i) what happens when this query is executed.
  ii) the output from this query.

```
SELECT COUNT(*) AS [Number of dogs]

FROM Dog

WHERE ownerNumber="XZQ395"
```

 b) State:
  i) what happens when this query is executed.
  ii) the output from this query.

```
SELECT ROUND(AVG(seedTime),2) AS
[Average seed time]

FROM Team
```

9 Using the query designs below and the Seudair data dictionary in Table 11.1, create SQL queries to:
 a) calculate the total amount for receipt number 5.

Field(s) and calculation(s)	Total=SUM(Transaction. quantity*Jewellery.price)
Table(s) and query	Receipt, Transaction, Jewellery
Search criteria	Receipt.receiptNumber=5
Sort order	

b) display the price of the most expensive piece of jewellery.

Field(s) and calculation(s)	Most expensive = MAX(price)
Table(s) and query	Jewellery
Search criteria	
Sort order	

c) count the number of necklaces designed by Harriet Henry.

Field(s) and calculation(s)	Number of necklaces = COUNT(*)
Table(s) and query	Designer, Jewellery
Search criteria	designerName= "Harriet Henry"
Sort order	

d) display the average price of gold wedding rings designed by Iain Ibbotsen.

Field(s) and calculation(s)	Average price gold wedding rings by Iain Ibbotsen = AVG(Jewellery.price)
Table(s) and query	Designer, Jewellery
Search criteria	Designer.designerName = "Iain Ibbotsen" and Jewellery.itemType = "wedding ring" and Jewellery.metalType = "Gold"
Sort order	

a SQL query to display the total number of tickets sold and the total amount of money made.

TICKET {<u>ticketNo</u>, ticketType, quantity, price, stageName*}

STAGE {<u>stageName</u>, location, underCover}

ACT {<u>actName</u>, musicGenre, members, setLengthMins, startTime, day, stageName*}

Field(s) and calculation(s)	Total tickets = SUM(quantity), Total money = SUM(quantity*price)
Table(s) and query	Ticket
Search criteria	
Sort order	

STROMIVAR ATHLETICS CLUB

EVENT		
eventCode	type	name
TR100	Track	100m
FISP	Field	Shot Put
FIHA	Field	Hammer throw
TR1500	Track	1500m
TRH110	Track	110m Hurdles
TR200	Track	200m

10 Using the query design and the design for the Ravimorts Music Festival database below, create

ATHLETE					
athleteNo	forename	surname	address	town	postcode
SAC0096	Sammy	Cruikshank	3 Tower Flats	Stromivar	SV1 4QK
SAC0045	Tiffany	Paterson	21 Inverton Road	Stromivar	SV1 5BN
SAC0158	Sau Wai	Chin	12 The Grange	Achnafort	SV3 6XZ
SAC0055	Awais	Abbas	22 Manor Park Road	Bellatron	SV6 5UJ
SAC0017	David	Colins	51b Baker Street	Achnafort	SV3 6LV
SAC0125	Emma	MacDuff	11 Haggs Lane	Stromivar	SV1 8LU
SAC0056	John	Godfrey	15 The Lane	Bellatron	SV6 7RQ
SAC0259	Alex	Brady	12 The Grange	Achnafort	SV3 6XZ

ENTRY				
entryNo	athleteNo	eventCode	time	distanceMetres
1	SAC0045	TR100	00:00:11.52	
2	SAC0096	TRH110	00:00:13.65	
3	SAC0158	FISP		15.2

4	SAC0055	FIHA		67.54
5	SAC0017	TR1500	00:03:52.52	
6	SAC0045	TR200	00:00:24.65	
7	SAC0125	TR200	00:00:24.23	
8	SAC0125	TR100	00:00:12.02	
9	SAC0259	FIHA		62.21
10	SAC0056	FIHA		70.2

Table 11.4 Stromivar Athletics Club sample data

11 Answer the following questions using the Stromivar Athletics Club sample data from Table 11.4.
   a) State:
      i) what happens when this query is executed.
      ii) the output from this query.

```
SELECT MIN(time) AS [Fastest time over
200m]

FROM Entry

WHERE eventCode="TR200"
```

   b) State:
      i) what happens when this query is executed.
      ii) the output from this query.

```
SELECT AVG(distanceMetres) AS [Average
hammer throw distance (m)]

FROM Entry

WHERE eventCode="FIHA"
```

Implementation of grouping and aliases

12 Using the query design below and the design for the Ravimorts Music Festival database in question 10, create SQL queries to display:
   a) the number of acts appearing on each stage.

Field(s) and calculation(s)	Stage.stageName, Number of acts = COUNT(Act.actName)
Table(s) and query	Stage, Act
Search criteria	
Grouping	Stage.stageName
Sort order	

   b) the total set length per stage starting with the longest.

Field(s) and calculation(s)	Stage.stageName, Total set length = SUM(Act.setLengthMins)
Table(s) and query	Stage, Act
Search criteria	
Grouping	Stage.stageName
Sort order	SUM(Act.setLengthMins) DESC

13 Using the query design below and the Seudair data dictionary in Table 11.1, create SQL queries to find the:
   a) total of each gemstone sold sorted from most to least popular showing the gemstone type and quantity sold.

Field(s) and calculation(s)	Jewellery.gemstone, Total Gemstones Sold = SUM(Transaction.quantity)
Table(s) and query	Jewellery, Transaction, Receipt
Search criteria	
Grouping	Jewellery.gemstone
Sort order	SUM(Transaction.quantity) DESC

   b) total of each item type sold.

Field(s) and calculation(s)	Jewellery.itemType, Total Items Sold = SUM(Transaction.quantity)
Table(s) and query	Jewellery, Transaction, Receipt
Search criteria	
Grouping	Jewellery.itemType
Sort order	

   c) sales from each manufacturer.

Field(s) and calculation(s)	Manufacturer.manufacturer, Total Sales = SUM(Transaction. quantity* Jewellery.price)
Table(s) and query	Manufacturer, Designer, Jewellery, Transaction
Search criteria	
Grouping	Manufacturer.manufacturer
Sort order	

14 State what happens when this query is executed on the Seudair database.

```
SELECT Shop.shopNumber,
SUM(Transaction.quantity* Jewellery.
price) AS [Total Sales per Shop(£)]

FROM Shop, Transaction, Receipt, Jewellery

WHERE Receipt.
receiptNumber=Transaction.
receiptNumber AND Jewellery.
itemCode=Transaction.itemCode AND
Receipt.shopNumber=Shop.shopNumber

GROUP BY Shop.shopNumber
```

15 Using the query design below and the Flyball for Dogs database structure in Table 11.2, create SQL queries to:

a) display the breeds of dog used in flyball racing sorted by the least to most popular.

Field(s) and calculation(s)	breed, Number of dogs = COUNT(*)
Table(s) and query	Dog
Search criteria	
Grouping	breed
Sort order	COUNT(*) ASC

b) display the number of awards won by dogs from least to most.

Field(s) and calculation(s)	Dog.dogName, Medals won = COUNT(*)
Table(s) and query	Dog, Award
Search criteria	
Grouping	Dog.dogName
Sort order	COUNT(*) ASC

Implementation of using the result of a previous query

16 Using the query design below and the Flyball for Dogs database structure in Table 11.2, create SQL queries to display the team names and seed times of teams whose dogs run faster than the average seed time in ascending order

Query 1: Average time

Field(s) and calculation(s)	Average seed time = AVG(seedTime)
Table(s) and query	Team
Search criteria	
Grouping	
Sort order	

Query 2: Faster teams

Field(s) and calculation(s)	teamName, seedTime
Table(s) and query	Team, [Average time]
Search criteria	seedTime < Average seed time
Grouping	
Sort order	seedtime ASC

17 Using the query design below and the Seudair database structure in Table 11.1, create SQL queries to:

a) display the most expensive piece(s) of jewellery and the designer(s). (Hint: you have already created part of this SQL query in Question 4b.)

Query 1: Highest price

Field(s) and calculation(s)	Most expensive = MAX(price)
Table(s) and query	Jewellery
Search criteria	
Sort order	

Query 2: Most expensive piece(s)

Field(s) and calculation(s)	Jewellery.itemName, Jewellery.itemType, Designer.designerName, Jewellery.price
Table(s) and query	Jewellery, [Highest price], Designer
Search criteria	Jewellery.price = Most expensive
Sort order	

b) display the number of pieces jewellery that are more expensive than the average price of all the jewellery.

Query 1: Average price jewellery

Field(s) and calculation(s)	Average price = AVG(price)
Table(s) and query	Jewellery
Search criteria	
Grouping	
Sort order	

Query 2: Number more expensive

Field(s) and calculation(s)	Pieces more expensive than average = COUNT(*)
Table(s) and query	Jewellery, [Average price jewellery]
Search criteria	price >Average price
Grouping	
Sort order	

c) the name, designer and price of all the engagement rings that are the same price as the cheapest engagement ring.

Query 1: Cheapest engagement ring

Field(s) and calculation(s)	Cheapest = MIN(price)
Table(s) and query	Jewellery
Search criteria	itemName= "engagement ring"
Grouping	
Sort order	

Query 2: All cheapest engagement rings

Field(s) and calculation(s)	Jewellery.itemName, Designer.designerName, Jewellery.price
Table(s) and query	Jewellery, [Cheapest engagement ring], Designer
Search criteria	Jewellery.itemName= "engagement ring" AND Jewellery.price = Cheapest
Grouping	
Sort order	

18 Using the query design below and the design for the Ravimorts Music Festival database in question 10, create SQL queries to display the acts whose set lengths are shorter than the average set length along with the stage on which they are appearing sorted from the longest set.

Query 1: Average set length

Field(s) and calculation(s)	Average length = AVG(setLengthMins)
Table(s) and query	Act
Search criteria	
Grouping	
Sort order	

Query 2 Short set length

Field(s) and calculation(s)	Act.actName, Stage.stageName, Act.setLengthMins
Table(s) and query	Act, [Average set length], Stage
Search criteria	Act.setLengthMins < Average length
Grouping	
Sort order	Act.setLengthMins DESC

19 State the output from the following query using the Stromivar Athletics Club sample data from Table 11.4.

MS Access

Query 1

```
SELECT AVG(Entry.distanceMetres) AS
[Average Distance]

FROM Entry, Event

WHERE Event.eventCode=Entry.eventCode
AND Event.name = "Hammer throw"
```

Query 2

```
SELECT Athlete.forename, Athlete.
surname, Entry.distanceMetres

FROM Athlete, Entry, [Query 1]

WHERE Athlete.athleteNo=Entry.
athleteNo AND Entry.distanceMetres >
[Average Distance]

ORDER BY Athlete.surname, Athlete.
forename
```

MySQL

```
SELECT Athlete.forename, Athlete.
surname, Entry.distanceMetres

FROM Athlete, Entry

WHERE Athlete.athleteNo=Entry.
athleteNo AND

Entry.distanceMetres>(SELECT AVG(Entry.
distanceMetres)

FROM Entry, Event

WHERE Event.eventCode=Entry.eventCode
AND Event.name = "Hammer throw")

ORDER BY Athlete.surname, Athlete.
forename
```

161

KEY POINTS

- The structure of a relational database including fields, validation and relationships must be created before any data can be entered.
- The two main operations in a database are search and sort.
- Querying using a search allows you to look for specific information in the database.
- A search can be simple or complex.
- A simple search is performed on only one field with a single condition on one or more tables.
- A complex search is searching on multiple fields or using multiple conditions on one or more tables.
- Relational operators may be used to create search conditions.
- Relational operators include: < less than; <= less than or equal to; = equal to; > greater than; >= greater than or equal to; ≠ (or < >) not equal to.
- Logical operators are used to join conditions in a complex search: AND – both conditions must be met; OR – one condition must be met.
- The wildcard operators, either * and ? for MS Access or % and for MySQL, can be used to represent any information: this allows users to search for results with similar information, such as names beginning with Jo*.
- In SQL the wildcard operators display all the fields from a table where the criteria are met.
- Sorting allows the user to arrange the records in a database into a certain alphabetic or numeric order, such as: ascending order (a to z or 0 to 9) or descending order (z to a or 9 to 0).
- A simple sort is performed on only one field; a complex sort on multiple fields.
- A query can involve both searching and sorting.
- SQL (Structured Query Language) is used for the creation and manipulation of databases.
- SELECT, INSERT, UPDATE and DELETE are four basic SQL commands.
- Equi-join allows data from linked tables to be queried together.

- Equi-join must have a matching primary and foreign key in the tables.
- Queries can also be used to calculate or compute an arithmetic expression from other fields (columns) in tables and display its result as part of the output from that query.
- Computed values can consist of fieldnames, numbers and arithmetic operators.
- An alias assigns a temporary name to the SELECT part of a query which is only displayed in that query.
- An alias appears after the field or expression it is to display in the output.
- Where the result of a calculation may produce more than the desired number of places after the decimal point, the ROUND function is used.
- Aggregate functions are a collection of functions that are used to perform calculations on a set of values across multiple rows in column.
- COUNT, SUM, MIN, MAX and AVG are five basic aggregate functions.
- COUNT() Counts the number of rows in a column.
- SUM() Sums/adds all the values in a column.
- MIN() Returns the lowest value in a column.
- MAX() Returns the highest value in a column.
- AVG() Calculates the average value across a set of values in a column.
- Grouping data is used to group together rows that contain the same values and present the results for each of these 'summaries'.
- GROUP BY must appear before the ORDER BY clause in a SQL query.
- Any non-aggregated field that appears in the SELECT clause with an aggregate function must appear in the GROUP BY part of the SQL statement.
- Use of sub-queries allows the result from one query to be used as part of another query.
- Sub-queries are also known as 'nested queries'.

Chapter 12 Database testing

This chapter looks at how a database is tested using supplied test data and queries.

The following topics are covered:

- describe and exemplify testing:
  - ensuring that SQL operations work correctly at this level.

Testing

The database must be tested to make sure it operates as intended and that all SQL queries produce the correct results.

Testing involves running queries to which the result is already known. This means that the database developer must already know the correct output of a query by working out these values manually. The correct values that match the manually calculated ones should be output from each table when queried. Whatever is to be deleted, altered or stored must be done correctly and, in addition, the rules of entity and referential integrity should be tested.

It is important that the database designer ensures that the data output is as expected, since a database and its queries that produce incorrect results are of no use to the client.

Using the Red Tiles Estate Agents database, we will test some queries to ensure that they run with the correct syntax and produce the expected output.

CHECKIST OF AREAS THAT SHOULD BE TESTED

- ✓ Fields/columns have been selected in SELECT clause.
- ✓ Correct tables.
- ✓ Use of the wildcard.
- ✓ Conditions which use logical and relational operators.
- ✓ Equi-joins.
- ✓ Output is correct using manually worked out results.
- ✓ Computed values produce the correct answer.
- ✓ If aliases are required, ensure they are included.
- ✓ Query will work as expected, i.e. DELETE/UPDATE correct columns/fields/columns are identified and deleted/updated.
- ✓ That queries which require an aggregate function have *only* the aggregate function in the SELECT statement.
- ✓ Correct aggregate function used.
- ✓ If a field/column is present in the SELECT clause with the aggregate function, make sure the same field/column appears in the GROUP BY clause.
- ✓ The order of GROUP BY and ORDER BY.
- ✓ Query and sub-query (using the result of a previous query) are correctly formed.

Test order

1 Open the database to be tested.
2 Ensure that the expected results have been created.
3 Implement the SQL query to be tested.
4 Check the test output against the expected results.
5 Report the findings.

Example tests

The examples that follow are common errors that occur when running queries in a database. See the download on *www.???.com* for full details of the Red Tiles Estate Agents tables to check the output.

WORKED EXAMPLE 1

Missing fields

This query should display all the clients and asking prices of two-bedroomed properties for sale in Portussie.

The expected output should be:

clientName	address	town	noOfBedrooms	askingPrice
Graham Goldfinch	2 Amethyst Park	Portussie	3	99000

The following query is entered and executed.

```
SELECT Client.clientName, Property.address, Property.town, Property.noOfBedrooms

FROM Property, Client

WHERE Property.clientCode=Client.clientCode AND Property.sold=False AND Property.town="Portussie"
```

The output from this query when it is executed is:

clientName	address	town	noOfBedrooms
▶ Graham Goldfinch	2 Amethyst Park	Portussie	3

This query output does not give the correct output as it is missing the askingPrice field. This must be added to the SELECT clause in the SQL query, i.e.

```
SELECT Client.clientName, Property.address, Property.town, Property.noOfBedrooms,
Property.askingPrice

FROM Property, Client

WHERE Property.clientCode=Client.clientCode AND Property.sold=False AND Property.town="Portussie"
```

clientName	address	town	noOfBedrooms	askingPrice
▶ Graham Goldfinch	2 Amethyst Park	Portussie	3	99000

WORKED EXAMPLE 2

Missing tables

This query should display the names of agents and clients who have properties for sale in Farkirk.

The expected output should be:

agentName	clientName	town
Susan Spade	Katrina Knot	Farkirk
Harriet Heart	Gabriel Gannet	Farkirk
Harriet Heart	Gabriel Gannet	Farkirk

The following query is entered and executed.

```
SELECT Agent.agentName, Client.
clientName, Property.town

FROM Agent, Client

WHERE Agent.agentNo=Property.agentNo
AND Client.clientCode=Property.
clientCode AND Property.town="Farkirk"
AND Property.sold=False
```

In MS Access a window opens waiting for input.

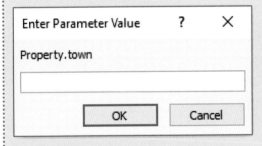

However, in MySQL an error is generated.

Error Code: 1054. Unknown column 'Property.town' in 'field list'

Neither MS Access nor MySQL produce any output. This is because the Property table has been omitted from the FROM clause and needs to be inserted.

```
SELECT Agent.agentName, Client.
clientName, Property.town

FROM Agent, Client, Property

WHERE Agent.agentNo=Property.agentNo
AND Client.clientCode=Property.
clientCode AND Property.town="Farkirk"
AND Property.sold=False
```

MS Access

agentName	clientName	town
Susan Spade	Katrina Knot	Farkirk
Desmond Diamond	Gabriel Gannet	Farkirk
Harriet Heart	Gabriel Gannet	Farkirk

MySQL

agentName	clientName	town
Susan Spade	Katrina Knot	Farkirk
Desmond Diamond	Gabriel Gannet	Farkirk
Harriet Heart	Gabriel Gannet	Farkirk

WORKED EXAMPLE 3

Use of the wildcard

This query should display client names and the details of all the properties that were sold in September 2019.

The expected output should be:

clientName	address	postcode	dateSold
Abdullah Auk	12 Opal Row	PT15 1BT	02/09/2019
Ernie Emu	17a Opalite Court	PT3 7EB	04/09/2019
Ogden Ostrich	11a Opalite Court	PT3 7EB	09/09/2019
Chizzy Chough	14 Pearl Close	ST18 3WD	06/09/2019
Samiah Stonechat	12 Pyrite Crescent	BV3 9GG	13/09/2019
Patsy Pelican	9 Pyrite Crescent	BV3 9GG	10/09/2019

The following queries are entered and executed in MS Access and MySQL respectively.

MS Access

```
SELECT Client.clientName, Property.address, Property.postcode, Property.dateSold
FROM Client, Property
WHERE Client.clientCode=Property.clientCode AND Property.dateSold LIKE "?/09/2019"
```

MySQL

```
SELECT Client.clientName, Property.address, Property.postcode, Property.dateSold
FROM Client, Property
WHERE Client.clientCode=Property.clientCode AND Property.dateSold LIKE '2019-09-_'
```

When the queries are executed, no values are returned.

MS Access

clientName ⌄	address ⌄	postcode ⌄	dateSold ⌄

MySQL

clientName	address	postcode	dateSold

This is because the wildcard has been incorrectly entered in the WHERE clause. In MS Access another ? should be added and in MySQL an additional _ (underscore) should be added into the date.

MySQL

This should produce the correct output as required.

MS Access

```
SELECT Client.clientName, Property.address, Property.postcode, Property.dateSold
FROM Client, Property
WHERE Client.clientCode=Property.clientCode AND Property.dateSold LIKE
"??/09/2019"
```

```
SELECT Client.clientName, Property.address, Property.postcode, Property.dateSold
FROM Client, Property
WHERE Client.clientCode=Property.clientCode AND Property.dateSold LIKE
'2019-09-_ _'
```

MS Access

clientName ⌄	address ⌄	postcode ⌄	dateSold ⌄
Abdullah Auk	12 Opal Row	PT15 1BT	02/09/2019
Ernie Emu	17a Opalite Court	PT3 7EB	04/09/2019
Ogden Ostrich	11a Opalite Court	PT3 7EB	09/09/2019
Chizzy Chough	14 Pearl Close	ST18 3WD	06/09/2019
Samiah Stonechat	12 Pyrite Crescent	BV3 9GG	13/09/2019
Patsy Pelican	9 Pyrite Crescent	BV3 9GG	10/09/2019

MySQL

clientName	address	postcode	dateSold
Abdullah Auk	12 Opal Row	PT15 1BT	2019-09-02
Ernie Emu	17a Opalite Court	PT3 7EB	2019-09-04
Ogden Ostrich	11a Opalite Court	PT3 7EB	2019-09-09
Chizzy Chough	14 Pearl Close	ST18 3WD	2019-09-06
Samiah Stonechat	12 Pyrite Crescent	BV3 9GG	2019-09-13
Patsy Pelican	9 Pyrite Crescent	BV3 9GG	2019-09-10

WORKED EXAMPLE 4

Conditions which use logical and relational operators

This query should display all the clients' name and addresses whose asking price for their flats is more than £100,000.

The expected output should be:

clientName	address	askingPrice	type	sold
Jeremy Jackdaw	3d Malachite Gardens	125000	Flat	False

The following query is entered and executed.

```
SELECT Client.clientName, Property.address, Property.askingPrice, Property.type,
Property.sold

FROM Client, Property

WHERE Client.clientCode=Property.clientCode AND Property.askingPrice<100000 AND
Property.sold=False AND Property.type= "Flat"
```

clientName	address	askingPrice	type	sold
Derek Dipper	4a Apatite Close	80000	Flat	0
Ricardo Rhea	3 Cat's Eye Alley	56000	Flat	0
Francis Fulmar	3b Iolite Alley	45000	Flat	0
Grainne Garganey	16 Iolite Road	65500	Flat	0
Pushpa Pipit	21c Sunstone Flats	75000	Flat	0
Pushpa Pipit	13d Sunstone Flats	75000	Flat	0

The results quite clearly show that flats over £100,000 have not been searched for. In fact, flats under £100,000 have been searched for. To correct this, the relational operator < (less than) in the WHERE clause should be replaced with > (greater than).

```
SELECT Client.clientName, Property.address, Property.askingPrice, Property.type,
Property.sold

FROM Client, Property

WHERE Client.clientCode=Property.clientCode AND Property.askingPrice>100000 AND
Property.sold=False AND Property.type= "Flat"
```

This should produce the correct output as required.

clientName	address	askingPrice	type	sold
Jeremy Jackdaw	3d Malachite Gardens	125000	Flat	0

WORKED EXAMPLE 5

Missing equi-join

This query should display all the agents who have sold houses in Dunmor.

The expected output should be:

agentName	address	town	sold	type
Beatrice Black	14 Labradorite Street	Dunmor	True	House
Gordon Green	5 Labradorite Street	Dunmor	True	House
Beatrice Black	82 Ruby Street	Dunmor	True	House

The following query is entered and executed.

```
SELECT Agent.agentName, Property.address, Property.town, Property.sold, Property.
type

FROM Agent, Property

WHERE Property.town="Dunmor" AND Property.sold=True AND Property.type="House"
```

When the query is executed the following output is displayed.

agentName	address	town	sold	type
Robert Rose	14 Labradorite Street	Dunmor	1	House
Robert Rose	5 Labradorite Street	Dunmor	1	House
Robert Rose	82 Ruby Street	Dunmor	1	House
Lawrence Lily	14 Labradorite Street	Dunmor	1	House
Lawrence Lily	5 Labradorite Street	Dunmor	1	House
Lawrence Lily	82 Ruby Street	Dunmor	1	House
Laura Lavender	14 Labradorite Street	Dunmor	1	House
Laura Lavender	5 Labradorite Street	Dunmor	1	House
Laura Lavender	82 Ruby Street	Dunmor	1	House
Louise Lilac	14 Labradorite Street	Dunmor	1	House
Louise Lilac	5 Labradorite Street	Dunmor	1	House
Louise Lilac	82 Ruby Street	Dunmor	1	House
Ben Brown	14 Labradorite Street	Dunmor	1	House
Ben Brown	5 Labradorite Street	Dunmor	1	House
Ben Brown	82 Ruby Street	Dunmor	1	House
Beatrice Black	14 Labradorite Street	Dunmor	1	House
Beatrice Black	5 Labradorite Street	Dunmor	1	House
Beatrice Black	82 Ruby Street	Dunmor	1	House
Gordon Green	14 Labradorite Street	Dunmor	1	House
Gordon Green	5 Labradorite Street	Dunmor	1	House
Gordon Green	82 Ruby Street	Dunmor	1	House
Olivia Orange	14 Labradorite Street	Dunmor	1	House
Olivia Orange	5 Labradorite Street	Dunmor	1	House
Olivia Orange	82 Ruby Street	Dunmor	1	House
Ryan Red	14 Labradorite Street	Dunmor	1	House
Ryan Red	5 Labradorite Street	Dunmor	1	House
Ryan Red	82 Ruby Street	Dunmor	1	House
Jeremy Jack	14 Labradorite Street	Dunmor	1	House

Notice the number of repetitions of the same addresses and multiple estate agents. This is because the equi-join has been omitted and no relationship has been established between the tables Agent and Property. To correct this, the equi-join must be included in the WHERE clause.

```
SELECT Agent.agentName, Property.address, Property.town, Property.sold, Property.
type

FROM Agent, Property

WHERE Property.agentNo=Agent.agentNo AND Property.town="Dunmor" AND Property.
sold=True AND Property.type="House"
```

This should produce the correct output as required and remove the duplicated values.

agentName	address	town	sold	type
Beatrice Black	14 Labradorite Street	Dunmor	1	House
Gordon Green	5 Labradorite Street	Dunmor	1	House
Beatrice Black	82 Ruby Street	Dunmor	1	House

WORKED EXAMPLE 6

Incorrect aggregate function

This query should count the number of properties that have been sold in the Red Tiles Estate Agency.

The expected output should be:

Number of sold properties
120

The following query is entered and executed.

MS Access

```
SELECT SUM(propertyID) AS [Number of
sold properties]

FROM Property

WHERE sold=True
```

MySQL

```
SELECT SUM(propertyID) AS 'Number of
sold properties'

FROM Property

WHERE sold=True
```

When the query is executed the following output is displayed.

Number of sold properties
10625

This has given total of all the propertyIDs where the sold value is True rather than counted the number of sold properties.

To correct this the correct aggregate function should be used, in this case the COUNT function.

```
SELECT COUNT(propertyID)

FROM Property

WHERE sold=True
```

This should produce the correct output as required.

Number of sold properties
120

WORKED EXAMPLE 7

Incorrect aggregate function

This query should display the highest asking price for a property.

The expected output should be:

Highest price(£)
655000

The following query is entered and executed.

```
SELECT MIN(askingPrice)
FROM Property
```

When the query is executed the following output is displayed.

MIN(askingPrice)
34000

There are two issues with this output. First, the highest asking price has not been displayed. It is the lowest. Second, there is no alias to change the heading to make it more readable.

To correct this, the aggregate function should be changed from MIN to MAX. An alias should be included at the end to produce a more readable output.

MS Access

```
SELECT MAX(askingPrice) AS [Highest
price(£)]
FROM Property
```

MySQL

```
SELECT MAX(askingPrice) AS 'Highest
price(£)'
FROM Property
```

This should produce the correct output as required.

Highest price(£)
655000

WORKED EXAMPLE 8

Incorrect use of DELETE

This query should delete the Topaz Terrace properties in Penkenneth from the Property table.

The expected and updated output should be:

propertyID	address	town	postcode
156	1 Tektite Yard	East Stanbridge	ST18 1JW
157	3a Topaz Court	East Stanbridge	ST18 7DK
158	**16 Topaz Terrace**	**Penkenneth**	**ST8 6EH**
159	**10 Topaz Terrace**	**Penkenneth**	**ST8 6EH**
160	7 Tourmaline Way	East Stanbridge	ST18 2KP
161	1 Tourmaline Way	East Stanbridge	ST18 2KP

Properties in green should be removed.

MS Access

```
DELETE * FROM Property
```

MySQL

```
DELETE FROM Property
```

When the query is executed the following output is displayed.

MS Access

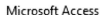

Microsoft Access ✕

⚠ **You are about to delete 166 row(s) from the specified table.**

Once you click Yes, you can't use the Undo command to reverse the changes. Are you sure you want to delete the selected records?

[Yes] [No]

MS Access will warn before you delete any rows. Make sure you check this before you click Yes.

MySQL

propertyID	address	town	postcode	firstListed	dateSold	askingPrice	soldPrice	sold	type	noOfBedrooms	description
NULL	NULL	NULL	NULL	NULL	NULL	NULL	NULL	NULL	NULL	NULL	NULL

MySQL provides no warning unless the table contains foreign keys which are primary keys in other tables. This will not allow the contents to be deleted. However, the contents of Property table do not have any foreign keys which are primary keys in any other tables and the contents are completely removed.

To correct this, the query must be amended as follows.

MS Access

```
DELETE *
FROM Property
WHERE address LIKE "*Topaz Terrace" AND town= "Penkenneth"
```

MySQL

```
DELETE
FROM Property
WHERE address LIKE "%Topaz Terrace" AND town= "Penkenneth"
```

This should produce the correct output as required.

propertyID	address	town	postcode
156	1 Tektite Yard	East Stanbridge	ST18 1JW
157	3a Topaz Court	East Stanbridge	ST18 7DK
158	16 Topaz Terrace	Penkenneth	ST8 6EH
159	10 Topaz Terrace	Penkenneth	ST8 6EH
160	7 Tourmaline Way	East Stanbridge	ST18 2KP
161	1 Tourmaline Way	East Stanbridge	ST18 2KP

propertyID	address	town	postcode
156	1 Tektite Yard	East Stanbridge	ST18 1JW
157	3a Topaz Court	East Stanbridge	ST18 7DK
160	7 Tourmaline Way	East Stanbridge	ST18 2KP
161	1 Tourmaline Way	East Stanbridge	ST18 2KP

Incorrect use of UPDATE

Similarly, care must be taken with UPDATE. Entering this query will set *all* sold prices to NULL or empty.

```
UPDATE property
SET soldPrice=NULL
```

171

WORKED EXAMPLE 9

Computed field with incorrect output

This query should display the difference between the sold price and the asking price to show whether or not the sold property has made more than its asking price.

The expected output should be:

address	town	postcode	Profit made(£)
4 Agate Avenue	Axelbridge	AX1 6BF	500
15a Agate Circus	Axelbridge	AX1 8NY	15000
3 Alexandrite Court	Thurdeen	AX3 4FV	3000
10 Alexandrite Court	Thurdeen	AX3 4FV	12000
771 Alexandrite Street	Thurdeen	AX3 9YT	2250
21 Amber Cross	Fort Mags	AX4 2QQ	500
18 Amber Park	Fort Mags	AX4 6GH	250

The following query is entered and executed.

```
SELECT address, town, postcode, askingPrice-soldPrice
FROM Property
WHERE sold=True
```

When the query is executed the following output is displayed.

address	town	postcode	askingPrice-soldPrice
4 Agate Avenue	Axelbridge	AX1 6BF	-500
15a Agate Circus	Axelbridge	AX1 8NY	-15000
3 Alexandrite Court	Thurdeen	AX3 4FV	-3000
10 Alexandrite Court	Thurdeen	AX3 4FV	-12000
771 Alexandrite Street	Thurdeen	AX3 9YT	-2250
3 Amber Cross	Fort Mags	AX4 2QQ	500
21 Amber Cross	Fort Mags	AX4 2QQ	-500
18 Amber Park	Fort Mags	AX4 6GH	-250

There are several issues with this query:

- The calculation has been performed the wrong way around, so all the properties look as if they have made a loss.
- There is no alias to display 'Profit made' as a column heading.
- The query is meant to display only the properties that made a profit and all the properties have been displayed. Note that 3 Amber Cross should not be present at all as it actually made a loss when sold.

To correct this, the query must be amended as follows.

```
SELECT address, town, postcode, soldPrice-askingPrice AS 'Profit made'
FROM Property
WHERE sold=True and soldPrice-askingPrice>0
```

This should produce the correct output as required.

address	town	postcode	Profit made
4 Agate Avenue	Axelbridge	AX1 6BF	500
15a Agate Circus	Axelbridge	AX1 8NY	15000
3 Alexandrite Court	Thurdeen	AX3 4FV	3000
10 Alexandrite Court	Thurdeen	AX3 4FV	12000
771 Alexandrite Street	Thurdeen	AX3 9YT	2250
21 Amber Cross	Fort Mags	AX4 2QQ	500
18 Amber Park	Fort Mags	AX4 6GH	250

WORKED EXAMPLE 10

GROUP BY/ORDER BY errors

This query should display the number of properties each of the clients has sold with Red Tiles Estate Agents from most to least and sorted within that in order of client name.

The expected output should be:

clientName	Number of properties
Abdullah Auk	4
Bjorn Buzzard	4
Rebecca Raven	4
Bertie Bullfinch	3
Rafael Robin	3
Ricardo Rhea	2
Andrew Avocet	1
Bashir Blackcap	1

The following query is entered and executed.

```
SELECT Client.clientName,
COUNT(Client.clientCode)

FROM Client, Property

WHERE Property.clientCode=Client.
clientCode AND Property.sold=True

ORDER BY COUNT(Client.clientCode) ASC,
Client.clientName ASC

GROUP BY Property.propertyID
```

When the query is executed the following output is displayed.

MS Access

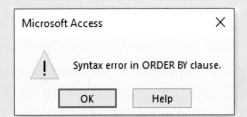

MySQL

Error Code: 1064. You have an error in your SQL syntax; check the manual

that corresponds to your MySQL server version for the right syntax to use

near 'GROUP BY Property.propertyID' at line 5

Neither database package will allow the query to run. The first issue is the order of GROUP BY and ORDER BY. Remember that GROUP BY *must* come before ORDER BY in the order of operations.

Altering the order will change the query to:

```
SELECT Client.clientName,
COUNT(Client.clientCode)

FROM Client, Property

WHERE Property.clientCode=Client.
clientCode AND Property.sold=True

GROUP BY Property.propertyID

ORDER BY COUNT(Client.clientCode) ASC,
Client.clientName ASC
```

When the updated query is executed the following output is displayed.

MS Access

Microsoft Access ✕

⚠ Your query does not include the specified expression 'clientName' as part of an aggregate function.

[OK]   [Help]

MySQL

clientName	COUNT(Clientt.clientCode)
Abdullah Auk	1
Abdullah Auk	1
Abdullah Auk	1
Abdullah Auk	1
Andrew Avocet	1
Bashir Blackcap	1
Bertie Bullfinch	1
Bertie Bullfinch	1
Bertie Bullfinch	1
Bethany Brambling	1
Bilal Bunting	1
Bjorn Buzzard	1
Bjorn Buzzard	1

MS Access is still reporting an error while MySQL simply produces the number 1 next to multiple copies of each client name.

This problem is caused by the incorrect non-aggregate term Property.propertyID in the GROUP BY clause. It should be grouped by the non-aggregate term Client.clientName from the SELECT clause.

Changing the GROUP BY clause will change the query to:

```
SELECT Client.clientName,
COUNT(Client.clientCode)

FROM Client, Property

WHERE Property.clientCode=Client.
clientCode AND Property.sold=True

GROUP BY Client.clientName

ORDER BY COUNT(Client.clientCode) ASC,
Client.clientName ASC
```

When the updated query is executed the following output is displayed.

MS Access

clientName	Expr1001
Andrew Avocet	1
Bashir Blackcap	1
Bethany Brambling	1
Bilal Bunting	1
Cameron Crossbill	1
Caroline Coot	1
Catherine Curlew	1
Chesney Chiffchaff	1
Chizzy Chough	1
Christopher Crossbill	1
Clarence Crow	1
Clothide Cuckoo	1

MySQL

clientName	COUNT(Clientt.clientCode)
Andrew Avocet	1
Bashir Blackcap	1
Bethany Brambling	1
Bilal Bunting	1
Cameron Crossbill	1
Caroline Coot	1
Catherine Curlew	1
Chesney Chiffchaff	1
Chizzy Chough	1
Christopher Cross...	1
Clarence Crow	1
Clothide Cuckoo	1

The output is still incorrect as neither has been sorted from largest to smallest and the column heading in both still does not have an alias displaying 'Number of properties'.

Making these last alterations will change the query to:

MS Access

```
SELECT Client.clientName,
COUNT(Client.clientCode) AS [Number of
properties]

FROM Client, Property

WHERE Property.clientCode=Client.
clientCode and Property.sold=True

GROUP BY Client.clientName

ORDER BY COUNT(Client.clientCode)
DESC, Client.clientName ASC
```

174

MySQL

```
SELECT Client.clientName,
COUNT(Client.clientCode) AS [Number of
properties]

FROM Client, Property

WHERE Property.clientCode=Client.
clientCode and Property.sold=True

GROUP BY Client.clientName

ORDER BY COUNT(Client.clientCode)
DESC, Client.clientName ASC
```

This should produce the correct output as required.

MS Access

clientName	Number of properties
Abdullah Auk	4
Bjorn Buzzard	4
Rebecca Raven	4
Bertie Bullfinch	3
Rafael Robin	3
Ricardo Rhea	2
Andrew Avocet	1
Bashir Blackcap	1

MySQL

clientName	Number of properties
Abdullah Auk	4
Bjorn Buzzard	4
Rebecca Raven	4
Bertie Bullfinch	3
Rafael Robin	3
Ricardo Rhea	2
Andrew Avocet	1
Bashir Blackcap	1

WORKED EXAMPLE 11

Errors using the result of a previous query

This query should calculate the average sold property price in the town of Axelbridge and then display all the properties currently for sale at or below that price.

The expected output should be:

Query 1

Average price in Axelbridge
201500

Query 2

address	town	postcode	askingPrice
21 Agate Avenue	Axelbridge	AX1 6BF	150000
4 Peridot Walk	Axelbridge	AX1 2JM	90000

The following query is entered for Query 1 and executed.

MS Access

Query 1: Average price Axelbridge

```
SELECT MIN(askingPrice) AS [Average
price in Axelbridge]

FROM Property

WHERE sold=False AND town=
"Axelbridge"
```

When the query is executed the following output is displayed.

Average price in Axelbridge
90000

Query 2: Properties available for less than the average price

```
SELECT address, town, postcode,
askingPrice

FROM Property, [Average price
Axelbridge]

WHERE sold=False AND
askingPrice>[Average price in
Axelbridge] AND town="Axelbridge"
```

address	town	postcode	askingPrice
21 Agate Avenue	Axelbridge	AX1 6BF	150000
1c Agate Circus	Axelbridge	AX1 8NY	250000
19 Peridot Place	Axelbridge	AX1 2JN	295000
14 Peridot Place	Axelbridge	AX1 2JN	220000

MySQL

```
SELECT address, town, postcode,
askingPrice

FROM Property

WHERE sold=False AND town="Axelbridge"
AND askingPrice>(SELECT
MIN(askingPrice) FROM Property WHERE
sold=False AND town= "Axelbridge")
```

address	town	postcode	askingPrice
21 Agate Avenue	Axelbridge	AX1 6BF	150000
1c Agate Circus	Axelbridge	AX1 8NY	250000
19 Peridot Place	Axelbridge	AX1 2JN	295000
14 Peridot Place	Axelbridge	AX1 2JN	220000

On closer inspection of Query 1 in MS Access *Average price Axelbridge* and the nested query in MySQL (highlighted in purple), it can be seen that there are several problems.

- The aggregate function is MIN and should be AVG.
- The askingPrice is being used for the AVG and not the soldPrice.
- Finally, the Boolean value for sold is incorrect as this selects all the unsold properties.

Query 2 in MS Access and the main part of the query in MySQL has only a minor problem in that the greater than (>) operator has been selected when it should have been the less than or equal to (<=).

To correct this, the queries must be amended as follows.

Query 1: Average price Axelbridge

```
SELECT AVG(soldPrice) AS [Average
price in Axelbridge]

FROM Property

WHERE sold=True AND town=
"Axelbridge"
```

Query 2: Properties available for less than the average price

```
SELECT address, town, postcode,
askingPrice

FROM Property, [Average price
Axelbridge]

WHERE sold=False AND
askingPrice<=[Average price in
Axelbridge] AND town="Axelbridge"
```

MySQL

```
SELECT address, town, postcode,
askingPrice

FROM Property

WHERE sold=False AND town="Axelbridge"
AND askingPrice<=(SELECT
AVG(soldPrice) FROM Property WHERE
sold=True AND town= "Axelbridge")
```

This should produce the correct output as required.

MS Access

Average price in Axelbridge ▾
201500

address ▾	town ▾	postcode ▾	askingPrice ▾
21 Agate Avenue	Axelbridge	AX1 6BF	150000
4 Peridot Walk	Axelbridge	AX1 2JM	90000

MySQL

address	town	postcode	askingPrice
21 Agate Avenue	Axelbridge	AX1 6BF	150000
4 Peridot Walk	Axelbridge	AX1 2JM	90000

CHECK YOUR LEARNING

Now answer questions (on pages 176–179) on testing

QUESTIONS

1 The following queries are to be implemented in the Seudair database. Sample data is provided in Figure 12.2 for each query.

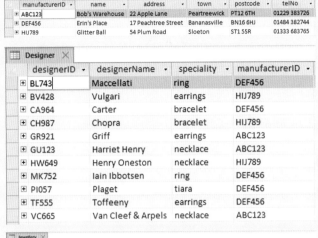

Figure 12.2 Seudair sample data

a) Describe how this SQL statement to display all the necklaces could be tested.

SELECT itemName, metalType, gemstone, price

FROM Jewellery

WHERE itemType = "necklace"

b) Describe how this SQL statement could be tested.

SELECT Designer.designerName, Jewellery.metalType, Jewellery.itemType

FROM Designer, Jewellery

WHERE Designer.designerID=Jewellery. designerID AND Jewellery.itemType = "ring"

c) This SQL query should display rings of any type together with any gemstones which are made of both gold and white gold. The expected and the actual outputs are shown below.

SELECT itemName, gemstone, metalType

FROM Jewellery

WHERE itemType = "ring" AND metalType LIKE "*ring"

Expected output

itemName	metalType	gemstone
engagement ring	Gold	Diamond
wedding ring	Gold	None
wedding ring	White gold	None
wedding ring	White gold	None
engagement ring	White gold	Diamond
engagement ring	White gold	Sapphire
wedding ring	Gold	none

ACTUAL OUTPUT

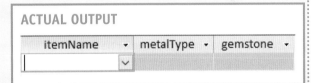

State the errors in the SQL query and write the corrected query.

d) This SQL query should display the total amount for receipt number 2. The expected and actual outputs are shown below.

SELECT COUNT(Transaction. quantity*Jewellery.price) AS 'Total amount owed'

FROM Receipt, Transaction, Jewellery

WHERE Jewellery.itemCode=Transaction. itemCode AND Receipt.receiptNumber=2

Expected output

Total amount owed
5880

ACTUAL OUTPUT

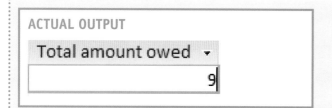

State the errors in the SQL query and write the corrected query.

e) The SQL queries below should first calculate the average price of wedding rings and then display designer name, metal types and price of those less than the average price in order of price from cheapest to dearest. The expected and actual outputs are shown below.

Query 1: Average price

```
SELECT ROUND(MAX(price),2) AS [Average]

FROM Jewellery
```

Expected output

Average
1662.5

ACTUAL OUTPUT

Average ▾
1850

Query 2: Wedding rings less than the average

MS Access

```
SELECT Designer.designerName,
Jewellery.itemName, Jewellery.
metalType, Jewellery.price

FROM Designer, Jewellery, [Average
price]

WHERE Designer.designerID=Jewellery.
designerID AND Jewellery.itemName =
"wedding ring" AND price>[Average]

ORDER BY Jewellery.price DESC
```

MySQL

```
SELECT Designer.designerName,
Jewellery.itemName, Jewellery.
metalType, Jewellery.price

FROM Designer, Jewellery

WHERE Designer.designerID=Jewellery.
designerID AND Jewellery.itemName =
"wedding ring" AND

price>(SELECT ROUND(MAX(price),2) FROM
Jewellery)

ORDER BY Jewellery.price DESC
```

Expected output

designerName	itemName	metalType	price
Iain Ibbotsen	wedding ring	Gold	1500
Iain Ibbotsen	wedding ring	Gold	1600

ACTUAL OUTPUT

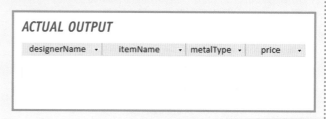

State the errors in the SQL queries and write the corrected queries.

2 The following queries are to be implemented in the Flyball for Dogs database.

a) This query should display all the dogs and the names of their owners in the Furr Goodness Sake team. Describe how this SQL statement could be tested.

```
SELECT Owner.forename, Owner.surname,
Dog.dogName, Team.teamName

FROM Owner, Dog, Team

WHERE Dog.teamNumber=Team.teamNumber
AND Dog.ownerNumber=Owner.ownerNumber
AND team.teamName= "Furr Goodness
Sake"
```

b) This SQL query should display all the awards won by Hamish the English Cocker Spaniel. The expected and actual outputs are shown below.

```
SELECT Dog.dogName, Dog.breed, Award.
award

FROM Dog, Award

WHERE Dog.dogName= "Hamish"
```

Expected output

dogName	Breed	award
Hamish	English Cocker Spaniel	Flyball Dog
Hamish	English Cocker Spaniel	Flyball Graduate
Hamish	English Cocker Spaniel	Flyball Silver
Hamish	English Cocker Spaniel	Flyball Gold

ACTUAL OUTPUT

dogName ▾	breed ▾	award ▾
Hamish|	English Cocker Spaniel	Flyball Dog
Hamish	Golden Retriever	Flyball Dog
Hamish	English Cocker Spaniel	Flyball Intermediate
Hamish	Golden Retriever	Flyball Intermediate
Hamish	English Cocker Spaniel	Flyball Graduate
Hamish	Golden Retriever	Flyball Graduate
Hamish	English Cocker Spaniel	Flyball Advanced
Hamish	Golden Retriever	Flyball Advanced
Hamish	English Cocker Spaniel	Flyball Silver
Hamish	Golden Retriever	Flyball Silver
Hamish	English Cocker Spaniel	Fylball Gold
Hamish	Golden Retriever	Fylball Gold

State the errors in the SQL query and write the corrected query.

3 The following queries are to be implemented in the Ravimorts Music Festival database.

a) Big Dave and the Bandits have had to cancel their set at the festival. Their details have to be removed from the Act table. This query is entered.

```
DELETE *

FROM Act
```

Explain why this query will not remove the act Big Dave and the Bandits and how it should be corrected.

b) This query should display all the acts that will play either The Big Top stage or the Curved Stage on Saturday together with the start time in order of first to last. The expected and actual outputs are shown below.

```
SELECT Stage.stageName, Act.actName,
Act.startTime

FROM Act, Stage

WHERE Stage.stageName=Act.stageName
AND Stage.stageName= "The Big Top" AND
Stage.stageName= "Curved Stage"
```

Expected output

Stage Name	Act	Start Time
The Big Top	The Factory	14:00
Curved Stage	Jammy Quai	15:00
Curved Stage	Cling Fu Fighting	20:00

ACTUAL OUTPUT

stageName ▾	actName ▾	startTime ▾

State the errors in the SQL query and write the corrected query.

KEY POINTS

- The database must be tested to ensure that it operates as intended.
- Testing involves performing queries and running statements, the answers to which have already been worked out manually.
- These answers are known as the expected output.
- The answers can then be compared to the output of SQL queries run on the database and its tables to ensure the output is correct.
- The output from running queries and statements is known as the actual output.
- Testing should demonstrate that the rules of entity and referential integrity perform as expected.

Chapter 13 Evaluation

This final chapter on databases looks at evaluation of queries and suitability of an implemented database. The following topics are covered:

- evaluate solutions at this level in terms of:
  - fitness for purpose
  - accuracy of output.

Once created, it is vital that a database should be evaluated in terms of **fitness for purpose** and **accuracy of output**. This should normally be completed as the testing phase is taking place, so that both developers and testers can assess whether what has been produced is what was requested.

A database is deemed fit for purpose if it is what the client requested in the requirements document in terms of the end-user and functional requirements and performs as expected when queried.

What the database produces when it is queried is important. If queries are run or SQL statements are performed which generate incorrect output, then either the database or tables within the database will have to be restructured or the query reformatted until the correct output is produced. A database that does not perform as required is of no use to the client. Database users are unlikely to pay for something that does not fulfil requirements.

What follow in this chapter are specific instances of queries which work but may or may not produce what was initially requested.

WORKED EXAMPLE 1

Fit for purpose and correct output

The end-user and functional requirements were as follows:

End-user requirements

Calculate the number of properties sold by each branch. Order by most sold.

Functional requirements

A query to sort search results on the total properties sold per branch.

The expected output should be:

branchCode	Number sold
RTE105	25
RTF102	20
RTF101	18
RTP103	13
RTD100	12
RTE106	12
RTD107	10
RTF104	10

The following query is implemented and executed:

MS Access

```
SELECT Branch.branchCode, COUNT(*) AS
[Number sold]

FROM Property, Agent, Branch

WHERE Agent.agentNo=Property.agentNo
AND Branch.branchCode=Agent.branchCode
AND Property.sold=True

GROUP BY Branch.branchCode

ORDER BY COUNT(*) DESC
```

MySQL

```
SELECT Branch.branchCode, COUNT(*) AS
'Number sold'

FROM Property, Agent, Branch

WHERE Agent.agentNo=Property.agentNo
AND Branch.branchCode=Agent.branchCode
AND Property.sold=True

GROUP BY Branch.branchCode

ORDER BY COUNT(*) DESC
```

When the query is executed, the following output is displayed.

ACTUAL OUTPUT

MS Access

branchCode	Number sold
RTE105	25
RTF102	20
RTF101	18
RTP103	13
RTE106	12
RTD100	12
RTF104	10
RTD107	10

MySQL

branchCode	Number sold
RTE105	25
RTF102	20
RTF101	18
RTP103	13
RTD100	12
RTE106	12
RTD107	10
RTF104	10

The actual output from the query exactly matches the expected output. Therefore, the query is both fit for purpose and has delivered accurate output.

Fit for purpose but incorrect output

The end-user and functional requirements were as follows:

End-user requirements

The highest and lowest prices of available properties.

Functional requirements

A query to show the maximum and minimum price of unsold properties.

The expected output should be:

Cheapest property	Dearest property
45000	295000

The following query is implemented and executed:

```
SELECT MIN(askingPrice),
MAX(askingPrice)

FROM Property

WHERE sold=False
```

When the query is executed, the following output is displayed.

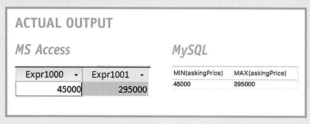

ACTUAL OUTPUT

MS Access

Expr1000 ▾	Expr1001 ▾
45000	295000

MySQL

MIN(askingPrice)	MAX(askingPrice)
45000	295000

The actual output from the query does not match the expected output. The column headings do not display the *Cheapest property* and *Dearest property* as required. However, the query is fit for purpose as it produces the correct number values as required.

To correct this the query should be altered as follows:

MS Access

```
SELECT MIN(askingPrice) AS [Cheapest
property], MAX(askingPrice) AS
[Dearest property]

FROM Property

WHERE sold=False
```

MySQL

```
SELECT MIN(askingPrice) AS 'Cheapest
property', MAX(askingPrice) AS
'Dearest property'

FROM Property

WHERE sold=False
```

This should produce the correct output as required and therefore the query is now both fit for purpose and produces accurate output.

MS Access

Cheapest property ▾	Dearest property ▾
45000	295000

MySQL

Cheapest property	Dearest property
45000	295000

WORKED EXAMPLE 3

Not fit for purpose but correct output

The end-user and functional requirements were as follows:

End-user requirements

Full details of a specific type of property for sale in a town within a certain price range.

Functional requirements

A complex query to search in a given town and property type within a set price range.

A query to search for prices of available houses between £50,000 and £200,000 in Auchabhainn is to be executed.

The expected output should be:

address	town	postcode	description	askingPrice
1 Jade Lane	Auchabhainn	ST9 6VG	3 bedrooms, 1 bathroom, kitchen, living room, conservatory	180500
14 Jade Lane	Auchabhainn	ST9 6VG	3 bedrooms, 1 bathroom, kitchen, living room, conservatory	182000

The following query is implemented and executed:

```
SELECT address, town, postcode, description, askingPrice

FROM Property

WHERE sold=False AND type="house" AND askingPrice>=50000 AND askingPrice<=200000
```

When the query is executed, the following output is displayed.

ACTUAL OUTPUT

MS Access

address	town	postcode	description	askingPrice
5 Ammolite Cross	Farkirk	PT5 8ST	3 bedrooms, 1 ensuite, 1 bathroom, kitchen, living room, lounge, conservatory	195000
3 Ammolite Cross	Farkirk	PT5 8ST	3 bedrooms, 1 ensuite, 1 bathroom, kitchen, living room, lounge, conservatory	195000
101 Beryl Street	Invertrose	PT3 5KP	3 bedrooms, 1 ensuite, 1 bathroom, kitchen, living room	160000
23 Chrysoberyl Street	Arnouston	BV2 3XZ	3 bedrooms, 1 ensuite, 1 bathroom, kitchen, living room, lounge, conservatory	199000
12 Feldspar Road	Kirkinallen	ST6 3TQ	3 bedrooms, 1 ensuite, 1 bathroom, kitchen, living room	168000
1 Jade Lane	Auchabhainn	ST9 6VG	3 bedrooms, 1 bathroom, kitchen, living room, conservatory	180500
14 Jade Lane	Auchabhainn	ST9 6VG	3 bedrooms, 1 bathroom, kitchen, living room, conservatory	182000
33 Malachite Street	Portacraig	BV5 3PQ	3 bedrooms, 1 bathroom, kitchen, living room	99500
15 Obsidian Avenue	Portacraig	BV5 9SF	3 bedrooms, 1 bathroom, kitchen, living room	113000
19 Pearl Close	East Stanbridge	ST18 3WD	4 bedrooms, 1 ensuite, 1 bathroom, kitchen, living room	145000
4 Peridot Walk	Axelbridge	AX1 2JM	3 bedrooms, 1 bathroom, kitchen, living room	90000
2 Serpentine Green	Gerryburgh	PT10 6JD	3 bedrooms, 1 bathroom, kitchen, living room, conservatory	130000
3a Topaz Court	East Stanbridge	ST18 7DK	3 bedrooms, 1 bathroom, kitchen, living room	85000
16 Topaz Terrace	Penkenneth	ST8 6EH	3 bedrooms, 1 bathroom, kitchen, living room, conservatory	125000
10 Topaz Terrace	Penkenneth	ST8 6EH	3 bedrooms, 1 bathroom, kitchen, living room, conservatory	125000

address	town	postcode	description	askingPrice
5 Ammolite Cross	Farkirk	PT5 8ST	3 bedrooms, 1 ensuite, 1 bathroom, kitchen, living room, lounge, conservatory	195000
3 Ammolite Cross	Farkirk	PT5 8ST	3 bedrooms, 1 ensuite, 1 bathroom, kitchen, living room, lounge, conservatory	195000
101 Beryl Street	Invertrose	PT3 5KP	3 bedrooms, 1 ensuite, 1 bathroom, kitchen, living room	160000
23 Chrysoberyl Street	Arnouston	BV2 3XZ	3 bedrooms, 1 ensuite, 1 bathroom, kitchen, living room, lounge, conservatory	199000
12 Feldspar Road	Kirkinallen	ST6 3TQ	3 bedrooms, 1 ensuite, 1 bathroom, kitchen, living room	168000
1 Jade Lane	Auchabhainn	ST9 6VG	3 bedrooms, 1 bathroom, kitchen, living room, conservatory	180500
14 Jade Lane	Auchabhainn	ST9 6VG	3 bedrooms, 1 bathroom, kitchen, living room, conservatory	182000
33 Malachite Street	Portacraig	BV5 3PQ	3 bedrooms, 1 bathroom, kitchen, living room	99500
15 Obsidian Avenue	Portacraig	BV5 9SF	3 bedrooms, 1 bathroom, kitchen, living room	113000
19 Pearl Close	East Stanbridge	ST18 3WD	4 bedrooms, 1 ensuite, 1 bathroom, kitchen, living room	145000
4 Peridot Walk	Axelbridge	AX1 2JM	3 bedrooms, 1 bathroom, kitchen, living room	90000
2 Serpentine Green	Gerryburgh	PT10 6JD	3 bedrooms, 1 bathroom, kitchen, living room, conservatory	130000
3a Topaz Court	East Stanbridge	ST18 7DK	3 bedrooms, 1 bathroom, kitchen, living room	85000
16 Topaz Terrace	Penkenneth	ST8 6EH	3 bedrooms, 1 bathroom, kitchen, living room, conservatory	125000
10 Topaz Terrace	Penkenneth	ST8 6EH	3 bedrooms, 1 bathroom, kitchen, living room, conservatory	125000

The actual output from the query gives not only the results for Auchabhainn but also all the other towns with house prices between £50,000 and £200,000. This makes the output accurate, as it is still possible to find the requested house prices, but it is not fit for purpose, as only the town of Auchabhainn was required in the query.

To correct this the query hould be altered as follows:

```
SELECT address, town, postcode, description, askingPrice

FROM Property

WHERE sold=False AND type="house" AND askingPrice>=50000 AND askingPrice<=200000
AND town="Auchabhainn"
```

This should produce the correct output as required and therefore the query is now both fit for purpose and produces accurate output.

MS Access

address	town	postcode	description	askingPrice
1 Jade Lane	Auchabhainn	ST9 6VG	3 bedrooms, 1 bathroom, kitchen, living room, conservatory	180500
14 Jade Lane	Auchabhainn	ST9 6VG	3 bedrooms, 1 bathroom, kitchen, living room, conservatory	182000

MySQL

address	town	postcode	description	askingPrice
1 Jade Lane	Auchabhainn	ST9 6VG	3 bedrooms, 1 bathroom, kitchen, living room, conservatory	180500
14 Jade Lane	Auchabhainn	ST9 6VG	3 bedrooms, 1 bathroom, kitchen, living room, conservatory	182000

WORKED EXAMPLE 4

Not fit for purpose and incorrect output

The end-user and functional requirements were as follows:

End-user requirements

The amount of commission each client should pay on house sales.

Functional requirements

A query to calculate client commission on houses sold.

A query to find the commission to be paid by clients in the month of September 2019 is to be executed. Clients pay commission at 3% on the sold price of a house.

The expected output should be:

Name of Client	Commission to pay September 2019
Abdullah Auk	7650.00
Ernie Emu	2347.50
Ogden Ostrich	2325.00
Chizzy Chough	4230.00
Samiah Stonechat	8700.00
Patsy Pelican	8880.00

The following query is implemented and executed:

MS Access

```
SELECT Client.clientName,
SUM(Property.askingPrice*0.03)

FROM Client, Property

WHERE Client.clientCode=Property.
clientCode AND Property.sold=True AND
Property.dateSold LIKE "??/09/2019"

GROUP BY Client.clientName
```

MySQL

```
SELECT Client.clientName,
SUM(Property.askingPrice*0.03)

FROM Client, Property

WHERE Client.clientCode=Property.
clientCode AND Property.sold=True AND
Property.dateSold LIKE "2019-09-__"

GROUP BY Client.clientName
```

When the query is executed, the following output is displayed.

ACTUAL OUTPUT

MS Access

clientName	Expr1001
Abdullah Auk	7650
Chizzy Chough	4260
Ernie Emu	2280
Ogden Ostrich	2265
Patsy Pelican	8850
Samiah Stonechat	8850

MySQL

clientName	SUM(askingPrice*0.03)
Abdullah Auk	7650.00
Ernie Emu	2280.00
Ogden Ostrich	2265.00
Chizzy Chough	4260.00
Samiah Stonechat	8850.00
Patsy Pelican	8850.00

The actual output from the query gives the wrong set of values for the commission and the display does not have the headings that were required. The means the query that has been implemented is neither fit for purpose nor producing accurate output. The reason the query has produced the wrong value is that the asking price and not the sold price has been included in the calculation and the aliases required for the column headings have been omitted.

To correct this the query should be altered as follows:

MS Access

```
SELECT Client.clientName AS [Name
of Client], SUM(soldPrice*0.03) AS
[Commission to Pay September 2019]

FROM Client, Property

WHERE Client.clientCode=Property.
clientCode AND sold=True AND Property.
dateSold LIKE "??/09/2019"

GROUP BY Client.clientName
```

MySQL

```
SELECT Client.clientName AS 'Name
of Client', SUM(soldPrice*0.03) AS
'Commission to Pay September 2019'

FROM Client, Property

WHERE Client.clientCode=Property.
clientCode AND sold=True AND Property.
dateSold LIKE "2019-09-__"

GROUP BY Client.clientName
```

This should produce the correct output as required and therefore the query is now both fit for purpose and produces accurate output.

MS Access

Name of Client ▾	Commission to Pay September 2019 ▾
Abdullah Auk	7650
Chizzy Chough	4230
Ernie Emu	2347.5
Ogden Ostrich	2325
Patsy Pelican	8880
Samiah Stonechat	8700

MySQL

Name of Client	Commission to Pay September 2019
Abdullah Auk	7650.00
Ernie Emu	2347.50
Ogden Ostrich	2325.00
Chizzy Chough	4230.00
Samiah Stonechat	8700.00
Patsy Pelican	8880.00

All the problems with the database we have looked at so far have been concerned with queries. However, the structure of the tables in the database also needs to be considered.

WORKED EXAMPLE 5

Test and evaluate tables

The end-user and functional requirements were as follows:

End-user requirements

Find specific features required in a property.

Functional requirements

A complex query to search for specific details required in a property.

A query to show available properties with one ensuite and no conservatory in Farkirk is to be executed. The query should display the client who is selling the house, its address and a description of the rest of the house.

The expected output should be:

clientName	address	town	postcode	description
Katrina Knot	19 Ammolite Avenue	Farkirk	PT5 5XY	3 bedrooms, 1 ensuite, 1 bathroom, kitchen, living room

The following query is implemented and executed:

MS Access

```
SELECT Client.clientName, Property.
address, Property.town, Property.
postcode, Property.description

FROM Property, Client

WHERE Property.clientCode=Client.
clientCode AND Property.description
LIKE "*1 ensuite*" AND Property.
sold=False AND Property.town="Farkirk"
```

MySQL

```
SELECT Client.clientName, Property.
address, Property.town,Property.
postcode, Property.description

FROM Property, Client

WHERE Property.clientCode=Client.
clientCode AND Property.description
LIKE "%1 ensuite%" AND Property.
sold=False AND Property.town="Farkirk"
```

When the query is executed, the following output is displayed.

ACTUAL OUTPUT

MS Access

clientName	address	town	postcode	description
Katrina Knot	19 Ammolite Avenue	Farkirk	PT5 5XY	3 bedrooms, 1 ensuite, 1 bathroom, kitchen, living room
Gabriel Gannet	5 Ammolite Cross	Farkirk	PT5 8ST	3 bedrooms, 1 ensuite, 1 bathroom, kitchen, living room, lounge, conservatory
Gabriel Gannet	3 Ammolite Cross	Farkirk	PT5 8ST	3 bedrooms, 1 ensuite, 1 bathroom, kitchen, living room, lounge, conservatory

MySQL

clientName	address	town	postcode	description
Katrina Knot	19 Ammolite Avenue	Farkirk	PT5 5XY	3 bedrooms, 1 ensuite, 1 bathroom, kitchen, living room
Gabriel Gannet	5 Ammolite Cross	Farkirk	PT5 8ST	3 bedrooms, 1 ensuite, 1 bathroom, kitchen, living room, lounge, conservatory
Gabriel Gannet	3 Ammolite Cross	Farkirk	PT5 8ST	3 bedrooms, 1 ensuite, 1 bathroom, kitchen, living room, lounge, conservatory

The actual output from the query shows all the properties in Farkirk that have both one ensuite and a conservatory, which is not what was required. This means the query that has been implemented does not produce accurate output. It could be argued that it is fit for purpose, as it is possible to pick out the properties with no conservatory. However, if there were more than three results, it could prove difficult.

The problem does not lie solely with the design of the SQL query but more so with the design of the Property table itself. It does not allow individual, possibly specialised, features to be selected, such as ensuite, lounge or conservatory.

To correct this query, the design of the PROPERTY entity and table should be altered as follows:

Attribute name	Key	Type	Size	Required	Validation
propertyID	PK	Number		Y	>0
address		Text	30	Y	maxLength=30
town		Text	30	Y	maxLength=30
postcode		Text	8	Y	maxLength=8
firstListed		Date		Y	
dateSold		Date		N	
askingPrice		Number		Y	>0
soldPrice		Number		N	>0
sold		Boolean		Y	True or False
type		Text	10	Y	Restricted choice: House, Flat, Apartment, Bungalow
noOfBedrooms		Number		Y	Restricted choice: 1,2,3,4,5
ensuite		Number		Y	Restricted choice: 0,1,2,3
lounge		Boolean		Y	True or False
conservatory		Boolean		Y	True or False
utility		Boolean		Y	True or False
description		Text	255	Y	maxLength=255
agentNo	FK	Text	4	Y	maxLength=4, existing agentNo from AGENT table
clientCode	FK	Text	6	Y	maxLength=6, existing clientCode from CLIENT table

And the SQL query implemented as follows:

```
SELECT Client.clientName, Property.address, Property.town, Property.postcode,
Property.description

FROM Client, Property

WHERE Client.clientCode=Property.clientCode AND Property.ensuite=1 AND Property.
sold=False AND Property.conservatory=False AND Property.town="Farkirk"
```

This should produce the correct output as required and therefore the query
is now both fit for purpose and produces accurate output.

MS Access

clientName	address	town	postcode	description
Katrina Knot	19 Ammolite Avenue	Farkirk	PT5 5XY	3 bedrooms, 1 ensuite, 1 bathroom, kitchen, living room

MySQL

clientName	address	town	postcode	description
Katrina Knot	19 Ammolite Avenue	Farkirk	PT5 5XY	3 bedrooms, 1 ensuite, 1 bathroom, kitchen, living room

CHECK YOUR LEARNING

Now answer questions on pages 11–13 on evaluation

QUESTIONS

1 A count is required to calculate the number of dogs in each division in the
Flyball for Dogs database.
The expected output is shown below.

Division Number	number of dogs
1	6
2	7
3	13

Small sample of data (for data types)

DIVISION

divisionCode	division	type	area
SSC1	1	Senior	Scotland

TEAM

teamNumber	name	captain	seedRanking	seedTime	registrationDate	type	divisionCode
001	Carswell Flyers	Roger Clarke	4	18.45	1998-05-17	Open	SSC1

DOG

UKFANumber	name	breed	ownerNumber	teamNumber
0163A	Hamish	English Cocker Spaniel	AEF152	001

The following query is entered and executed.

```
SELECT Division.division, SUM(Dog.
UKFANumber)

FROM Division, Team, Dog

WHERE Division.divisionCode=Team.
divisionCode AND Team.teamNumber=Dog.
teamNumber

GROUP BY Division.division
```

This query produces the output shown below.

ACTUAL OUTPUT

Microsoft Access   ✕

⚠ Data type mismatch in criteria expression.

OK   Help

Evaluate the query in terms of fitness for purpose and accuracy of output.

2 A query has been produced to show the total manufacturer sales each shop has made using the Seudair database.
The expected output is shown below.

shopNumber	Manufacturer name	Total sales
1	Glitter Ball	2390
2	Erin's Palace	6310
2	Glitter Ball	2130
3	Erin's Palace	12500
4	Erin's Palace	3300

The following query is entered and executed.

```
SELECT Shop.shopNumber, Manufacturer.
name AS [Manufacturer name],
SUM(Transaction.quantity*Jewellery.
price) AS [Total sales]

FROM Manufacturer, Designer,
Jewellery, Transaction, Receipt, Shop

WHERE Manufacturer.
manufacturerID=Designer.manufacturerID
AND Designer.designerID=Jewellery.
designerID AND Jewellery.
itemCode=Transaction.itemCode AND
Transaction.receiptNumber=receipt.
receiptNumber

GROUP BY Shop.shopNumber,
Manufacturer.name
```

This query produces the output shown below.

ACTUAL OUTPUT

shopNumber	Manufacturer name	Total sales
1	Glitter Ball	2390
2	Erin's Place	6310
2	Glitter Ball	2130
3	Erin's Place	12500
4	Erin's Place	3300

Evaluate the query in terms of fitness for purpose and accuracy of output.

3 The queries which are to be evaluated in this question are based on the TeeVeeFi database.

a) A query has been designed to calculate the total number of customers on a specific contract. The expected output is shown below.

package	Total customers
White	2
Black	3
Blue	2
Red	2
Gold	3

The following query is entered and executed.

```
SELECT COUNT(*)

FROM Account

GROUP BY package
```

This query produces the output shown below.

ACTUAL OUTPUT

Expr1000
3
2
3
2
2

Evaluate the query in terms of fitness for purpose and accuracy of output.

b) A query has been designed to work out which are the most popular films based on number of views and sorted in order of popularity.

The expected output is shown below.

Film	Nuber of views
Hotel Croatia	5
Defrosted	4
Shred	3
Eric at Sea	3
The 13 Bakers	2

The following query is entered and executed.

```
SELECT Programme.type, COUNT(*) AS
[Number of views]

FROM Programme, Usage

WHERE Programme.programmeID=Usage.
programmeID AND Programme.type=
"Film"

GROUP BY Programme.name

ORDER BY COUNT(*) DESC
```

This query produces the output shown below.

ACTUAL OUTPUT

name	Expr1001
The 13 Bakers	2
Shred	3
Eric at Sea	3
Defrosted	4
Hotel Croatia	5

Evaluate the query in terms of fitness for purpose and accuracy of output.

c) A query has been designed to display the amount owed by customers whose monthly payment has not yet been made.

The expected output is shown below.

title	forename	surname	Monthly payment outstanding	billPaid
Ms	Maddy	Paterson	15	False
Mr	Henry	Hillary	25	False
Mr	Craig	Rees	5	False
Mrs	Judith	Green	10	False
Mr	Rudi	O'Reilly	5	False
Mr	Gavin	Carter	10	False
Miss	Molly	Good	15	False

The following query is entered and executed.

```
SELECT Customer.title, Customer.
forename, Customer.surname,
costPerMonth AS [Monthly payment
outstanding], Account.billPaid

FROM Customer, Account

WHERE Customer.customerID=Account.
customerID AND Account.
billPaid=True
```

This query produces the output shown below.

ACTUAL OUTPUT

title	forename	surname	Monthly payment outstanding	billPaid
Mrs	Laura	Williams	20	☑
Mrs	Sandra	Macari	20	☑
Mr	Simon	Anderson	10	☑
Ms	Vicky	Macdonald	25	☑
Mr	D'Arcy	Whitaker	25	☑

Evaluate the query in terms of fitness for purpose and accuracy of output.

KEY POINTS

- A database must be evaluated in terms of both fitness for purpose and accuracy of output.
- A database is deemed fit for purpose if it is what the client requested in the requirements document in terms of the end-user and functional requirements and performs as expected when queried.
- If any queries are run or SQL statements performed which generate incorrect output, then either the database or its tables will have to be restructured or the query reformatted until the correct output is produced.

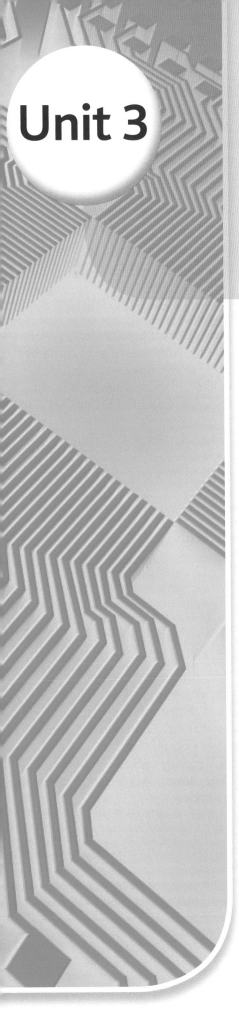

Web design and development

Chapter 14 Analysis

> This chapter looks at analysing the requirements of a web-based solution.
>
> The following topics are covered:
>
> ● Identify the end-user and functional requirements of a website problem that relates to design and implementation at this level.

End-user and functional requirements

You can find detailed definitions for end-user requirements and functional requirements in Chapter 9.

The end-user requirements for the website list what it should contain (images, sounds and videos) and what it should look and feel like. The functional requirements specify which pages are to be created, what each page should display and what the page should do.

Personas should be created at this stage to identify the user(s) or target audience of the website being created. This will make testing at the later stages of the development process more straightforward. See Chapter 19 for more information on personas.

Example of end-user and functional requirements

This example will be used in the web design and development chapters, making it easier to follow the complete process from analysis to evaluation.

Bob de Warner owns a small chain of bakery shops. He would like a website developed to bring his baked products to a wider audience. Bob and his staff would like the website to allow potential customers to see which products are available in shops and which are available to order online. The website should provide images of the baked goods available, a small selection of popular cake recipes and a page for ordering celebration cakes. It should also provide links on each page to Bob's pages on social media platforms and information on how to find Bob's shops.

Some of Bob's regular customers and his staff have been asked about what they would like to see on the website in addition to the above requests. The results of these interviews are as follows:

Figure 14.1 Bob de Warner's logo

- I'd really like to know a little bit about Bob and when he started up.
- It would be helpful if the cake recipes could also have instructional videos.
- Can the products be split into different sections like bread, cakes and biscuits?
- We sell different varieties of bread, cakes and biscuits. Pages for each of these would allow our customers to see what is available in our shops.
- We sell a large selection of small cakes and biscuits. Is there a way some of the images can be made larger so customers can see them more clearly plus a description of each?
- I like the idea of ordering my birthday cake online. Can these be delivered as well as picked up from the shop?

Further interviews with Bob and his staff have revealed that the varieties of bread, cakes and biscuits are quite extensive.

- Bread is available in several varieties: white, brown, wholemeal, sourdough and multigrain.
- Cakes are categorised as large cakes and small cakes. Large cakes are further divided into large cakes and celebration cakes.
- Celebration cakes include birthday, engagement, wedding, anniversary and christening cakes.
- Biscuits are available as plain and fancy.
- Bob has also decided that he would like to provide three simple recipes for a Victoria sponge, a chocolate fudge cake and gingerbread.

End-user requirements

Pulling all this information together generates a list of end-user requirements.

- The client would like to have a website to advertise his bakery shops and products for sale.
- Users are interested in buying baked goods.
- Users would like to know about the origins of Bob and his first shop.
- The client would like users to be able to see all the baked goods available in shops.
- The client would like users to be able to see the cakes available to be ordered online.
- The client would like the baked goods to be separated into Bread, Cakes and Biscuits.
- The client would like to have one page for recipes and one for ordering celebration cakes.
- Users should be able to view separate pages for each of the different varieties of Breads, Cakes and Biscuits plus Recipes and Ordering.

- Users should be able to view: White, Brown, Wholemeal, Sourdough and Multigrain breads.
- Users should be able to view the following types of cakes: Large Cakes and Small Cakes.
- Users should be able to see examples of Large Cakes and Celebration Cakes.
- Users should be able to view images of examples of small cakes.
- Users should be able to view the following types of biscuits: Plain and Fancy.
- The client would like users to be able to select small images of baked goods to see larger versions on the page with a description of each.
- Users should be able to order celebration cakes online using a simple form.
- Users should be able to select from Birthday, Engagement, Wedding, Anniversary and Christening cakes when ordering celebration cakes.
- The client would like to provide three popular cake recipes: Victoria Sponge, Chocolate Fudge Cake and Gingerbread.
- Users would like the cake recipes to include instructional videos.
- Users should be able to click on links to the social media pages.
- Users should be able to find Bob de Warner shops.

Functional requirements

Pulling all this information together generates a list of functional requirements.

- The pages in the website should contain information about Bob's bakery shops.
- The website will display information about the goods for sale in Bob's bakery shops.
- The home page will display introductory information about Bob's bakery shops and the history of his bakery shops.
- The website will contain pages on: Bread, Cake, Biscuits, Recipes and Ordering online.
- The Bread page will provide clickable buttons to display either White, Brown, Wholemeal, Sourdough or Multigrain bread types.
- The Bread page will show rollover images of each bread type and display information on each type.
- The Cake page will contain links to Large Cakes and Small Cakes sub-pages.
- The Large Cakes sub-page will display clickable images to show examples of Large and Celebration Cakes.
- The Small Cakes sub-page should show examples of the small cakes available to buy.

- The Biscuits page will provide clickable buttons to select either Plain or Fancy biscuits.
- The images on the Small Cakes and Biscuits pages should be thumbnails which may be rolled over to view a larger image and description of each.
- The Ordering page should provide a simple form for customers to order celebration cakes.
- The form should provide a simple selection of celebration cakes: Birthday, Engagement, Wedding, Anniversary and Christening.
- The Recipes page should allow selection of recipes for Victoria Sponge, Chocolate Fudge Cake and Gingerbread from an on-screen menu.

- Each recipe on the Recipe page should display recipe instructions and an instructional video on how to make each cake.
- Each page should have a link in the footer to social media pages.
- The Find Us page should display locations (addresses) of shops.

CHECK YOUR LEARNING

Now answer questions 1–5 below

QUESTIONS

1 Who is the end-user of a website?
2 Why is it important to ensure that the end-user requirements are correct?
3 What is meant by the term functional requirements?
4 InverBlair Council has commissioned a new website to coincide with 20th year of their free-to-view airshow in June 2021. The airshow is an annual event which runs over the first weekend in June. Web developers have discussed the website with the organisers and have listed a small selection of all the statements below:
- We'd like a general introduction to the airshow with a welcome statement from InverBlair Council's Provost on the main page of the website.
- We need to show a programme of events for each of the two days – Saturday and Sunday – so our visitors can decide when they want to visit the airshow.
- Visitors need to be able to book tickets with a secure website if they want a special access pass.
- Some of our visitors have a special interest in specific planes from WW1, WW2 and current fighter jets. The Red Arrows will also display at the close of the airshow on the Sunday. We'd like to be able to have a page that will show a little of the history of these planes with photographs and videos of each of the planes.
- The airshow will also have other planes and displays as part of the experience such as seaplanes, aerial display teams and wing walkers. Some photographs of these on the page would allow potential spectators to see each of these before their visit.
- So that we can improve, a feedback form from our visitors is absolutely vital.
From the statements given above, identify three end-user requirements.

5 The Northern League of Unusual Sports (NoLUS) are holding their annual competition on the Isle of Wigg this year. The committee have commissioned web developers to create their website to advertise the event and to attract paying spectators along for the three-day event. A small selection of the statements from the committee and some local competitors are listed below.
- We'd like our spectators to be able to find out a little bit about what unusual sports are and what is unusual about them.
- We've agreed that the sports included in this year's competition will be shin kicking, extreme ironing, toe wrestling, bog snorkelling, lawnmower racing, wife carrying, chess boxing and black pudding throwing. Information for each of these with photographs and videos from last year's competition are vital to allow spectators to see what is involved in each of these unusual sports.
- For each of the days, Friday to Sunday, we need to include a programme of events.
- I'm a professional cheese roller and I'd like to include a page with information about cheese rolling as a sport that everyone can come and have a free try on the day.
- We also have Ultimate Frisbee™ as this year's demo sport for possible inclusion in the next year's competition in Muckling. It would be helpful to have a detailed page of information on how to play the sport with a video showing what is involved in Ultimate Frisbee™.
- Spectators can buy a one, two or three-day ticket but this would need to be purchased on a secure website.
From the statements given above, identify three functional requirements.

193

KEY POINTS

- The end-user requirements for the website list what it should contain (images, sounds and videos) and what it should look and feel like.
- Functional requirements specify which pages are to be created, what each page should display and what the page should do.
- A persona is created during analysis to identify the user(s) or target audience of the website being created.

Chapter 15 Design

This chapter looks at designing the navigational and web page structure of a website.

The following topics are covered:

- Describe and exemplify the website structure of a multi-level website with a home page and two additional levels, with no more than four pages per level.
- Describe, exemplify and implement, taking into account end-user requirements and device-type, an effective user-interface design (visual layout and readability) using wire-framing to include:
  - a horizontal navigational bar
  - relative horizontal and vertical positioning of the media
  - form inputs
  - file formats of the media (text, graphics, video, and audio).
- Describe, exemplify and implement prototyping (low-fidelity) from wireframe design at this level.

Website structure

Once the analysis is complete, the next stage is to consider the design of the website. When designing a website, a developer should consider both the structure of the website and how the user will navigate between each of the many possible pages and levels within the website and the design of each of those individual pages.

There are many different ways that the design for a website can be illustrated. The most common and logical structure for websites is the hierarchical structure. A hierarchical (or tree) structure is shown in Figure 15.1. A hierarchical structure allows fast movement between pages using navigation bars and can be easily expanded to allow more information to be added in different levels.

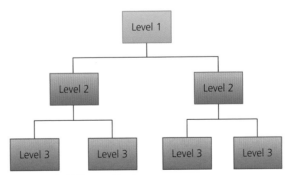

Figure 15.1 Hierarchical structure

A linear (or sequential) structure is shown in Figure 15.2. A linear structure is useful for processes that may be followed in a set order, like reading a story or making a purchase by entering delivery details followed by payment information and then finally confirming the transaction. If required, a linear structure allows the user to go back to the previous page. Linear structures can be time-consuming, so it is better to keep such sequences short.

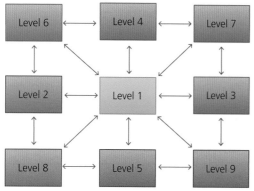

Figure 15.2 Linear structure

A web structure is shown in Figure 15.3. Web structures allow multiple direct connections between web pages.

Figure 15.3 Web structure

At Higher level, you will use a multi-level hierarchical structure with the horizontal navigation bar indicated as shown below in Figure 15.4. This shows the multi-level navigational structure for Bob de Warner's website with the main topics and sub-topics identified in the end-user and functional requirements in Chapter 14. The following pages were identified for development:

- Home page
- Bread
- White
- Brown
- Wholemeal
- Sourdough
- Multigrain
- Cakes
- Large cakes
- Small cakes
- Biscuits
- Plain biscuits
- Fancy biscuits
- Recipes
- Ordering
- Find us

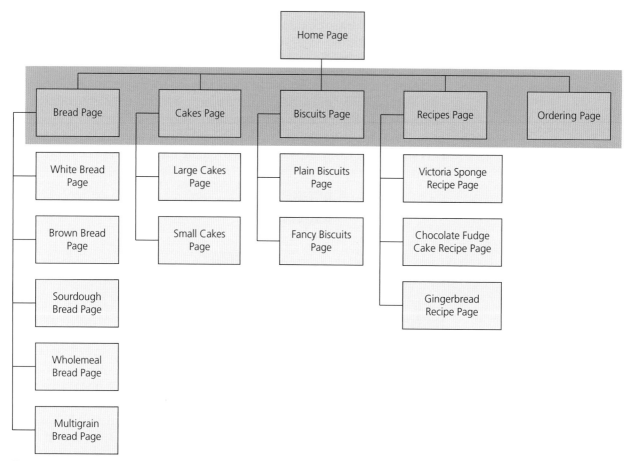

Figure 15.4 Hierarchical structure with horizontal navigation bar

To show which pages are to be present in the navigation bar, a shaded background is included with horizontal lines to show how they are linked. This navigation bar also includes the home page. The vertical lines show how the sub-pages are linked from each main page. The horizontal lines show how each main page is linked to every other main page in the website.

The current design means creating several pages for both the bread and recipe sections. A better way to implement this and to reduce the number of pages that need to be stored, is to use JavaScript™. When an element on the page is selected, a different page will be displayed. See Chapter 18 for JavaScript implementation. The design for the navigation of the website can be updated as shown in Figure 15.5.

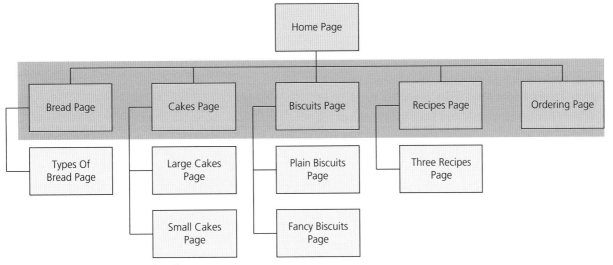

Figure 15.5 Updated navigational structure

Wireframe design

Once the navigational structure has been decided, a design for the content of each of the pages must be created. A wireframe is a low-fidelity design technique where the web developer will draw a greyscale, graphical skeleton of the layout. It is made up of lines and boxes and also shows the interaction of each of the elements in a web page. It is important as it allows the web developer to provide their client with a visual understanding of how the page will look and function and allows them to make basic changes in layout before the next phase is considered.

A wireframe should include the horizontal and vertical positions of:

- the navigation bar
- text that will appear on the page
- media elements: images, video and audio (including sizes where appropriate)
- the file types (and names) of each of the media elements
- any interactive parts of the page
- any hyperlinks
- each of the form elements.

In order to maintain consistency, the positioning of contents of the top, navigation and bottom of page should remain the same on each page.

Figure 15.6 shows a simple outline for the design of a basic web page. Notice how the header, navigation bar and footer are positioned. These web parts will not change regardless of the page viewed. Other simple layouts can be created depending on the website required, but this is the basic layout you will use for Higher Computing Science.

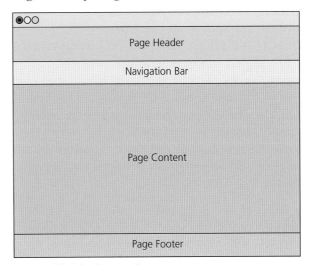

Figure 15.6 Basic page layout

When designing the wireframe, it is also important to take into account the types of devices on which the website will be viewed. To provide an effective design for a user-interface may mean that a simplified version has to be designed for viewing on mobile devices rather than one on which everything would be displayed.

Visual layout is the appearance of the website on each device or how the page is organised. A screen which is crammed full of text and images is more difficult to read than one which makes effective use of white space. White space is the part of the screen which does not contain any content. Effective use of white space is a key element of visual layout design and it helps focus the reader's attention upon what is important on the page.

Websites are considered to be readable when they are easy to read and understand. Readability may be tested by looking at the level of difficulty of the language used. One way of doing this is to measure the reading age of the text using word-processing software or a dedicated website. Using short words and sentences improves readability. This paragraph has a reading age of 14.

Be careful not to confuse the readability of a website with the readability of program code. Readability of program code may be improved by adding internal commentary.

File formats of media

Computers use a range of media or data types. These include text, images, video and audio and should be indicated in the wireframe where necessary.

Text

Any character which appears on a computer keyboard, for example upper-case letters (ABCDEFGHIJKLMNOPQRSTUVWXYZ), lower-case letters (abcdefghijklmnopqrstuvwxyz), numbers, punctuation marks and special characters, like the hash tag (#), are text. Remember that numbers stored as text may not be used in calculations. Text for a web page should be created separately in a word-processing package and checked before copying into each page because many web design packages do not contain a spellchecker.

Images

The diagrams and other pictures in this book are images. Image files for a website are generally saved as JPEG (Joint Photographic Expert Group), PNG (Portable Network Graphic) or GIF (Graphics Interchange Format) file types as they are standard file types which can be viewed in any browser. In addition, the file size for each of these types of image files is significantly smaller as they are usually compressed. This means that they will be faster to load in a browser.

Video

Movies or videos are a type of data produced by a digital video camera, some digital still cameras, tablet computers and mobile phones. Video data is made up of a sequence of moving or 'live' action images.

Animation is data made up of moving images. Animation is the creation of apparent movement through the presentation of a sequence of slightly different still pictures. One method of producing animation is rapidly changing between two or more still images, like a flick (flip) book. Computer animation is used in the film and television industry to mix computer-generated images with 'live' action.

MP4 (MPEG-4 Motion Picture Experts Group) files are one video file type used in websites. MPEG is called a container file because it contains both video and audio in one file. It is also a compressed file type which makes it more suitable for loading and playing in websites as the file size is smaller.

Other types that may be used include: AVI (Audio Video Interleave), FLV (Flash Video Format), MOV (Apple Quicktime Video) and WMV (Windows Media Video). For the purposes of this textbook we will be using MP4 files for the website.

Figure 15.7 MPEG-4 logo

Audio

This includes music, voice recording, or any other noise produced by a computer. MP3 (MPEG-1 Audio Layer-3) is currently the most popular file format on the web for distributing CD-quality sound.

MP3 files are compressed to around one tenth of the size of the original file, yet preserve the quality. Again, this means that as the file size is smaller, any audio can be loaded and played more quickly from the internet. Other file types for audio include: WAV (WAVeform audio file format), AIFF (Audio Interchange File Format), FLAC (Free Lossless Audio Codec) and Ogg Vorbis.

Figure 15.8 MP3 logo

Wireframe for the home page

The end-user and functional requirements state that the home page should contain information about the shops and Bob's history.

Figure 15.9 shows the design for the Home Page for Bob's website. It includes the header, the horizontal navigational bar and footer as well as the layout for each of the media elements to be included on the page. Subsequent wireframe designs will only show the layout for a selection of the pages without the header, horizontal navigational bar and footer as these do not change.

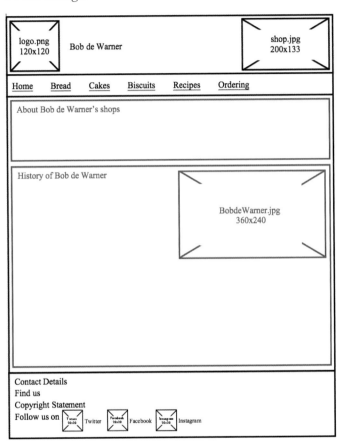

Figure 15.9 home page design

Notice that the wireframe above includes all of the required elements including the data types of each element where necessary. Figures 15.10 to 15.13 show the wireframe designs for the Bread, Small Cakes, Recipe and Ordering pages and the end user and functional requirements for each of the pages. On each page, as well as the position of each element, the file names and file types are also included.

Bread page

The end-user and functional requirements for the bread page state that:

- users should be able to view the different types of bread: White, Brown, Wholemeal, Sourdough and Multigrain.
- the bread page will provide clickable buttons to display either White, Brown, Wholemeal, Sourdough or Multigrain bread types.
- the Bread page will show rollover images of each bread type and display information on each bread type.

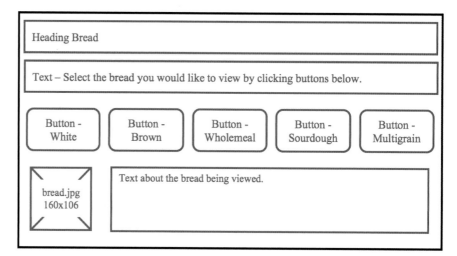

Figure 15.10 Bread page wireframe

Small cakes page

The end-user and functional requirements for the Small Cakes page state that:

- users should be able to view images of examples of small cakes.
- the client would like users to be able to select small images of baked goods to see larger versions on the page with a description of each.
- the Small Cakes sub-page should show examples of the small cakes available to buy.
- the images on each of the Small Cakes and Biscuits pages should be thumbnails which may be rolled over to view a larger image and description of each.

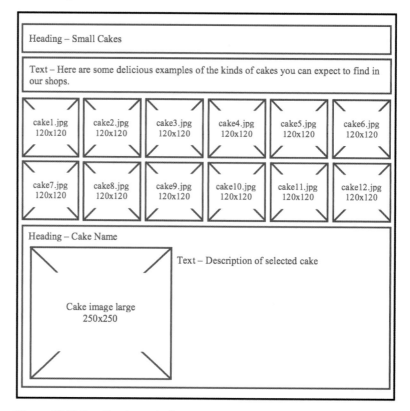

Figure 15.11 Small cakes wireframe

Recipes page

The end-user and functional requirements for the Recipes page state that:

- the client would like to provide three popular cake recipes: Victoria Sponge, Chocolate Fudge Cake and Gingerbread.
- users would like the cake recipes to include instructional videos.
- the Recipes page should allow selection of recipes for Victoria sponge, Chocolate Fudge Cake and Gingerbread from an on-screen menu.
- each recipe on the Recipes page should display recipe instructions and an instructional video on how to make each cake.

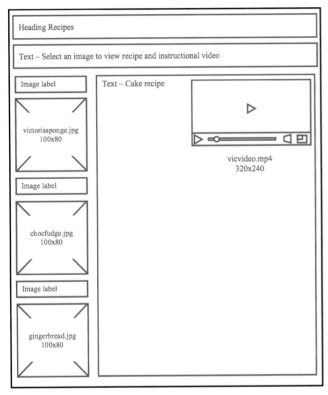

Figure 15.12 Recipes wireframe

Ordering page (form inputs)

The end-user and functional requirements for the Ordering page state that:

- users should be able to order celebration cakes online using a simple form.
- users should be able to select from Birthday, Engagement, Wedding, Anniversary and Christening cakes when ordering celebration cakes.
- the Ordering page should provide a simple form for customers to order celebration cakes.

- the form should provide a simple selection of different types of celebration cakes: Birthday, Engagement, Wedding, Anniversary and Christening.

The Ordering wireframe design shows the position of all the required form inputs including drop-down menus, radio buttons, text and number inputs plus the 'Send order' button to send the order to the server (see Chapter 18).

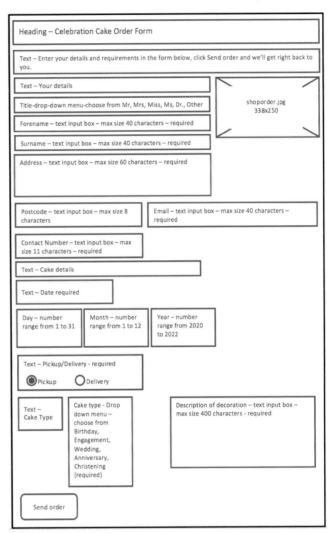

Figure 15.13 Ordering wireframe

Low-fidelity prototype

A low-fidelity prototype is an easy way to translate basic ideas from a wireframe into a basic, testable product. The main difference between a wireframe and a low-fidelity prototype is that the low-fidelity prototype offers interactivity.

It can be created using pen and paper but can also be produced electronically using either specialist prototyping software (with templates) or presentation software. Both of these methods have their advantages and disadvantages and which one to choose is up to the design team.

A paper-based prototype requires two people to demonstrate how the website should work. One person pretends to click on 'hyperlinks' while the other person plays the part of the website and moves from page to page. At this stage developers will use personas created at the Analysis stage to test whether the end user and functional requirements are being met. See Chapter 19 for more information on personas.

The advantages of a paper-based prototype are that:

● it is cheap to implement
● it is fast to create
● it allows more people to take part in (and understand) the design process as no special skills are required
● the fact that everything is written down means that the process is self-documenting.

There are, however, a couple of disadvantages to this method. It is not:

● always clear to users which parts of the paper design are interactive without using their imagination
● possible to represent complicated animations or transitions between pages when using paper.

An electronic prototype will incorporate basic interactivity between web pages and can be used as the basis for creating a **high-fidelity** prototype.

The advantages of an electronic prototype are that:

● only one person is required to demonstrate the prototype
● it is easy to make changes to a design without having to redraw everything on paper.

The disadvantages are the direct opposite of the advantages of using a paper-based method:

● more expensive to implement
● slower to create
● fewer people are directly involved
● the documentation must be created separately.

In general, a low-fidelity prototype should help to identify issues with navigation. Specifically, it should highlight **orphan pages** and **dead links**.

Figure 15.14 shows examples of the paper version of the low-fidelity prototype for Bob's Home and Bread pages on the website.

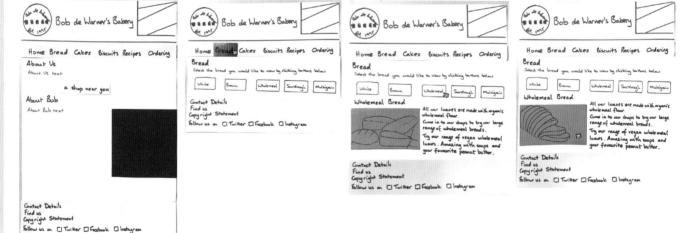

Figure 15.14 Low-fidelity prototype

High-fidelity prototyping

A high-fidelity prototype is a highly interactive version of the website which has a large amount of functionality. It is quite close to how the finished website will look and feel.

Again, it means the developer can demonstrate the website to the client before any code is written and will still allow changes to be made easily. Figure 15.15 shows an example of a high-fidelity prototype.

Figure 15.15 High-fidelity prototype

CHECK YOUR LEARNING

Now answer questions 1–17 (on pages 204–205)

QUESTIONS

1 What is meant by website structure?
2 Explain the difference between a hierarchical and linear navigation website structure. You may draw a diagram to illustrate your answer.
3 State one advantage of a
   a) hierarchical navigation website structure.
   b) linear navigation website structure.
4 The Northern League of Unusual Sports (NoLUS) website is to be designed with a multi-level structure. It will consist of a home page with a horizontal navigation bar with links to six main pages: Sports, Programme, Ultimate Frisbee™, Come and Try and Booking. The sports page will have links to Shin Kicking, Extreme Ironing, Toe Wrestling, Bog Snorkelling, Lawnmower Racing, Wife Carrying, Chess Boxing and Black Pudding Throwing sub-pages. The Ultimate Frisbee™ page will have links to two sub-pages showing information about the sport and videos.
   Draw the design for a multi-level structure for the Northern League of Unusual Sports website.
5 Radio Caledonia are a well-established radio network across Scotland. They broadcast in both English and Gaelic. The owners of the network are developing a new website with pages for each of their stations in English. The website will consist of a home page with a horizontal navigation bar with links to four main pages: *Rèidio gu tuath*, *Rèidio gu deas*, *Rèidio an iar* and *Rèidio an ear*. The *Rèidio an ear* page will have links to four sub-pages showing pages on Local, National and International News, Talk and Sport and the *Rèidio an iar* page will have links to three popular composer sub-pages on Bach, Beethoven and Mozart. Listeners can contact *Rèidio gu deas* to request songs on the Fifteen Minutes of Fab slot by filling in a form accessed from that station's web page.
   Draw the design for a multi-level structure for the Radio Caledonia website.
6 What is a wireframe?
7 Which elements should be included in a wireframe?
8 What is visual layout?
9 What is readability?
10 How may readability be measured?

11 The wireframe for the History of planes at the Inverblair Airshow is created. This is shown below.

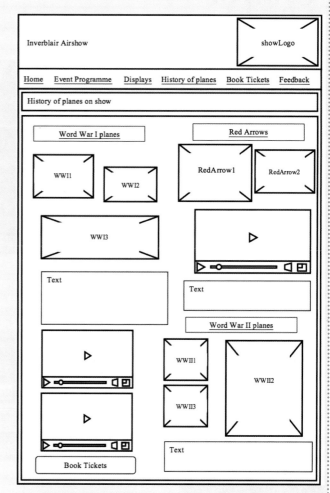

State why the design for this user interface is not effective.

12 Create a wireframe for the ultimate Frisbee™ web page for NoLUS to contain the following elements: the main website heading (Northern League of Unusual Sports) with the NoLUS logo (200x150 pixels), links to the other pages, information about Ultimate Frisbee, two images of Ultimate Frisbee (300x200 pixels) and two videos (320x240 pixels). Your design should also include standard footer.

13 Create a wireframe for the 'Fifteen minutes of fab' form for Radio Caledonia. There is no requirement to create the header, navigation bar or footer. The form should contain the following elements.

- Title (Choose from Ms, Mr, Mrs, Miss, Other)
- Forename (max 30 characters)
- Surname (max 30 characters)
- Email address (max 40 characters)
- Choice of eight pieces of music (max size 500)
- Preferred weekday to play choices (Mon-Fri)

14 What is purpose of a low-fidelity prototype?

15 What can a run-through of a low-fidelity prototype identify?

16 a) State two ways in which a low-fidelity prototype can be created.

b) State one advantage and one disadvantage of each method you named in part (a).

17 Create a low-fidelity prototype using either concrete materials or low-fidelity prototype software for the website wireframes shown below (three from Radio Caledonia as a sample – home page and *Rèidioan iar* page).

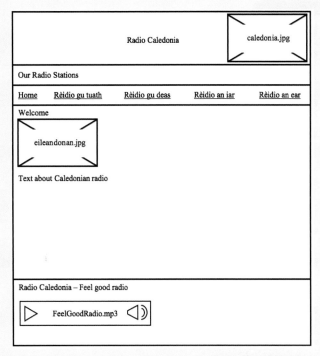

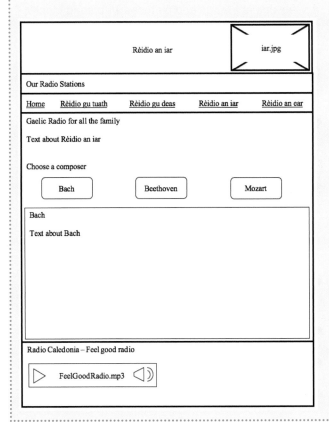

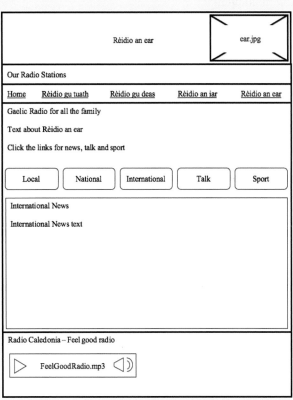

KEY POINTS

- A developer should consider both the structure of the website and the navigation during the design phase.
- Types of navigation structure include hierarchical, linear and web.
- Hierarchical navigation allows fast movement between pages and can be easily expanded to allow more information to be added.
- Linear navigation is useful for processes that may be followed in a set order, like reading a story or making a purchase.
- Web navigation allows multiple direct connections between pages.
- A multi-level hierarchical structure shows a horizontal navigation bar with main topics and sub-topics.
- The navigation bar includes the home page and is shaded in the navigational structure.
- Vertical lines show how sub-pages are linked from the main page.
- Horizontal lines show how each main page is linked to every other main page in the website.
- A wireframe is a low-fidelity design technique where a greyscale, graphical skeleton of the layout is drawn.
- It uses labelled blocks to show the layout of each page on the website without any of the actual content of the page being present.
- A wireframe should include the horizontal and vertical positions of:
  - the navigation bar
  - text that will appear on the page
  - media elements: images, video and audio (including sizes where appropriate)
  - the file types (and names) of each of the media elements
  - any interactive parts of the page
  - any hyperlinks
  - each of the form elements.
- Each page should maintain the position of the contents of the top, navigation and bottom in order to remain consistent.
- Types of devices on which the website will be viewed must be taken into account during design.
- Visual layout is the appearance of the website on the screen or how the display is organised.
- A screen which is crammed full of text and graphics, is more difficult to read than one which makes effective use of white space.
- A website is readable when it is easy to read and understand.
- Readability may be tested by looking at the level of difficulty of the language used.
- Computers use a range of media or data types. These include text, images, video and audio.
- Any character which appears on a computer keyboard is text.
- Images includes diagrams, photographs and any other pictures.
- Video data is made up of a sequence of moving or 'live' action images.
- Audio includes music or any other noise produced by a computer.
- A standard file format is a way of storing data so that it can be understood by and transferred between different application packages.
- Images:
  - Joint Photographic Expert Group (JPEG) is good for natural, real-life images.
  - GIF (Graphics Interchange Format) works well for line drawings and pictures with solid blocks of colour, like cartoons.
  - GIF is limited to 256 colours.
  - Portable Network Graphics (PNG) incorporates the advantages of GIF files, without the limitations, i.e. more than 256 colours may be represented.
- Video:
  - The Motion Picture Expert Group video format is called MPEG.
  - MPEG-4 (MP4) is a standard used to store video.
- Audio:
  - WAVeform audio file format (WAV) is the native sound format for Windows®.
  - MP3 (MPEG-1 Audio Layer-3) files are compressed to around one tenth of the size of the original file yet preserve the quality.
- Prototypes allow the designer to demonstrate to a client how their website will look and feel before it has been created.
- Feedback from the client allows changes to be easily made to the design.
- Low-fidelity prototypes translate a wireframe into a basic, testable product.
- Low-fidelity prototypes can either be paper-based or electronic.
- Low-fidelity prototypes show basic interactivity between web pages (where a wireframe does not).
- Low-fidelity prototypes should help to identify issues with navigation.
- Low-fidelity prototypes should highlight orphan pages and dead links.

Chapter 16 Implementation (HTML)

This chapter looks at implementing the design of a website using HTML.

The following topics are covered:

- Describe, exemplify and implement HTML code:
  - nav
  - header
  - footer
  - section
  - main
  - form
  - id attribute.
- Describe, exemplify and implement form elements:
  - form element: input
    - text
    - number
    - textarea
    - radio
    - submit.
  - form element: select.
- Describe, exemplify and implement form-data validation:
  - length
  - presence
  - range.
- Read and explain code that makes use of the above HTML.

HyperText Mark-up Language (HTML)

HTML is used to create documents or web pages, which may be viewed by using a web browser. HTML uses elements to carry out the mark-up functions. An HTML document usually has three main elements: the document type declaration, the head and the body. Each part or element of an HTML document is separated or delimited by a tag. Each tag has a start like this <> and most tags require an end tag, like this </>. Start and end tags are also called open and closing tags.

At Higher level, we use **HTML5 semantic elements**. This means that the three main elements used before now increases to five and better describes how the page should look.

HTML5 semantic elements

In Chapter 15, we looked at the basic layout for a web page. To achieve this layout, HTML5 semantic elements should be used. An HTML semantic element is an HTML tag which clearly describes the area of the webpage in a way which is easy to understand. You will not need to know this term for Higher, but you will need to know the effect of semantic elements and where they should be placed in the web page.

Semantic elements that you need to know and use are:

- nav
- header
- footer
- section
- main

Semantic element	Description
<nav>	Contains the main navigation bar that generally appears on each web page. It does not have to contain all the hyperlinks that are present on each page, simply those that are part of the main structure of the website.
<header>	Usually contains the header information for a web page to appear at the top of every web page. It can contain the logo and some text. On some websites it will contain a search bar and navigation (although at Higher this is done separately).
<footer>	Contains footer information to appear at the bottom of every web page such as copyright information, contact details, etc.
<section>	Used to separate a web page into different parts for easy identification and for use in CSS. For example, a page might be split into different areas for a heading, content and conclusion.
<main>	Contains the content for each web page.

Further information on other semantic elements and why they were introduced for HTML5, can be found on these websites:

- https:// www.w3schools.com/html/html5_semantic_elements.asp
- https:// www.w3docs.com/learn-html/semantic-elements-in-html5.html
- https://guide.freecodecamp.org/html/html5-semantic-elements/

We can now update the basic layout of our web page to look like Figure 16.1 with all the main HTML elements.

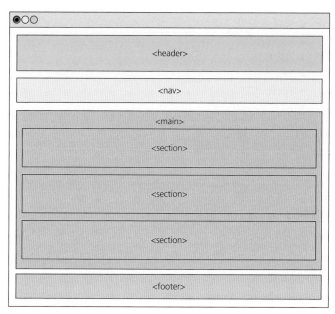

Figure 16.1 HTML elements

Basic website design

The code for the basic design based on the wireframe for Bob de Warner's website can be set up as shown below.

```
<!DOCTYPE html>

<html>

<head>

    <title>This will contain the title of each page.</title>

    <!--link to CSS file should be placed here-->

</head>

<body>

<!-- Header of each web page-->

    <header>

    <!--The logo or banner image can be placed either here or after the website title-->

    <h1>The name of the website should be placed here.</h1>

    </header>
```

```
<!--Navigation bar-->
<nav>
        <ul>   <!--An unordered list here for the elements of the navigation bar-->
                <li><a href=" Hyperlink to sub page 1.html"> </a></li>
                <li><a href=" Hyperlink to sub page 2.html"> </a></li>
                <li><a href=" Hyperlink to sub page 3.html"> </a></li>
                <li><a href=" Hyperlink to sub page 4.html"> </a></li>
                <li><a href=" Hyperlink to sub page 5.html"> </a></li>
                <li><a href=" Hyperlink to sub page 6.html"> </a></li>
        </ul>
</nav>
<!--Changeable main content of each web page-->
<main>
        <section>
        This should contain the main linked content for the page in here.
        </section>
        <section>
        And more content could be placed in here.
        </section>
</main>
<!--Web page footer-->
<footer>
        Finally, the footer information such as copyright and contact information in here.
        </footer>
</body>
</html>
```

The wireframe for Bob's Home page is set out as shown in Figure 16.2.

The areas in black are those which will need to be replicated across every page. This will improve the consistency of the website as the header, navigation bar and footer will appear in the same place on every page.

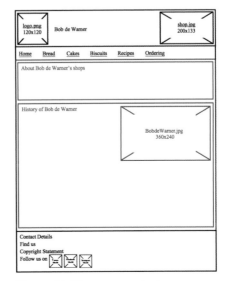

Figure 16.2 home page design

The code can now be updated to look as follows:

```html
<!DOCTYPE html>
<html>
<head>

    <title>Home Page</title>
    <!--link to CSS file should be placed here-->
</head>
<body>
    <!-- Header of each web page-->
    <header>

        <img src="../images/logo.png">
    <h1>Bob de Warner's Bakery</h1>
    <img src="../images/shop.jpg">
    </header>
    <!-- Navigation Bar-->
    <nav>

        <ul> <!--An unordered list here for the elements of the navigation bar-->
            <li><a href="home.html">Home</a></li>
            <li><a href="bread.html">Bread</a></li>
            <li><a href="cakes.html">Cakes</a></li>
            <li><a href="biscuits.html">Biscuits</a></li>
            <li><a href="recipes.html">Recipes</a></li>
            <li><a href="ordering.html">Ordering</a></li>
        </ul>
    </nav>
    <!--Changeable main content of each web page-->
    <main>
        <section>
        This should contain the main linked content for the page in here.
        </section>
        <section>
        And more content could be placed in here.
        </section>
    </main>
    <!--Web page footer-->
    <footer>
        <ul>
        <li><a href="contact.html">Contact Details</a></li>
        <li><a href="findus.html">Find Us</a></li>
        <li><a href="copyright.html">Copyright Statement</a></li>
        <li>Follow us on</li>
        <li><a href="https://twitter.com/home"><img src="../images/twitter.png"
            >Twitter</a></li>
```

```
    <li><a href="https://en-gb.facebook.com/BobdeWarner/"><img src="../images/
        facebook.png">Facebook</a></li>

    <li><a href="https://www.instagram.com/bobdewarner.bakery/?hl=en"><img
        src="../images/instagram.jpg">Instagram</a></li>

    </ul>

    </footer>

</body>

</html>
```

This will produce the page shown in Figure 16.3.

Figure 16.3 Home page with no styling

This page bears no resemblance to the wireframe shown in Figure 16.2. This is because there is no styling included in the file, so the page not only looks very plain, but the entire page is difficult to see in the browser window as the images are too large and the content is all stacked on top of each other.

Styling in CSS for this page will be added in Chapter 17 to address the issues for the web page. Note that the HTML code for this web page should be reused in every other page so that consistency is maintained across the website.

Form

The **form** element allows the web developer to create a page where the client can collect data from the user of the website. This could be anything from a sign-up to a newsletter to a complaints page.

```
<form action="">
```

This would normally tell the HTML page where to send the form-data in the **action** attribute. The form-data is sent to the URL (Uniform Resource Locator) of a form processor which makes use of a PHP script to handle it. However, as PHP is outwith the scope of the Higher course, when the form is submitted it will not send the data anywhere. PHP is covered in detail in Advanced Higher Computing.

DID YOU KNOW?

PHP

PHP:Hypertext Preprocessor is a server scripting language used to make dynamic web content. It can be used, among other things, to collect form-data or send and receive cookies. For more information on PHP go to:

- https:// www.w3schools.com/PHP/php_intro.asp
- https:// www.php.net/

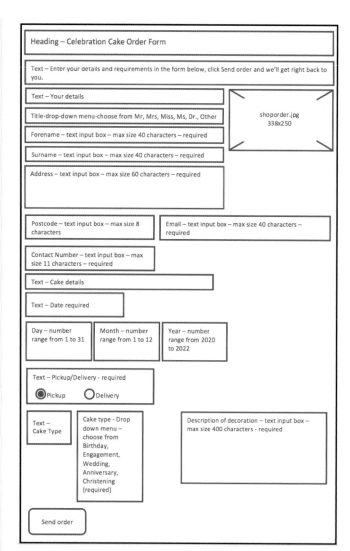

Figure 16.4 Order wireframe

To implement the input areas for the order page, a number of different elements should be used. Where required, form elements will be validated using length, presence and range checks.

Form element: <input>

Used for simple data entry into a form. It can be of several different types: text, number, radio and submit plus the textarea multiple line input are those used at Higher.

Text

A text type allows the form to accept text input and is made up of several attributes, for example:

```
<input type="text" name="forename"
size="20" maxlength="20" required>
```

type="**text**" identifies the input for this part as text. If no input type is selected, then text is selected by default.

name="forename" is included to identify this part of the form when it is sent to the server to be processed.

Each name attribute should be unique and not be duplicated anywhere else on the form. Although at Higher, the form is not submitted to any server for processing it should still be included.

size="20" should define, in the case of a text type, the size of the text element in the browser, i.e. the text box visible.

maxlength="20" will define the number of characters that can be entered. This is a **length check** in HTML.

required is used if data has to be entered into the form and will not allow the user to complete the form unless these boxes are completed. This is a **presence check** in HTML.

Figure 16.5 shows how a text input type will display in a browser.

Forename

Figure 16.5 Text input

The value attribute can be used to pre-populate a text input type as shown in Figure 16.6.

```
<input type="text" name="forename"
value="Enter forename" size="20"
maxlength="20" required>
```

Forename

Enter forename

Figure 16.6 Pre-populate text input

Number

If a **number** type is chosen, then the limits of entry can be restricted to between two values; **min** and **max** are used to perform a **range** check in HTML, e.g. min="1" max="31".

```
<input type="number" name="day" min="1"
max="31" required>
```

Figure 16.7 shows how the number input type will display in a browser.

Date required
Day ☐ Month ☐ Year ☐

Figure 16.7 Number input

The value attribute can again be used to pre-populate the numeric input type associated with the Year input box as shown in Figure 16.8.

```
<input type="number" name="year"
value="2020" min="2020" max="2022"
required>
```

Date required
Day 1 Month 1 Year 2020

Figure 16.8 Pre-populate numeric input

Radio

If a **radio** type is selected, then a series of radio buttons will be displayed.

type="radio" identifies the input for this type as a radio button.

name="del" means that the radio buttons are treated as a group and ensures that only one button may be selected at a time.

id="pickup" is used here to identify each of the options in the radio buttons.

value="pickup" is a unique value that would be sent to the server when the form is submitted to identify which radio button was selected.

```
<input type="radio" name="del" id="pickup"
value="pickup" required>Pickup

<input type="radio" name="del"
id="delivery" value="delivery">Delivery
```

Figure 16.9 shows how the radio input type will display in a browser.

Pickup/Delivery (please select one) ○ Pickup ○ Delivery

Figure 16.9 Radio button input

If required, then the **checked** attribute can be used to pre-populate one radio button in the form as shown in Figure 16.10.

```
<input type="radio" name="del" id="pickup"
value="pickup" checked required>Pickup
```

Pickup/Delivery (please select one) ⦿ Pickup ○ Delivery

Figure 16.10 Pre-populated radio button

Submit

If a **submit** type is selected, then a clickable button is displayed on the screen to allow the form-data to be submitted. Clicking submit will ensure that the browser checks for form-data that may be missing from required entries.

A small section of JavaScript is included so that a confirmation window appears to the user to let them know their form-data has been submitted.

```
<input type="submit" onclick="alert('Order
sent. ')" value="Send order">
```

As before with the id attribute, the form-data is not actually submitted at Higher and is covered in the Advanced Higher course.

Figure 16.11 shows how the submit input type will display in a browser.

Figure 16.11 Submit input

Textarea

The **textarea** input defines a multiple line input in a form. It could be used for addresses, for customers to write a review or where a longer text entry may be required.

```
<textarea name="description" rows="10"
cols="80" maxlength="500"></textarea>
```

The **rows** attribute dictates how many rows will be displayed, e.g. rows="10".

The **cols** attribute dictates how many rows will be displayed, e.g. cols="80".

Figure 16.12 shows how the textarea type will display in a browser.

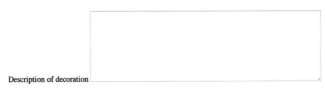

Description of decoration

Figure 16.12 Textarea type

The textarea type can also be pre-populated with some text if required by entering a short sentence between the opening and closing elements as follows.

```
<textarea name="description" rows="10"
cols="80" maxlength="500">No special
requirements</textarea>
```

Figure 16.13 Pre-populated textarea

Further information on other form elements including further input types can be found at:

- https://www.w3schools.com/html/html_form_elements.asp
- https://developer.mozilla.org/en-US/docs/Web/HTML/Element/Input

Form element: <select>

The **select** element defines a drop-down list which will allow a selection of possible inputs.

```
<select name="title">
```

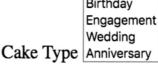

Figure 16.14 Drop-down list

Option

The **option** elements define the contents of the drop-down list. The default setting is for the first in the list to be selected.

```
<option value="birthday"> Birthday
</option>

<option value="engagement"> Engagement
</option>

<option value="wedding"> Wedding
</option>

<option value="anniversary"> Anniversary
</option>

<option value="christening"> Christening
</option>
```

However, it is possible to define a pre-selected option, if required, using the **selected** attribute.

```
<option value="birthday"
selected>Birthday</option>
```

When put together, the HTML code looks as follows.

```
<select name="title">

    <option value="birthday" selected>
    Birthday </option>

    <option value="engagement">
    Engagement</option>

    <option value="wedding">Wedding
    </option>

    <option value="anniversary">
    Anniversary</option>

    <option value="christening">
    Christening</option>

</select>
```

Figure 16.15 shows how the select type will display in a browser.

Figure 16.15 Select type

Multiple items can be chosen from the drop-down list if the **multiple** attribute is used.

```
<select name="title" multiple>
```

Cake Type
Birthday
Engagement
Wedding
Anniversary

Figure 16.16 Multiple selections

It is also possible to define how many items from the drop-down list may be displayed in the browser at any given time.

```
<select name="title" size="3">
```

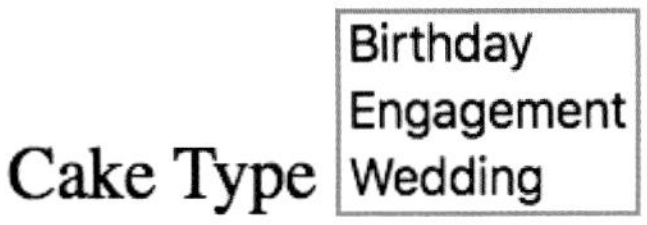

| Cake Type | Birthday
Engagement
Wedding |

Figure 16.17 Three items viewed in browser

Id attribute

id attributes are used specifically to identify elements on the web page. When implementing radio buttons on a form, it is used to uniquely identify each radio button (see page 213). They are also used in JavaScript code and functions and to allow styles to be applied to an element from a stylesheet.

See Chapters 17 and 18 for more information on id attributes in use in CSS and JavaScript.

Figure 16.18 shows the basic layout of the form for the website. Notice that the layout is not yet the same as the wireframe (see Figure 16.4) as there has been no styling applied yet. However, the contents of the page are all present.

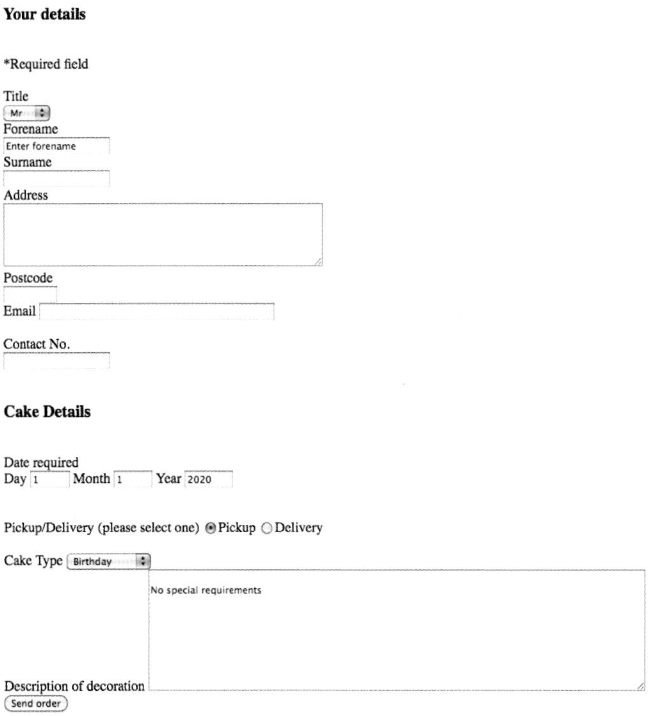

Your details

*Required field

Title
Mr

Forename
Enter forename

Surname

Address

Postcode

Email

Contact No.

Cake Details

Date required
Day 1   Month 1   Year 2020

Pickup/Delivery (please select one) ⦿ Pickup ○ Delivery

Cake Type Birthday

No special requirements

Description of decoration
Send order

Figure 16.18 Ordering page

NOTE

This chapter is not meant to be a comprehensive treatment of HTML. Your teacher or lecturer will provide you with further examples and exercises.

CHECK YOUR LEARNING

Now answer questions 1–3 (on page 215)

QUESTIONS

1 State the main semantic elements used in an HTML5 document.
2 What does the element **<form action="">** perform on form submission?
3 A form is to be created for pet owners at a veterinary surgery to rate the treatment their pet received. Write the HTML form code for the survey:
   a) where the owner can enter their name and name of their pet. Both inputs should be a required entry and should accept a maximum of 30 characters and the input box size should be 30.
   b) where the owner can enter the kennel name of their pet. It should accept a maximum of 30 characters and the input box size should be 30.
   c) which will allow the owner to enter how they rated their visit to the surgery. Ratings are required and should be between 1 and 10 where 1 is poor and 10 is excellent.
   d) where the owner can select which vet they saw. Choose from Mr Brock, Mr Hillier, Ms Collins and Mrs Green. This is required and should allow the owner to select more than one vet.
   e) where the owner can make a comment about the treatment they and their pet have received. It should be pre-populated with the text 'Enter your comments about your pet's treatment.'. Owners should be able to enter up to 500 characters.
   f) to select whether or not a follow up appointment has been booked. 'No' should automatically be selected.
   g) to submit the form. It should thank the owners for submitting their comments.

KEY POINTS

- HyperText Mark-up Language (HTML) is used to create web pages which may be viewed by using a web browser.
- Each part or element of an HTML document is separated by a tag.
- Each tag has a start, like this <> and an end tag, like this </>.
- Some tags have attributes, which provide additional information about an element.
- Attributes can contain values and are enclosed in quotes.
- HTML semantic elements are HTML tags which clearly describe the area of the webpage in a way that is easy to understand.
- An HTML document has five main elements:
  - nav
  - header
  - footer
  - section
  - main
- <nav> contains the main navigation bar that generally appears on each web page.
- <header> usually contains the header information for a web page to appear at the top of every web page.
- <footer> contains footer information to appear at the bottom of every web page.
- <section> is used to separate a web page into different parts for easy identification.
- <main> contains the content for each web page.
- The form element allows the web developer to create a page where the client can collect data from the user of the website.
- Input form elements consist of:
  - text
  - number
  - radio
  - submit
  - textarea
- A text type allows the form to accept text input:
  - type="text" identifies the input as text
  - name="xxx" identifies the part of the form to be sent to the server to be processed
  - size="20" defines the size (the text box visible on the page) of the text element
  - maxlength="20" defines the maximum number of characters that can be entered (length check)
  - required means the box must be completed (presence check).
- A number type allows the form to accept number input:
  - type="number" identifies the input as a number
- min and max can be used to restrict numbers to between two values (range check).
- A radio type displays a series of radio buttons:
  - type="radio" identifies the input as a radio button
  - name="x" ensures radio buttons as treated as a group
  - id="y" identifies the options in each radio button
  - value="z" the unique value sent to the server to identify which radio button was selected.
- A submit type displays a clickable button on the screen to allow the form-data to be submitted:
  - type="submit" identifies the input as a submit button.
- The textarea input defines a multiple line input in a form and is used where a longer text entry may be required:
  - name="description" identifies the part to be sent to the server
  - rows="10" defines how many rows will be displayed
  - cols="80" defines how many columns will be displayed
  - maxlength="500" defines the maximum number of characters that can be entered (length check).
- The textarea type can also be pre-populated with some text if required by entering a short sentence between the opening and closing elements.
- The form element <select> defines a drop-down list which will allow a selection of possible inputs.
- The <option> elements define the contents of the drop-down list.
- id attributes are used to specifically identify elements on the web page.

Chapter 17 Implementation (CSS)

This chapter looks at controlling the appearance and position of elements on web pages in a website using Cascading Style Sheets.

The following topics are covered:

- Describe, exemplify and implement efficient inline, internal and external Cascading Style Sheets (CSS) using grouping and descendant selectors to:
  - control appearance and positioning:
    - sizes (height, width)
    - float (left, right)
    - clear (both)
    - display (block, inline, none)
    - margins/padding
  - create horizontal navigation bars:
    - list-style-type: none
    - hover.
- Read and explain code that makes use of the above CSS.

Styling

HTML is used to describe the structure and content of a web page. Pages created in HTML are plain in appearance when displayed in browser software. That is, there are no colour backgrounds or text; no different fonts or font colours and all content is usually linear in appearance, i.e. images and text appear one underneath the other.

To enhance the look and feel of web pages, Cascading Style Sheets (CSS) are included and linked to websites and their constituent web pages.

What is CSS?

CSS is a language used to describe how a web page will be presented in a browser. It can include fonts, colours and the layout of each web page. CSS can be used by HTML and any other XML-based language (eXtensible Markup Language), such as SVG or XML.

Why use CSS?

It allows the web developer to control the layout of all the web pages in a website at a stroke by making simple changes to the CSS file. It can save a great deal of time, as it means that web developers do not have to go through each web page separately to make changes.

It also means that web pages can be downloaded much more quickly by the browser, as any CSS files are downloaded once and then referred to multiple times by each web page which uses its styles.

Types of CSS

There are three different ways to apply CSS to an HTML document:

- inline
- internal (embedded)
- external (linked).

Inline styling

Inline styles are used within HTML tags. The style attribute is included in the line of code you wish to style. For example:

```
<p style="color:#340913; text-align:center">

Fancy a fancy biscuit or something for dunking in your beverage?<br>

Pop into one of our shops for a selection of our lovely, tasty biscuits.<br>

Buttery shortbread to go with a fresh coffee or an empire biscuit for elevenses.<br>

Come in and try one!</p>
```

will display the text shown on the Biscuits page as in Figure 17.1.

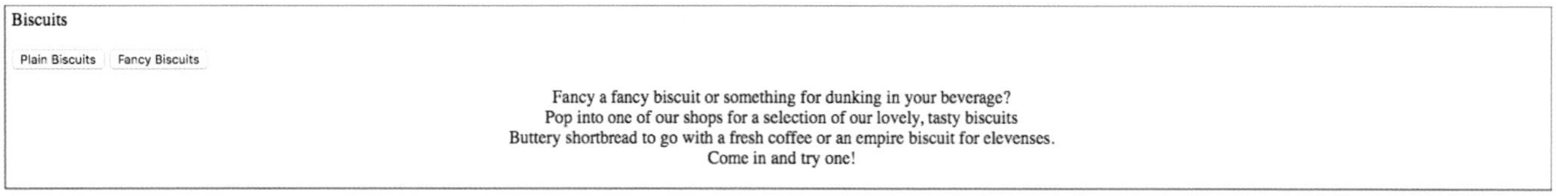

Biscuits

Plain Biscuits   Fancy Biscuits

Fancy a fancy biscuit or something for dunking in your beverage?
Pop into one of our shops for a selection of our lovely, tasty biscuits
Buttery shortbread to go with a fresh coffee or an empire biscuit for elevenses.
Come in and try one!

Figure 17.1 Inline styling

Inline styling should be avoided where possible as it is considered better practice for HTML not to contain the design parts of a website. Using inline styling also makes it much more difficult to achieve uniformity across web pages. Avoiding the use of inline styling means that it is only necessary to update one page rather than several thousand in the case of a large website.

Internal styling

Internal or embedded styles are defined in the <head> tag of a website and are used to apply to the whole page.

The <style> tag is used to contain the styling for the page where each section to be styled is identified by one of the HTML tags. These are HTML selectors. We will look more closely at selectors on page 220.

```
<head>
    <style>
        img{height:200px; width:300px}
    </style>
</head>
```

This internal style will make all the images 200 by 300 pixels after the <img> tag. Figure 17.2 shows how this affects the Biscuits page before and after the internal style has been applied.

Before

Shortbread

Cookies

After

Shortbread

Cookies

Empire Biscuit

Figure 17.2 Internal styling

Although using internal styling makes an HTML document appear less cluttered than inline styling, it still causes problems with uniformity across web pages within a website. It will also take longer for a web page to load, because all the styling has to be loaded at the head of the page before the rest of the page is loaded.

External styling

External or linked styles are created as a separate file. A CSS file will contain all the style rules for every page in the website and every page in the website will have a link to the CSS file.

The reference to the CSS file is contained within the <head> tags using a <link> tag.

The stylesheet contains the styling for the page. Some simple styles to change the font on the Biscuits page are shown here.

HTML

```
<head>

<title>Biscuits</title>

<link rel="stylesheet" type="text/css"
href="../css/styles.css">

<style>

img{height:200px;width:300px}

</style>

</head>
```

CSS (styles.css file)

```
body{font-family:Candara,Arial,sans-serif}
```

Figure 17.3 shows how this now affects the Biscuits page.

Bob de Warner's Bakery

Home
Bread
Cakes
Biscuits
Recipes
Ordering
Biscuits
Plain Biscuits Fancy Biscuits

Fancy a fancy biscuit or something for dunking in your beverage?
Pop into one of our shops for a selection of our lovely, tasty biscuits
Buttery shortbread to go with a fresh coffee or an empire biscuit for elevenses.
Come in and try one!

Shortbread

Figure 17.3 External styling

Note that, if more than one style is used then the order of application is as follows:

1 inline
2 internal
3 external.

This means that even if you are using an external stylesheet to define how the page looks, any inline styles written into the code will overwrite the other style settings.

CHECK YOUR LEARNING

Now answer questions 1–9 (on page 234) on styling

Selectors

HTML selector

An HTML selector is a way of identifying styles in internal and external stylesheets. They make use of the HTML tags to style sections of code in the web page.

Every selector contains properties which are written in curly brackets {}. These properties include changing font size, family, colour, alignment, margins, padding and also changing background colours, among others.

HTML selector rules in CSS are written like this:

```
header{background-color:#fbdfe6}

body{font-family: Candara, Arial, sans-serif}
```

The browser will apply these rules as follows. The header section of the web page will display in the chosen background colour and any text that appears in the body section of the HTML document will display using the font Candara.

Note the values that are given to the font-family property. This is to ensure that there is compatibility with all browsers.

The first value is the font that the developer would like to use on the web page. The next one in the list is the one that should be tried next by the browser, with the final one being a font in the family if none of the other ones are available. This is useful if the client chooses an unusual font which may not be able to be displayed in all browsers.

Note that there are only a few fonts which are used in common across a number of systems.

These are called web-safe fonts. Web-safe fonts include Arial, Candara, Courier, Georgia, Times and Verdana. You can find out more about web safe fonts at https://www.cssfontstack.com.

Class selector

The class selector allows the developer to pinpoint exactly where in the HTML document the style is to be applied. It uses a full stop before the class selector name. The HTML selector is more of a broad brushstroke and it is difficult to apply multiple different styles to different parts of the web page.

The class selector can be used by both internal and external styling and will overrule any other style applied to that part of the HTML document.

A class selector rule is written as shown here in a CSS document:

```
.largeHeading{color:#fbdfe6;font-size:28px;
font-weight:bold}
```

To implement this in a web page, it should be included like this:

```
<p class="largeHeading">About us</p>
```

Figure 17.4 shows how these would affect the home page in the website.

Home
Bread
Cakes
Biscuits
Recipes
Ordering

About us

With a reputation for high-quality baked goods, Bob de Warner bakery shops can be found country-wide. From our fabulously tasty pastries to our award-winning bread, there is something to suit everyone. Look for our shops in selected high streets. Find out if we have a shop near you where our friendly, highly trained staff will be happy to help with all your needs.

About Bob

Figure 17.4 Class selector applied

Id selector

The id selector is used to identify and style one element in an HTML document. It uses the hash (#) character to identify each element to be styled. The main difference between id and class selectors is that an id only identifies one element for styling whereas a class selector can be used in many different elements.

As with the class selector, the id selector can be used in both internal and external stylesheets.

```
#bob{height:240px;width:360px;float:right;
margin-left:20px}
```

To implement this in a web page, it should be included like this:

```
<img id="bob" src="../images/Bob.jpg">
```

221

Figure 17.5 shows how this would affect the home page in the website.

Home
Bread
Cakes
Biscuits
Recipes
Ordering

About us

With a reputation for high-quality baked goods, Bob de Warner bakery shops can be found country-wide. From our fabulously tasty pastries to our award-winning bread, there is something to suit everyone. Look for our shops in selected high streets. Find out if we have a shop near you where our friendly, highly trained staff will be happy to help with all your needs.

About Bob

Bob started baking as a young child with his father who owned a small bakery in a High Inchirvine in Scotland. He left school and was lucky enough to secure a place in Paris at the famous Ecole de Monsieur Le Patissier.
This started Bob on his, now famous, career path. He found that he was able to improve on age-old recipes and experimented with flavours and designs never before seen in the baking school.
Once qualified, he left to work back in London with the award-winning pastry chef Henri Rees in Palais du Sucre. After five years working with Henri, Bob finally felt he had the skills required to open his first bakery. Returning to his Scottish roots, Bob's first bakery in the centre of Glasgow was a roaring success and this success continued as he opened one, then two and finally multiple bakeries around Scotland.
Bob attributes his success to the high-quality ingredients used in each baked good, attention to detail and his own well-trained bakers.
Bob still bakes in the kitchen of his main shop but can often be found in his other shops on a regular basis.
Contact Details
Find Us
Copyright Statement
Follow us on

Figure 17.5 Id selector applied

We will look in detail at the different styles covered in these examples later in this chapter.

Grouping and descendant selectors

When writing CSS styles, you will make use of **grouping** and **descendant selectors** to apply styles. Before we start to look in detail at any more CSS, it makes sense to define what is meant by, and the difference between, grouping and descendant selectors. The main differences between the two selectors is in the way they are written and how they are applied.

Grouping selector

A grouping selector is one in which groups of html elements are to have the same CSS styles applied to them. It increases the efficiency of reading the styles rather than having the same ones repeated over and over.

Before the grouping selector is applied, the stylesheet looks like this:

```
main{background-color:#d61a46}

section{background-color:#d61a46}

section{padding:10px}

p{padding:10px}

h2{padding:10px}
```

After grouping the styles together, they will look like this:

```
main, section{background-color:#d61a46}

section, p, h2{padding:10px}
```

Notice that there are commas between each html element. This means that exactly the same styling will be applied to each of these elements.

The first grouping selector will apply the same colour styles to both the main and section elements.

The second grouping selector will apply padding (see later in the chapter) to the section, p and h2 elements.

Descendant selector

A descendant selector is used to identify one part of a web page specifically to style it separately from the rest. It makes using the same code across multiple different web pages far more efficient than continuing to add multiple id or class selectors.

Descendant selectors look like the ones shown here:

```
nav ul li{float:left;width:120px;text-align:center}

main section h2{text-align:center}
```

Notice that there are *no* commas between each html element. This means that each style will only be applied to each of these parts of the web page and nowhere else. This means that the first descendant selector will only apply the style to the list element in the unordered list in the navigation bar. The second will only apply the style to the h2 element that appears in the sub-section element in main section.

CHECK YOUR LEARNING

Now answer questions 10–14 (on pages 234–235) on selectors

Controlling appearance and positioning of elements

Once the basic HTML has been written and all the elements of the pages have been included, then web developers need to look at the positioning of each of the elements in the website. Currently everything displays one element underneath another on every web page, which does not match the wireframes.

There are a number of different ways to control the appearance and position of the elements on a web page.

Colour schemes

It is important to choose a colour scheme carefully so that the colours work well together. Colour wheels can be used to help decide which colours work well together. Monochromatic colour schemes use variations (hues, tints and shades) of the same colour throughout the website. Analogous colour schemes use colours which are next to one another on the colour wheel. Complementary colour schemes use colours which are on opposite sides of the colour wheel.

Figure 17.6 shows three colour wheels displaying monochromatic, analogous and complementary colours.

You can find out more about the different types of colour schemes at:

- https://www.w3schools.com/colors/colors_schemes.asp
- https://color.adobe.com/create/color-wheel

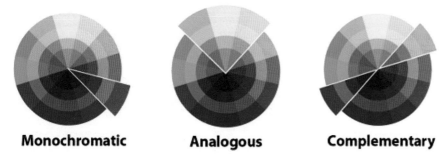

Monochromatic   **Analogous**   **Complementary**

Figure 17.6 Colour wheels

A monochromatic colour scheme has been chosen for Bob de Warner's website, the colours for which can be seen in Figure 17.7 and the home page in Figure 17.8.

Figure 17.7 Colour scheme for website

Colours in CSS may be identified in three different ways:

color:pink

color:#fbdfe6

color:rgb(251,223,230)

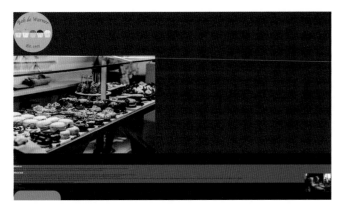

Figure 17.8 Updated Home page

Image sizes

Figure 17.9 shows the wireframe for the Home page again. There are two images at the top that are to appear on every page. Figure 17.10 shows the Home page as displayed in the browser. The images are very large compared to the wireframe and the size of each needs to be reduced.

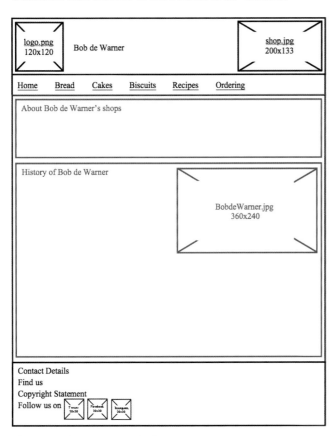

Figure 17.9 Home page design

Figure 17.10 Header on the Home page

CSS can be used to reduce the size of each image using the height and width properties. This can be assigned in either pixels (e.g. 300px) or as a percentage of the original image size (e.g. 25%).

For example, altering the height and width using classes:

```
.logo{height:120px;width:120px}

.banner{height:133px;width:200px}
```

Figure 17.11 now shows the web page with the size of each image reduced.

Figure 17.11 Reduced image sizes

Element sizes

Every HTML element automatically expands to the width of the browser page. However, sometimes this is not required, and the content of the pages needs to be reduced. This can also be controlled by using the same CSS height and width properties as before but this time assigning them to the element's header, body, etc., for example:

```
body  {width:900px}

header{height:140px}
```

```
footer{height:90px}

nav{height:50px}
```

Figure 17.12 shows how this affects the Home page.

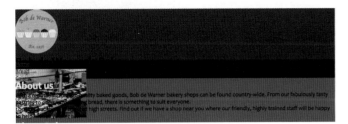

Figure 17.12 Element sizes reduced

Float

The elements for these pages are still very linear; they display one element underneath the other and, as can also be seen, all the content overlaps and cannot be read. The wireframe for this page (see Figure 17.9) requires the logo and shop images to be displayed on the left and right of the website heading. To do this a float property should be applied. This will allow the images to be floated to the left and right of the heading, for example:

```
.logo{float:left;height:120px;width:120px}

.banner{float:right;height:133px;width:200px}
```

Before

Figure 17.14 Ordering page

Display property

The display property controls the layout of a web page. It is arguably the most important styling tool in CSS. Each element placed on a web page is in the form of a rectangular box. Display controls how that box behaves.

There several values associated with the display property:

● block
● inline
● none.

The default value for most elements is either inline or block depending on the browser used to view the web page.

Figure 17.13 shows how this affects the header in the Home page.

Figure 17.13 Float property applied to the Home page

clear:both

In the Ordering page, the float property has been applied to the description of decoration, but in order that the styling does not apply to other elements in the page, i.e. the submit button, a clear:both rule is used to negate the impact of the float property otherwise it will continue to float the rest of the elements, for example:

```
<div style="clear:both">

    <input type="submit"
onclick="alert('Order sent.')" value="Send
order">

</div>
```

Figure 17.14 shows before and after applying the clear:both property.

After

display:block

When styling a web page, some elements of a web page are automatically set to block, i.e. they will, by default, take up the full width of the container element. A container element normally includes tags such as <div>, <section> and <ul> and also text elements <h1> and <p>. This means that anything contained in these elements will force anything that appears on the web page to appear on the next line rather than in line with that container element. This default setting is set automatically by the **User Agent (UA)** stylesheet in the browser in which the user is viewing the web page. The UA stylesheet is the default setting for displaying the web page in a browser when there is no other stylesheet present with rules to be followed.

Figure 17.15 shows how display:block can be used to display text with the <span> tag. Without display:block, the text appears in one line. display:block ensures that the second <span> tag takes up the full container for that element.

```
<span>Top Line</span>

<span style="display: block;">Middle
Line</span>

<span>Bottom Line</span>
```

Before | **After**

Top Line Middle Line Bottom Line | Top Line Middle Line Bottom Line

Figure 17.15 display:block element with text

Figure 17.16 shows how display:block is used on the Ordering page to display the image, where it forces the image to go over to a new line and does not overlap.

```
<p style="display:block">Enter your
details and requirements in the form
below, click Send order, and we'll get
right back to you.</p>
```

Figure 17.16 display:block property with an image

display:inline

Inline styling is usually the default set by the UA stylesheet. Inline elements generally do not interrupt the flow of the web page and ensure that, rather than taking up the entire width of the element, they only take up as much space as is required by the text in the container element. <span> and <a> are inline elements as they do not force the browser to take a new line when included in the HTML code of the web page. Instead they are included as part of the text without breaking the flow.

```
Look for our shops in selected high
streets. Find out if we have <a
href="findus.html"> a shop near you</a>
where our friendly, highly trained staff
will be happy to help with all your needs.
```

Figure 17.17 shows how the anchor <a> inline element can be used to display a hyperlink as part of the text.

About us

With a reputation for high-quality baked goods, Bob de Warner bakery shops can be found country-wide. From our fabulously tasty pastries to our award-winning bread, there is something to suit everyone.
Look for our shops in selected high streets. Find out if we have a shop near you where our friendly, highly trained staff will be happy to help with all your needs.

Figure 17.17 Inline text

The display:inline property can be assigned to an element that is not normally an inline element to ensure that it does not use up the full width of the container element.

Figure 17.18 shows how display:inline is used on both the Home and Ordering pages to allow the image to overlap with the container element.

```
<p style="display:inline">Enter your
details and requirements in the form
below, click Send order, and we'll get
right back to you.</p>
```

Figure 17.18 display:inline

display:none

The display:none property will hide the container which uses it. It means that anything contained in a <div> or <section> tag for example, will not be displayed on screen, almost as if it is not there. We will look at this property in more detail in Chapter 18 when we'll use it in conjunction with JavaScript to hide elements on the page which can be viewed when certain actions are performed.

```
<section id="lemon" style="display:none">
```

Margins and padding

As discussed earlier in the chapter, all of the HTML elements used are considered to be rectangles or boxes. This is known as the **box model** and is used to refer to the design and layout of each page.

The box model is made up of margins, border, padding and the content of each elements. Figure 17.19 shows the layout of the box model.

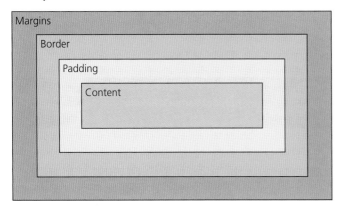

Figure 17.19 The box model

As with the display property, each browser has default settings for both margins and padding. To override this setting and to ensure that margins and padding are set by the web developer and not the browser, the universal selector (*) should be set in the stylesheet as follows:

```
* {margin:0; padding:0}
```

Margins

Margins are used to specify the space around an element. Margins are transparent on web pages; only

their effects are shown. The margin can be set all around the element but can also be set to specify each side of the element separately. That is:

- margin
- margin-top
- margin-right
- margin-bottom
- margin-left

Margin properties can have their values written in px, pt, cm or can be set as a percentage (%) of the width of the containing element.

Setting a uniform sized margin around the h1 element can be written as:

```
h1{margin:10px}
```

Each margin can also be set individually as margin-top, margin-right, margin-bottom and margin-left. For example:

```
h2{margin-top:20px; margin-right:15px;
margin-bottom:15px; margin-left:10px}
```

These four values can also be written in shorthand provided the order is as above.

```
h2{margin:20px 15px 15px 10px}
```

The body margin property should be set to auto. This will horizontally centre the element inside its container, which means that the element's position will automatically be set by the browser and the space that is left is split between the left and right margins.

```
body {margin:auto}
```

If this is not set, then each web page will be automatically set to the left-hand side of the browser. Figure 17.20 shows before and after this is implemented.

Before

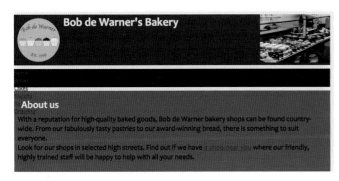

After

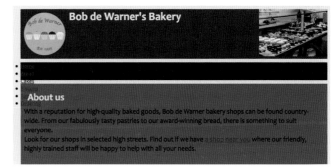

Figure 17.20 margin:auto

In this example, on the Small cakes page, before the margin is implemented, the images are next to one another as shown in Figure 17.21.

Figure 17.21 Before margins are implemented

Implementing a CSS rule with a margin of 10 pixels shown below has the effect shown in Figure 17.22.

```
.small{height:120px;width:120px;margin:10px}
```

Before

Figure 17.23 Setting h1 margin

If margins are set for elements that are next to one another they will overlap, i.e. if element 1 has a margin of 10px and element 2 has a margin of 10px then the margin between the two elements will be still be 10px. This is because margins *push* away from other elements and *not* away from other margins.

Figure 17.24 shows how this works for two elements with a margin of 10px.

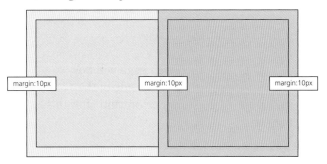

Figure 17.24 Overlapping margins

Borders

The border property is visible and sets the outside of an element's border. The style, width and colour of the element can be set and viewed on the web page.

On the Bread web page, a border has been used to create the border for a button. It has a border width of 2 pixels, the first one has a solid border, the second is dotted and the third is dashed. The colour is the

Figure 17.22 After margins are implemented

This example shows how identifying the left and top margins affects the h1 element in the header element on each page.

```
h1 {margin-left:120px; margin-top: 50px;}
```

Its effect is shown in Figure 17.23.

After

main colour for the page, which is #340913. To set the border-fill colour, the command 'background-color: #fbdfe6' is used.

```
border: 2px solid #340913;
border: 2px dotted #340913;
border: 2px dashed #340913;
```

The effects of these commands are shown in Figure 17.25.

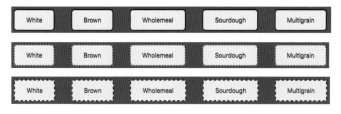

Figure 17.25 Borders

> **NOTE**
> Border properties are not part of the Higher Computing Science course but are included here for completeness.

Padding

The padding sets the space around the *content* of each element. Padding, like margins, is transparent. The padding can be set all around the content but can also be used to specify each side of the content separately. That is:

- padding
- padding-top
- padding-right
- padding-bottom
- padding-left

Padding properties can have their values written in px, pt, cm or can be set as a percentage (%) of the width of the containing element.

Setting a uniform sized padding around the contents of section, p and h2 elements can be written as:

```
section, p, h2{padding:10px}
```

Figure 17.26 shows the Home page before the padding is set. As can be seen, the text on the page is lined up straight down the edge of the element with no gap.

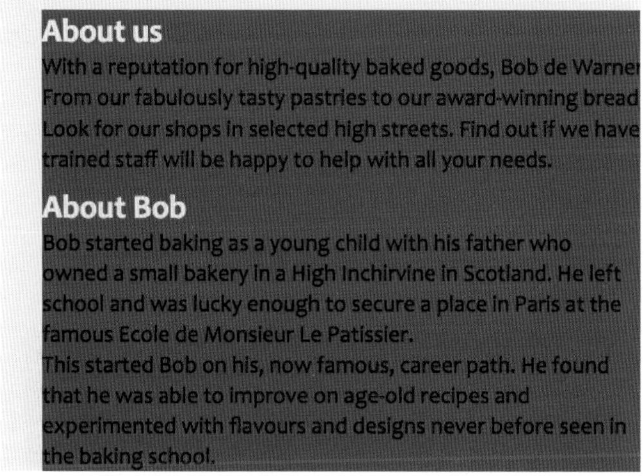

About us

With a reputation for high-quality baked goods, Bob de Warner
From our fabulously tasty pastries to our award-winning bread
Look for our shops in selected high streets. Find out if we have
trained staff will be happy to help with all your needs.

About Bob

Bob started baking as a young child with his father who
owned a small bakery in a High Inchirvine in Scotland. He left
school and was lucky enough to secure a place in Paris at the
famous Ecole de Monsieur Le Patissier.
This started Bob on his, now famous, career path. He found
that he was able to improve on age-old recipes and
experimented with flavours and designs never before seen in
the baking school.

Figure 17.26 Before padding

Figure 17.27 shows the same part of the Home page after the CSS padding rule has been implemented. This now shows the content having been pushed away from the edge of the element.

Before

Figure 17.28 Setting the footer padding

If padding is set for elements that are next to one another, they will *not* overlap, i.e. if element 1 has padding of 10px and element 2 has padding of 10px

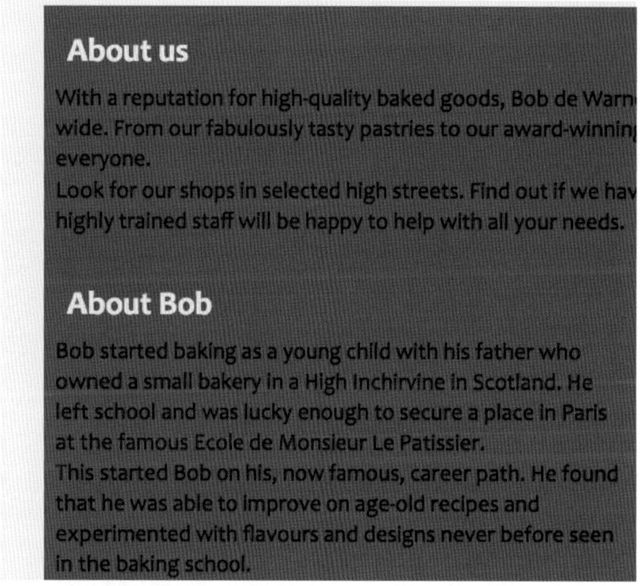

About us

With a reputation for high-quality baked goods, Bob de Warn
wide. From our fabulously tasty pastries to our award-winning
everyone.
Look for our shops in selected high streets. Find out if we hav
highly trained staff will be happy to help with all your needs.

About Bob

Bob started baking as a young child with his father who
owned a small bakery in a High Inchirvine in Scotland. He
left school and was lucky enough to secure a place in Paris
at the famous Ecole de Monsieur Le Patissier.
This started Bob on his, now famous, career path. He found
that he was able to improve on age-old recipes and
experimented with flavours and designs never before seen
in the baking school.

Figure 17.27 After padding

Padding can also be set individually as padding-top, padding-right, padding-bottom and padding-left, for example:

```
p{padding-top:10px; padding-right:5px;
padding-bottom:15px; padding-left:5px}
```

These four values can also be written in shorthand provided the order is as above.

```
p{padding:10px 5px 15px 5px}
```

This example shows how identifying the left and top padding affects the footer on each page.

```
footer{padding-left:10px; padding-top:20px}
```

Its effect is shown in Figure 17.28.

After

then the padding between the two elements will be 20px. This is because the padding is set around the content of the element.

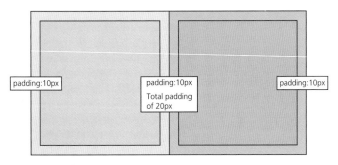

padding:10px padding:10px padding:10px

Total padding of 20px

Figure 17.29 Padding between elements

CHECK YOUR LEARNING

Now answer questions 15–21 (on pages 236–237) on controlling appearance and positioning of elements

Create horizontal navigation bars

List-style-type:none

At the moment, as can be seen in Figure 17.30 and on each page of the website, the navigation bar is displayed over the top of the next section, is in the default blue colour, is difficult to read and is bulleted.

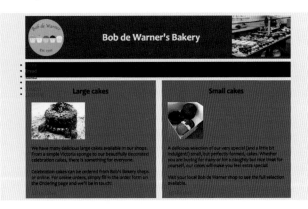

Figure 17.30 Current vertical navigation

The code for each of these links is written as shown here:

```
<nav>
<ul>
<li><a href="home.html">Home</a></li>
<li><a href="bread.html">Bread</a></li>
<li><a href="cakes.html">Cakes</a></li>
<li><a href="biscuits.html">Biscuits</a></li>
```

```
<li><a href="recipes.html">Recipes</a></li>
<li><a href="ordering.html">Ordering</a></li>
</ul>
</nav>
```

According to each wireframe, the navigation bar is to be displayed horizontally. To alter this, the style of the navigation bar needs to be altered.

First of all, the bullet points should be removed. It is possible to change the type of bullet points used by using the CSS property list-style-type. Some different ones are:

List Style	Example
list-style-type: circle	• Home
list-style-type: square	• Home
list-style-type: lower-roman	i. Home
list-style-type: lower-alpha	a. Home

However, in this case, each element of the navigation bar should have no bullet points displayed. A descendant selector is used to style the navigation bar:

```
nav ul{list-style-type:none}
```

A similar command is used to style the footer. This changes the navigation bar as shown in Figure 17.31.

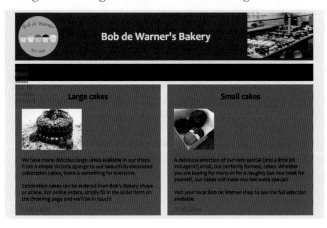

Figure 17.31 Bullet points removed

Now that the bullet points have been removed from each hyperlink in the navigation bar, the list must now be displayed horizontally.

Using the float property, each element in the navigation bar can be displayed alongside the other, i.e.

```
nav ul li{float:left}
```

will produce the navigation bar shown in Figure 17.32.

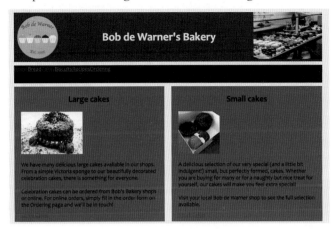

Figure 17.32 Navigation bar floated elements

This can be altered to

```
nav ul li{float:left;width:120px;
text-align:center}
```

so that the elements are not directly next to one another, as can be seen in Figure 17.33.

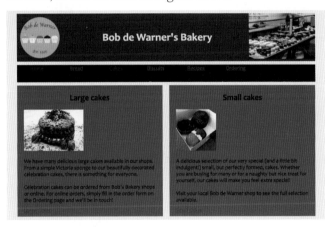

Figure 17.33 Navigation bar spaced out

Hover

Although the navigation bar is now much easier to view, the links themselves are still difficult to view against the background colour of the navigation bar.

To create an area around which to hover, the following CSS should be used. This will ensure that the box surrounding the hyperlink in the navigation bar also becomes a hyperlink. Note that descendant selectors are used again only to identify the hyperlinks in the navigation bar.

```
nav ul li a{display:block}
```

To move the hyperlinks away from the top of the navigation bar, some padding is added.

```
nav ul li a{display:block;padding:10px}
```

To change the colour of the hyperlinks, the following CSS style can be added.

```
nav a{color:#fbdfe6;font-size:22px}
```

And finally, the CSS style

```
nav ul li a:hover {background-color:#ec6988;
color:#340913}
```

can be added to give the effect shown in Figure 17.34. The **hover** selector is used to interact with an element when the mouse is moved over the element. It does not necessarily activate the element as in this case, but it can be set to do so.

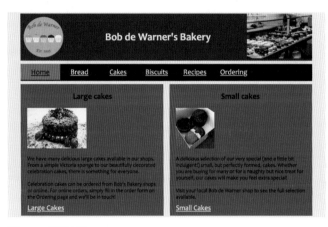

Figure 17.34 Hover

> **NOTE**
>
> The hyperlinks in each of the sections has been styled to match the colour scheme of the website using the
>
> style `main section a{color:#fbdfe6; font-size:22px}.`

> **CHECK YOUR LEARNING**
>
> **Now answer question 22 (on page 237) on create horizontal navigation bars**

Page layouts using CSS styling

A combination of all of the above may be used to achieve the layouts for some of the pages. Some examples of each follow. Note that there are other ways in which to achieve the same layouts, but the HTML and CSS that was used to create these pages is shown here.

Ordering page

The wireframe and web page layouts, once both HTML and CSS are completed, are shown in Figure 17.35.

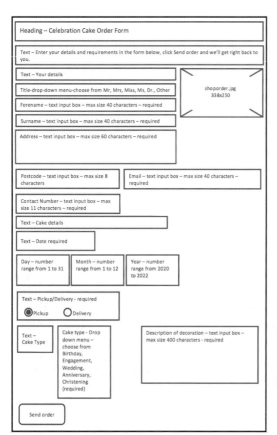

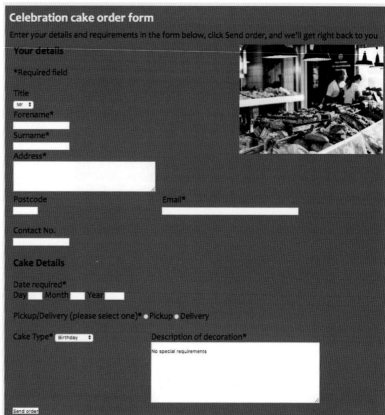

Figure 17.35 Ordering wireframe and page

For example, to move the Email and Description of decoration sections to the right-hand side of the ordering form, this class selector has been used in the stylesheet.

```
.formpart{width:300px;float:left;padding-right:50px}
```

Cake page

The Cake page has two separate boxes displayed side by side. Figure 17.36 shows both the wireframe and the corresponding web page, after HTML and CSS are completed.

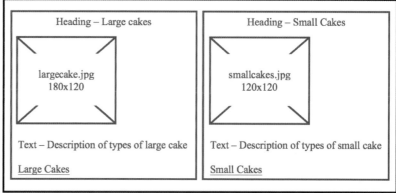

Figure 17.36 Cakes wireframe and page

In this case two id selectors were used to split the web page into two distinct parts. The two sections have been floated left and right and sizes given to each section.

```
#cakeleft{float:left;width:420px}

#cakeright{float:right;width:420px}
```

Recipe page

The Recipe page displays the recipe list on the left-hand side with the recipe and video on the right-hand side.

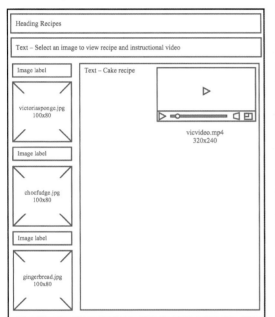

Figure 17.37 Recipes wireframe and page

On this page the panel on the left has an id selector to allow the images and headings to appear on the left. Both the recipe and video use class selectors so that they will appear on the right-hand side of the page.

```
#recipeleft{float:left}

.recipe{font-size:20px;margin-left:260px;
padding-top:10px}

.videoright{float:right}
```

> **CHECK YOUR LEARNING**
>
> **Now answer question 23 (on page 237) on page layouts using CSS styling**

QUESTIONS

Styling

1 What does CSS stand for?
2 What is CSS used for in a website?
3 State three ways in which CSS can be applied to a website.
4 State the effect these lines of inline styling would have on the phrase 'Caledonian Radio'.

a)
```
<p style="color:blue; text-align:center"> Caledonian Radio</p>
```

b)
```
<p style="background-color:yellow; color:magenta;text-align:right;font-size:24px"> Caledonian Radio</p>
```

5 Why should inline styling be avoided?
6 Where is the <style> tag placed when internal styling is used?
7 State the effect this section of internal styling would have on a web page.

```
<style>
    h1{color:red;font-size:28px;font-weight:bold}

    a{ background-color:black;color:magenta;font-size:22px}

    img{height:200px; width:300px}
</style>
```

8 An external stylesheet contains these rules:

```
div{color:yellow; font-family: Geneva, sans-serif; font-size:16pt}

h1{background-color:blue; color:yellow}
```

State what will happen to the linked pages if the rules are changed to the ones below:

```
div{color:orange; font-family: Georgia, serif; font-size:18pt; font-weight:bold}

h1{background-color:black; color:green}
```

9 What is the order in which styles should be applied?

Selectors

10 Using html selectors, write the rule to style the following tags:
  a) <h1> Make the text colour orange, font size 24 points, background colour black
  b) <p> Centre the text, text colour rgb(255,3,255), make the font Calibri
  c) <img> Change the size of the image to 300x200 pixels
11 The HTML code for the Come and Try page of the NoLUS (Northern League of Unusual Sports) website is shown below.

```
<html>
  <head>
    <title>Come and try</title>
  </head>
  <body>
    <header>
      <h1>Northern League of Unusual Sports</h1>
    </header>
    <nav>
      <ul>
        <li><a href="home.html">Home</a></a></li>
        <li><a href="sports.html">Sports page</a></a></li>
        <li><a href="frisbee.html">Ultimate Frisbee</a></li>
        <li><a href="programme.html">Programme</a></li>
        <li><a href="comeandtry.html">Come and try</a></li>
        <li><a href="booking.html">Booking</a></li>
```

```
        </ul>
    </nav>
    <main>
        <h1>Come and try — Cheese rolling</h1>
        <section> <!--section one-->
            <p>An introduction to the world-famous cheese-rolling event. The
original and best is held annually on the Spring Bank Holiday at Cooper's Hill
near Gloucester. It was originally held for the residents of the local village of
Brockworth, Gloucestershire. However, participants now come from as far away as
the USA and New Zealand to chase the large cheese round down the hill. The event
at Cooper's Hill involves chasing a 7 to 9 pound (about 3-4kg) round of Double
Gloucester cheese down the very steep hill. The cheese starts rolling first before
the first competitor is allowed to start and can reach speeds of up to 70mph.</p>
<p>It was cancelled in 2009 after health and safety concerns, because in recent years,
some competitors have suffered from broken bones — the highest casualty list being in
1997 when 33 competitors had to be treated for injuries.</p>
<p>The winner, of course, wins the round of Double Gloucester!</p>
<p>Come and try our slightly smaller event with smaller rounds of cheese. There will
be mini competitions down our hill for children and adults alike. Events start each
day at 2 p.m. Check out the Programme of events to see when each race will take
place on each day.</p>
        </section>
        <section><!--section two-->
            <img src="images/cheeseroll1.jpg">
            <img src="images/cheeseroll2.jpg">
        </section>
        <section><!--section three-->
            <video width="320" height="240" controls>
              <source src="cheeseroll1.mp4" type="video/mp4">
            </video>
        </section>
    </main>
    <footer>
        <ul>
            <li><a href="contact.html">Contact us</a></a></li>
            <li><a href="map.html">Site map</a></li>
            <li><a href="copyright.html">Copyright Notice</a></li>
        </ul>
    </footer>
 </body>
</html>
```

In the questions which follow, write CSS rules for an external stylesheet to style the HTML tags, classes, ids and sections.

a) i) <body> Make the page background colour azure.
   ii) <p> Change the font of all paragraphs to Calibri, 14 points, coloured honeydew and centred.

b) Create class selector rules to style:
   i) Section one and three – make the first and third section background colours darkslategray where class="onethree"
   ii) Section two – make the second section background colour seagreen where class="two"
   iii) Navigation bar and footer– make the navigation bar and footer background colour darkcyan where class="navfoot"
   iv) Make a rule called cheeseimg to style the images' size 300x200 pixels where class="cheeseimg"

c) Create id selector rules to style the:
   i) Navigation bar hyperlinks – make the font Candara, 14 points and colour honeydew where id="navhyp"
   ii) Footer hyperlinks – make the font Candara, 12 points and colour honeydew where id="foothyp"
   iii) Come and Try-Cheese Rolling <h1> - make the font Candara, 18 points, background colour seagreen and the font colour honeydew where id="cheeseheading".

12 Some of the CSS rules used to style the margins and paddings of the Airshow's website are shown here. Rewrite the CSS rules in the most efficient way using grouping selectors.

a)
```
body {margin:auto}
h1 {margin-left:120px;margin-top:50px}
header{margin-top:10px;
margin-bottom:10px }
main{margin-top:10px; margin-
bottom:10px }
section{margin-bottom:10px}
nav{margin-top:5px}
footer{margin-top:5px}
```

b)
```
section{padding-left:10px; padding-
right:5px}
p{padding:10px}
h2{padding:10px}
footer{padding-left:10px; padding-
top:20px;padding-bottom:5px}
```

13 Caledonian Radio have chosen a variety of colours for backgrounds and fonts for their website. Rewrite these CSS rules in the most efficient way using grouping selectors.

```
body{color: #FFF5FC}
h1{color:#191970}
section{background-color: #B0719E}
p{color: #F6FFF5}
h2{color:#191970}
```

14 The navigation bar on each web page of the Northern League of Unusual Sports uses descendant selectors, as shown here.

```
nav ul li a{display:block;padding:10px}
```

Explain why descendant selectors are used to display the navigation bar.

Controlling appearance and positioning of elements

15 Write an id selector called 'plane' to change the size of an image to 640x480 pixels.
16 Write a class selector called 'helicoptervid' to change the size of the video window to 400x300 pixels.
17 Write html selectors to set the:
   a) body width to 800 pixels
   b) header height to 200 pixels
   c) footer height to 100 pixels
   d) navigation bar height to 130 pixels
18 Rewrite this margin in shorthand form.

```
p{margin-top:10px; margin-right:20px;
margin-bottom:10px; margin-left:15px}
```

19 Describe what happens when this margin is set for the html body element.

```
body {margin:auto}
```

20 Caledonia Radio's header currently looks like the image in Figure 17.38.

SBC - Radio Caledonia

Welcome!

Figure 17.38 Header of Caledonia Radio

It should look like the annotated wireframe shown in Figure 17.39.

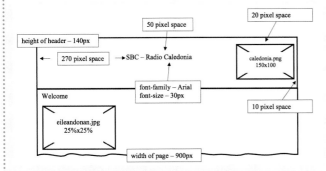

Figure 17.39 Annotated wireframe header

a) Copy and complete the id selector calbanner and amend the original HTML code to float the banner to the left of the browser window and change the size of the image to 150x100 pixels.

```
HTML

<header>

<h1>SBC – Radio Caledonia</h1>

<img src="../images/caledonia.png">

</header>

CSS

#calbanner{float:_____;
width:_____; height:_____}
```

b) The header element now looks as shown in Figure 17.40.

Figure 17.40 Header of Caledonia Radio

i) Identify the problem shown in Figure 17.40.
ii) Name and describe the element that needs to be added to allow the image to be in the correct position. Explain why you chose this CSS element.
iii) Copy and complete the CSS below to change where the image and page heading will be displayed in the browser.

```
h1{_____;font-
family:Arial;font-size:30px;}
```

c) Figure 17.41 shows the page after the CSS styles in part (b)(iii) were applied.

Figure 17.41 Header of Caledonia Radio

The size of the header is too small to fit both the heading and the image. It should be altered to the height shown in the wireframe in Figure 17.39. The page should only have a width of 900 pixels. Copy and complete the CSS rules below to effect this change on the page.

```
body {margin:_____}

body {_____:900px}

header{height:_____}
```

d) Figure 17.42 shows the position after the last CSS rules were applied.

SBC - Radio Caledonia

Welcome!

Figure 17.42 Header of Caledonia Radio

Margins and padding should now be used to move the text to the position indicated on the wireframe. Explain the difference between margins and padding.

e) Copy and complete the CSS below to change where the image and page heading will now be displayed in the browser as per the annotated wireframe in Figure 17.39.

```
header{margin-_____:_____}

h1{padding-_____:_____;
padding-_____:_____}

#calbanner{_____-
right:_____; float:right;
width:150px;height:100px}
```

21 What effect would the clear (both) rule have on a web page?

Creating horizontal navigation bars

22 a) Using descendant selectors, write the CSS rule to remove the bullet points from the hyperlinks in an unordered list in a footer.
b) Using descendant selectors, write the CSS rule to create a hover area around a hyperlink in an unordered list in the navigation bar. The background colour should be dark red and the text colour should be linen.

Page layouts using CSS styling

23 Figure 17.43 shows an annotated wireframe of part of the feedback form for the Inverblair Airshow. Each <section> has been assigned a class selector to identify it.

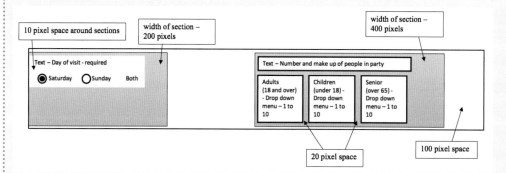

Figure 17.43 Feedback form part 1

a) A CSS file has been created to style the elements of this part of the page so that the *Day of visit* <section> is placed next to the *Party* <section> on the page. The html and class selectors which will style this are shown here.

Copy and complete the html and class selectors to style the page so that it appears as in the annotated wireframe.

```
section{_____}
.party{_____}
.people{_____}
.left{_____;}
```

b) State what effect the following style rules will have on the Feedback page.

i) `p{padding:10px}`

ii) `h1{display:inline;float:left;color:aliceblue}`

c) Figure 17.44 shows an annotated wireframe of another part of the same feedback form for the Inverblair Airshow. This single <section> has been further sub-divided into <div> elements each of which has been assigned an id selector.

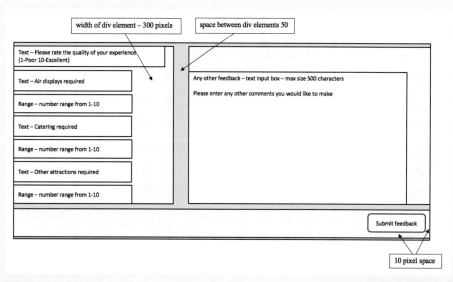

Figure 17.44 Feedback form part 2

The id selectors which will style this in <div> elements are shown here:

Copy and complete these id selectors to style the page so that it appears as in the annotated wireframe.

```
#rate{_____}
#feedback{_____ }
#button{_____}
```

KEY POINTS

Styling

- CSS is a language used to describe how a web page will be presented in a browser.
- CSS allows the web developer to easily control the layout of all the web pages in a website.
- There are three different ways to apply CSS to an HTML document:
  - inline
  - internal (embedded)
  - external (linked).
- Inline styles are used within HTML tags.
- Internal or embedded styles are defined in the <head> tag of a website and are used to apply to the whole page.
- Internal styling uses the <style> tag.
- External or linked styles are created as a separate file.

Selectors

- An HTML selector is a way of identifying styles in internal and external stylesheets.
- The class selector allows the developer to pinpoint exactly where in the HTML document the style is to be applied.
- The class selector uses a full stop before the class selector name.
- The id selector is used identify and style one element in an HTML document.
- The id selector uses the hash (#) character to identify each element to be styled.
- The font-family property contains a list of fonts to be tried when loading a web page.
- The font-size property indicates the size of the font to be used.
- A grouping selector is one in which groups of html elements are to have the same CSS styles applied to them.

Controlling appearance and positioning of elements

- A descendant selector is used to specifically identify one part of a web page to style it separately from the rest.
- The color property indicates the colour of the font to be displayed.
- Colour schemes should be carefully selected so that the colours work well together.
- CSS can be used to reduce the size of each image using the height and width properties.
- CSS can be used to reduce the size of the header, body, main and footer elements.
- The float property allows images to be floated to the left or right.

- The clear:both rule is used to negate the impact of a float property.
- The display property controls the layout of a web page.
- The display property has three values:
  - block
  - inline
  - none.
- The display:block property takes up the full width of the container element.
- The display:inline property only takes up as much space as is required by the text in the container element.
- The display:none property will hide the container which uses it and will display nothing on screen.
- The box model is made up of margins, border, padding and the content of each elements.
- Margins are used to specify the space around an element and are transparent.
- The margin can be set all around the element using *margin*.
- Each side of the element can be specified separately:
  - margin-top
  - margin-right
  - margin-bottom
  - margin-left.
- Margin properties' values are written in px, pt, cm or can be set as a percentage (%) of the width of the containing element.
- The body margin property should be set to auto.
- The padding sets the space around *content* of each element and are transparent.
- The padding can be set all around the content using *padding*.
- Each side of the content can be specified separately:
  - padding-top
  - padding-right
  - padding-bottom
  - padding-left.
- Padding properties' values are written in px, pt, cm or can be set as a percentage (%) of the width of the containing element.

Create horizontal navigation bars

- List-style-type:none removes bullet points from a bulleted list.
- A float property is used to display the navigation bar horizontally.
- The hover selector is used to interact with an element when the mouse is moved over the element.

Page layouts using CSS styling

- There may be more than one way to achieve the same effect using CSS.

239

Chapter 18 Implementation (JavaScript)

> This chapter looks at creating web pages that include interactivity.
>
> The following topics are covered:
>
> - Describe, exemplify and implement coding of JavaScript functions related to mouse events:
>   - onmouseover
>   - onmouseout
>   - onclick.

Scripting languages

A scripting language is a programming language that allows the user to carry out or automate tasks, which would otherwise have to be done as a series of single steps. Scripting languages may be used to automate tasks in application packages, web browsers and operating systems. Examples of scripting languages include JavaScript®, VBScript® and AppleScript®.

JavaScript

JavaScript was invented for use in web browsers. It was created by Brendan Eich in 1995, while working at Netscape. The purpose of JavaScript is to make web pages more dynamic and interactive. For instance, when viewing a web page, a script may be activated by the user when clicking a button or rolling the mouse pointer over or away from a particular area on the web page.

A simple example of this interaction is shown in the script below:

```
<!DOCTYPE html>

<html>

<body>

<h2 id="text">Click the button below for a message</h2>

<button type="button" onclick='document.
getElementById("text").innerHTML = "Computing Science is
amazing!!"'>Click Me for a message!</button>

</body>

</html>
```

Click the button below for a message

Click Me for a message!

Computing Science is amazing!!

Click Me for a message!

Figure 18.1 Simple JavaScript interaction

Advantages of JavaScript

JavaScript has a number of advantages. These include:

- it may be included in the HTML code of a web page.
- the code will operate without an internet connection, without having to communicate with a server and is relatively fast, as the code is processed by the browser software.
- it can load only the required content and the whole web page need not be reloaded.
- it is a fully-featured programming language; you may be using JavaScript as your main programming language for this course.

Disadvantages of JavaScript

- Security: hackers can use JavaScript to run malicious code or malware on a user's computer. However, users can disable the JavaScript code from working by changing the settings in the browser.
- Advertising: JavaScript may be used to create adverts and pop-up windows, which can annoy users.
- Layout: the output from JavaScript may look different on different browsers.

Whether the following feature of JavaScript is an advantage or a disadvantage, is left for the reader to decide. JavaScript can be used to write cookies, which are used to identify and track visitors to web pages, by storing data on the user's computer. This may be convenient for users who frequently visit a site, such as for online shopping. You can read more about cookies in Chapter 24.

Figure 18.2 Cookies in Google Chrome™

REMINDERS

Remember not to confuse the programming language Java™ with the scripting language JavaScript. Java is a compiled language used to create stand-alone programs, including applets. JavaScript is used with a web browser program and is an interpreted language.

In a similar fashion to CSS (see Chapter 17), we will look at three ways to apply JavaScript to an HTML document:

- inline HTML
- internal script
- external file.

HTML events

In order to implement each of these methods, an event needs to be triggered. An event is how HTML uses JavaScript to run code when the user or browser does something in a web page. Clicking a button is one example of an event. A message that appears when a web page has completed loading or when the user closes a browser window are other examples. Events in JavaScript are run by **event handlers**. An event handler is JavaScript code which is in the HTML document and not inside script tags. It means that when the user moves the mouse over or clicks on, for example, an image, then some JavaScript code is executed.

In order to make sure that different web browsers deal with each type of event in the same manner, a standardised model has been set up. This model is known as the Document Object Model (DOM). The DOM contains a specific set of events that can trigger JavaScript.

For Higher Computing Science we will look at three different events:

- onmouseover: triggered when the user moves their mouse onto and then hovers over an object such as an image.
- onmouseout: triggered when the user moves their mouse away from an object on the screen.
- onclick: triggered when an element such as a button, link or image is clicked by the user.

You can find out about more HTML events at https:// www.w3schools.com/tags/ref_eventattributes.asp.

Inline HTML

Inline JavaScript involves entering the code for the event straight into the HTML. On the ordering page, this script is included as a clickable button to 'send' the order.

```
<input type="submit" onclick="
alert('Order sent. ')" value="Send order">
```

When this script is run on the ordering page, an alert box is generated with the message 'Order sent' as shown in Figure 18.3.

Figure 18.3 Ordering page

Rollover images using inline JavaScript

Bread page – change the image

This script is included as an inline script to switch between two images.

```
<img class="breadimages" src="../images/white1.jpg" onmouseover=" this.src='../images/
white2.jpg'" onmouseout="this.src='../images/white1.jpg'">
```

This script will initially display the one image of bread. When the onmouseover event is triggered by the user moving the mouse over the first image, the image will change to a different image of bread. When the onmouseout event is triggered by the user moving the mouse away, the original bread image will be displayed.

Figure 18.4 demonstrates how this inline JavaScript changes the image of one bread image on the bread page when the onmouseover event is triggered.

this – refers to the object being handled, in this case the <img> element.

src – refers to the file path where the original and replacement images are found.

Before

After

Wholemeal bread

All our loaves are made with organic wholemeal flour

Come in to our shops to try our large range of wholemeal breads.

Try our range of vegan wholemeal loaves. Amazing with soups and your favourite peanut butter!

Figure 18.4 Bread page onmouseover event

Biscuits page – change the size of an image

This final example makes use of the 'this.style' element and will change the size of each of the images from small to large.

style – the CSS style to be applied to this element.

width='300px' – change the width of the image to 300 pixels.

```
<img class="biscuits" src="../images/
shortbread.jpg" style="margin-left:10px"
onmouseover="this.style.width>='300px';this.
style.height='200px'" onmouseout="this.
style.width>='200px';this.style.
height='133px'">
```

When the onmouseover event is triggered by the user moving the mouse over the image, the image will increase in size to 300x200 pixels. When the onmouseout event is triggered by the user moving the mouse away, the original image will be displayed.

Figure 18.5 demonstrates how this inline JavaScript changes the size of the image on the biscuits page when the onmouseover event is triggered.

As can be seen, this makes for an extremely long line of HTML code. While this works, it is not particularly efficient or readable, as it has to be repeated for each image whose size is to be changed. It can also mean that loading of the web page is slow and can make maintenance tricky. We will look at how this can be implemented using internal JavaScript with a function.

Before

After

Figure 18.5 Biscuit page onmouseover event

Internal script

Internal JavaScript uses individual statements to define functions which can be placed inside the <head> or <body> section of an HTML page and can be referred to at points in the HTML document. All JavaScript statements should be written between <script> tags.

Within the <script> tags, a JavaScript **function** can contain any number of JavaScript statements. A function is a piece of JavaScript that can be referred to and run as many times as required. The function runs when an event such as a button onclick or onmouseover event occurs. Because the function can be referred to as many times as required in the HTML document, it makes it much more efficient than rewriting the same code over again.

Using the rollover example from before, this could be written:

```
In the head tags
```

```
function large(thisBiscuit)
    {thisBiscuit.style.width='300px';
    thisBiscuit.style.height='200px';
    }
function small(thisBiscuit)
    {thisBiscuit.style.width='200px';
    thisBiscuit.style.height='133px';
    }
```

```
In the body tags
```

```
<img class="biscuits" src="../images/shortbread.jpg" style="margin-left:10px"
onmouseover="large(this)" onmouseout="small(this)">
```

In the head, the function is created and the script required is inserted. In this case the script sets and resets the size of the image when the mouse is moved over and away from the image. The function only needs to be written once and can be called as many times as is required in the body section of the HTML code, rather than rewriting the same code over and over again.

This – is an actual parameter and passes the value (in this case the image) to the function.

In this example, when the onmouseover(this) event is triggered, the function large(thisBiscuit) is called and the size of the image changes from 200x133 pixels to 300x200 pixels. When the onmouseout(this) event is triggered, the function small(thisBiscuit) is called and the image size changes back to 200x133 pixels.

Figure 18.6 shows how the page looks in the browser before and after the onmouseover event. Notice that the way in which the interaction works is no different but the code is much more efficient.

Before

After

Figure 18.6 Biscuits page with functions

Reveal hidden elements

Recipes page

In the head tags

```
<head>
<script>
function Victoria(){
document.getElementById("vicsp").style.display="block";
document.getElementById("choccake").style.display="none";
document.getElementById("gingerb").style.display="none";
}
function Chocolate(){
document.getElementById("vicsp").style.display="none";
document.getElementById("choccake").style.display="block";
document.getElementById("gingerb").style.display="none";
}
...
</script>
</head>
...
```

> JavaScript functions which will run depending on which image is clicked. Notice the id attributes in brackets which will identify the element to run once clicked, e.g. choccake will find the element with the same id attribute in the <body>.

In the body tags

```
<div>
    <h2>Victoria Sponge</h2>
        <img src="../images/vicsponge.jpg" onclick="Victoria()">
</div>
<div>
        <h2>Chocolate Cake</h2>
        <img src="../images/chocolatecake.jpg" onclick="Chocolate()">

</div>
<div>
        <h2>Gingerbread</h2>
        <img src="../images/gingerbread.jpg" onclick="Gingerbread()">
</div>
...
<section id="vicsp" style="display:block">
```

> When the image of the chocolate cake is clicked on, the function Chocolate is run in the <head> tags.

> Displays this recipe when the page loads.

```
        <div class="videoright">

                <video width="320" height="240" controls>

                <source src="../videos/vicvideo.mp4" type="video/mp4">

                </video>

        </div>

        <div class="recipe">

                <h3>Ingredients - Victoria Sponge<h3>

                <ul>

                <li>200g butter</li>

                <li>200g caster sugar</li>

                <li>200g self-raising flour</li>

                <li>3 eggs</li>

                <li>1tsp vanilla essence</li>

                <li>Strawberry jam</li>

                <li>300ml of whipping cream</li>

                <li>Caster sugar to sprinkle on top</li>
```

> Section of HTML that has the id="choccake" referred to in the function in the <head> section

```
                </ul>

...

<section id="choccake" style="display:none">

<div class="videoright">

    <video width="320" height="240" controls>

    <source src="../videos/chocvideo.mp4" type="video/mp4">

    </video>

    </div>
```

> This is hidden until the chocolate cake is clicked on. It then replaces the Victoria sponge recipe with the Chocolate cake recipe on the right-hand side of the display by referring to the id attribute "choccake" and displaying the appropriate text and video.

```
    <div class="recipe">

            <h3>Ingredients - Chocolate Cake</h3>

            <ul>

...
```

Before

After

Figure 18.7 Recipes page before and after the onclick event

As an alternative, document.getElementById is used to specifically identify part of an HTML document. However, instead of simply applying the JavaScript to the current element, it must have an associated id attribute in order that the relevant element may be identified and run.

External file

The final method of defining and using JavaScript is by means of an external file. In this method the scripts are defined in a separate file and a link to the file is then placed inside the <script> tags using the src attribute in the <head> tags.

Using a file means that the script can be referred to in many HTML files without having to be rewritten. It also means that the script only has to be updated once for it to be applied to each of the HTML files.

Finally, it separates the HTML and the JavaScript code which means that all pages should be faster to load once the JavaScript file has been downloaded.

In both the Bread and Small Cakes, an external JavaScript file has been used to operate clicking the buttons and moving the mouse over the images of the mini-cakes to give information about each cake. Note: on both pages images and text are hidden when the page first loads. Only triggering the events cause elements to be displayed.

This means that for each of these pages, the JavaScript code is separate and can be easily updated. It also means that there is not a large amount of code, particularly on the small cakes page, in the <head> section of the HTML document.

Reveal hidden elements with an external JavaScript

In the head tags

Contains the link to the JavaScript file.

Bread page

```
<script src="../javascript/bread.js"></script>
```

Small cakes page

```
<script src="../javascript/smallcakes.js"></script>
```

In the body tags

Contains the function calls and sections of text and images to display.

Bread page

247

```
<button class="button" onclick="showwhitebread()">White</button>
<button class="button" onclick="showbrownbread()">Brown</button>
...
<section id="wholemeal" style="display:none">
<p class = "largeHeading">Wholemeal bread</p>

...

</section>

...
```

> Each of these lines run the function indicated when the onclick event is triggered.

Small cakes page

```
<img class ="small" src="../images/LemonTart.jpg" onmouseover="showlemontart()">
<img class ="small" src="../images/MiniLemonMerginuePie.jpg" onmouseover="showlmp()">
...
<section id="lemon" style="display:none">
<p class = "largeHeading">Lemon Tart</p>
...
</section>
```

> Each of these lines run the function indicated when the onmouseover event is triggered.

In the external JavaScript file

Contains the functions which will identify which element to display on the page when either event occurs.

Bread page

```
function showwholemealbread(){
document.getElementById("white").style.display="none";
document.getElementById("brown").style.display="none";
document.getElementById("wholemeal").style.display="block";
document.getElementById("sourdough").style.display="none";
document.getElementById("multigrain").style.display="none";
}
```

> As before, document.getElementById will identify the element with a specific id in the HTML code and display what appears in that element.

Small cakes page

```
function showlemontart(){
document.getElementById("lemon").style.display="block";
document.getElementById("lmp").style.display="none";
document.getElementById("cheesecake").style.display="none";
document.getElementById("raspberry").style.display="none";
document.getElementById("duo").style.display="none";
document.getElementById("pear").style.display="none";
document.getElementById("bombe").style.display="none";
document.getElementById("vanilla").style.display="none";
document.getElementById("egg").style.display="none";
document.getElementById("flan").style.display="none";
document.getElementById("apple").style.display="none";
document.getElementById("eclair").style.display="none";
}
```

Notice that the external script does not contain the script tags, simply the function to run the script. The code inside the body tags does not change at all. It behaves as if the script was still present in the code itself and not in a separate file.

Figures 18.8 and 18.9 show how both these pages look before and after the JavaScript function has been run.

Before

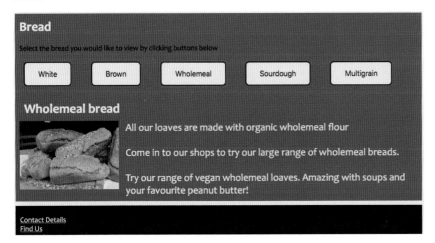

After

Figure 18.8 Onclick event on bread page

Before   **After**

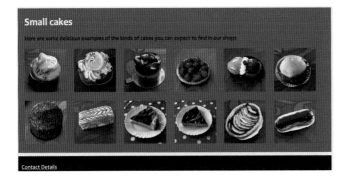   

Figure 18.9 Onmouseover event on small cakes page

CHECK YOUR LEARNING

Now answer questions 1–20 below

QUESTIONS

1 What is a scripting language?
2 Name two scripting languages.
3 What is the purpose of JavaScript?
4 State two advantages of JavaScript.
5 State two disadvantages of JavaScript.
6 State the three main ways in which JavaScript can be applied to a HTML document.
7 What is an event?
8 What is an event handler?
9 State three types of events.
10 Describe what will happen when this JavaScript event is run.

```
<h2 onclick="this.innerHTML = 'You
clicked me!!'">Click me quick!</h2>
```

11 Describe what will happen when this JavaScript event is run.

```
<img src="../images/studio1.png"
onmouseover="this.src='../images/studio2.
png'" onmouseout="this.src='../images/
studio1.png'">
```

12 Describe what will happen when this JavaScript event is run.

```
<img src="../images/chessboxing.
jpg" onmouseover="this.style.
width='400px';this.style.
height='266px'" onmouseout="this.style.
width='200px';this.style.height='133px'">
```

13 Why is excessive use of inline JavaScript not considered to be good practice?
14 Where can internal JavaScript functions be placed in an HTML document?
15 Which tags should be used to contain a JavaScript function?
16 Describe what will happen when this JavaScript function is run.

```
<html>
<head>
<script>
function blue(thisText)
    {thisText.style.color='blue';
        }
function red(thisText)
    {thisText.style.color='red';
    }
</script>
</head>
<body>
<h1 style="color:red"
onmouseover="blue(this)"
onmouseout="red(this)">Change my
colour!</h1>
</body>
</html>
```

17 Inverblair would like users of their website to be able to click on small images of planes to be able to see larger versions of the same image. The JavaScript shown here increases the size of the image. Rewrite the JavaScript using functions with parameter passing in the <head> tags and calls to the functions in the <body> tags.

```
<img src="images/vulcan.jpg" width='300'
height='200'

onclick="this.style.width='900px';this.
style.height='600px'"

onmouseout="this.style.width='300px';this.
style.height='200px'">
```

18 Write JavaScript functions to change from the image frog.jpg to toad.jpg from the *images* folder using onmouseover and onmouseout events. Assume that the script is run from an HTML file stored in an *HTML* folder.

19 State two advantages of using an external JavaScript file over an internal JavaScript file.

20 One of the user requirements from the Northern League of Unusual Sports was to have information about each sport with photographs and videos from last year's competition. Describe what will happen when the following scripts are implemented.

HTML file

```
…

<p class="largeHeading">Sports you can see this year</p>

<p class="text"> Move your mouse over the small images to find out a little more
about the sports you can see at the NoLUS championships.</p><br>

<img  class ="small" src="images/shinkick.jpg" onmouseover="showShinKicking()">

<img  class ="small" src="images/iron.jpg" onmouseover="showExtremeIroning()">

<img  class ="small" src="images/toe.jpg" onmouseover="showToeWrestling()">

<img  class ="small" src="images/bog.jpg" onmouseover="showBogSnorkelling()">

<img  class ="small" src="images/lawn.jpg" onmouseover="showLawnmowerRacing()">

<img  class ="small" src="images/carry.jpg" onmouseover="showWifeCarrying()">

<img  class ="small" src="images/chessb.jpg" onmouseover="showChessBoxing()">

<img  class ="small" src="images/pudding.jpg" onmouseover="showBlackPudding()">

</section>

<section id="shin" style="display:none">

     <p class = "largeHeading">Shin kicking</p>

     <img class="large" src="images/shinkick.jpg">

…

<section id="pudding" style="display:none">

     <p class = "largeHeading">Black pudding throwing</p>

     <img class="large" src="images/pudding.jpg">

     <p class="sporttext">Yes you heard it right!<br><br>

     Much throwing around of our famous Lancashire black pudding.

     <br><br>

     Competitors must hurl a black pudding at a Yorkshire pudding balanced on a 10m
plinth.

     The winner is the person who dislodges the most Yorkshire puddings.</p>

     <video width="320" height="240" controls>

          <source src="videos/bpuddingvideo.mp4" type="video/mp4">

     </video>

</section>
```

JavaScript file

```javascript
function showShinKicking(){
document.getElementById("shin").style.display="block";
document.getElementById("ironing").style.display="none";
document.getElementById("toe").style.display="none";
document.getElementById("bog").style.display="none";
document.getElementById("lawnmower").style.display="none";
document.getElementById("carry").style.display="none";
document.getElementById("chessbox").style.display="none";
document.getElementById("pudding").style.display="none";
}
...

function showBlackPudding(){
document.getElementById("shin").style.display="none";
document.getElementById("ironing").style.display="none";
document.getElementById("toe").style.display="none";
document.getElementById("bog").style.display="none";
document.getElementById("lawnmower").style.display="none";
document.getElementById("carry").style.display="none";
document.getElementById("chessbox").style.display="none";
document.getElementById("pudding").style.display="block";
}
```

KEY POINTS

- A scripting language is a programming language that allows the user to carry out or automate tasks.
- JavaScript was created for use in web browsers.
- The purpose of JavaScript is to make web pages more dynamic and interactive.
- JavaScript advantages include:
  - it may be included in the HTML code of a web page
  - the code will operate without an internet connection
  - it can load only the required content of a web page
  - it is a fully featured programming language.
- JavaScript disadvantages include:
  - security: hackers can use JavaScript to run malware
  - advertising: JavaScript may be used to create pop-up windows
  - layout: the output from JavaScript may look different on different browsers.

- JavaScript can be used to write cookies, which are used to identify and track visitors to web pages.
- JavaScript is used with a web browser program and is an interpreted language.
- There are three ways to apply JavaScript to an HTML document:
  - inline HTML
  - internal script
  - external file.
- JavaScript is used with a web browser program and is an interpreted language.
- HTML events are executed using JavaScript.
- An event is how HTML uses JavaScript to run code when the user or browser does something in a web page.

- Events in JavaScript are run by event handlers.
- An event handler is JavaScript code which is in the HTML document and not inside script tags.
- Three commonly used event types are:
  - onmouseover
  - onmouseout
  - onclick.
- Inline JavaScript involves entering the code for the event straight into the HTML.
- Internal JavaScript uses individual statements to define functions which can be placed inside the <head> or <body> section of an HTML page.
- Each statement should be written between <script> tags.
- A function is a piece of JavaScript that can be referred to and run as many times as required.
- External JavaScript scripts are defined in a separate file and a link to the file is placed inside the <script> tags using the src attribute in the <head> tags.
- The external script does not contain the script tags, simply the function to run the script.

Chapter 19 Testing

This chapter looks at how website testing takes place. The following topics are covered:

- Describe, exemplify and implement usability of a prototype testing using:
  - personas
  - test cases
  - scenarios.
- Describe and exemplify testing implemented websites using:
  - input validation
  - navigational bar works
  - media content displays correctly.
- Describe and exemplify compatibility testing:
  - device-type: tablet, smartphone, desktop
  - browser.

Testing

The website must be tested to make sure that it meets the original design and it operates as intended, for instance, input is validated in forms, navigation works and media content (images, videos and sounds) displays correctly.

Low fidelity prototype testing

Usability testing

Websites are tested in terms of their usability, that is, how easy the website is to use and achieve specific goals with actual users or the clients who have commissioned the website. Usability testing is started at the very beginning of the process particularly when using Agile methodology. Usability testing continues throughout the development process as the project is broken down into smaller chunks for both developers and clients. See Chapter 1 for more on Agile methodology.

More specifically, usability testing starts at the wireframe stage where users are involved in testing the page layout (how the information is presented to the user) and simple navigational structure. Once a low-fidelity prototype has been created, the client can test areas like navigation, colour scheme chosen and any interaction. Progression is then made to a high-fidelity (clickable) prototype and eventually the final build of the product where users can interact fully with the website.

During usability testing of the low fidelity prototype, the client is asked to complete a set of tasks whilst being observed by the developer. During the testing, notes are taken where the client experiences problems or are confused by what they are being asked to do but no interaction takes place as the developer will not be present when users are actually using the website.

If, as the tests progress with other users, the same problems or confusion arise, recommendations will be made and action taken to resolve the issues encountered. It is important not ask for opinions, as the user is not being asked whether or not they like the content of the website, it is more about whether or not they can perform certain tasks with ease.

It is much cheaper and easier to fix a paper-based low-fidelity prototype, rather than at the end of the website's development.

Personas

Personas are fictitious users which are created to accurately represent the individuals or audience who are likely to be using the website and can be related to the age and experience of the user. If the website is created with a specific persona in mind, then it gives developers a clear idea of the target audience. Personas should be created at the analysis stage to focus on those who are likely to be the main users of the website instead of trying to represent as many users as possible.

For example, one persona for Bob's website could be a student who would like to bake a chocolate cake for a party and needs a simple recipe. A second could be a customer who wants to buy a birthday cake for his daughter and would like to order it online to be collected in the shop. And a final one could be an elderly customer of Bob's shops who wants to see the selection of small cakes that are available.

Test cases

Test cases are used when specific features of the website need to be tested and a series of instructions need to be followed to complete the task. These test cases would be created from the initial user requirements. Some examples are shown below.

From the functional requirements:

- Each recipe sub-page should display recipe instructions and an instructional video on how to make each cake.

'Click on the Recipes link. Select Gingerbread from the images on the left of the window. Click the video on the right-hand side of the window.'

or

From the end-user requirements:

- Users would like to be able to select small images of baked goods to see larger versions on the page with a description of each.

'Click on the Cakes link. Click on the Small Cakes link. move the pointer over a raspberry tart.'

or

- The Ordering page should provide a simple form for customers to order celebration cakes.

'Click on the Ordering link. Enter your name, address, contact telephone number and email address. Enter the date 14th July 2021. Select Pickup. Select Birthday from the Cake type drop-down menu. Enter the description 'Happy 15th Birthday Emma' in the Description of decoration box. Click the Send order button.'

Scenarios

Scenarios are open-ended tasks in which the user has to perform a series of tasks based on a situation. For example, these could be something like:

'Order an Anniversary cake for a specific date with an appropriate message on the cake.'

or

'Find a cake recipe that takes less than an hour to make.'

or

'Find an example of a wedding cake in celebration cakes.'

For more information on how user testing should be performed visit: https://www.smashingmagazine.com/2018/03/guide-user-testing/

To see an example of how usability testing can be done with a paper prototype, visit this YouTube link to BlueDuckLabs: https://www.youtube.com/watch?v=9wQkLthhHKA.

Figure 19.1 Website testing

Implemented website testing

Once the website has been implemented, a number of tests need to be carried out. These include testing:

- input validation
- navigation bar working
- media content displays correctly.

Testing any form of software whether or not it is a website will normally involve some kind of test plan.

In testing websites, it is usually a good idea to draw a table of what has to be tested with expected and actual results for each noted. For example:

- When testing input validation, each element in the form would be tested to ensure that only valid data can be input.
- When testing navigation, each of the hyperlinks on each page would be tested.
- When testing media content, each page's content (images, videos, audio and text) would be listed in the table.

Input validation: forms

Forms that are created require some validation so that the data entered is correct. Validation cannot correct errors in spelling or users entering incorrect personal details. However, it can be set up so that data which can be validated is accepted. For example, dates, limits on text length or items chosen from drop-down menus cannot be incorrectly entered before the data is transmitted to the server. Chapter 16 looked at the following kinds of input validation for the ordering form on Bob's website:

- restricted choice check
- range check
- length check
- presence check.

Each of the areas that used these checks must be tested to ensure that these do, in fact, work.

In the examples which follow, each test has been carried out to make sure that the data that is entered is correct.

Figure 19.2 shows the ordering wireframe as a comparison for each check.

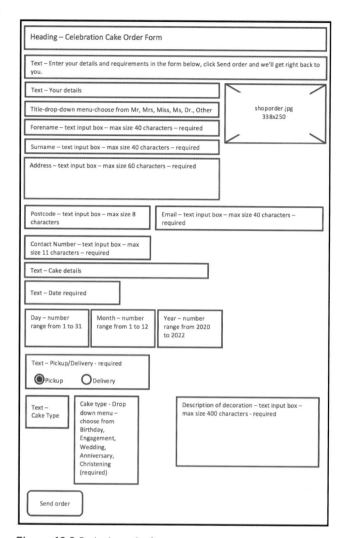

Figure 19.2 Ordering wireframe

Restricted choice check

A restricted choice check is used when the designer wants to limit the user to a specific set of inputs. It avoids the user entering a value that does not exist. Figure 19.3 shows the restricted choices placed on three of the entries in the form. It is not possible to enter any other text other than what is shown in the drop-down menus and radio buttons. Each of the choices in both the drop-down menu and radio buttons should be tested. In this form it is not possible to make multiple choices or for multiple options to appear. However, if these are part of a form then they should also be tested.

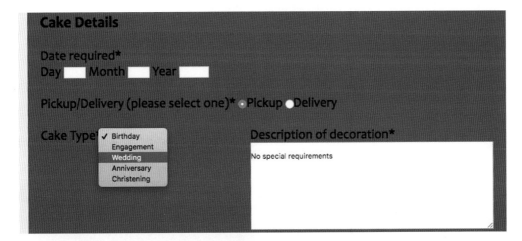

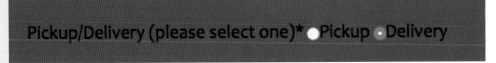

Figure 19.3 Restricted choice check

Range check

A range check will avoid incorrect numeric data from being input and sent to the server. When the 'Send order' button is clicked, the browser will show any validation errors in the form. This is also known as *client-side validation* and can be performed using JavaScript. If the data is invalid, most browsers will indicate the error in the browser. However, there are some which will not. I leave it up to the reader to check this when recommending the best browser in which to view the website. Figure 19.4 shows the lower and upper limits of data permissible and also what will happen when data out of range is entered.

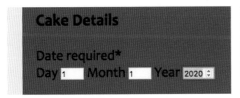
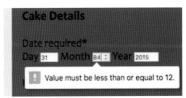

Figure 19.4 Range check

Length check

A length check is done where only a specified number of characters can be entered in the input box. The test data that will be used to test each of the field boxes is shown in Table 19.1. Each piece of test data will ensure that only the maximum number of characters is accepted according to the wireframe.

Field	Test data	Characters used	Characters permitted	Expected result	Actual result
Forename	Nigella Thomasina Charlotte Wilhelmina Veronica	47	40	Nigella Thomasina Charlotte Wilhelmina V	Fail
Surname	Pinkington-Higginbottom-Smythe-Hamilton Jnr	42	40	Pinkington-Higginbottom-Smythe-Hamilton	Fail
Address	The Priory House 23a Stable Street Little Longsbottom Wittingford	62	60	The Priory House 23a Stable Street Little Longsbottom Wittingford	Fail
Postcode	abcdefghijklmnopqrstuvwxyz	26	8	abcdefgh	Fail
Contact Number	01234567890123456789	20	11	01234567890	Pass
Email	testthis.emailaddress@testing.website.co.uk	43	40	testthis.emailaddress@testing.website.co.uk	Fail

Table 19.1 Test data used to test field boxes

The results of the tests are shown in Figure 19.5.

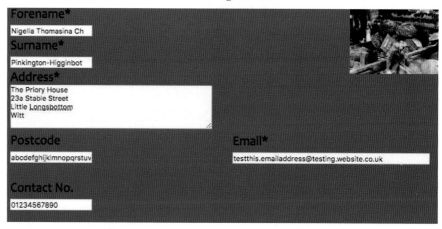

Figure 19.5 Length check

As can be seen, many of the input boxes have problems.

- The Forename and Surname boxes limit the number of characters to 20 not 40 as shown in the wireframe.
- The Postcode box allows many more than the wireframe's 8 characters.
- The Email address allows too many characters to be entered where only 40 characters are permitted.
- Finally, the Address box does not allow enough characters to be entered and the Address has been truncated. This was not picked up during wireframe testing. It would be sensible to change this to 100 characters to allow for longer addresses.

The HTML code for these areas is shown below.

```
Forename*<br>
    <input type="text" name="forename" size="20" maxlength="20"required><br>
Surname*<br>
    <input type="text" name="surname" size="20" maxlength="20"required><br>
Address*<br>
    <textarea name="address" rows="5" cols="50" maxlength="60" required>
    </textarea><br>
<div class="formpart">
Postcode<br>
    <input type="text" name="postcode" size="20">
</div>
<div class="formpart">
Email*
<input type="text" name="email" size="50" maxlength="50"required>
</div>
<div style="clear:both"><br>
Contact No.<br>
<input type="text" name="contact" size="20" maxlength="11">
</div>
```

To correct all these errors, the maxlength should be altered or, in the case of the Postcode, inserted.

Figure 19.6 shows the form after corrected length checks have been implemented.

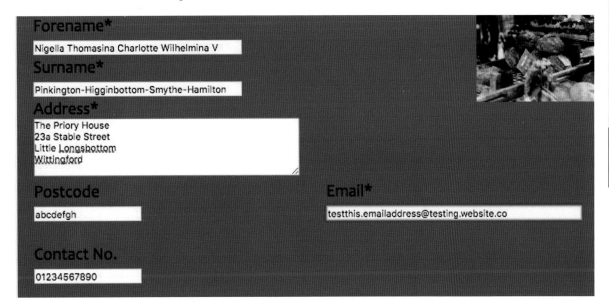

Figure 19.6 Corrected length check

Presence check

This will check that the user has been entered where input is required. Again, this validated by the browser and any errors reported on clicking the 'send order' button. Figure 19.7 shows what will happen when the field is left blank.

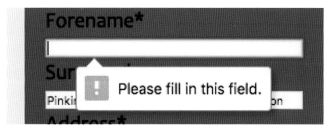

Figure 19.7 Presence check

Navigation

Testing the navigation involves testing that all the links work whether they are in the navigational bar or included as part of other pages.

Navigational bar

Each link in the navigational bar should be tested to ensure that they lead to the correct page. A table similar to that shown in Table 19.2 should be created and should contain each link in the navigational bar.

Page tested		Home			
Test	Expected Result	Actual Result	Pass/ Fail	Date	Action Taken
Bread link	Bread page displayed	Bread page displayed	Pass	06/03/2020	None
Cakes link	Cakes page displayed	Cakes page displayed	Pass	06/03/2020	None
Biscuits link	Biscuits page displayed	Biscuits page displayed	Pass	06/03/2020	None
Recipes link	Recipes page displayed	Recipes page displayed	Pass	06/03/2020	None
Ordering link	Ordering page displayed	Ordering page displayed	Pass	06/03/2020	None

Table 19.2 Home page links tested

For example, clicking on the bread link in Bob's website should lead to the bread page as shown in Figure 19.8.

Before

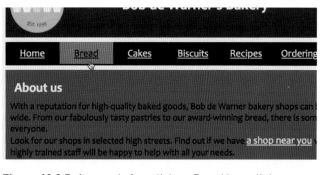

After

Figure 19.8 Before and after click on Bread hyperlink

Home page

The Home hyperlink should be tested on each page to make sure that each page can return to the Home page. Since the hyperlink to return to the Home page is included in the navigational bar on Bob's website, it should work but it is sensible to test this regardless. Again, a table like that shown in Table 19.3 should be created for this test on each page as shown below for the Bread page.

Page tested		Bread			
Test	Expected Result	Actual Result	Pass/ Fail	Date	Action Taken
Home link	Home page displayed	Home page displayed	Pass	06/03/2020	None

Table 19.3 Bread page links tested

Internal links

Any links that are included as part of each web page but are not part of the navigational bar should be tested. The Cakes page contains two internal hyperlinks that should be tested to ensure that they go to the correct page when clicked.

Table 19.4 shows how this would be done for the Cakes page. This also incorporates the internal links in the footer. These should be tested along with the Home page as the code for this is copied to each page created.

Page tested	Cakes				
Test	Expected Result	Actual Result	Pass/ Fail	Date	Action Taken
Large Cakes link	Large cakes page displayed	Large cakes page displayed	Pass	10/03/20	None
Small Cakes link	Small cakes page displayed	Small cakes page displayed	Pass	10/03/20	None
Contact Details link	Contact page displayed	Page not found	Fail	10/03/20	Contact page to be created and linked
Find Us link	Find us page displayed	Find us page displayed	Pass	10/03/20	None
Copyright Statement link	Copyright page displayed	Page not found	Fail	10/03/20	Copyright page to be linked correctly

Table 19.4 Cakes page links tested

Each link must be clicked to test that they produce the desired web page and any which are *dead links*, i.e. there is no associated web page when clicked, should be identified and either the link created or, in the case that no page exists as above, the page created. Figure 19.9 shows internal links on the Cakes page.

Orphan pages

An orphan page is one which is not linked to any other pages in the website. The Copyright page has been created and is shown in Figure 19.10.

Figure 19.9 Cakes page internal links

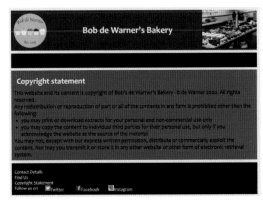

Figure 19.10 Copyright page

As can been seen in Table 19.5, however, it fails every test as the navigational bar is missing from the web page and there is no way to link directly from the Copyright page to the other main pages in the website.

Page tested	Copyright				
Test	Expected Result	Actual Result	Pass/ Fail	Date	Action Taken
Bread link	Bread page displayed	Navigational bar missing	Fail	15/03/2020	Navigational bar to be included in web page code
Cakes link	Cakes page displayed	Navigational bar missing	Fail	15/03/2020	Navigational bar to be included in web page code
Biscuits link	Biscuits page displayed	Navigational bar missing	Fail	15/03/2020	Navigational bar to be included in web page code
Recipes link	Recipes page displayed	Navigational bar missing	Fail	15/03/2020	Navigational bar to be included in web page code
Ordering link	Ordering page displayed	Navigational bar missing	Fail	15/03/2020	Navigational bar to be included in web page code

Table 19.5 Copyright page links tested

External hyperlinks

An external hyperlink is one that takes the user from the website they are using on one server to another website on another server. Each page on Bob's website has a set of external links in the footer to go to social media sites on which he has feeds, images and information. Each of these must also be tested using a table to ensure that they direct the user to the correct page on each of these social media sites.

Table 19.6 shows how each of these should be tested.

Page tested	Copyright				
Test	Expected Result	Actual Result	Pass/ Fail	Date	Action Taken
Twitter link	Twitter page displayed	Twitter page displayed	Pass	15/03/2020	None
Facebook link	Facebook page displayed	Facebook page displayed	Pass	15/03/2020	None
Instagram link	Instagram page displayed	Instagram page displayed	Pass	15/03/2020	None

Table 19.6 Social media links tested

All social platform links work and therefore no further testing is required for external links as the same html code exists on each page.

Media content

It is essential that the content of each page displays as it was designed to. This means that text, audio, video and images both still and animated should display correctly, be present and also in the intended position on the page as dictated by the wireframe.

Figure 19.11 shows the annotated wireframe for the small cakes page and the web page itself. The wireframe and implemented web page should be compared to make sure that it has been implemented as requested.

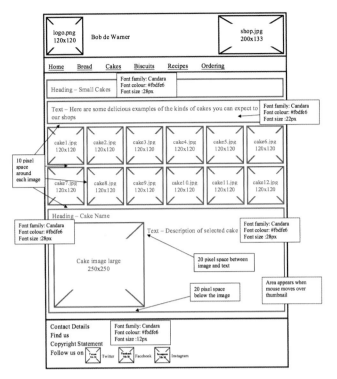
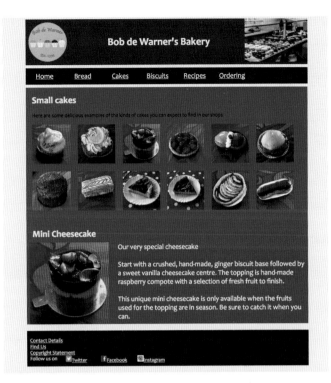

Figure 19.11 Annotated small cakes page wireframe and web page

Table 19.7 shows how the media for this would be tested. Note this also contains the images and text from the header and footer as well as the small cakes content.

Page tested	Small Cakes				
Test	Expected Result	Actual Result	Pass/ Fail	Date	Action Taken
Logo displayed	BdW logo appears floated left	BdW logo appears in correct position	Pass	17/03/2020	None
Heading displayed	Main heading displays centred	Heading displays in centre of page	Pass	17/03/2020	None
Shop image displayed	Image of shop floated right	Shop image appears in correct position	Pass	17/03/2020	None
Sub-heading displayed	'Small cakes' heading displays	Sub-heading displays correctly	Pass	17/03/2020	None
Intro text displayed	Intro text displays	Intro text is too small and wrong colour	Fail	17/03/2020	Change font size and colour to match wireframe
Small cakes thumbnails displayed	Thumbnails of small cakes display	Small cake images appear correctly	Pass	17/03/2020	None
Small cakes text appears	When mouse moves over small image, correct text appears underneath	Correct text appears for the first two but is incorrect thereafter	Fail	17/03/2020	Enter correct text for other cakes
Small cakes text in correct position	Text appears to the right of the large image	Text is correctly positioned	Pass	17/03/2020	None
Small cakes large image appears	When mouse moves over small image, large image appears underneath	Correct image appears	Pass	17/03/2020	None
Social media small images	Images of Twitter, Facebook and Instagram are displayed	Correct images and sizes appear	Pass	17/03/2020	None

Table 19.7 Small cakes page media tested

Files types for media content

There are many different file types that can be associated with images, videos and audio. When choosing which file type for creating and storing any of these, it is a good idea to choose a standard file format. That is, one which will be supported by any browser in which the user chooses to view the website.

When choosing a file format for an image, you should stick to JPG, GIF and PNG standard file formats.

Table 19.8 shows a selection of standard file formats for videos and audio which are all compatible with and supported by the HTML5 standard.

NOTE

Not all standard file formats are compatible with HTML5 and some may require a browser plug-in to be viewed or play. A browser plug-in, also known as a browser add-on, is a small program which extends the functionality of the browser. This means that the browser can play videos or audio that it would not otherwise be able to.

File type	File format	File extension	Description
Video	MP4 or MPEG-4	.mp4	Developed by the Moving Picture Experts Group. MPEG files are compressed to save backing storage space. MPEG is called a container file because it contains both video and audio in one file. Used by TV hardware and video cameras.
	Ogg	.ogg	Theora Ogg was developed by the Xiph.org Foundation. Theora Ogg is a container format and is free, open and unpatented.
	WebM	.webm	Developed initially by On2, Xiph.org and Matroska and then later by Mozilla Firefox, Opera and Google. WebM files are supported by most browser software. WebM is a container format and is used by YouTube.
Audio	MP3	.mp3	Developed by Moving Picture Experts Group: MPEG-1 Audio Layer 3. MP3 files are compressed to around one tenth of the size of the original file but are able to preserve the quality.
	WAV	.wav	Developed by IBM and Microsoft: WAVeform audio file format. WAV is the native sound format for Windows.
	Ogg	.ogg	Ogg Vorbis was developed by the Xiph.org Foundation. Vorbis is the audio compression scheme used to store and play digital music.

Table 19.8 Audio and video file formats compatible with HTML5

CHECK YOUR LEARNING

Now answer questions 1–13 (on pages 269–270) on usability testing

Compatibility testing

Device type

Consumers can now get their information in many different ways and on many different devices, such as smartphones, tablets, laptops and desktops, and how each website displays, differs from device type to device type. Even within each device type, there are different operating systems, screen sizes, memory and processor types. For example, an Android smartphone's browser will display a website differently from an Apple iPhone's iOS browser. Both of these will also render the website differently from the browser on a desktop computer. Because of this issue, many websites also provide a mobile (compatible) site. This means that should the user inadvertently navigate to the desktop version of the website, they will be prompted, by means of a pop-up, to navigate to the mobile (compatible) version.

There are also different ways of interacting with those devices, for example smartphones and tablets largely use a touchscreen for interaction, whereas a desktop will use a mouse.

All these many factors mean that different versions of each website should be produced and tested so that they display correctly on each device type. Sometimes, however, this won't be necessary if the target user of the website is not someone who uses such devices and it may be that a smartphone-enabled website is not always required. However, in general, it makes sense for the website developer to consider all options when developing the website and for the client to carefully consider their audience.

Responsive web design techniques involve using HTML and CSS techniques to resize or hide elements in a website so that it may display at its best on all device types.

Figure 19.12 Mobile and desktop versions

Browsers

Often websites don't display the way they should in a browser. Common problems include where and how the text displays both size and alignment and differences in how the CSS styles and colours are interpreted by the browser. In addition, menus may not be in the correct place or, more simply, images may not appear.

Figure 19.13 shows how Bob's website displays on Mozilla Firefox™, Google Chrome™ and Safari®. Notice how the colours in the **<main>** part of the website display differently in Firefox compared to Chrome and Safari.

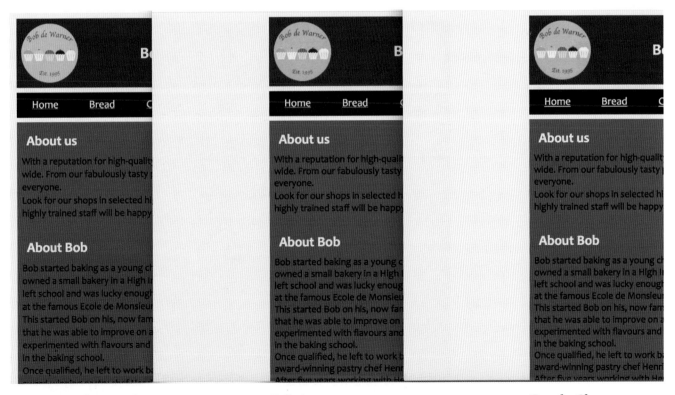

Mozilla Firefox   Safari   Google Chrome

Figure 19.13 CSS in different browsers

Figure 19.14 shows how the text in each browser differs. Mozilla Firefox and Google Chrome are able to display an apostrophe where Safari cannot and supplies the characters â€™ instead.

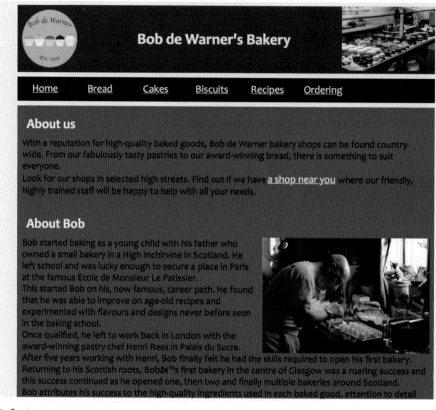

Safari

Google Chrome

Mozilla Firefox

Figure 19.14 Text in different browsers

It is important that these features are tested in different browsers, as it is of no use simply making a website that will only work in one browser. Cross-browser compatibility testing ensures that websites work across different web browsers and versions.

To solve the problem of characters not displaying correctly in Safari, Text Encoding should either be set as Unicode (UTF-8) in the browser itself or included as part of the HTML file in the **<head>** tags as a **meta** element with a **charset** attribute, for example:

```
<!DOCTYPE html>

<html>

<head>

<meta charset="utf-8"/>

<title>Bob's Home Page
</title>
```

The **meta tag** provides metadata about the web page. **Metadata** is data about data and is not displayed on the page. Usually, the meta tags will provide information about the author of the web page or any keywords. In this case, it provides the browser with information about this web page, i.e. that this HTML page will use the Unicode (UTF-8) character set and how to display the content of the page. You can read more about Unicode in Chapter 21.

DID YOU KNOW?

How to make money from user testing

You can actually make money by testing websites that other people have created. The link below is one of many websites that people can upload their own website to and request to have it tested by you, the user. Website owners provide a scenario for each test. Users make a video of their tests, provide feedback based on their experience and are paid according to a suggested price. https://usertestingmarket.com/3d/user_tests/

For more information on cross-browser testing check out:

- https://developer.mozilla.org/en-US/docs/Learn/Tools_and_testing/Cross_browser_testing/Introduction
- https://www.w3schools.com/html/html_responsive.asp

The next website will tell you how the browser you are using to view websites scores on their tests and how well it supports the HTML5 standards and all the specifications related to HTML5. It tests and scores areas like video support, audio support, security and web payments.

- https://html5test.com/

Figure 19.15 shows how Mozilla Firefox, Google Chrome and Safari score on each of the tests and how well they support the HTML5 standard.

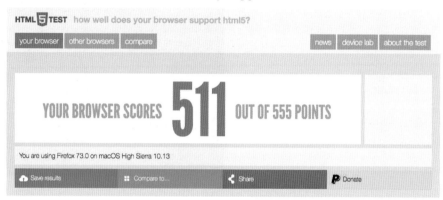

Mozilla Firefox score

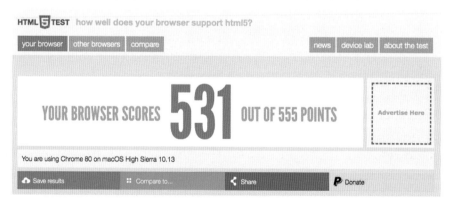

Google Chrome score

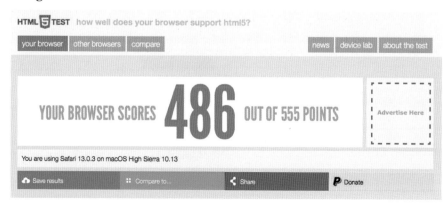

Safari score

Figure 19.15 HTML5 test comparisons

CHECK YOUR LEARNING

Now answer questions 14–16 (on page 270) on compatibility testing

And finally, this last website gives the UK government's advice on how to design websites for different browsers and devices:

● https://www.gov.uk/service-manual/technology/designing-for-different-browsers-and-devices

QUESTIONS

Usability testing

1 At which point in the development of a website should usability testing take place?
2 On what is usability testing based?
3 Why should the developer not provide any assistance when the website is being tested?
4 Describe what is meant by the term:
   a) Persona
   b) Test case
   c) Scenario
5 Describe a suitable persona to test the Caledonia Radio website. The home page is shown in Figure 19.16.

Figure 19.16 Radio Caledonia Home Page

6 Based on the organisers' statements on page 193 in Chapter 14, describe a suitable test case that could be used to test the InverBlair Airshow website.
7 Describe a suitable scenario that could be used to test the InverBlair Airshow website.
8 A booking form has been created for the Northern League of Unusual Sports and is shown in Figure 19.17. Name and describe the type of validation should be included in these fields:
   a) title
   b) number of tickets
   c) forename and surname
   d) any special requirements

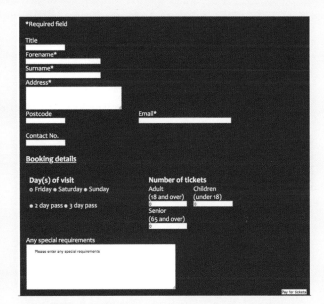

Figure 19.17 Booking form

9 Describe how navigation testing should take place.
10 Describe what is meant by:
   a) a dead link.
   b) an orphan page.
11 a) Create a test table to show the navigation testing that should take place on the part of the home page of the Inverblair Airshow website.

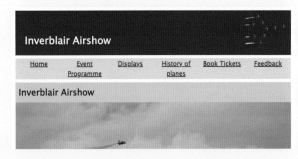

   b) Fill in the Actual results as follows:
   ● Event Programme, Displays and Feedback links all work as expected
   ● History of planes is a dead link as the link to the history page has been spelled incorrectly
   ● Book Tickets page is an orphan page
   Complete the table and suggest what action should be taken to remedy these two problems.

12 Describe what is meant by media testing.

13 Another part of the home page from Inverblair's Airshow website is shown in Figure 19.18 below. It is meant to show a video with highlights from last year's airshow. However, the video does not play when clicked.

This year's display will start with the RAF Falcons Parachute Display Team who will land on Inverblair's beach and will also include the Eurofighter, WWII flypast, Gyrocopter, de Havilland Dragon Rapide, aerial acrobatics plus many more. Both Saturday and Sunday's displays will be rounded of in style with the Red Arrows. The night-time aerobatics fireworks display team Aerosparx will complete Saturday's programme along with a Fireworks display at 10pm.

Saturday's programme will commence with the RAF Falcons at 12pm and the aerial displays will start at 1pm and finish at 10pm.

Sunday's programme will commence at 1pm with the aerial displays.

For more details, check the Programme of Events page.

Our usual, local and international team of experts will talk you through all the displays, so absolutely no specialist knowledge is required. So come along and have a fun and memorable day out with all your family!

Highlights from last year's airshow

Figure 19.18 Home page video

The file format of the video is .mov, as can be seen in the HTML code:

```
<video controls>
    <source src="../videos/lastyear.mov"
type="video/mov">
Your browser does not support the video
tag
</video>.
```

a) Explain why the movie will not play in the browser.
b) Suggest what should be done to solve this problem and rewrite the HTML code.

Compatibility testing

14 Describe what is meant by compatibility testing with respect to:
    a) device type
    b) browsers.

15 Figure 19.19 shows the sports page from the Northern League of Unusual Sports website. State two compatibility issues that may arise when viewing this page on a smartphone rather than a desktop computer.

16 Figure 19.20 shows two versions of the Radio Caledonia home page in Safari and Google Chrome. Describe the compatibility issue being shown here.

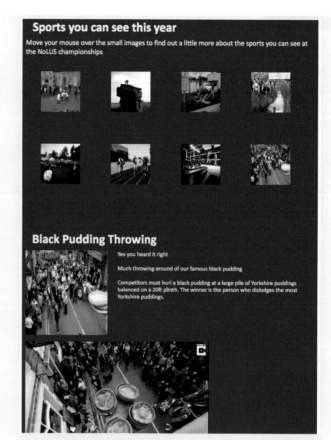

Sports you can see this year

Move your mouse over the small images to find out a little more about the sports you can see at the NoLUS championships

Black Pudding Throwing

Yes you heard it right

Much throwing around of our famous black pudding

Competitors must hurl a black pudding at a large pile of Yorkshire puddings balanced on a 20ft plinth. The winner is the person who dislodges the most Yorkshire puddings.

Figure 19.19 NoLUS sports page

SBC - Radio Caledonia

Our radio stations

| Home | RÃ¨idio gu tuath | RÃ¨idio gu deas | RÃ¨idio an iar | RÃ¨idio an ear |

Welcome

FÃ ilte to the Caledonia family of radio stations. Whether you are are looking for easy listening on RÃ¨idio gu tuath, want something a little louder on RÃ¨idio gu deas or even a little more sophisticated on RÃ¨idio an iar.

You can also find local, national and international news on RÃ¨idio an ear.

Safari

SBC - Radio Caledonia

Our radio stations

| Home | Rèidio gu tuath | Rèidio gu deas | Rèidio an iar | Rèidio an ear |

Welcome

Fàilte to the Caledonia family of radio stations. Whether you are looking for easy listening on Rèidio gu tuath, want something a little louder on Rèidio gu deas or even a little more sophisticated on Rèidio an iar.

You can also find local, national and international news on Rèidio an ear.

Google Chrome

Figure 19.20 Radio Caledonia home page

KEY POINTS

- The website must be tested to make sure that it meets the original design and it operates as intended.
- The media on the website (graphics, audio or video) should be tested to make sure they open and play back correctly on each web page.

Usability testing

- Usability testing is testing how easy the website is to use and achieve specific goals with the users or the clients who commissioned the website.
- At the wireframe stage, the user tests the layout and simple navigational structure.
- At the low-fidelity prototype stage, areas like navigation, colour scheme chosen and any interaction are tested.
- During usability testing, the client is asked to complete a set of tasks whilst being observed by the developer.
- During usability testing, action will be taken to resolve any issues encountered.
- A persona is a fictitious user created to accurately represent the individuals or audience who are likely to be using the website and can be related to the age and experience of the user.
- Test cases are used when specific features of the website need to be tested and a series of instructions need to be followed to complete the task.
- Test cases are created from initial user requirements.
- Scenarios are open-ended tasks in which the user has to perform a series of tasks based on a situation.

Input validation-forms testing

- Forms require some validation so that the data entered is correct.
- Input validation involves:
  - restricted choice check
  - range check
  - length check
  - presence check.

- Each of these checks must be tested to make sure they highlight basic errors.

Navigation testing

- Navigation testing involves testing that all links work correctly.
- A dead link is where there is no associated web page when clicked.
- An orphan page is one which is not linked to any other pages in the website.

Media content

- File types for media content should be chosen so that they can be viewed in any browser.
- Standard file formats include:
  - Images: JPG, GIF and PNG
  - Video: MP4 or MPEG-4
  - Audio: MP3 and WAV.

Compatibility testing

- Websites will display differently from device type to device type.
- Each device type may have different operating systems, screen sizes, memory and processor types.
- Websites should be produced and tested so that they display correctly on each device type.
- Responsive web design techniques involve using HTML and CSS to resize or hide elements in a website so that it may display at its best on all device types.
- Common display problems with browsers include:
  - how and where the text displays
  - the size of the text
  - differences in colour
  - menus not in the correct place
  - images not appearing.
- Cross-browser compatibility testing ensures that websites work across different web browsers and versions.
- The meta tag provides metadata about the web page.
- Metadata is data about data and is not displayed on the page.

Chapter 20 Evaluation

This chapter looks at how to evaluate a website against the original requirements. The following topics are covered:

- Evaluate solutions at this level in terms of:
  - fitness for purpose
  - usability.

Evaluation

Once a website has been programmed, tested and all features and functions added, it must be then be evaluated in terms of fitness for purpose and usability.

This means that the website designers must decide whether or not what has been created matches both the end-user and functional requirements. For example, are users of the website easily able to find what they are looking for without too many mouse clicks?

How the website functions and what it displays when it is being browsed is important. Does the new website look the same as the original wireframe and low-fidelity prototype designs? Does everything work, for instance do scripts run as intended? Does the CSS look the way it is meant to?

To help explain this we will revisit the original end-user and functional requirements for Bob's website from Chapter 14.

	End-user requirements	Functional requirements
1	The client would like to have a website to advertise his bakery shops and products for sale.	
2	Users are interested in buying baked goods.	
3	Users would like to know about the origins of Bob and his first shop.	The Home page will display introductory information about Bob's bakery shops and the history of his bakery shops.
4	The client would like users to be able to see all the baked goods available in shops and cakes available to order online.	
5	The client would like the baked goods to be separated into Bread, Cakes and Biscuits.	The website will contain pages on: Bread, Cake, Biscuits, Recipes and Ordering online.
6	the client would like to have one page for recipes and one for ordering celebration cakes.	
7	Users should be able to view separate pages for each of the different varieties of Breads, Cakes and Biscuits plus Recipes and Ordering.	
8	Users should be able to view the following types of Bread: White, Brown, Wholemeal, Sourdough and Multigrain.	The Bread page will provide clickable buttons to display either White, Brown, Wholemeal, Sourdough or Multigrain bread types. The Bread page will show rollover images of each bread type and display information on each bread type.
9	Users should be able to view the following types of cakes: Large cakes and Small cakes.	The Cake page will contain links to Large cakes and Small cakes sub-pages.
10	Users should be able to see examples of Large cakes and Celebration cakes.	The Large cakes sub-page will display clickable images to show examples of Large and Celebration cakes.

	End-user requirements	Functional requirements
11	Users should be able to view images of examples of Small cakes.	The Small cakes sub-page should show examples of the small cakes available to buy.
12	Users should be able to view the following types of biscuits: Plain and Fancy.	The Biscuits page will provide clickable buttons to select either Plain or Fancy biscuits.
13	The client would like users to be able to select small images of some baked goods to see larger versions on the page with a description of each.	The images on the Small cakes and Biscuits pages should be thumbnails which can be rolled over to view a larger image and description of each.
14	Users should be able to order celebration cakes online using a simple form.	The Ordering page should provide a simple form for customers to order celebration cakes.
15	Users should be able to select from Birthday, Engagement, Wedding, Anniversary and Christening cakes when ordering celebration cakes.	The form should provide a simple selection of different types of celebration cakes: Birthday, Engagement, Wedding, Anniversary and Christening.
16	The client would like to provide three popular cake recipes: Victoria sponge, Chocolate fudge cake and Gingerbread.	The recipes page should allow selection of recipes for Victoria sponge, Chocolate fudge cake and Gingerbread from an on-screen menu.
17	Users would like the cake recipes to include instructional videos.	Each recipe on the Recipe page should display recipe instructions and an instructional video on how to make each cake.
18	Users should be able to click on links to the social media pages.	Each page should have a link in the Footer to social media pages.
19	Users should be able to find Bob de Warner bakery shops.	The find us page should display locations (addresses) of shops.

Table 20.1 Bakery website end-user and functional requirements

Fitness for purpose

To check fitness for purpose we need to revisit the functional requirements. This is because the functional requirements are a detailed list of how the website should be implemented.

As this is quite an extensive list, we will sample two of the functional requirements to see if they are fit for purpose.

Biscuits page rollover images

The functional requirements for this page are shown below. The Biscuits page will be checked to see if it is fit for purpose. A small image of each Biscuit should display and on rollover, a larger image of a biscuit plus a description should be displayed.

13 The images on the Small cakes and Biscuits pages should be thumbnails which can be rolled over to view a larger image and description of each.

Figure 20.1 shows the implemented web page for the Biscuits page.

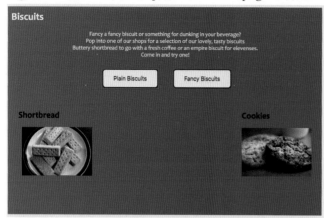
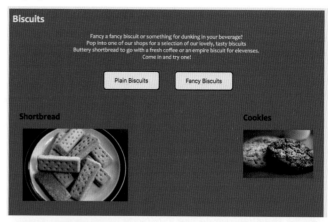

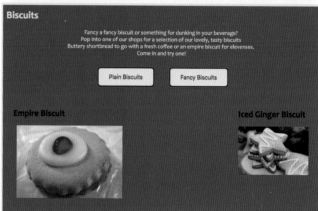

Figure 20.1 Biscuits page (before and after rollover)

As can be seen, this page is not fit for purpose. Two biscuit categories are provided but only two biscuit types appear when each type is clicked and there is no information about any of the biscuits on the page when each of the biscuits is selected. The only part of the page that does function as required is the rollover where a large version of each biscuit displays.

Recipes page

The functional requirements for this page are shown below. The Recipes page will be checked to see if it is fit for purpose when each recipe on the left-hand side of the screen changes to the correct recipe when selected.

16 The Recipes page should allow selection of Recipes for Victoria sponge, Chocolate fudge cake and Gingerbread from an on-screen menu

Figure 20.2 shows the implemented web page for the Recipes page.

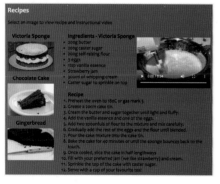
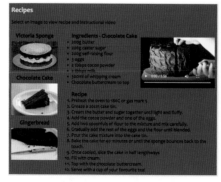
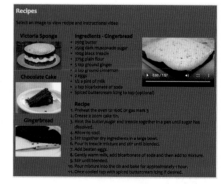

Figure 20.2 Recipes page (after each recipe is selected)

The Recipes page is fit for purpose as the correct Recipes are displayed when the recipe on the left of the window is clicked and videos also run when clicked.

Usability

To check for usability, we revisit the end-user requirements. This is because the end-user requirements are a detailed list of what the user requested for their website. For usability, we will sample two of the end-user requirements to see if the website is usable.

Find Us page

The end-user requirements for the Find Us page are shown below. The Find Us page will be checked to see if it provides the information about where Bob's bakery shops are located.

19 The Find Us page should display locations (addresses) of shops.

Figure 20.3 shows the Find Us page after it has been implemented. This is quite obviously not usable as there are no locations of any bakery shops. In fact, it just contains filler text. The addresses have not been included so it fails to provide the correct information.

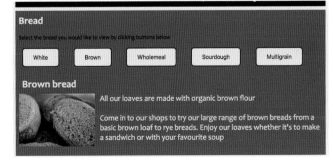

Figure 20.3 Find us page

Bread page

The end user requirements for the Bread page are shown below. The Bread page will be checked to ensure that it provides the five different types of bread list in these requirements.

8 Users should be able to view the following types of bread: White, Brown, Wholemeal, Sourdough and Multigrain.

Figure 20.4 shows the Bread page after it has been implemented. It has, as per the end-user requirements, the five different types of bread that can be selected. This makes this page usable as it provides exactly what was requested.

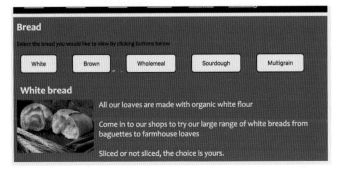

Figure 20.4 Bread page

Each page in the website should be evaluated for fitness for purpose and usability to ensure that it matches both the end-user and functional requirements exactly. There are some deliberate errors in the implementation of Bob's website which would not normally occur in professional website design and implementation, as this would have been carefully checked and tested as the design process progressed.

CHECK YOUR LEARNING

Now answer questions 1–3 below

QUESTIONS

1 Describe why it is important to evaluate a website in terms of both the end-user and functional requirements.

2 The organisers of the Northern League of Unusual Sports have complained to the developers that the Ultimate Frisbee™ page is not fit for purpose. The functional requirement for this page is shown here.

- The Ultimate Frisbee page should have detailed information on how to play the sport including a video of what is involved.

Figure 20.5 shows the page after it has been implemented. Describe why the organisers believe that the Ultimate Frisbee™ web page is not fit for purpose.

| Home | Sports Page | Ultimate Frisbee | Programme | Come and Try | Booking |

Ultimate (Frisbee)

Our introductory sport this year is a non-contact sport that involves flying discs known to us as Frisbees.

Originally known as Ultimate Frisbee and now know as simply **Ultimate**, this sport was developed in 1968 by students at Columbia High School in Maplewood New Jersey.

Ultimate is quite unique in that it generally does not have any referees, instead players themselves decide on whether or not a point has been scored, or if a foul has occurred. It very much relies on the principal of fair play.

It has some similarities with other sports. For example a player may not move whilst they are holding the disc. Teams are referred to as offensive or defensive depending on who has the disc.

Come along and see our teams playing Ultimate.

Figure 20.5 Ultimate

3 The Programme of Events page for the Inverblair Airshow is shown in Figure 20.6. One of the council members has fed back that the page contains everything that was requested but the layout could be better. Comment on:
a) the usability of the page.
b) what could be done to improve the usability.

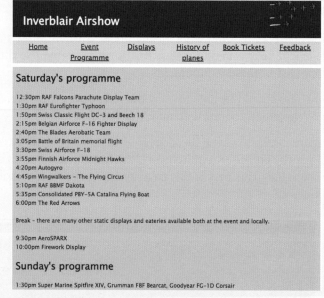

Figure 20.6 Programme of events

KEY POINTS

- Websites should be evaluated in terms of fitness for purpose and usability.
- To check fitness for purpose, the functional requirements should be revisited.
- The functional requirements are a detailed list of how the website should be implemented.
- To check for usability, the end user requirements should be revisited.
- The end-user requirements are a detailed list of what the user requested for their website.

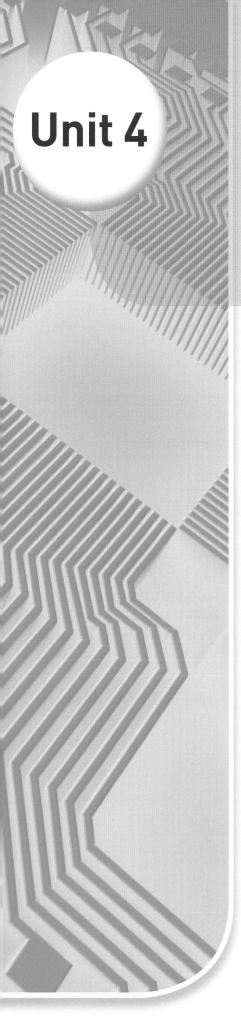

Computer systems

Chapter 21 Data representation

This chapter explains how the method of data representation in a computer system depends on the type of data that is being used. The types of data which we will consider in this chapter are:

1 numbers
2 text
3 graphics.

The following topics are covered:

- Describe and exemplify the use of binary to represent positive and negative integers using two's complement, including the range of numbers that can be represented using a fixed number of bits.
- Conversion of two's complement numbers from binary to denary and vice versa.
- Describe and exemplify floating-point representation of positive and negative real numbers, using the terms mantissa and exponent.
- Describe the relationship between the number of bits assigned to the mantissa/exponent, and the range and precision of floating-point numbers.
- Describe Unicode used to represent characters and its advantage over extended ASCII code (8-bit) in terms of numbers of characters.
- Describe the relative advantages and disadvantages of bitmapped graphics versus vector graphics.

1 Numbers

The binary system

Regardless of the type of data, all data is ultimately stored as binary numbers. Let's look at the binary system before we consider how these different number types are represented.

The two-state machine

A computer system is known as a *two-state machine* because the processing and storage devices in a computer system have one feature in common: they have two states only. These two states are 'on' and 'off' and are represented using the digits 1 for 'on' and 0 for 'off'. This system of using only two numbers is called the binary system because the word binary means 'two states'. In the same way as a light bulb can have two states 'on' or 'off', a binary number has two values 1 or 0, 'on' or 'off'.

Why do computers use the binary system?

Computers use the binary number system because it is easy to represent the two states 'on' or 'off' inside a computer. These two states are represented by voltages. Zero (0) volts is used to represent 0, and a voltage, usually between 1 and 5 volts, depending on the type of computer, is used to represent 1.

Advantages of using the binary system

- Fewer rules need to be built into the processor for the operations add, subtract, multiply and divide on two digits (0, 1) than if all ten digits (0–9) were used.
- Any slight drop in the voltage does not change the data, since any voltage above 0 volts is used to represent 1.
- The two states are easy to represent in storage devices, for instance the direction of polarisation on a magnetic medium or whether or not a charge is stored in a cell in solid-state drives.

Disadvantage of using the binary system

- A large number of digits is required to represent numbers.

Bits

A single unit in binary is called a **bit**. The word bit is made up from the two words BInary digiT.

Unlike computers, people use the decimal or **denary** number system. Decimal means ten, so people count in units, followed by tens, hundreds, thousands, etc.

For example, the number 2407 is made up like this:

| 1000 | 100 | 10 | 1 | these are the place values |
| | 2 | 4 | 0 | 7 | these are the digits |

This means $2 \times 1000 + 4 \times 100 + 0 \times 10 + 1 \times 7$. This is easy for us to understand because we are familiar with the decimal system. Thinking about place values in this way will help us to understand the binary system.

Binary works in a similar way, except that binary place values do not go up in tens, they go up in twos. Let's look at a binary number made up of four bits:

| 8 | 4 | 2 | 1 | these are the place values |
| 1 | 1 | 0 | 1 | these are the bits |

Each bit has its own place value, starting with units, then twos, fours, eights and so on.

The binary number in the example is 1101. This means:

$1 \times 8 + 1 \times 4 + 0 \times 2 + 1 \times 1$ which is 13 in decimal.

Bytes

A binary number which is made up of eight bits (for instance 1101 0110) is called a **byte**. What is the largest number a byte can hold? Let's work it out. A byte has eight bits, so if each bit had the value 1, this would give 1111 1111. Now consider the place values for the eight bits:

| 128 | 64 | 32 | 16 | 8 | 4 | 2 | 1 | these are the place values |
| | 1 | 1 | 1 | 1 | 1 | 1 | 1 | 1 | these are the bits |

So, we have $128 + 64 + 32 + 16 + 8 + 4 + 2 + 1$ which is 255 in decimal.

Note that a byte can have the value zero, so a byte can hold a range of values from zero (0000 0000) to 255 (1111 1111) making a total of 256 different numbers.

More and more bytes

One **Kilobyte** is **1024 bytes** (because $2^{10} = 1024$). One Kilobyte is also called one **Kb** for short. In the same way, one **Megabyte** (**Mb**) is 1024 Kilobytes (1024 × 1024 bytes), one **Gigabyte** (**Gb**) is 1024 Megabytes (1024 × 1024 × 1024 bytes) and a **Terabyte** (**Tb**) is 1024 Gigabytes (1024 × 1024 × 1024 × 1024 bytes). A **Petabyte** (**Pb**) is 1024 Terabytes (1024 × 1024 × 1024 × 1024 × 1024 bytes).

At the time of writing this book, the main memory of a typical microcomputer is measured in Gigabytes, with desktop computer memory ranging from 4 to 64 Gigabytes. The backing storage capacity is measured in Gigabytes and Terabytes, with typical hard disk capacities ranging from 512 Gigabytes to 3 Terabytes and solid-state drive capacities ranging from 512 Gigabytes to 8 Terabytes.

Converting between units

To change:

- bits to bytes, divide by 8
- bytes to bits, multiply by 8
- bytes to Kilobytes, divide by 1024
- Kilobytes to bytes, multiply by 1024.

All larger units are multiples of 1024.

Where do the place values come from?

The place values come from the number base which, in the case of the binary number system, is the number 2. Each different place value can be created by starting from 2^0, like this:

Power of 2	Place value
11	2048
10	1024
9	512
8	256
7	128
6	64
5	32
4	16
3	8
2	4
1	2
0	1

and so on.

Power of 2	Place value	Notes
0	1	
1	2	
2	4	
3	8	
4	16	
5	32	
6	64	
7	128	
8	256	Range of numbers represented by 1 byte
9	512	
10	1024	1024 bytes = 1 Kilobyte
11	2048	
12	4096	
13	8192	
14	16384	
15	32768	
16	65536	
17	131 072	
18	262 144	
19	524 288	
20	1 048 576	1024 Kilobytes = 1 Megabyte
21	2 097 152	
22	4 194 304	
23	8 388 608	
24	16 777 216	'True' colours
25	33 554 432	
26	67 108 864	
27	134 217 728	
28	268 435 456	
29	536 870 912	
30	1 073 741 824	1024 Megabytes = 1 Gigabyte
31	2 147 483 648	
32	4 294 967 296	
33	8 589 934 592	
34	17 179 869 184	
35	34 359 738 368	
36	68 719 476 736	
37	137 438 953 472	
38	274 877 906 944	
39	549 755 813 888	
40	1 099 511 627 776	1024 Gigabytes = 1 Terabyte

Table 21.1 Binary place values up to 40 bits

Note that the left-most bit in a binary number is called the **most significant bit (MSB)** because it has the highest place value and that the rightmost bit is called the **least significant bit (LSB)**.

It is easy to work out 2^{32} bytes, because 2^{32} bytes = $2^{30} \times 2^2$ = 1 Gb × 4 = 4 Gb.

A useful rule to remember is that:

- 2^{10} bytes = 1 Kb (1024)
- 2^{20} bytes = 1 Mb (1,048,576)
- 2^{30} bytes = 1 Gb (1,073,741,824)
- 2^{40} bytes = 1 Tb (1,099,511,627,776).

Therefore, we can say that, using 32 bits, for example, the largest number that may be represented is:

1111 1111 1111 1111 1111 1111 1111 1111 in binary or 4,294,967,295 in decimal.

If we include 0, there is a total range of 4,294,967,296 different numbers.

Changing between binary and decimal representations

It is easy to change a binary number into decimal: just write down the place values and add them up like this:

Place values	128	64	32	16	8	4	2	1	
Binary number	0	1	0	0	0	0	1	1	
Decimal	0	+64	+0	+0	+0	+0	+2	+1	= 67

Method 1

One way to change a decimal number into binary is to write down the place values and then subtract each place value from the number in turn, like this:

Suppose the number is 99. Look at the place values: 128 is larger than 99, so put a 0 at place value 128.

Now subtract 64 from 99, so that 99 – 64 = 35; put a 1 at place value 64.

Now subtract 32 from 35, so that 35 – 32 = 3; put a 1 at place value 32.

Now move to the next suitable place value, which is 2, 3 – 2 = 1; put a 1 at place value 2.

Now we are left with 1 – 1 = 0; put a 1 at place value 1.

Result:

Place values	128	64	32	16	8	4	2	1	
Binary number	0	1	1	0	0	0	1	1	= 99

Method 2

Another way to change a decimal number into binary is using the remainder method. In this method we continually divide the decimal number by two making a note of the divided number and its remainder (either 1 or 0) like this:

Decimal number		Remainder
99	÷2	
49	÷2	1
24	÷2	1
12	÷2	0
6	÷2	0
3	÷2	0
1	÷2	1
0		1

The remainder should then be read from bottom to top to reveal the binary number: 110011.

Real numbers and integer numbers

Numbers may be classified as real numbers or integer numbers. Real numbers include *all* numbers, both whole and fractional. Integer numbers are a subset of real numbers which include only whole numbers, either positive or negative. The distinction is important because the method used to represent integer numbers in computer systems is different from the method used to represent real numbers.

Representing integers

Positive numbers

Positive numbers are represented in the binary system as described earlier, using a set number of places.

Size of integers

The size of the number which may be represented depends on the number of bytes which are available in the computer's memory to store it. If the computer designer or programmer has allocated two bytes to store a number, then numbers from 0000 0000 0000 0000

up to 1111 1111 1111 1111 may be stored (0 to 65,535 in decimal – a total of 65,536 different numbers).

Negative numbers

Representing negative numbers in a computer system makes it necessary to store the sign of the number, i.e. whether the number if positive (+) or negative (–). Taking the previous example, one of the 16 bits available would have to be used to store the sign, leaving 15 bits for the actual number. This would reduce the size of the numbers that could be represented to a range of:

1111 1111 1111 1111 to 0111 1111 1111 1111
or $-(2^{15} - 1)$ to $+ 2^{15} - 1$
or -32767 to $+ 32767$ (in decimal)

where 1 represents the negative sign and 0 represents the positive sign.

As a general rule, when using this **signed bit representation**, for the number of bits n, the range of numbers would be:

$$-(2^{n-1} - 1) \text{ to } +(2^{n-1} - 1)$$

This signed bit system has a number of disadvantages, not least of which are the two values for zero:

1000 0000 0000 0000 (negative zero)

and

0000 0000 0000 0000 (positive zero).

A system of representation which avoids this problem is called **two's complement**.

It is easy to obtain the two's complement of a number by following these steps.

Method 1

Positive number in 8 bits	0000 0111	+7
Change all the ones to zeros and vice versa	1111 1000	
Then add 1	+ 1	
Negative number	1111 1001	–7

Method 2

Another method of obtaining the two's complement of a number is to have the left-most (or the most significant) bit represent –128, for example:

–128	64	32	16	8	4	2	1	
1	0	0	0	0	0	0	0	= –128

Note that the rest of the place values are positive.

Again, taking the same example of –7, this method gives:

–128	64	32	16	8	4	2	1
1	1	1	1	1	0	0	1

So, we have:

–128	+64	+32	+16	+8	+0	+0	+1	= –7

Table 21.2 shows how some positive and negative integers are stored.

Decimal	Two's complement
127	0111 1111
64	0100 0000
2	0000 0010
1	0000 0001
0	0000 0000
–1	1111 1111
–2	1111 1110
–64	1100 0000
–127	1000 0001
–128	1000 0000

Table 21.2 Comparing positive and negative integers

Advantages of two's complement

- There is only one value for zero.
- Arithmetic carried out using two's complement numbers is correct.
- To change a number back from two's complement you just repeat the same process as you followed to create it.

Notice that two's complement representation also retains the left-most bit as the signed bit.

Representing real numbers

Fractions

Fractions in denary (decimal) use a decimal point and look like this:

fraction	1/10	1/100	1/1000	1/10000	1/100000
decimal	0.1	0.01	0.001	0.0001	0.00001

Fractions in binary use a binary point and look like this:

fraction	decimal	binary fraction
1/2	0.5	0.1
1/4	0.25	0.01
1/8	0.125	0.001
1/16	0.0625	0.0001
1/32	0.03125	0.00001
1/64	0.015625	0.000001
1/128	0.0078125	0.0000001

Floating-point representation

Let's start by looking at real numbers in decimal. Any decimal number can be represented with the decimal point in a fixed position and a multiplier, which is a power of 10. For example:

$$20.125 = 0.20125 \times 100 = 0.20125 \times 10^2$$

This is a decimal number and so uses powers of ten. Ten is the base. Any number can be represented in any number base in the form:

$$m \times \text{base}^e$$

Where **m** is called the mantissa and **e** is the exponent. The mantissa is the actual number and the exponent is the power to which the base is raised. For the binary system, the base would be 2. Furthermore, since the base is *always* 2, the base can be ignored and does not need to be stored in the computer alongside the number.

Taking the above example of decimal 20.125, in binary or base two this would be:

$$10100.001 = 0.10100001 \times 2^5 = 0.10100001 \times 2^{101}$$

(Remember 101 in binary = 5 in decimal.)

If the position of the point is always kept the same and the number base is always two, then all that needs to be stored is the mantissa and the exponent. So using the above example:

10100.001 can be stored as   1010 0001   101
                                         mantissa   exponent

Therefore, any number can be stored in a computer's memory as two binary numbers, the mantissa and the exponent. This way of representing numbers is called **floating-point representation**.

Floating-point and Higher Computing Science

Various standards and conventions exist regarding the use of floating-point representation. The following format is used in the Higher Computing Science course.

The mantissa is stored using signed bit representation (in 1+15 bits) and the exponent is stored using two's complement (in 8 bits).

Using the example above (of 20.125) with 16 bits to store the mantissa and 8 bits to store the exponent, then each part of the number is stored as follows:

- The left-most bit of the mantissa is used to store the sign.
- The other 15 bits are used to store the mantissa itself.
- 8 bits are used to store the exponent as a two's complement number.

Figures 21.1a to d explain in detail the process of storing four different numbers in floating-point, starting with 20.125.

Storing 20.125 using floating-point representation with a 16-bit mantissa and an 8-bit exponent

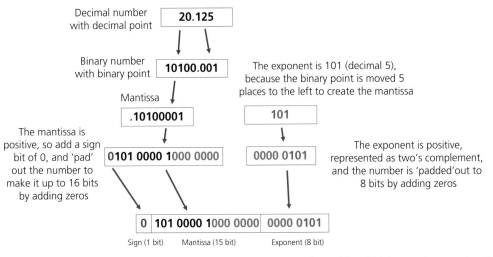

Figure 21.1a Storing 20.125 using floating-point representation with a 16-bit mantissa and an 8-bit exponent

Storing -4200.25 using floating-point representation with a 16-bit mantissa and an 8-bit exponent

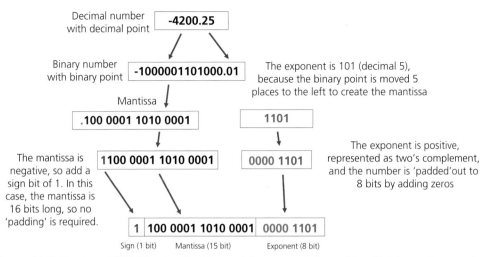

Figure 21.1b Storing −4000.25 using floating-point representation with a 16-bit mantissa and an 8-bit exponent

Storing −0.00375 using floating-point representation with a 16-bit mantissa and an 8-bit exponent

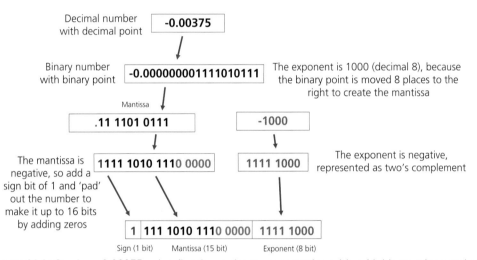

Figure 21.1c Storing −0.00375 using floating-point representation with a 16-bit mantissa and an 8-bit exponent

Storing 0.06257 using floating-point representation with a 16-bit mantissa and an 8-bit exponent

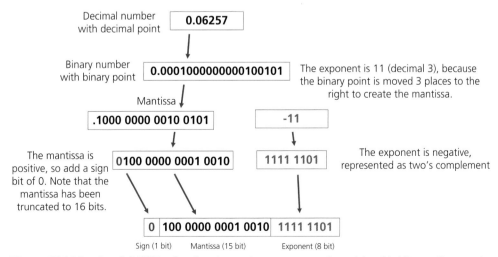

Figure 21.1d Storing 0.06257 using floating-point representation with a 16-bit mantissa and an 8-bit exponent

Note that, in the last example the mantissa has been *truncated* or shortened by removal of the least significant bit in order to fit the space allocated to it in the computer's memory.

Precision and range of floating-point representation

Just as the computer designer or programmer has to make a decision about how many bytes in memory should be used to store integers, a similar decision has to be made for real numbers stored in floating-point representation.

Increasing the number of bytes for the mantissa would increase the **precision**, since this would allow more digits of the numbers to be stored.

Increasing the number of bytes for the exponent would increase the **range** of numbers which could be stored.

Using the Higher Computing Science format above, with a 15-bit mantissa and an 8-bit exponent, the largest number that could be stored is:

$$\text{111 1111 1111 1111} \times 2^{1111\ 1111}$$

Increasing the number of bits for the mantissa to 20, leaving only 3 bits for the exponent, changes this to:

$$\text{111 1111 1111 1111 1111} \times 2^{111}$$

So, the precision of the stored number is increased, and the range is decreased.

When the number of bytes is fixed, the precision is limited, and calculations carried out using numbers represented by floating-point representation may not always give an accurate answer. The last example in Figure 21.1 shows that one of the bits is lost from the mantissa when it is shortened or truncated because the number is too large to fit into the available storage. One method of checking the accuracy of storage of a number in floating-point representation is to convert the number into floating-point representation and then back into decimal and compare the result.

Many computer systems and languages make use of so-called **double precision arithmetic**. Double precision arithmetic uses 64 bits to store numbers, with 1 sign bit, an 11-bit exponent and a 52-bit mantissa.

You should note that the examples above have been simplified to make it easy to understand the basic principles involved in floating-point representation of numbers. There is insufficient space in this book to give a complete and detailed account of floating-point representation.

CHECK YOUR LEARNING

Now answer questions 1–9 (on pages 288–289) on storage of numbers

2 Text

A byte is the space in a computer's memory which is used to hold one character. A **character** is a symbol or letter on the computer keyboard. Characters include the digits 0 to 9, letters and punctuation marks. They are called numeric, alphabetic and special characters respectively. A mixture of alphabetic and numeric characters is called alphanumeric. A, B, C, a, b, c, 0, 1, 2, 9, &, £, * are all characters.

The computer must be able to represent all the characters we wish to use. A list of all the characters which a computer can process and store is called the **character set**. Different types of computer may have slightly different character sets. To allow a computer to represent all the characters, a different code number is given to each character.

The most popular form of this code is the American Standard Code for Information Interchange or ASCII. ASCII is a 7-bit code. Using a 7-bit code allows 2^7 or 128 different codes, so ASCII can represent 128 characters. If more than 128 characters are required, then 8 bits can be used, giving 2^8 or 256 possible characters. This is called extended ASCII, and allows additional characters, such as those with accents Ê, 5, or special symbols, like ™ and © to be represented.

Many different computers use ASCII to represent text. This makes it easier for text to be transferred between different computer systems.

Some ASCII characters do not print on the screen in the normal way. They are known as **control characters** because they control certain operations of the computer system. In ASCII, codes from 0 to 31 are used as control characters. The origin of control characters is found in the history of computers when output was obtained on a mechanical **teletype** printer rather than a screen. Control characters were used to control the movement of the print head and the paper, for example a carriage return character moved the paper up one line and also moved the print head to the left-hand side.

Character	Binary	Decimal
enable printer	000 0010	2
disable printer	000 0011	3
bell	000 0111	7
tab	000 1001	9
Cursor down	000 1010	10
Cursor up	000 1011	11
Clear screen	000 1100	12
Return	000 1101	13
space	010 0000	32
!	010 0001	33
C	010 0010	34
0	011 0000	48
1	011 0001	49
2	011 0010	50
3	011 0011	51
?	011 1111	63
@	100 0000	64
A	100 0001	65
B	100 0010	66
C	100 0011	67
W	101 0111	87
X	101 1000	88
Y	101 1001	89
Z	101 1010	90
a	110 0001	97
b	110 0010	98

Table 21.3 Sample of ASCII

Unicode (universal character set)

This book is written in English and uses characters from the Roman or Latin character set. Many other languages, such as Japanese, use completely different types of characters.

The Unicode character set is designed to represent the writing schemes of all of the world's major languages. The first 128 characters of Unicode are identical to ASCII. This allows for compatibility between Unicode and ASCII. Unicode is a 16-bit code and can represent 65,536 different characters.

The advantage that Unicode has over extended ASCII is that many more characters (or every possible character) may be represented. A disadvantage is that Unicode takes up at least twice as much storage space as ASCII (16 bits compared to 8 bits).

The Unicode standard continues to be developed and is at version 13.0 at the time of writing this book. Early versions of Unicode contained fewer than 65,536 characters, and so all of the characters could be represented by 16 bits (remember that $2^{16} = 65,536$). Unicode now contains around 140,000 characters, including a wide variety of symbols and emoji and therefore more than 16 bits are required to represent all of these characters. Unicode standards include UTF-8, UTF-16 and UTF-32.

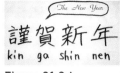

Figure 21.2 A seasonal greeting from Japan

Figure 21.3 Unicode

How individual emoji with the same Unicode identity are represented can vary between applications and platforms. Some examples of this are shown in Figure 21.4.

Figure 21.4 Emoji are small digital images used to express an idea or emotion. The most popular emoji is 😂 known as the 'face with tears of joy'. The emoji variations shown above are taken from https://emojipedia.org/diving-mask/

The development of a universal character code has implications for most computer software companies. Examples include companies who create typefaces, operating systems and especially social media applications.

There is a great deal more to Unicode than can be described in a few lines in this book. You can find out more about it at www.unicode.org/ and http://en.wikipedia.org/wiki/unicode.

CHECK YOUR LEARNING

Now answer questions 10–12 (on page 289) on storage of text

3 Graphics

Graphics, like any information displayed on a computer screen, are made up of tiny dots called **pixels**. Pixel is short for picture element. Imagine the whole of the computer screen being made up of many thousands of pixels. Each pixel may be set to 'on' or 'off' depending on whether the value of the pixel in the computer's memory is 1 or 0.

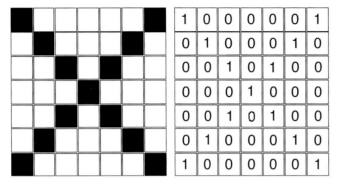

Figure 21.5 How graphics are stored in the computer's memory

Look at Figure 21.5, which shows how graphics are stored in the computer's memory. The picture is drawn on a 7×7 grid. Grid squares which are 'on' are represented by a 1 and grid squares which are 'off' are represented by 0. The amount of memory required to store this graphic would be 7×7 bits, which is 49 bits.

Graphics resolution

The quality of the picture is determined by the resolution of the graphics available. The smaller the size of the pixels, the finer the detail that can be displayed on the screen. Small pixels mean high resolution, as can be seen in Figure 21.6. Large pixels mean low resolution. One way of describing the resolution of the screen is to give the number of pixels horizontally and vertically. For instance, a screen display operating at 800×600 pixels (SVGA) is a lower resolution than 1024×768 pixels (XGA). Another way of describing the resolution is to give the total number of pixels available, although this description is usually applied to devices such as cameras, as in 'a 20 Megapixel camera'.

Figure 21.6 A high-resolution graphic

Increasing the resolution of a graphic has consequences. As the number of pixels increases, so does the storage space that will be required to store the graphic.

Bitmapped and vector graphics

Graphics packages can be classified into two main types, **bitmapped** and **vector**. Both types of package are used to produce pictures, but they store the graphics in a different way. Bitmapped packages paint pictures by changing the colour of the pixels which make up the screen display. Vector packages work by drawing objects on the screen. Bitmapped packages and vector graphics packages are commonly known as *Paint* and *Draw* packages, respectively. Vector packages are sometimes also called *object-oriented* graphics.

Other differences between bitmapped and vector graphics

When two shapes overlap on the screen in a bitmapped package, the shape which is on top rubs out the shape underneath. When the same thing is done in a vector graphics package, the shapes remain as separate objects. They can be separated again and both shapes stay the same (see Figure 21.7).

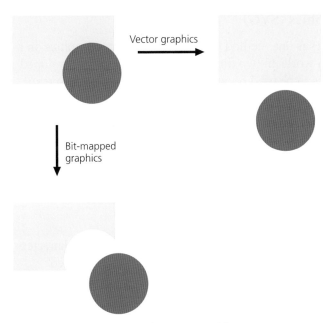

Figure 21.7 Bitmapped and vector graphics

When you save a file created by a bitmapped package, then the whole screen is saved, whether or not it contains any images. This results in a relatively large file size being produced. The objects produced by a vector graphics package have their descriptions stored as a file of data called object attributes. These object attributes take up far less backing storage space than a file created by a bitmapped package, since only the object attributes rather than the whole screen need be stored. Figure 21.8 shows an object and its attributes. You can read more about vector graphics later in this chapter.

Object attributes :

Object number : 1
Type of object : Polygon
Start X coordinate : 802
Start Y coordinate : 804
Number of sides : 9
Angle : 40
Length of side : 120
Line thickness : 6
Fill pattern : 57
Pen pattern : 1

Figure 21.8 Object attributes

When you create a picture using a bitmapped package, its resolution is fixed at that time. If you then go on to print the picture, the original resolution will be maintained in the printout. The resolution of a printer is measured in dots per inch (dpi). For the purpose of comparison, we will also refer to screen resolution as dots per inch rather than pixels. Suppose the resolution of the microcomputer screen is 72 dpi in two dimensions and the printer which you are using is an ink jet, set at its default value of 360 dpi. When your picture is printed it will be at the screen resolution of 72 dpi, because in order to print, the processor sends the bitmap to the printer.

When a picture is created using a vector graphics package, the resolution of the screen has no effect on the resolution of the printout. The picture will be printed out at the full resolution available on the printer. This feature is called **resolution independence**. Resolution independence is possible using vector graphics because when the picture is printed, the processor sends the file of object attributes which represent the picture to the printer.

Figure 21.9 Individual pixels in a bitmapped image

When editing a picture created by a bitmapped graphics package, it is possible to zoom in as far as the individual pixels and make changes (see Figure 21.9). When editing a picture produced by a vector graphics package, it is possible to zoom in to enlarge portions of the picture on the screen, but it is not possible to edit any pixels. It is possible to edit the individual objects which make up the picture, or alter any of the attributes, such as line width.

Figure 21.10 Vector graphics

Figure 21.11 Graphic image from SVG code

Scalable vector graphics (SVG)

Scalable vector graphics is one method of representing vector graphics on a computer system. **SVG** works in two dimensions (2D). SVG was developed to allow vector graphics to be used on **web pages**. SVG files are plain text files, written in **mark-up language**, and, just like **HTML**, they may be edited using a **text editor** like *TextEdit* or *Notepad*. When SVG files are saved, they use filenames ending in .SVG. SVG graphics may be displayed in a **web browser**.

A listing of some code in SVG and the resulting graphic image is shown below:

```
<circle cx= "200 "cy= "200" r="100" fill="green"/>
```

The SVG code which draws the green circle in Figure 21.11 is 49 characters long and therefore requires a storage space of 49 bytes using extended ASCII. Storing the same graphic as a bitmapped image requires 176 Kilobytes, more than 3000 times the storage space.

The storage requirement of the tiger image in Figure 21.10 is 98 Kilobytes for the vector graphics (SVG code) and 995 Kilobytes if bitmapped graphics are used. One reason why code takes up much less storage than bitmapped images is that each character in the code only requires one byte of storage, whereas a single pixel in a bitmap graphic may require as much as three bytes (24 bits).

> **CHECK YOUR LEARNING**
>
> **Now answer questions 13–20 (on pages 289–290) on storage of graphics**

QUESTIONS

Storage of numbers

1 Convert the following binary numbers into denary (decimal – all positive numbers):
   a) 1011
   b) 1001 1111
   c) 1010 1010
   d) 1111 1110
2 Convert the following denary (decimal) numbers into binary:
   a) 122
   b) 193
   c) 256
   d) 1023
3 Express the following denary numbers in binary using 8-bit two's complement notation:
   a) −6
   b) −25
   c) −92
   d) −120

4 Express the following denary (decimal) numbers as binary using a binary point:
   a) 0.25
   b) 7.375
   c) 15.53125
5 Convert the following real numbers into binary using floating-point representation. There are 16 bits available for the mantissa (including the sign bit) and 8 bits for the exponent. You may find the following URL useful: www.rapidtables.com/convert/number/decimal-to-binary.html.
   a) 0.00275
   b) 134.25
   c) −617.83
   d) −0.0937
6 A binary number made up of only four bits is called a nibble. It is called this because it is half of a byte.
   a) What is the largest binary number a nibble can hold?
   b) What range of numbers may be held in a nibble?

7 a) In floating-point representation, what will be the effect of increasing the number of bits used to store the exponent?

b) Look back at the examples of floating-point representation shown in Figure 21.1. Note that the left-most bit in the mantissa is always 1. Explain how a computer designer could make use of this feature and what effect this may have on the number stored.

8 What range of numbers can be represented in floating point if 4 bytes is available for the mantissa and 1 byte for the exponent? State any assumptions you make, for example, whether or not you are using two's complement representation.

9 a) Using a high-level programming language such as PYTHON or BASIC, try out some calculations using real numbers and compare the answers with those you have calculated yourself. Look at the documentation for the language and note the range and precision of the numbers which can be stored. Repeat the process using an application package which can handle numbers (like a spreadsheet). Note any differences in precision or range.

b) When the number 1.23 is converted from decimal into binary, the result is 1.001110101110000101. If this number is converted back into decimal, the result is 1.229999542236328125. Use the website www.rapidtables.com/convert/number/decimal-to-binary.html or a calculator to try out other examples of your own, then answer this question.

Why is it possible to say that 'calculations carried out using numbers represented by floating point may not always give an accurate answer'?

Storage of text

10 What is a:

a) character?

b) character set?

c) control character?

11 a) What does the abbreviation ASCII stand for?

b) How many characters can ASCII represent?

c) Give a reason for your answer to b).

d) Describe one method of increasing the number of characters that may be represented by ASCII.

e) What is the ASCII for:

i) e?

ii) E?

Express your answers in decimal or binary.

12 a) What is Unicode?

b) State one advantage of Unicode over ASCII.

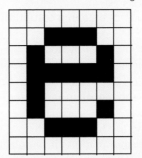

Figure 21.12 Character bitmap

c) The character shown in Figure 21.13 has been stored using:

i) a bitmap

ii) ASCII

iii) Unicode.

In each case calculate (or show) the number of bits required for representing the character.

d) Which method is most efficient (uses least storage space)?

Storage of graphics

13 Why are bitmapped graphics so-called?

14 How are vector graphics stored?

15 With respect to graphics, what is:

a) resolution?

b) resolution independence?

i) Which type of graphics provides resolution independence?

16 Which of the following statements are true of:

a) bitmaps?

b) vector images?

1 pixels can be edited

2 pixels cannot be edited

3 resolution independent

4 resolution dependent

5 overlapping parts of the image may be separated cleanly

6 file size is constant regardless of the complexity of the image

7 file size increases as the complexity of the image increases

17 Jemima has installed a graphics package on her laptop computer. The graphics package has online help, but it does not indicate whether it is a bitmapped or vector package. Describe two tests Jemima could carry out in order to find this out.

KEY POINTS

- The internal representation of data in a computer system is in binary.
- Computers use the binary number system because it is easy to represent the two states 'on' or 'off' inside a computer, fewer rules need to be built into the processor and a drop in the voltage does not change the data.
- One disadvantage of using the binary number system is that a large number of digits is required to represent numbers.
- Types of data which are represented in a computer system include numbers, text and graphics.
- Numbers may be stored as integer or floating-point representation (real numbers).
- Negative numbers are stored using two's complement.
- Fractions in binary use a binary point.
- Floating-point representation uses a mantissa and an exponent.
- The mantissa holds the number and the exponent holds the power.
- In Higher Computing Science, the mantissa is stored using signed bit representation in 16 bits and the exponent is stored using two's complement in 8 bits.
- Increasing the number of bytes used for the mantissa will increase the precision of the number being stored and hence decrease the range since fewer bits will be available to store the exponent.
- Increasing the number of bytes used for the exponent will increase the range of the number being stored and hence decrease the precision since fewer bytes will be available to store the mantissa.
- To change:
  - bits to bytes, divide by 8
  - bytes to bits, multiply by 8
  - bytes to Kilobytes, divide by 1024
  - Kilobytes to bytes, multiply by 1024.
- All larger units are multiples of 1024.
- Text may be stored as integer values using the American Standard Code for Information Interchange (ASCII).
- ASCII is a 7-bit code.
- Extended ASCII uses 8 bits.
- A character is a symbol or letter on the computer keyboard.
- Control characters control certain operations of the computer system.
- Unicode is a 16-bit system which can represent 65,536 characters.
- The advantage that Unicode has over ASCII is that many more characters (or every possible character) may be represented.
- Graphics may be either bitmapped or vector.
- Graphics are made up of tiny dots called pixels.
- The quality of the picture is determined by the resolution of the graphics available.
- The smaller the size of the pixels, the finer the detail that can be displayed on the screen.
- Bitmapped packages paint pictures by changing the colour of the pixels that make up the screen display.
- Bitmapped graphics have a direct relationship between the bits in the computer's memory and the picture displayed on the computer screen.
- Vector packages work by drawing objects on the screen.
- Scalable vector graphics (SVG) is one method of representing vector graphics on a computer system.
- Differences between bitmap and vector:
  - Overlapping shapes may be separated in vector.
  - Bitmap saves the whole screen.
  - Bitmap resolution is fixed; vector is resolution independent.
  - Bitmap can zoom to show and edit pixels.

Chapter 22 Computer structure

This chapter explains the concept of the fetch–execute cycle and the factors affecting computer performance. In order to do this, we will look first at the structure of a computer system.

The following topics are covered:

- Describe the concept of the fetch–execute cycle.
- Describe the factors affecting computer system performance:
  - number of processors (cores)
  - width of data bus
  - cache memory
  - clock speed.

Computer structure

The **processor** is the main part of the computer, consisting of the **control unit**, the **arithmetic and logic unit (ALU)** and the **registers**.

A computer may have more than one processor or **core**. This can help improve the performance of the computer by increasing its processing power.

Figure 22.1 shows how a processor connects to the input, output and backing storage devices of the computer.

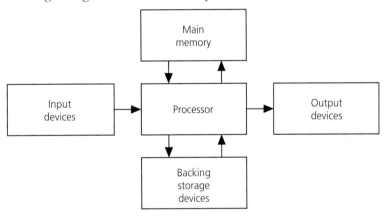

Figure 22.1 Block diagram of a computer system

Processor structure

The **control unit** in the processor controls all the other parts of the processor and makes sure that the program instructions of the computer are carried out in the correct order. The control unit makes sure everything happens in the correct place at the correct time.

The **arithmetic and logic unit**, or ALU, carries out the calculations (arithmetic) and performs the logical operations.

The **registers** are a group of **storage locations** in the processor which are used to hold data being processed, instructions being executed and addresses to be accessed. The precise details of what these registers are and how they function is not required at Higher level. However, some of these registers are named in Figure 22.2 to help with the explanation of the fetch–execute cycle.

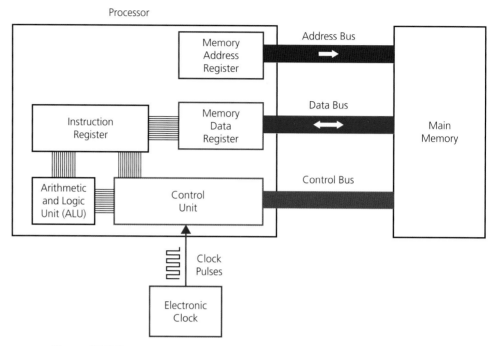

Figure 22.2 Processor structure

Main memory

The main memory of a computer is a general term for any type of computer memory other than backing storage. The place where each item is stored in a computer's memory is important because the computer has to be able to find any given item of data or an instruction. Main memory consists of a number of **storage locations**, each of which is identified by a unique **address**. An address is a binary number used to identify a storage location in main memory. The ability of the processor to identify each storage location is called its **addressability**.

Types of main memory

Main memory consists of **Random Access Memory (RAM)** and **Read Only Memory (ROM)**. RAM is a type of computer memory which holds its data as long as the computer is switched on. When the computer is switched off, any data held in RAM is lost. RAM is **volatile** memory. The purpose of RAM is to hold the computer's programs and data while they are being processed. ROM is a type of computer memory which holds its data permanently. When the computer is switched off, any data held in ROM is preserved. ROM is **permanent** memory. **Flash ROM** is a special type of ROM which may be reprogrammed. Flash ROM is not normally used for main memory but instead is the backing storage medium in solid-state drives (SSDs), USB flash drives, memory cards and phones.

Buses

Three sets of wires called **buses** connect the processor to the memory and input/output devices. These are the **address bus**, the **data bus** and the **control bus**. Figure 22.3 shows how the buses are connected to these devices.

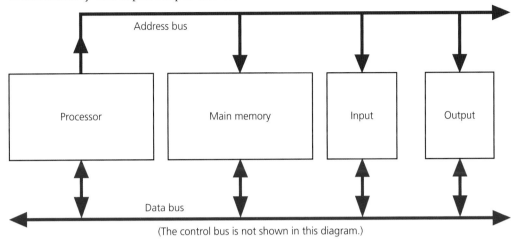

Figure 22.3 Address bus and data bus connections

Address bus

The address bus carries the address information from the processor to the main memory and any other devices attached to the bus. The address bus is *unidirectional* or one-way only. The number of wires in the address bus (the width of the bus) determines the number of storage locations which the processor can address. A microcomputer with 64 wires in the address bus is said to have a 64-bit address bus. Each of the wires in the bus can be switched on (set to 1 in binary) or off (set to 0 in binary). A 64-bit address bus can therefore address a series of memory locations starting from address:

0000 0000 0000 0000 0000 0000 0000 0000 0000 0000 0000 0000 0000 0000 0000 (decimal 0)

up to and including address:

1111 1111 1111 1111 1111 1111 1111 1111 1111 1111 1111 1111 1111 1111 1111 (decimal $2^{64}-1$)

making a total of 2^{64} addresses.

Every time a bit is added to the width of the address bus, the address range doubles. Increasing the width of the address bus, for instance, from 64 bits to 128 bits, will increase the total number of memory locations which the processor can address from 2^{64} in decimal, to 2^{128} in decimal.

Data bus

The data bus carries data to and from the processor, main memory and any other devices attached to the data bus. The data bus is therefore *bi-directional* or two-way. Each storage location in memory can hold a quantity of data called a **word**. A word is the number of bits that can be processed by the processor in a single operation. This is the same as the number of wires in (the width of) the computer's data bus. The width of the computer's data bus and hence the **word length** may consist of as many as 64 bits.

The number of wires in the data bus determines the quantity of data which the bus can carry. A microcomputer with a 64-bit data bus can carry 64 bits of data or instructions at a time. Increasing the number of wires in the data bus will increase the quantity of data which the bus can carry. This is one method of increasing the performance of a computer system.

Control bus

The control bus is made up of a number of separate wires or lines, each with its own function. These include **read**, **write** and **clock**. You do not need to know about any of the other control lines for your Higher course. The read line is used by the processor to indicate that a **memory read** operation is to take place. The write line is used by the processor to indicate that a **memory write** operation is to take place (see *The fetch–execute cycle* below). The clock line carries a series of clock pulses at a constant rate. These pulses are used to keep the processor and its related components in step with one another. The **clock speed** (or **rate**) is the frequency at which the clock generates pulses. Frequency is measured in hertz, and a computer's clock rate is measured in *Gigahertz* (GHz). Increasing the clock rate will increase the speed at which the computer operates. This is another method of increasing the performance of a computer system. See Figure 22.2.

The fetch–execute cycle

The processor of the computer is able to carry out a process only when it is given a set of instructions. A set of instructions which controls the operation of the processor is called a **program**. By changing the program which is stored or held in the computer's main memory, a computer can carry out a completely different process. This is known as the **stored program concept**.

Each program instruction is stored in a separate storage location in the computer's main memory. In order for the processor to carry out a process, it must be supplied with instructions from the memory, one at a time, in the correct order. This method of operating a computer was first described by *John Von Neumann (1903–57)*, and nearly all modern computers are based on this *Von Neumann* architecture.

The fetch–execute cycle is the name given to the way in which the processor takes in an instruction from memory (**fetch**) and carries out that instruction (**execute**). The fetch–execute cycle consists of two parts or phases. The fetch phase is where the instruction is copied from memory into the instruction register inside the processor. The execute phase follows next, in which the instruction is decoded by the control unit of the processor and carried out. It is sometimes useful to think of it as the **fetch–decode–execute cycle**. Looking back at Figure 22.2 will help you to understand this process.

Steps in the fetch–execute cycle

1 The processor sets up the address bus with the required memory address. It does this by placing a value in the memory address register.
2 The control unit of the processor activates the read line on the control bus.
3 The instruction is transferred from memory to the memory data register in the processor via the data bus and stored in the instruction register (*fetch phase*).
4 The instruction is decoded and then carried out or executed (*execute phase*).

The fetch–execute cycle including memory read and write operations

The fetch–execute cycle described above, involves only a memory read operation. Here is an example which also involves a memory write operation. Suppose that the instruction held in the computer's memory is: *Put the value 101 into memory location 1100* and that this instruction is held in memory location 1111.

The steps involved are:

1 The processor sets up the address bus with the required memory address. It does this by placing a value in the memory address register (1111).
2 The control unit of the processor activates the read line on the control bus.
3 The instruction is transferred from memory to the memory data register in the processor via the data bus and stored in the instruction register (*fetch phase*).
4 The instruction is decoded and then carried out or executed (*execute phase*).
5 The processor sets up the address bus with the required memory address. It does this by placing a value in the memory address register (1100).
6 The processor sets up the data bus with the value to be written to memory. It does this by placing the value in the memory data register (101).
7 The control unit of the processor activates the write line on the control bus.
8 The contents of the memory data register (101) are transferred to the required storage location in the computer's memory (1100).

> ## CHECK YOUR LEARNING
>
> **Now answer questions 1–10 (on page 299) on computer structure and the fetch–execute cycle**

Factors affecting system performance

Many different factors can affect the performance of a computer system. The factors which we will look at are:

- number of processors (cores)
- width of the data bus
- cache memory
- clock speed.

Number of processors (cores)

The first microcomputer systems contained only a single processor or central processing unit (CPU). In order to increase computer performance, manufacturers of computer systems added extra processors. This can may be done by either installing multiple separate processors or building two (*dual*), four (*quad*), or more processors or **cores** into a single processor chip.

Installing multi-core processors is the more efficient method, because the cores are much closer together than if separate processors were used. The shorter distance allows signals to run at a higher clock speed, thus increasing the performance of the computer system. In addition, placing more than one core on a single chip improves the energy efficiency, because only one cooling system will be required.

In theory, having access to more than one processor or core means that separate tasks may be processed at the same time (*in parallel*). This has the potential to greatly increase the performance of a computer system.

However, merely installing multiple processors or multi-core processors into a computer system will *not* result in any improvement in performance unless the software (*the application which is running, or the operating system, or both*) is able to recognise their presence and take advantage of them. For instance, a program which renders graphics for a movie, will not run any faster on a computer with multiple processors or cores unless the software is able to divide the task into separate parts and allocate each part of the task to a separate core.

Utilities like *Windows Task Manager* and *About This Mac* may be used to display a variety of detailed information including the number of processor cores, clock speed, main memory and cache sizes (see Figure 22.4).

macOS High Sierra
Version 10.13.6

iMac (27-inch, Mid 2011)
Processor 3.4 GHz Intel Core i7
Memory 12 GB 1333 MHz DDR3
Startup Disk Macintosh SSD
Graphics AMD Radeon HD 6970M 2048 MB
Serial Number C02G603HDHJW

System Report...   Software Update...

iMac

Hardware Overview:

Model Name:	iMac
Model Identifier:	iMac12,2
Processor Name:	Intel Core i7
Processor Speed:	3.4 GHz
Number of Processors:	1
Total Number of Cores:	4
L2 Cache (per Core):	256 KB
L3 Cache:	8 MB
Memory:	12 GB
Boot ROM Version:	87.0.0.0.0
SMC Version (system):	1.72f2

Figure 22.4 Multi-core computer systems details

Supercomputers

Figure 22.5 The Summit Supercomputer at Oak Ridge National Laboratory, USA

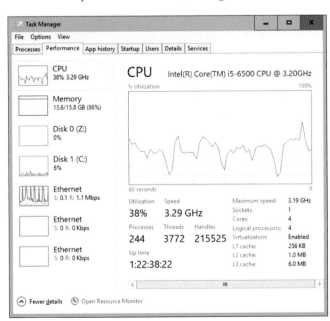

If you have enough processors, it is possible to link them together and produce a **supercomputer**. Supercomputers operate at extremely high speeds and are used for intensive and very demanding applications, including weather forecasting, oil exploration, quantum mechanics and cryptanalysis. Figure 22.5 shows the fastest supercomputer in June 2020. It is interesting to note that this supercomputer is made up of 7,299,072 processor cores, each running at a clock speed of 2.2 GHz. If you look at www.top500.org you can see the current list of supercomputers. Part of this list is shown in Table 22.1.

Rank	System	Cores	Rmax (TFlop/s)	Rpeak (TFlop/s)	Power (kW)
1	Supercomputer Fugaku - Supercomputer Fugaku, A64FX 48C 2.2GHz, Tofu interconnect D, Fujitsu RIKEN Center for Computational Science Japan	7,299,072	415,530.0	513,854.7	28,335
2	Summit - IBM Power System AC922, IBM POWER9 22C 3.07GHz, NVIDIA Volta GV100, Dual-rail Mellanox EDR Infiniband, IBM DOE/SC/ Oak Ridge National Laboratory United States	2,414,592	148,600.0	200,794.9	10,096
3	Sierra - IBM Power System AC922, IBM POWER9 22C 3.1GHz, NVIDIA Volta GV100, Dual-rail Mellanox EDR Infiniband, IBM / NVIDIA / Mellanox DOE/NNSA/LLNL United States	1,572,480	94,640.0	125,712.0	7,438
4	Sunway TaihuLight - Sunway MPP, Sunway SW26010 260C 1.45GHz, Sunway, NRCPC National Supercomputing Center in Wuxi China	10,649,600	93,014.6	125,435.9	15,371

Table 22.1 Four of the top 500 supercomputers in June 2020 (www.top500.org)

DID YOU KNOW?

Quantum computers

A great deal of research is taking place involving *quantum computers*, which operate in a totally different manner to those described in this chapter. In September 2019, it was alleged that a *quantum computer* had achieved so-called *quantum supremacy*, by taking only 200 seconds to solve a problem that would require approximately 10,000 years to process using the current fastest supercomputer.

Width of the data bus

The width of the data bus determines the quantity of data which the bus can carry at any one time. A microcomputer with a 32-bit data bus can carry 32 bits of data or instructions at a time. This means it has a **word length** of 32 bits.

Increasing the data bus width will increase the quantity of data which the bus can carry at any one time. Doubling the width, assuming that all other factors remain the same, will, in theory, double the quantity of data which may be transferred between the processor and the memory during the fetch–execute cycle. This will have a significant effect on the performance of the computer system.

Large data bus widths are used to speed up data transfer between the processor's internal registers. The buses inside a processor may be 256 bits wide. Large buses are also used to communicate with cache memory. If the normal data bus width of a microcomputer is 64 bits, then the bus which connects the Level 2 cache (see below) to the processor may be 128 bits wide.

Cache memory

Significant improvements in system performance may be gained by the use of **cache memory**. It is much faster for the processor to access data and instructions held in cache memory than in main memory.

Cache memory is a relatively small amount of memory, for instance, between 32 and 64 Kilobytes, which is used as a temporary store for often-used instructions. Cache memory may be referred to as Level 1, 2 or 3, which indicates its relative proximity to the processor. Level 1 cache is usually built into the processor chip and connected to the processor's registers by a bus which may be 128 or 256 bits wide. Level 2 and 3 cache may also be on the chip or very close to it. Each core in a multi-core processor typically has a dedicated Level 1 cache. Higher cache levels are shared between cores.

The operation of cache memory is explained in Figure 22.6.

1 The cache fetches the next instruction from main memory in advance of the processor. (Level 1 cache is checked first, followed by Level 2 and so on.)
2 Processor checks to see if the next instruction is in the cache.
3 If the instruction is found (known as a **cache hit**), then the instruction is fetched from the cache – a very fast process.
4 If the instruction is not found, this is a **cache miss**. In which case the cache has to fetch the instruction from the main memory – a much slower process.

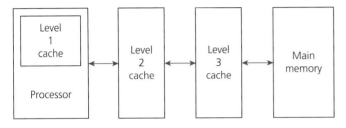

Figure 22.6 The operation of cache memory

The computer's processor operates so many times faster than the speed of access to main memory that it is possible for the processor to carry out hundreds of instructions during the time taken to recover from a cache miss. So much so, that the processor may run out of instructions to process – this is known as a **CPU stall**.

Clock speed

The computer's clock signal is carried by one of the lines on the control bus (see Figure 22.2). The clock generates a series of clock pulses at a constant rate. The clock speed (or rate) is the frequency at which the clock generates pulses. Frequency is measured in hertz, and a computer's clock rate is measured in either *Megahertz* (MHz) or *Gigahertz* (GHz) (1 GHz = 1000 MHz). Everything that the processor does is kept precisely in time with the clock. The fetch–execute cycle described earlier in this chapter is a good example of how this works.

Suppose a processor's clock rate is 1 GHz. This means that the clock is generating pulses one thousand million times a second. One single pulse is called a **clock cycle**. Fetching a single instruction from the computer's memory takes a length of time measured in clock cycles, say 10 clock cycles. So our example

processor will be able to fetch one hundred million of these instructions in one second. If the clock rate was increased to 2 GHz, then the processor would be able to fetch two hundred million of the same instructions in one second.

This shows just how significant the effect of increasing the clock rate can have on a computer's overall performance. You should note that in fact, different instructions will take different numbers of clock cycles to fetch.

At the time of writing this book, typical microcomputers had a clock rate of over 3 GHz. It should be noted, however, that a microcomputer's clock rate is always quoted as that of the processor. In fact, a microcomputer's buses may have separate clocks, each working at a much slower rate than the processor's clock. A typical microcomputer's data bus, for example, might have a clock rate of 800 MHz. This difference between the clock rates of the processor and the bus can result in a processor *bottleneck* which can reduce a computer system's overall performance, because the data cannot be transferred as fast as the processor can process it.

The general principle of chemistry that '*a reaction can only proceed as fast as the speed of its slowest step*' also applies to computers. Regardless of how fast the processor may be able to process instructions, if, say, the memory access speed is slow, then that will limit the computer system's overall performance. The slowest component in any system, therefore, may be regarded as the *limiting factor*.

It is relatively easy to obtain an increase in computer performance by increasing the clock speed of a processor. However, manufacturers have found that this increase cannot go on indefinitely. Technical problems are being experienced with heat dissipation and increased power consumption, among other difficulties. The faster a processor runs in terms of clock speed, the more heat it produces and the more energy it consumes. Some processors are even liquid-cooled, using equipment like a miniature refrigerator.

Underwater Data Centre

Figure 22.7 Microsoft's Underwater Data Centre

In summer 2018, the Microsoft Corporation sank a shipping container-sized data centre into the North Sea off the coast of Orkney. Project Natick is powered by renewable energy and is made up of '12 racks containing 864 standard Microsoft datacenter servers with FPGA acceleration and 27.6 petabytes of disk. This Natick datacenter is as powerful as several thousand high-end consumer PCs and has enough storage for about 5 million movies.'

Microsoft's reasoning is as follows: 'More than half of the world's population lives within about 120 miles of the coast. By putting datacenters in bodies of water near coastal cities, data would have a short distance to travel to reach coastal communities, leading to fast and smooth web surfing, video streaming and game playing as well as authentic experiences for AI-driven technologies.'

You can find out more at https://natick.research. microsoft.com/

Measuring computer speeds

It is relatively easy to quote processor clock speeds as a measurement of how fast a computer system is operating. However, it is not reliable, because the overall performance of the computer depends on much more than just the processor. Doubling the clock speed or the width of the data bus, for instance, will not result in the doubling of the overall speed of operation of a computer system.

MIPS stands for **Millions of Instructions Per Second** and is a measure of performance based on the average number of machine code instructions executed. Like clock speed, MIPS is only a useful measure of computer performance if in all other respects the rest of the test conditions remain the same.

If you look back at the list in Figure 22.6, you will see that the unit of measurement used to compare the different machines is the TFlop or Teraflop, which is one trillion (10^{12}) floating-point operations per second.

These measurements do not really mean much to the ordinary user. While it may impress some people to be able to say that their latest processor is 10 times faster than an *Intel Core i9-9980XE Skylake × 18-Core 3.0 GHz (4.4 GHz Turbo),* or whatever, it is of more importance to the user how fast applications run, and this depends on the performance of the whole computer system, not just one particular component. It is much more useful and informative to use a **benchmark**, which is a standard set of computer tasks designed to allow a computer's performance to be measured.

The Standard Performance Evaluation Corporation (**SPEC**) is one example of an organisation which produces standard benchmarks. Their **CPU2017** suite of benchmarks is designed to reveal details of a whole machine's performance that cannot be learnt simply by knowing a processor's clock speed. If performance depended only on GHz, there would be no performance difference between two identical processors and a faster processor would always win. You can find out more about SPEC at www.spec.org/cpu2017/.

Many published comparative reviews of computer systems use so-called real-world tests, which involve timing the performance of certain applications carrying out demanding tasks that occupy a great deal of processor time.

Even taking all this into account, a modern computer system is very much over-specified for common tasks like surfing the web or word processing. Extreme specifications and top-of-the-range performance are only important for demanding users such as graphics or video professionals.

CHECK YOUR LEARNING

Now answer questions 11–25 (on page 299) on factors affecting system performance

QUESTIONS

Computer structure and the fetch-execute cycle

1 A computer's processor has three main parts. Name each of these three parts and describe their function.
2 With respect to a computer, what is a core?
3 Two types of main memory are RAM and ROM.
   a) What do the terms RAM and ROM mean?
   b) State one difference between RAM and ROM.
   c) State one difference between ROM and flash ROM.
4 What is a bus in a computer system?
5 A computer has three buses. Name each of these buses and describe their function.
6 Which bus can be described as:
   a) unidirectional?
   b) bi-directional?
   c) a collection of single lines?
7 a) With respect to a bus, what is meant by the term width?
   b) State one effect of increasing the:
      i) unidirectional bus width?
      ii) bi-directional bus width?
8 What is meant by the terms:
   a) address?
   b) addressability?
   c) storage location?
   d) word?
9 What is:
   a) the clock?
   b) the clock speed (rate)?
   c) the name of the unit used to measure the clock speed?
   d) a clock cycle?
10 List the steps involved in the fetch–execute cycle.

11 In the fetch–execute cycle, what happens during execute?

Factors affecting system performance

12 State four factors which affect systems performance.
13 Explain why it is more efficient for a computer to use a multi-core processor instead of separate processor chips.
14 What is parallel processing?
15 Under what circumstances might increasing the number of processors in a computer system NOT result in an improvement in overall performance?
16 State one application which is suitable for a supercomputer.
17 What is determined by the width of the data bus?
18 What is cache memory used for?
19 Where is cache memory located in a computer system?
20 What is a cache hit?
21 What is a CPU stall?
22 State one reason why adding cache memory can improve system performance.
23 Explain why improving system performance is not simply a matter of increasing the clock speed of the processor indefinitely.
24 State two measures of performance.
25 Orla has a 3.2 GHz Epsilon PC and Poppy has a 3.4 GHz Sigma PC. Poppy says her computer is faster than Orla's because it has a higher clock rate.
   a) Who do you think is correct? Give a reason for your choice.
   b) What type of test could be done to help decide who is correct?

KEY POINTS

- The processor of a computer includes the arithmetic and logic unit, control unit and registers.
- The control unit controls all the other parts of the processor and makes sure that the program instructions of the computer are carried out in the correct order.
- The arithmetic and logic unit carries out the calculations and performs the logical operations.
- The registers are a group of storage locations in the processor which are used to hold data being processed, instructions being executed and addresses to be accessed.
- The place where each item is stored in a computer's memory is important because the computer has to be able to find any given item of data or an instruction.
- An item is stored in memory in a storage location.
- Each storage location has its own unique address in the computer's main memory.
- An address is a binary number used to identify a storage location in main memory.
- The method a computer uses to identify storage locations is called its addressability.
- Main memory consists of a number of storage locations, each with a unique address.
- Main memory consists of Random Access Memory (RAM) and Read Only Memory (ROM).
- RAM holds its data as long as the computer is switched on.
- ROM holds data permanently.
- Flash ROM is a special type of ROM which may be reprogrammed.
- Wires called buses connect the processor to the memory and input/output devices of the computer.
- The address bus carries the address information from the processor to the main memory and any other devices attached to the bus.
- The address bus is unidirectional.
- The number of storage locations in the computer's memory that a processor can identify depends on the number of bits in the address or the number of wires in the address bus.
- The data bus carries data to and from the processor, main memory and any other devices attached to the data bus.
- The data bus is bi-directional.
- The control bus is made up of a number of separate wires or lines, each with its own function, including read, write and clock.
- The read line is used by the processor to indicate that a memory read operation is to take place.

- The write line is used by the processor to indicate that a memory write operation is to take place.
- The clock line carries a series of clock pulses at a constant rate in order to keep the processor and its related components in step with one another.
- A computer operates by fetching and executing instructions from a stored program.
- The fetch–execute cycle is the name given to the way in which the processor takes in an instruction from memory (fetch) and carries out that instruction (execute).
- The steps involved in the fetch–execute cycle are:
  1 The processor sets up the address bus with the required memory address. It does this by placing a value in the memory address register.
  2 The control unit of the processor activates the read line on the control bus.
  3 The instruction is transferred from memory to the memory data register in the processor via the data bus and stored in the Instruction Register (fetch phase).
  4 The instruction is decoded and then carried out or executed (execute phase).
- The factors which can affect the performance of a computer system are: the number of processors or cores, the width of the data bus, the use of cache memory and clock speed.
- Having access to more than one processor or core means that separate tasks may be processed at the same time which may greatly increase the performance of a computer system.
- The width of the data bus determines the quantity of data which the bus can carry at any one time.
- Increasing the data bus width will increase the quantity of data which the bus can carry at any one time, thus improving the computer system's performance.
- Cache memory is a relatively small amount of memory, which is used as a temporary store for often used instructions.
- It is much faster for the processor to access data and instructions held in cache memory than in main memory.
- The clock generates a series of clock pulses at a constant rate and everything that the processor does is kept precisely in time with the clock.
- Increasing the clock rate will speed up the fetch–execute cycle.
- Three measures of computer performance are: clock speed, MIPS, TFLOPS, and benchmarks.

Chapter 23 Environmental impact

This chapter describes the impact on the environment of the use of intelligent systems for heating, traffic control and car management.

The following topics are covered:

- Describe the environmental impact of intelligent systems:
  - heating systems
  - traffic control systems
  - car management systems.

Environmental terms

An **intelligent system** is a computer system which is programmed in such a manner that it can emulate and automate some intelligent aspects of human behaviour.

The **environmental impact** is the effect that a particular activity has on its surroundings.

The **carbon footprint** is the amount of **greenhouse gases** (including carbon dioxide and methane) produced by people or a particular activity. Greenhouse gases have an environmental impact because they absorb heat and can therefore cause climate change.

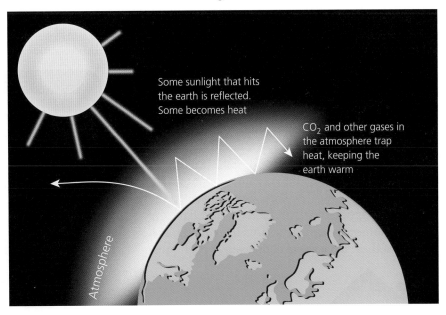

Some sunlight that hits the earth is reflected. Some becomes heat

CO_2 and other gases in the atmosphere trap heat, keeping the earth warm

Atmosphere

Figure 23.1 The greenhouse effect

You can find out more about climate change here: https://climate.nasa.gov/causes/.

What may be done in order to reduce the carbon footprint?

Actions that may be taken to reduce the carbon footprint include:

- using clean energy sources such as geothermal, hydrogen, hydropower, wave, wind and solar, instead of fossil fuels and biomass which produce greenhouse gases.
- improving home insulation and programming thermostats to reduce heating requirements.
- installing more efficient heating systems which produce more output for less input, such as more energy efficient gas boilers, air and ground source heat pumps.
- make more use of battery and gravity storage to assist with power supply management at times of peak demand.
- walking or cycling instead of driving to school or work.
- using zero-exhaust-emission electric battery or hydrogen-powered vehicles instead of petrol or diesel-powered ones.

Heating systems

Smart meters

A **utility meter** is an *analogue* device which measures and displays the consumption of gas or electricity in a premises by means of rotating dials. These are commonly known as 'dumb meters'. A **smart meter** is a *digital* device which performs the same function and is also connected to a communications network. A smart meter communicates its measurements to the customer via an in-home display (IHD) and to the applicable energy supplier through the data and communications company (DCC) hub. The DCC hub is installed in the premises alongside the smart meter(s) and IHD and creates a home area network (HAN). Figure 23.2 shows how all of these devices are connected to each other.

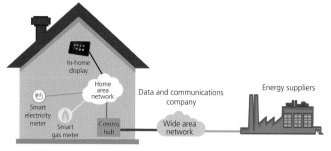

Figure 23.2 How a smart meter communicates

A smart meter automatically sends readings to the supplier as often as every 30 minutes. This removes the obligation from customers to provide meter readings to the supplier and the requirement for estimated readings or bills and reduces the need for suppliers to employ people to take meter readings. While there are many differing types in the market, some examples of smart meters for electricity and gas are shown in Figure 23.3.

Figure 23.3 Smart meters for electricity and gas

The readings from the smart meter are used by the supplier to calculate the cost and to bill the customer. The IHD allows the customer to continually monitor their energy use throughout the day. Figure 23.4 shows a typical smart meter IHD, which is normally issued to the customer free of charge.

Figure 23.4 Smart meter in home display

The readings also available to the customer via their online account page or dedicated app too. It is also possible to set a budget for energy use. It is hoped that making customers more aware of their energy use will prompt them to reduce their consumption. Figure 23.5 shows an example of how these readings may be used to inform the customer.

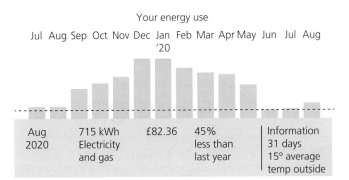

Your energy use

Aug 2020	715 kWh Electricity and gas	£82.36	45% less than last year	Information 31 days 15° average temp outside

Figure 23.5 Energy use graph

Homes which are capable of producing more electricity than they consume, for instance, via solar photovoltaic panels, can also use a smart meter to monitor the quantity of electricity that is exported to the national grid.

Smart thermostats

A control system is necessary to ensure that a heating system is used efficiently, and that expensive energy is not wasted on heating an empty home, for example. A **thermostat** is a device used to regulate temperature. A **smart thermostat** is one which uses **sensors** and **intelligent programming** to learn how your home heats up and your preferred temperature in particular rooms at different times throughout the day. Smart thermostats operate by being connected wirelessly to both your home's heating system and broadband router or hub. They may be controlled manually or remotely by using an app on your watch, phone or tablet (see Figure 23.7). Many smart thermostats may also be voice controlled via a smart speaker. You can tell your smart thermostat when you are going on holiday, so that it will stop heating while you are away. A smart thermostat can also recognise when you are on your way home and turn on the heating. This is known as **geofencing**. Geofencing uses GPS (global positioning system) to create a virtual geographic boundary around an area and enables the software to trigger an action when, for example, your phone enters (or leaves) the area. The app which controls the activity of the smart thermostat may also be linked to other devices and sensors around the home. For example switching lights on and off, controlling electrical plugs, doorbells and security cameras.

Figure 23.6 shows two types of smart thermostats.

Figure 23.6 Smart thermostats (Hive and Nest)

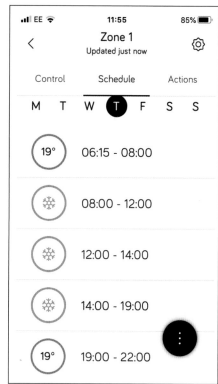

Figure 23.7 Controlling a smart thermostat using an app (Hive)

CHECK YOUR LEARNING

Now answer questions 1–9 (on page 309) on heating systems

Traffic control

Transport causes more greenhouse gas emissions than any other sector. In 2018, transport produced 26 per cent of greenhouse gas emissions, compared with 25 per cent from energy generation. Poor air quality is said to be linked to 40,000 premature deaths each year.

In 2015, there were an estimated 1.3 billion motor vehicles on the world's roads and that number is expected to rise to over 2 billion by 2040. Intelligent systems are being used to reduce road congestion in a number of ways.

National governments have set various end dates for the sales of new petrol and diesel cars in order to tackle climate change. In Scotland, this is expected to be in 2032. The UK committee on climate change has called for 60 per cent of new cars to have ultra-low emissions by 2030.

You can read more about the proposed ban on petrol and diesel vehicles at www.bbc.co.uk/news/uk-40726868.

Smart traffic lights

Smart traffic lights incorporate traffic sensors which can identify different road users and adapt the traffic management system to their needs. Over 400 of these sensors have been installed at the major junctions in the town of Milton Keynes, England. The system counts and classifies road users and measures the time it takes for vehicles to travel between junctions, allowing it to predict traffic conditions with 89 per cent accuracy. The system is also capable of identifying different categories of parking spaces, such as disabled, electric and car share. The operation of smart traffic lights is shown in Figure 23.8.

You can find out more about this system at https://vivacitylabs.com.

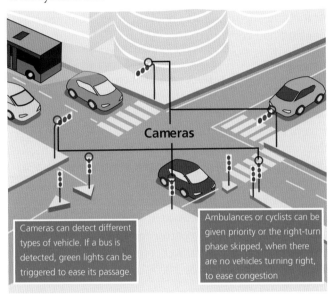

Cameras

Cameras can detect different types of vehicle. If a bus is detected, green lights can be triggered to ease its passage.

Ambulances or cyclists can be given priority or the right-turn phase skipped, when there are no vehicles turning right, to ease congestion

Figure 23.8 Smart traffic lights in operation

Smart motorways

A **smart motorway** is one which uses traffic management methods to increase capacity and reduce congestion in busy areas. A system known as MIDAS (Motorway Incident Detection and Automatic Signalling) constantly monitors the road traffic by using sensors.

There are four types of sensor in use.

1   Loops of copper wire beneath the surface of the road can detect how often a vehicle passes over them and how quickly it is moving. This system can also measure the length of the vehicles and so roughly determine the type of vehicle.
2   Radar beams projected from the side of the road can be used to provide similar information as the loops of wire, with the advantage that they are easy to maintain and less likely to suffer damage.
3   Automatic Number Plate Recognition (ANPR) cameras detect the number plate of each vehicle and

time how long it takes to travel between each set of cameras.
4   Speed cameras record images and speeds of vehicles travelling above the limit.

MIDAS then processes this data and can respond by displaying reduced speed limits on overhead gantries, for instance to 60, 50 or 40 mph. As a courtesy to drivers, there is a delay between the change to the new speed limit and the speed cameras being updated to reflect this in order to allow traffic to slow down safely without sudden braking. A smart motorway gantry is shown in Figure 23.9.

Figure 23.9 Smart motorways control traffic flow by displaying speed limits and lane closures on overhead gantries

The hard shoulder is a narrow emergency lane along the left of a motorway, separated by a solid white line. You can see the hard shoulder on the left of Figure 23.9.

DID YOU KNOW?

How to use the hard shoulder on motorway

1   Pull onto the hard shoulder if you cannot make it to a service station.
2   Park as far to the left as possible, with your wheels turned away from traffic.
3   Put on your hazard lights to help other drivers see you are there.
4   Get out of your car from the left-hand passenger door and stand on the verge, as far away from the traffic as possible.
5   Look for a motorway marker post (white with blue and red markings) to confirm your location.
6   Use an emergency SOS phone or your own phone to call for help.
7   Stay behind the barrier, as far away from traffic as possible.

There are three types of smart motorway in use.

1   Controlled motorway (CM): three (or more) lanes are used for traffic and the hard shoulder is for use only in an emergency such as a breakdown. See Figure 23.10.

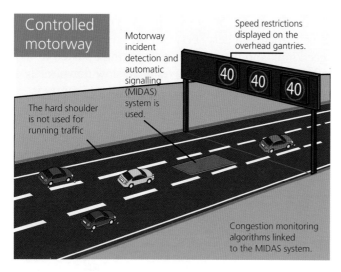

Figure 23.10 Controlled motorway

2   Dynamic hard shoulder/Hard shoulder running (DHS/HSR): the hard shoulder is used as a normal running lane during busy times but is reserved for emergencies at all other times. See Figure 23.11.

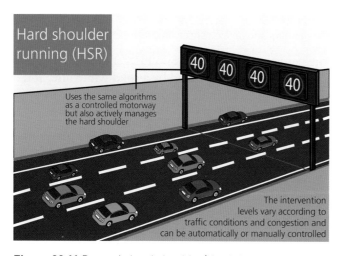

Figure 23.11 Dynamic hard shoulder/Hard shoulder running motorway

3   All lane running (ALR): the hard shoulder is used as an additional lane for cars to drive in normally. Special lay-bys called emergency refuge areas (ERAs) at distances of 1.5 miles apart may be used in the event of an emergency. It is proposed to reduce this distance to 1 mile. See Figure 23.12.

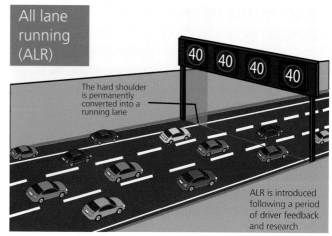

Figure 23.12 All lane running motorway

At the time of writing this book in 2019, Highways England had converted over 400 miles of motorway. This figure is expected to double by 2025.

However, MIDAS is not capable of either reacting to a crash or closing lanes on the motorway. This may only be done by a human in a control room who looks at a bank of CCTV monitors and receives updates from the police and members of the public. It was reported that in one instance, a broken-down vehicle remained unnoticed for as long as one hour. In response to this, Highways England are introducing stationary vehicle detection (SVD) which can alert operators by setting off an alarm in the control centre. You can read more about the use of SVD at www.theaa.com/about-us/newsroom/news/17-minutes-to-spot-a-live-lane-breakdown-on-smart-motorways.

While the purpose of smart motorways is to control traffic flow and improve road safety, opinions are divided between the general public and the road authority. Many people believe that turning a hard shoulder into an additional lane for traffic is dangerous in the event of an emergency. Furthermore, a survey of 2000 motorists in 2019 showed that more than half of the drivers are uncertain as to the correct method of driving on a smart motorway, to the point of not using the hard shoulder even when permitted to do so by the overhead signs.

Further information

You can find out more about one family's experience at www.channel4.com/news/familys-motorway-horror.

And more about what is being written about smart motorways at www.dailymail.co.uk/money/cars/article-7579021/One-ten-drivers-feel-safer-smart-motorways-finds-new-survey.html.

You can read about Highways England's response at www.gov.uk/government/news/safety-on-smart-motorways.

In its response to these concerns, in October 2019, the government announced that there would be an investigation into the safety of smart motorways by the Department for Transport, which you can read more about at www.autoexpress.co.uk/car-news/107769/smart-motorway-safety-to-be-subject-of-government-investigation.

Satellite navigation

Most new cars are either fitted with satellite navigation systems or are capable of connecting to a phone or tablet which can provide the same service through an app. In addition to allowing drivers to choose a preferred route to their destination, satellite navigation systems can display traffic information updated in real time. This provides advance warning of instances of traffic congestion, breakdowns, road works and road closures. Avoiding congested routes improves journey time and so reduces emissions and therefore reduces the environmental impact of the journey. Figure 23.13 shows a satellite navigation display and real time traffic information and route planning is shown in Figures 23.14 and 23.15.

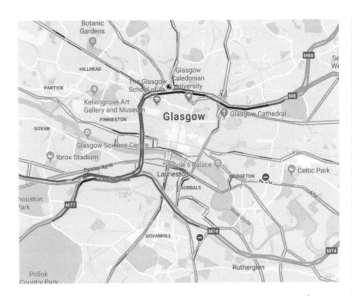

Figure 23.14 Real time traffic information (Google Maps)

Figure 23.15 Route planning with Google Maps

Figure 23.13 Satellite navigation in use (Garmin)

307

CHECK YOUR LEARNING

Now answer questions 10–20 (on page 309) on traffic control

Car management systems

Start-stop (or stop-start) systems

When the engines of petrol- and diesel-powered vehicles are running, they are constantly producing harmful emissions from the exhaust system. When such a vehicle stops temporarily at a junction, for example, then the engine continues to run or 'idle' at a slow speed in order to provide power to the rest of the car's equipment such as lights and the satellite navigation system.

A **start-stop** system automatically detects when a car is stationary and out of gear, for instance at a junction, and cuts the engine in order to reduce fuel consumption and emissions. The engine will automatically restart when the clutch pedal is depressed (or when the brake is released in an automatic), or if more power is demanded than can be met by the car's battery, such as turning on the air conditioning system. A start-stop system is not required in battery-powered cars since their electric motors only operate when the car is moving. A typical start-stop indicator display is shown in Figure 23.16.

In 2015, the US Department of Energy estimated that more than 6,000,000,000 gallons (22,712,470,704 litres) of fuel are wasted every year from idling engines. Each gallon of fuel used produces 20 pounds (9 kilograms) of carbon dioxide.

Figure 23.16 A car instrument panel showing a start-stop indicator (A)

Engine management systems

The **engine control unit** (ECU) on a petrol or diesel engine is the part of the engine management system which controls fuel supply, fuel injection, air supply, ignition and exhaust gas recycling. The engine control unit uses sensors to constantly monitor the state of the engine while it is running. The ECU provides precise control over the amount of fuel used in order to improve the performance of the engine and minimise the emission of harmful exhaust gases. The operation of an ECU is shown in Figure 23.17.

You can read about engine control units in more detail at www.ecutesting.com/categories/ecu-explained/.

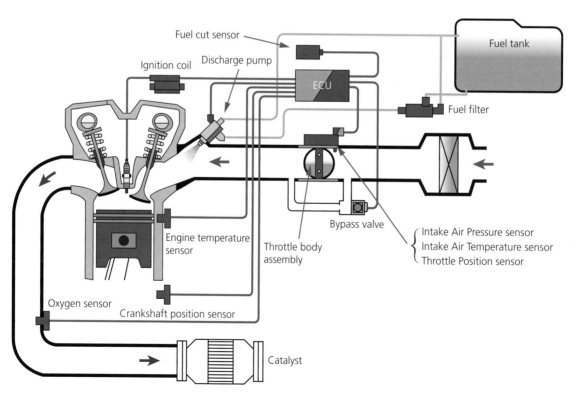

Figure 23.17 Engine control unit (ECU)

CHECK YOUR LEARNING

Now answer questions 21–23 (below) on car management systems

QUESTIONS

Heating systems

1 What is meant by the terms:
   a) intelligent system?
   b) environmental impact?
   c) carbon footprint?
2 Name two greenhouse gases.
3 Explain how greenhouse gases have an impact on the environment.
4 State two actions that may be taken in order to reduce the carbon footprint.
5 What is a smart meter?
6 How does a smart meter communicate information?
7 a) With whom/what does a smart meter communicate information?
   b) State one parameter that the user of a smart meter can alter.
8 What is a thermostat?
9 What features make a thermostat smart?

Traffic control

10 Which sector causes the most greenhouse gas emissions?
11 State one action being taken by national governments in order to tackle climate change.
12 What is incorporated into smart traffic lights?
13 What is a smart motorway?
14 Name four types of sensor used to monitor road traffic.

15 What action may be taken by a road traffic monitoring system when it detects congestion?
16 With respect to a motorway, what is the hard shoulder?
17 Name three types of smart motorway.
18 Why are humans still required in motorway control rooms?
19 State one reason why public opinion on the safety of smart motorways may be divided.
20 State one reason why the use of satellite navigation systems may reduce the environmental impact of a journey.

Car management systems

21 a) Which two types of vehicle engine produce harmful emissions?
   b) Explain why the use of a start-stop system can reduce the quantity of harmful emissions from such engines.
   c) Describe a situation in which a start-stop system in a vehicle powered by such engines may not operate.
   d) Name one type of vehicle which does not require a start-stop system.
22 Name five variables controlled by an engine control unit.
23 Explain how an engine control unit minimises the emission of harmful exhaust gases.

KEY POINTS

- An intelligent system is a computer system which is programmed in such a manner that it can emulate and automate some intelligent aspects of human behaviour.
- The environmental impact is the effect that a particular activity has on its surroundings.
- The carbon footprint is the amount of greenhouse gases (including carbon dioxide and methane) produced by people or a particular activity.
- Actions that may be taken to reduce the carbon footprint include:
  - using clean energy sources
  - improving home insulation
  - installing more efficient heating systems
  - making more use of power storage technology to even out demand
  - walking or cycling instead of driving
  - using zero exhaust emission vehicles.

Heating systems

- A smart meter is a digital device which measures the consumption of gas or electricity and is connected to a communications network.
- A smart meter communicates its measurements to the customer via an in-home display and to the applicable energy supplier through the data and communications company hub.
- A control system is necessary to ensure that a heating system is used efficiently and that expensive energy is not wasted.
- A thermostat is a device used to regulate temperature.
- A smart thermostat is one which uses sensors and intelligent programming to learn how your home heats up and your preferred temperature in particular rooms at different times throughout the day and may also detect when you are on your way home by using geofencing.
- Smart thermostats operate by being connected wirelessly to both your home's heating system and broadband router or hub.

Traffic control systems

- Transport creates more greenhouse gas emissions than any other sector.
- National governments have set end dates for the sales of new petrol and diesel cars in order to tackle climate change.
- Smart traffic lights incorporate traffic sensors which can identify different road users and adapt the traffic management system to their needs.
- A smart motorway uses traffic management methods to increase capacity and reduce congestion in busy areas.
- A system constantly monitors the road traffic using sensors and can automatically reduce the speed limit.
- Smart motorways can make use of the hard shoulder as an additional lane for traffic.
- People are still required in a control room to decide what to do in a road traffic emergency.
- Opinion is divided on the benefits of smart motorways in terms of road safety.
- Satellite navigation systems allow drivers to choose a preferred route to their destination and can display traffic information updated in real time.
- Avoiding congested routes improves journey time and so reduces emissions and therefore reduces the environmental impact of the journey.

Car management systems

- A start-stop system automatically detects when a car is stationary and out of gear, for instance, at a junction, and cuts the engine in order to reduce fuel consumption and emissions.
- The engine control unit provides precise control over the amount of fuel used in order to improve the performance of the engine and minimise the emission of harmful exhaust gases.

Chapter 24 Security risks and precautions

This chapter describes security risks and precautions. The following topics are covered.

- Describe and identify the implications for individuals and businesses of the Computer Misuse Act 1990:
  - unauthorised access to computer material
  - unauthorised access with intent to commit a further offence
  - unauthorised modification of programs or data on a computer.
- Describe and identify the security risks of:
  - tracking cookies
  - DOS (denial of service) attacks:
    - symptoms: slow performance, inability to access
    - effects: disruption to users and businesses
    - costs: lost revenue, labour in rectifying fault
    - types of fault: bandwidth consumption, resource starvation, Domain Name Service (DNS)
    - reasons: financial, political, personal.
- Describe how encryption is used to secure transmission of data:
  - use of public and private keys
  - digital signatures
  - digital certificates.

The Computer Misuse Act 1990

Since this Act was passed, individuals may be prosecuted for carrying out certain activities relating to computers which are classified as illegal. Any conviction which is made is a result of the application of this Act

The Computer Misuse Act 1990 makes it a criminal offence:

- *to gain unauthorised access to computer material.* If a person hacks, or even just <u>attempts to hack,</u> a computer system which does not belong to them or without the owner's permission, then they are liable to prosecution under the Act.
- *to gain unauthorised access with intent to commit or facilitate commission of further offences.* If a person hacks with the intent of, for example stealing money from an online bank account, then they may be prosecuted under the Act, <u>even if the intended transfer of funds does not actually take place</u>.
- *to carry out unauthorised acts with intent to impair the operation of a computer or causing or creating risk of serious damage or making, supplying or obtaining articles for use in the commission of these offences.* If a person writes or distributes any harmful program, such as any type of malware, or carries out a denial of service (DOS) attack, then they are liable to prosecution under the Act.

Malware is software which can damage a computer. Malware includes viruses, worms, Trojans, spyware, key loggers, ransomware and adware. You can read more about DOS attacks later on in the chapter.

You can find out detailed information on the legal implications of the Computer Misuse Act 1990 here: www.cps.gov.uk/legal-guidance/computer-misuse. Although the information provided in this web page specifically mentions England and Wales, please note that these legal provisions have also been agreed by the Scottish Parliament.

You can read about some of the examples of prosecutions which have taken place under the Computer Misuse Act 1990 here: www.computerevidence.co.uk/Cases/CMA.htm.

These types of crime are widespread because so many computers may be accessed through networks such as the internet. There are a variety of estimates as to the cost and extent of malware and criminal activities on computers.

Varonis is a cybersecurity company which helps organisations to protect their data. The company's website contains a list of current statistics on various forms of cybercrime. You can find out more about this here: www.varonis.com/blog/cybersecurity-statistics/.

Implications of the Computer Misuse Act 1990 for individuals

Individuals should take precautions to ensure that whatever data they have stored on their own computer systems or connected devices remains as private as possible. Suitable precautions include the use of passwords, biometrics, anti-virus software, firewalls, web proxies and encryption.

Passwords

Passwords should be difficult for others to guess. A mixture of random numbers, upper- and lower-case letters, punctuation marks and special characters is best. It is also very important to change your password on a regular basis. Using a different password for different websites is also advisable. Using only one password for everything greatly increases the damage that could be done, should that password be discovered.

Password manager software has been developed because of the difficulty of remembering so many different user identities and passwords for each website. Password manager software stores all of the passwords and login details and automatically logs the user in to previously visited websites.

Some browser software contains password management features that will offer to store a user's login details. It is not recommended that you use this feature if you work on a shared computer.

You can check out the security of a password on a number of websites, such as www.howsecureismypassword.net and www.passwordmeter.com.

Table 24.1 shows a list of the most common passwords of 2019. Is your password among the top 10?

Rank	Password
1	123456
2	123456789
3	qwerty
4	password
5	1111111
6	12345678
7	abc123
8	1234567
9	password1
10	12345

Table 24.1 The ten most common passwords of 2019

Biometrics

One alternative to passwords is the use of **biometrics**. Biometrics uses a person's physical characteristics in order to provide evidence of their identity. Examples of biometric data which may be used in this manner include facial recognition, fingerprints, retinal scan or voice-prints.

Biometrics may be physiological or behavioural. Physiological biometrics include a person's face, fingerprints, hands, irises and DNA. Behavioural biometrics include keystrokes, signature and voice.

It may be possible to imitate a person's handwriting and therefore their signature, but it is more difficult to imitate someone's irises or their DNA. A signature biometric may also record the way a person writes their signature *while they are doing it,* which will be different from the way a forger will write it, although both the genuine and the forged signatures may appear to be identical on paper.

In order to create biometric data, a person must have their physical characteristics scanned into a computer, which then adds them to a database. The data in the database is normally encrypted. When a person's identity is being verified, one or more characteristics will be scanned again and compared with what is held in the database against that person's name. If the details match, then the person is accepted.

It is now commonplace for phones to use biometrics such as fingerprints and facial recognition. Some uses of biometrics in schools include access control, attendance/registration and school meals systems.

Advantages of biometrics

- More secure than a password or card which can be stolen or lost.
- Difficult to forge some biometrics, for instance DNA, as opposed to handwriting

Disadvantages of biometrics

- If someone steals your biometric data, you cannot get new data, for example if a hacker manages to tamper with or change the biometric of your face, you cannot get a new one!
- You may be in physical danger, like the car owner who had part of his index finger chopped off by thieves trying to steal his car in 2005.

Anti-virus software

Anti-virus software protects a computer system against attack or infection from viruses and other types of malware. Sources of infection include software downloads and spam email messages. Anti-virus software should be able to detect malware and remove it from a computer system. It is important to keep anti-virus software up to date by means of regular downloads.

Anti-virus software is also included in *security suites*. A security suite is a collection of software which is sold together as a single package and contains programs which protect computers against a variety of malware. A typical security suite may include anti-virus, firewall, anti-spam, anti-spyware, parental controls, privacy and phishing protection. Additional programs may include features such as password management, online backup and tune-up.

Like anti-virus software, security suites also offer online support, including software updates which take account of the fact that new malware is constantly being developed.

Firewalls

A **firewall** is a system designed to prevent unauthorised access to or from a private network, such as in a school or local authority. The firewall contains rules and conditions which specify what is and is not allowed to pass through. All messages which pass through the firewall are examined to check whether or not they meet these rules and conditions. Those messages which do not are blocked. The main use of a firewall in a school or home network is to prevent unauthorised (outside) internet users from gaining access to the network.

Firewalls can be created in *hardware* or *software*. Hardware firewalls are located in the router which connects the network to the internet. A hardware firewall therefore provides protection for the whole network, regardless of the number of computers or other devices connected. A hardware firewall operates independently of the computers, so it has no effect on their performance. Software firewalls may use some system resources such as memory, storage space and processing, which may have an effect on a computer's performance, although less so if the firewall is part of the computer's own operating system. A hardware firewall cannot be easily affected by malware, unlike a software firewall. A software firewall can protect portable computers when they are used away from a hardware firewall-protected network. In practice, it is normal to have both types of firewall installed, in order to provide the maximum possible amount of protection.

Web proxies

A **web proxy** is often used along with a firewall. A web proxy is a server used to access web pages requested by other computers on a network. This means that the computers outside the network only come into contact with the web proxy and not the computers on the inside of the proxy. A web proxy is often used to control a user's access to web pages by means of content filtering. Most schools allow pupils and staff access to the internet only through such a server, which not only blocks websites deemed to be unsuitable, but records the web address or URL of every page accessed by its users. Some schools and local authorities use a **walled garden**, which only allows access to an approved set of URLs. The term 'walled garden' is also used to refer to any closed system or platform. For instance, the *iOS* app store only allows applications approved by *Apple* to be downloaded and run on their devices. The *Amazon Kindle* e-reader and a wide variety of games consoles operate in the same manner.

Implications of the Computer Misuse Act 1990 for businesses

The implications of gaining unauthorised access to a business's computer system include:

- risk of the computer system being put out of action resulting in a loss of income for the company until repairs have been carried out.
- cost of repairing the computer system, restoring the data and improving the security of the system to reduce the chance of unauthorised access in the future.
- losing customers to alternative businesses or suppliers whose computer systems are unaffected by hacking.
- losing trade secrets which may be of value to a competitor's business.
- customers being put at risk if their personal details (including passwords) are revealed.

CHECK YOUR LEARNING

Now answer questions 1–17 (on page 325) on the Computer Misuse Act 1990

The security risks of tracking cookies

Cookies

A **cookie** is a small text file which is sent from a website and stored on the user's computer by a web browser application. Cookies were originally designed to hold items which the user had placed in an online shopping basket. Cookies can record a user's login information and keep a record of which web pages have been visited previously. Cookies are not malware, but they can have consequences in terms of user privacy. There are several different types of cookie, but we will concentrate on two: the first-party cookie and the third-party or **tracking cookie**.

First-party cookies

A **first-party cookie** can improve a user's web browsing experience, because it allows a website to recognise a user by remembering their log-in data and applies any settings required, such as language, shopping basket content or recent search terms. The first-party cookie

will stop operating when the user leaves the website. It will only be read and possibly updated when the website is revisited.

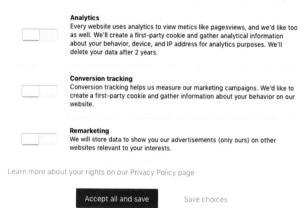

No ads on this website! Just pageviews

This website protects your privacy by adhering to the European Union General Data Protection Regulation (GDPR)...but we'd also like to see how many people visit our website by viewing analytics & conversion data. This means NO ads on our website. Please state below which processes you consent to. We will not use your data for any other purposes.

Analytics
Every website uses analytics to view metics like pageviews, and we'd like too as well. We'll create a first-party cookie and gather analytical information about your behavior, device, and IP address for analytics purposes. We'll delete your data after 2 years.

Conversion tracking
Conversion tracking helps us measure our marketing campaigns. We'd like to create a first-party cookie and gather information about your behavior on our website.

Remarketing
We will store data to show you our advertisements (only ours) on other websites relevant to your interests.

Learn more about your rights on our Privacy Policy page

[Accept all and save]   Save choices

Figure 24.1 Informing users about the use of cookies on a website

An example of what a first-party cookie does is to remember a user's acceptance of the use of cookies as required by General Data Protection Regulation (GDPR). The permission given by the user will be stored and not displayed again unless the user deletes the cookie.

First-party cookies benefit the operator of the website because they make it easier to use. Data obtained about the behaviour of users may also help operators to improve the design of the website. A first-party cookie may only be created and viewed by the website that the user is currently visiting and not by anyone else (such as a third party).

Third-party (tracking) cookies

Third-party cookies are also known as tracking or targeting cookies. Third-party cookies are not created by the operator of a website but instead by an advertiser (a third party). Third-party cookies collect information about the user, mainly for marketing use, such as age, origin, gender and user behaviour on the web. In addition, third-party cookies also collect the same information as first-party cookies. The reason why so much information is collected is in order to build up a complete as possible **user profile** and ultimately create a **unique identifier** for the user.

Many web pages (and spam emails) also contain so-called **tracking pixels** which are transparent and 1×1 pixel in size. All the user has to do to activate the HTML code associated with the tracking pixel is to visit the web page (or open the email). It is not necessary to click anywhere on the page. Tracking pixels can acquire data such as the operating system, type of device and browser, screen resolution, time, extent of activity on the website and Internet Protocol (IP) address (identifying the user's Internet Service Provider [ISP] and location).

Examples of third parties who may leave tracking cookies include:

- *Advertiser retargeting services*; these actively follow users around the web and display advertisements for products or services the user has viewed earlier. Retargeting also works across social media and email.
- *Social button plugins*; these are buttons on the browser which enable users to login, like or share content on social media. These plugins all place tracking cookies on a user's device.
- *Online chat popups*; these leave a cookie in order to improve the user experience. The next time the user visits the chat, the previous conversation may be recalled.

> **DID YOU KNOW?**
>
> **Do second-party cookies exist?**
>
> Second-party cookies do not exist. However, if the data gathered by a first-party cookie is sold or transferred from the company that created it to another company, (usually by means of an agreement to share data) then this is known as second-party data. The other company would then use the data to target advertisements at users.

The Norwegian Consumer Council published a detailed report on 14 January 2020 concerning the activities of the online advertising industry.

> In this report, we demonstrate how every time we use our phones, a large number of shadowy entities that are virtually unknown to consumers are receiving personal data about our interests, habits, and behaviour.

You can read the report here: www.forbrukerradet.no/out-of-control/.

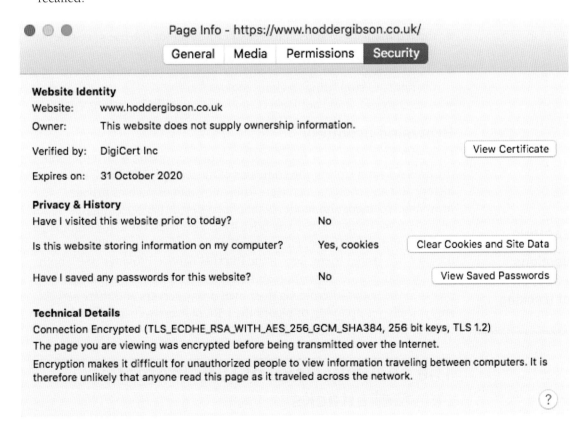

Figure 24.2 Web page information

Advantages of tracking cookies

For users:

- personalised advertising means that users will only see advertisements that will interest them.

For website operators:

- the provision of ads is carried out by the advertising server, not the website.
- advertising income may increase if users are more likely to click on relevant advertisements.

For advertisers:

- advertisements may actually prompt users to purchase the goods or services being advertised, increasing their income.

Disadvantages of tracking cookies

For users:

- the accumulation and storage of personal data may breach data protection law.

For website operators:

- users may be unhappy about third-party cookies being used to track their behaviour and hold their personal data and may avoid some websites because of this.

For advertisers:

- the requirement to constantly seek permission for the use of cookies and having to agree to this may be annoying for some users.
- changing legislation, attitudes and technologies may cause website operators to stop using tracking cookies.
- some browsers (and adblockers) automatically block tracking cookies.

Browsing privately

Most web browsers allow users to select a privacy option which prevents the browser from storing the addresses of the web pages visited, the search history and any cookies. These are known by names such as **private browsing** and **incognito mode**. It should be noted that selecting this option *only affects the computer or device being used*. This is useful if, for example, a shared computer is in use. However, all of the websites will still know that the user has visited them, as will the Internet Service Provider (ISP), both landline and mobile. Education authorities and employers usually allow access to the wider internet via their own **proxy servers** and these servers are typically set up to log or record the URL of every website visited against the user's login credentials.

> **CHECK YOUR LEARNING**
>
> **Now answer questions 18–26 (on page 325) on the security risks of tracking cookies**

The security risks of DOS (denial of service) attacks

A **DOS attack** is a procedure that tries to interrupt or suspend the services of a **host computer**. A host computer is a physical device which, when connected to a network, such as the internet, provides services to another connected computer. In this case, a host computer could be one which holds a company's website, or **web server**.

> **NOTE**
>
> The SQA Higher Computing Science Course Specification (2018–19) Version 2.1, upon which this textbook is based, makes no distinction between DOS and DDOS. This chapter uses both of these terms.

Symptoms of a DOS attack

A DOS attack involves sending so many requests to a host computer that it becomes unable to provide access to legitimate requests or slows the performance of the host so much that it becomes unusable. In some cases, a DOS attack can crash the affected computer, particularly when the attack includes malware. One other symptom of a DOS attack is receiving an excessive number of spam emails.

Distributed denial of service (DDOS) attack

A DDOS attack takes place when many different computers carry out a DOS attack on a single host computer. A variety of methods may be used to carry out a DDOS attack. These include:

- a **worm** such as *Mydoom*, which attacks a preprogrammed (fixed) target computer.
- a **Trojan**, which takes over a computer and turns it into a **zombie**. A zombie is a computer connected to the internet that is under the control of a hacker and is used to distribute malware, send out spam or steal your private information.

- a specific piece of software called a DDOS tool which connects to a handler or master computer, which, in turn, controls a number of zombie computers, collectively called a **botnet** or **zombie army**. The person in control of a botnet is a **bot herder**. A botnet can be targeted against any computer. The owner of a zombie computer may be completely unaware that their computer has been used in this manner. However, a computer used as a zombie will not operate properly, certainly not to its full efficiency. Virtually any device that is connected to the internet via the so-called **Internet of Things** (IoT) may be used in this manner; security lights, cameras, digital video recorders, routers and printers are devices that are vulnerable to attack because they often contain factory-set administrator passwords which are not updated by the user to something more secure.

What is the difference between DOS and DDOS?

The difference between these two types of denial of service attack is that a DOS attack is carried out by a single computer and a DDOS attack is carried out by many separate (distributed) computers simultaneously. As may be expected, it is much more difficult to defend against a DDOS attack, because of the number of computer systems involved.

Defending against attack

A number of different methods may be used to defend against or limit the effect of a DOS attack, including the use of a firewall. What the defence is trying to do is to block the attack, which is unwanted traffic, and allow access to genuine internet traffic.

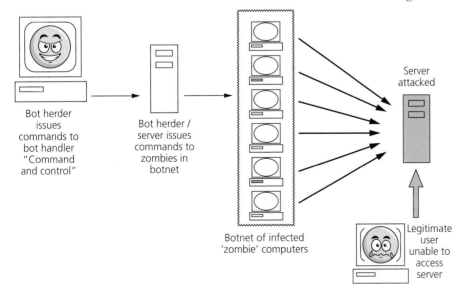

Bot herder issues commands to bot handler "Command and control"

Bot herder / server issues commands to zombies in botnet

Botnet of infected 'zombie' computers

Server attacked

Legitimate user unable to access server

Figure 24.3 Operation of a botnet

A movie from Kaspersky Labs® showing a simple animation of a DOS attack can be seen here: www.youtube.com/watch?v=yLbC7G71IyE.

Botnets

How a botnet is created

1 A hacker creates an email with a link to a website containing a hidden virus. This is sent to several home and business computers.
2 A user opens the email and clicks on the link; immediately their computer becomes infected by the virus.
3 The botnet is created; the virus software makes the computers into slave machines or zombies, waiting for commands from the hacker. Each slave machine has the potential to infect many others.

What happens next?

4 Spammers, who are trying to sell something, for instance prescription drugs, pay the hacker to send out spam via the botnet.
5 Hackers can also make money selling data stolen from infected computers, such as identity and bank details, and using them to launch attacks.
6 Hackers extort money from companies by threatening to attack their website using the botnet; a DDOS attack. The creators of botnets may also rent them out to other criminals in order to carry out attacks. These are known as DDOS-for-hire (or booters or stressors).

Example DDOS extortion letter

We are the Baddies and we have chosen your company as a target for our next DDoS attack.

Your network will be subject to a DDoS attack starting on Wednesday. (This is not a hoax, and to prove it we will start a small attack that will last for 30 minutes.)

We will refrain from attacking your servers for a small fee. The current fee is 2 Bitcoin (BTC). The fee will increase by 1 BTC for each day after the deadline has passed without payment.

Please send BTC to this address: 3J99t1WpEZ83CNmQviecltyiWrnqRhWSLy.

Once you have paid, we will automatically get informed. Please note that you have to make payment before the deadline or the attack WILL start!

If you decide not to pay, we will start the attack and uphold it until you do, there's no counter measure to this, you will only end up wasting more money trying to find a solution. We will completely destroy your reputation and make sure your services remain offline until you pay. Do not reply to this email, don't try to reason or negotiate, we will not read any replies. Once you have paid, we won't start the attack and you will never hear from us again. Please note that Bitcoin is anonymous and no one will find out that you have complied.

You can read more about botnets here: www.infosecurity-magazine.com/next-gen-infosec/ddos-botnets-damage-1-1/.

Effects of a DOS attack

The effects of a DOS attack include:

- *disruption to users* – users of a website affected by a DOS attack will find that the website either operates very slowly or that it has become totally inaccessible. This means that access to the website, which is a service, is effectively denied to the user, hence the name 'denial of service'.
- *disruption to businesses* – businesses will be disrupted because legitimate users will be unable to access the company's website, for instance, in order to purchase goods or services.

Costs of a DOS attack

The costs of a DOS attack include:

- *lost revenue*; the amount of money that a company or business may lose as a result of a DOS attack.
- *labour in rectifying fault*; the amount of money that a company or business needs to spend in order to recover from a DOS attack and put measures in place in order to prevent it from happening again. Recognising this, many companies have set up businesses based on providing services which protect against DOS attacks. The URLs of just a few of these companies are shown here:
  - www.akamai.com/uk/en/
  - www.radware.com
  - www.imperva.com
  - https://sucuri.net
  - www.symantec.com/security-center
  - www.kaspersky.co.uk
  - www.cloudflare.com/en-gb/
  - www.ibm.com/uk-en/cloud/cloud-internet-services

The costs of a DOS attack may be estimated by entering figures into this online calculator: www.akamai.com/uk/en/products/security/calculate-the-cost-of-ddos-attacks.jsp.

Types of fault

The types of fault experienced by computer systems, servers and networks involved in a DOS attack include:

Bandwidth consumption

This is a DOS attack which sends so many packets of data that the target organisation's service becomes overwhelmed. It depends on the attacker having access to a much higher bandwidth than the victim. Such an attack is typically carried out by a botnet (see Figure 24.3).

If the victim's service is cloud-based, then this type of attack may well result in a greater cost because the cloud provider will (quite legitimately) charge the victim for the increased traffic. Bandwidth consumption is also known as a **volumetric attack**.

The first one terabit per second (TBPS) DOS attack was recorded in 2018.

Resource starvation

Resource starvation attacks prevent availability by consuming services or processing power of the victim computer. One example of resource starvation is the so-called Transmission Control Protocol (TCP), together with Internet Protocol (IP):

- is the main method by which communications are established and maintained over the internet. TCP is used to establish a connection between a client and a server using a three-way handshake via SYN (synchronise) and ACK (acknowledge) packets. A SYN packet is sent from the client to the server. If the SYN packet is received, then a SYN/ACK is sent back to the IP address requested by the SYN. If the SYN/ACK is received, then a final ACK packet is sent.
- A SYN flood attack works by not responding to the server with the expected ACK packet. This can happen either by not sending an ACK or by sending a SYN to the server containing a false (or spoofed) IP address, which means that the computer located at the spoofed IP address will not send the ACK, because it did not send the SYN to start with.

- An attacker keeps on flooding the target server with repeated SYN requests until the server's TCP connection buffer maximum is reached and the system can no longer accept TCP connections. The resource that is being 'starved' in this example is the capacity of the connection buffer. This means that the server is effectively down and can no longer be accessed by legitimate users.

Another example of resource starvation involves subscribing a victim's email address to a large number of mailing lists in order to increase the amount of email traffic to that address. This type of attack may be carried out against a single person or a server. Even if a large number of messages can be handled by the victim's mail server, the victim's desktop email client will continue to fill with unwanted messages, consuming network and computer resources.

Domain name service (DNS)

Domain name services (or systems or servers) act like address books for the internet. For example, the domain name 'hoddergibson.co.uk' is easy for us to remember but is resolved (or translated) by a DNS into the IP address '107.162.140.19' in a process known as DNS lookup or DNS query.

A DNS **flood attack** overwhelms a single DNS with a large number of valid lookup requests, making it difficult for the server to distinguish between the attack and normal heavy workload. If legitimate users cannot access the DNS, then they will be unable to access websites.

The high bandwidth connections provided by IoT devices like webcams and digital video recorders are often used to carry out DNS flood attacks.

This link lists websites which provide real-time animation of worldwide DOS attacks here: https://geekflare.com/real-time-cyber-attacks/.

> **NOTE**
>
> There is not enough space in this chapter to provide specific details on all of the different types of fault that may be experienced by computers and servers who become victims of DOS attacks, but the ones covered here are those required for this course. You may like to research others for yourself.

Reasons for DOS attacks

DOS attacks do not happen at random. Criminals choose their victims deliberately; these are often so-called 'high-profile' targets such as e-commerce websites, banks and credit card companies. The reasons for DOS attacks include:

Financial

- Enacted by criminals in order to bully the victims and extort money, often demanding payment in the form of cryptocurrency such as Bitcoin. Unfortunately, simply paying the extortionists what they demand often results in further attacks.
- In order to damage or shut down a company's website in the hope that business traffic will come to a competing company's website.

Political

- In order to influence public confidence in government or the outcome of a democratic election. Often carried out by state-sized or state-sponsored actors (hackers), these attacks may also target another country's infrastructure, such as the national energy grid.
- Carried out because they do not agree with a particular company's activities, for example, testing of products on animals. The individuals or organisations carrying out attacks for these reasons are known as 'hacktivists', a term created by combining 'hacker' with 'activist'.

Personal

- In order to take revenge on a company from someone bearing a grudge, for instance, a former employee who has been dismissed or overlooked for a promotion. This is known as an 'insider threat'.

Distraction

- A DOS attack may also be used to distract the attention of security staff from another type of hack, such as stealing customer data. This is known as a 'smoke screen'.

Fun

- A hacker may have no discernible reason for carrying out an attack other than they enjoy doing it.

CHECK YOUR LEARNING

Now answer questions 27–36 (on page 326) on the security risks of DOS (Denial of Service) attacks

How encryption is used to secure transmission of data

Encryption means putting data into a code to prevent it from being seen by unauthorised users. **Decryption** means changing an encrypted message back into readable text. When you type a password to access a network, it is encrypted before it is sent to the **file server** to prevent it from being read en route. One common use of encryption is to protect email messages and files that are sent over a network. Other common uses of encryption are to protect storage media such as hard disks and flash ROM. Should the computer containing the media, or the media itself, be stolen, then it will be practically impossible to read the data stored in it without access to the correct password.

Files may be encrypted using an **application package**, like *Symantec Drive Encryption*®, or using a security feature built into the computer's operating system, like *FileVault*®. When the encrypted message reaches its destination, then the same encryption software is used to decrypt the message and turn it back into readable text.

A **key** is a piece of information which allows the sender to encrypt a message and the receiver to decrypt a message. A key is made up of a long string of random bits. In general, it may be said that the longer the key used to encrypt a message, the more difficult it will be to decrypt it. The minimum recommended length (number of bits) of a key is 128 bits. However, this may change as more sophisticated systems are created that may be able to crack these keys. Using a fast computer to attempt to decrypt a message by trying a lot of possibilities is known as a **brute force attack**.

Use of public and private keys

Public key encryption or **public key cryptography** uses two uniquely related keys, the **public key** and the **private key**. The public key is made generally available to everyone. The private key is kept confidential by its owner. The public key and the private key are mathematically related in such a manner that whatever message is encrypted with the public key may only be decrypted by the corresponding private key.

For instance, if John wants to send a message to Jane, and be sure that only Jane can read the message, he will encrypt the text with Jane's public key. Only Jane may access her corresponding private key and so she is the only person able to decrypt the message back into the original text. Should the message be intercepted by Rosie en route from John to Jane, the message will be unreadable because Rosie does not have access to Jane's private key.

The WhatsApp messaging app uses end-to-end encryption which makes use of public and private keys to ensure the security of any text, audio or video message sent using the app.

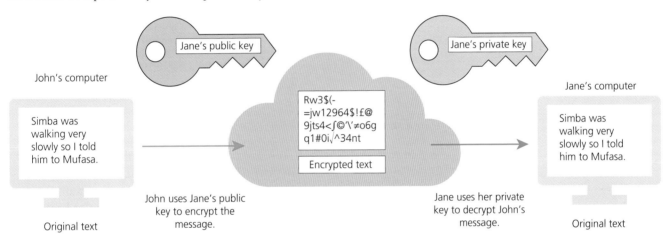

Figure 24.4 Public and private key encryption

DID YOU KNOW?

How private and public keys are created

One method of producing private and public keys involves using prime numbers. A prime number is one which is only divisible by itself or by 1. Examples of prime numbers include 2, 3, 5, 7, 11, 13, 17, 19, 23, 29, 31, 37, 41, 43, 47, 53, 59, 61, 67, 71, 73, 79, 83, 89, and 97. However, these small numbers are not used to produce keys because they would be too easy to 'crack'. A private key is generated using two very large prime numbers, typically more than 100 digits long. The public key is then created by multiplying the two prime numbers together to obtain the product. It is very difficult to work out which two large prime numbers were used to create the public key. This is known as prime factoring. The public key may be shared with anyone as required. As long as the private key (the original two prime numbers) is kept secure, then any messages encrypted by it are private.

Digital signatures

A **digital signature** is a method of ensuring that a message or software or digital document is valid and has not been tampered with. In many countries, a digital signature is considered to be just as legally binding as a handwritten one.

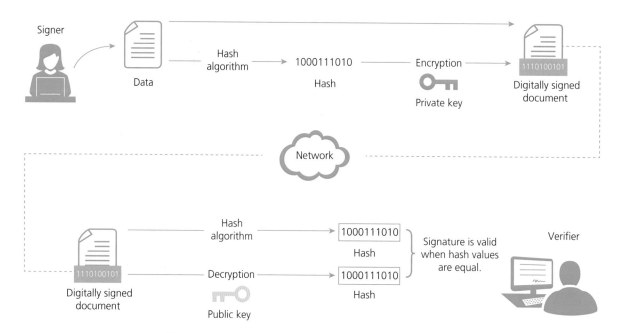

Figure 24.5 Creating and checking a digital signature

Digital signatures are based on the same private and public keys we looked at earlier in this chapter. In order to create a digital signature, the signing software or **hash algorithm**, creates a code of fixed length (for example 256 bits) from the original message. This is called a **hash code** or **hash value**. Unlike encryption (and decryption), hashing is a *one-way process*. The hash value is unique to the data that has been encoded, so that even a change of one single character in the original message will result in a completely different hash value.

Here is an example of a hash value for the word 'John':

```
a8cfcd74832004951b4408cdb0a5dbcd8c7e52d43f7fe
244bf720582e05241da
```

And here is an example of a hash value for the word 'Joan':

```
2d0f4c4eb78ce93adc09b60c696c76d0476185983c956
a6f2a5bbf0afb9dbc2e
```

If you would like to try this out for yourself, shown below is a short program in Python which will produce hash values.

```
from hashlib import sha256

h = sha256()

h.update(b'John')

hash = h.hexdigest()

print(hash)
```

The next step in the process is to use the message signer's private key to encrypt the hash value. This encrypted hash value, together with the *hash algorithm*, is the *digital signature*. The recipient of the message may now use the signer's public key to decrypt the hash value. In order to verify the digital signature, the recipient (or verifier) recalculates a second hash value and compares this new value with the decrypted value. If both hash values match, then that proves that the data hasn't changed since it was signed. One important aspect of applying a digital signature to communications is known as *non-repudiation*. Non-repudiation means that once an individual or an organisation has signed a message they cannot deny having done so.

If the two hash values do not match, then either the data has been tampered with (it lacks *integrity*) or the digital signature was created with a different private key (it is not *authentic*).

However, digital signatures also have some disadvantages, which include:

● there is no method of removing (or revoking) a digital signature, making decisions permanent.
● lack of confidentiality; the use of public keys means that anyone with a public key can decrypt the data.

Figure 24.6 Digital signatures are permanent

Digital certificates

A digital signature is used to verify that data is being sent securely. However, a digital signature does not itself prove the identity or trustworthiness of the sender of the data. A **digital certificate** is used to verify the identity of its owner.

Digital certificates are issued by recognised authorities, such as the government. In order to be granted a digital certificate, the authority must first be satisfied that the person or organisation making the request is exactly who they say that they are.

Digital certificates allow their holder's identity to be verified because they include:

● personal information to identify the owner
● information which identifies the issuing authority and how they may be contacted

- features which make them difficult to copy or forge
- the ability to be withdrawn at any time by the authority
- the ability to be checked for validity by contacting the authority
- a definite time limit after which the certificate is invalid.

Figure 24.7 shows a digital certificate in use in a web browser. The information in the digital certificate shown here may be accessed by clicking on the padlock icon in the web address bar.

Figure 24.7 A digital certificate in use in a web browser

Websites which do not have a current or valid digital certificate, should not be used for secure information such as credit card numbers or bank account details. A valid digital certificate will be issued by a reputable organisation and not be out of date or expired. Web browsers will warn the user if they detect a problem with a certificate or if the website is not secure. Remember that a website which shows a padlock icon, but does not display any certificate information, may be fraudulent. Note also that there is no consistency in the significance of different coloured padlock icons.

Security protocols

A protocol is a set of rules that determine how something is to be done, for instance, communication protocols are used when sending messages via the internet. Examples of communications protocols include: simple mail transfer protocol (SMTP), post office protocol (POP), hypertext transfer protocol (HTTP), internet protocol (IP), transmission control protocol (TCP) and file transfer protocol (FTP).

A security protocol is a sequence of operations that makes sure data is protected. Security protocols are often used together with communications protocols, to ensure that sensitive data, such as credit card numbers, is kept private while it is being transmitted over a network. Examples of security protocols include transport layer security (TLS) and secure sockets layer (SSL). The hypertext transfer protocol secure (HTTPS) is produced by the combination of SSL/TLS and HTTP.

A security protocol guarantees the security of data in transit, but it does not prove that the person or organisation is trustworthy; that is the function of the digital certificate.

Now answer questions 37–47 (on page 326) on how encryption is used to secure transmission of data

QUESTIONS

The Computer Misuse Act 1990

1 List three criminal offences covered by the Computer Misuse Act 1990.
2 State your opinion as to whether or not these scenarios are criminal offences under the Computer Misuse Act 1990.
   a) attempting to hack a computer system that does not belong to you
   b) attempting to steal money from an online bank account
   c) spreading malware
   d) carrying out a DOS attack.
3 What is malware?
4 List three types of malware.
5 Name three precautions which can help to keep data held on computer systems private.
6 One feature of browser software is the storage of user's login details. Under what circumstance is the use of this feature insecure?
7 What are biometrics?
8 Name one physiological and one behavioural biometric.
9 State one advantage and one disadvantage of the use of biometrics.
10 Name two sources of malware.
11 Why is it necessary for ant-virus software to be regularly updated?
12 What is a firewall?

13 Explain the operation of a firewall.
14 Where is a hardware firewall located?
15 What is a web proxy?
16 Name two features that may be provided to a school by a web proxy.
17 State two implications of gaining unauthorised access to a business's computer system.

The security risks of tracking cookies

18 What is a cookie?
19 State the function of a first-party cookie.
20 State the function of a third-party or tracking cookie.
21 Why are tracking cookies also known as third-party cookies?
22 What effect has the General Data Protection Regulation (GDPR) had on a website's use of cookies?
23 a) Describe the size and colour of a tracking pixel.
   b) State one reason why tracking pixels are like this.
   c) What data may tracking pixels acquire?
24 State one example of a third party who may leave tracking cookies.
25 State one advantage and one disadvantage of the use of tracking cookies for:
   a) users
   b) website operators
   c) advertisers.

26 Why is selecting the 'privacy' mode on a browser not really private?

The security risks of DOS (Denial of Service) attacks

27 What is a DOS attack?
28 What is a DDOS attack?
29 State two symptoms of a DOS attack.
30 What is a:
   a) zombie?
   b) botnet?
   c) bot herder?
31 a) Apart from a computer system, name two other types of devices that may be used by a hacker to carry out a DOS attack.
   b) Explain why some Internet of Things (IoT) devices may be used in this manner.
32 State one main difference between DOS and DDOS.
33 Describe one method of carrying out a DDOS attack.
34 Lost revenue is one cost of a DOS attack. Name one other cost of a DOS attack.
35 a) Name three types of fault that may be experienced by computer systems involved in a DOS attack.
   b) Which type of fault may be created by a SYN flood attack?
36 Financial gain is one reason why criminals may carry out DOS attacks. Name two other reasons and provide one example for each.

How encryption is used to secure transmission of data

37 What is meant by the terms:
   a) encryption?
   b) decryption?
   c) brute force attack?
38 a) In terms of encryption, what is a key?
   b) What is the minimum recommended length of a key?
39 a) Explain the relationship between a public and a private key.
   b) Describe the process of encryption and decryption using a public and a private key.
   c) What happens if the encrypted message in b) above is intercepted by a hacker?
40 What is the function of a digital signature?
41 Explain how a digital signature may be created.
42 Explain how a digital signature may be verified.
43 What is meant by the term 'non-repudiation'?
44 State two disadvantages of digital signatures.
45 What is the function of a digital certificate?
46 State two items of information included in a digital certificate.
47 How may a digital certificate be viewed when using a browser?

KEY POINTS

The Computer Misuse Act 1990

- The Computer Misuse Act 1990 makes it a criminal offence:
  - to gain unauthorised access to computer material
  - to gain unauthorised access with intent to commit or facilitate commission of further offences
  - to carry out unauthorised acts with intent to impair the operation of a computer or causing or creating risk of serious damage or making, supplying or obtaining articles for use in the commission of these offences.

Implications of the Computer Misuse Act 1990 for individuals

- Individuals should take precautions to ensure that whatever data they have stored on their own computer systems remains private.
- Passwords should be difficult to guess – a mixture of random numbers, letters and punctuation marks is best.
- It is very important to change your password on a regular basis.
- Biometrics is using a person's physical characteristics in order to provide evidence of their identity.
- Biometrics include facial recognition, fingerprints, retinal scan or voiceprints.
- Biometrics are more secure than a password and are more difficult to forge, but biometrics data cannot be replaced if it becomes compromised.
- Anti-virus software protects a computer system against attack or infection by viruses and other types of malware.
- A firewall is a system designed to prevent unauthorised access to or from a private network.
- The firewall contains rules and conditions, which specify what is and is not allowed to pass through.
- Firewalls can be created in hardware or software – hardware firewalls are located in the router.

- A web proxy is used to access web pages requested by computers on a network – the computers outside the network only come into contact with the web proxy.

Implications of the Computer Misuse Act 1990 for businesses

- The implications of gaining unauthorised access to a business's computer system include:
  - The computer system may be put out of action
  - The cost of repair
  - Loss of customers to competitor businesses
  - Loss of trade secrets
  - Loss of customer's personal details.

The security risks of tracking cookies

- A cookie is a small text file which is sent from a website and stored on the user's computer.
- A first-party cookie allows a website to recognise a user by remembering their log-in data and applies any settings required.
- Third-party cookies are also known as tracking cookies.
- Third-party cookies are created by advertisers and collect information about users.
- Examples of third parties who may leave tracking cookies include:
  - Advertiser re-targeting services
  - Social button plugins
  - On-line chat popups
- Advantages of tracking (third party) cookies include:
  - Personalised advertising
  - The provision of ads is carried out by the advertising server
  - Advertising income may increase
  - Advertisements may actually prompt users to purchase goods.
- Disadvantages of tracking (third party) cookies
  - The accumulation and storage of personal data may breach data protection law
  - Users may be unhappy about cookies being used to track their behaviour and hold their personal data
  - The requirement to seek permission for the use of cookies may be annoying
  - Changing legislation may cause website operators to stop using tracking cookies
  - Some browsers automatically block tracking cookies.

The security risks of DOS (Denial of Service) attacks

- A DOS attack is a procedure, which tries to interrupt or suspend the services of a *host computer*, which is connected to the Internet.
- A DOS attack involves sending so many requests to a host computer, that it becomes *unable to provide access* to legitimate requests or *slows the performance* of the host so much that it becomes unusable.
- A DDOS attack takes place when many different computers carry out a DOS attack on a single host computer.
- It is more difficult to defend against a DDOS attack, because of the number of computer systems involved.
- A firewall may be used to defend against or limit the effect of a DOS attack.
- The effects of a DOS attack include disruption to users and businesses.
- The costs of a DOS attack include lost revenue and the cost of the labour involved in rectifying the fault and protecting against future attacks.
- The types of fault experienced by computer systems, servers and networks involved in a DOS attack include:
  - bandwidth consumption – A DOS attack which sends so many packets of data that the target organisation's service becomes overwhelmed
  - resource starvation – these attacks prevent availability by consuming services or processing power of the victim that are required by legitimate users. One example of resource starvation is the so-called TCP SYN flood attack.
  - Domain Name Service (DNS) - A flood attack overwhelms a single DNS with a large number of lookup requests, making it difficult for the server to distinguish between the attack and normal workload. If legitimate users cannot access the DNS, then they will be unable to access websites.
- The reasons for DOS attacks include:
  - financial – enacted by criminals in order to bully the victims and extort money, or in order to shut down a company's website so that business traffic will come to a competing company's website

- political – in order to influence public confidence in government. Often carried out by state-sized or state-sponsored actors (hackers), these attacks may also target another country's infrastructure
- because they do not agree with a particular company's activities, for example, testing of products on animals. The individuals or organisations carrying out attacks for these reasons are known as 'hacktivists'
- personal – in order to take revenge on a company from someone bearing a grudge. This is known as an 'insider threat'
- distraction – in order to distract the attention of security staff from another type of hack
- 'fun' – a hacker may just enjoy doing it.

How encryption is used to secure transmission of data

- Encryption means putting data into a code to prevent it from being seen by unauthorised users
- Decryption means changing an encrypted message back into readable text
- Passwords are encrypted to prevent them from being read
- Encryption is to protect email messages and files that are sent over a network.
- A key is a piece of information which allows the sender to encrypt a message and the receiver to decrypt a message
- A key is made up of a long string of random bits - the longer the key, the more difficult it will be to decrypt it
- Using a fast computer to attempt to decrypt a message by trying a lot of possibilities is known as a brute force attack

Use of public and private keys

- Public Key Encryption uses two uniquely related keys, the public key and the private key
- The public key is made generally available to everyone and the private key is kept confidential by its owner
- The public key and the private key are mathematically related in such a manner that whatever message is encrypted with the public key may only be decrypted by the corresponding private key.

Digital signatures

- A digital signature is a method of ensuring that a message or software or a digital document is valid and has not been tampered with.
- In order to create a digital signature, the signing software or hash algorithm, creates a hash code of fixed length from the original message.

- Hashing is a *one-way process*.
- The hash value is unique to the encoded data, so a change of one single character will result in a completely different hash value.
- The next step is to use the message signer's private key to encrypt the hash value.
- This encrypted hash value, together with the hash algorithm, is the digital signature.
- The recipient of the message may now use the signer's public key to decrypt the hash value.
- In order to verify the digital signature, the recipient recalculates a second hash value and compares this new value with the decrypted value.
- If both hash values match, then that proves that the data hasn't changed since it was signed.
- Non-repudiation means that once an individual or an organisation has signed a message, then they cannot deny having done so.
- Disadvantages of digital signatures include:
  - No method of revoking a digital signature, making decisions permanent
  - Anyone with a public key can decrypt the data.

Digital certificates

- A digital signature does not prove the identity of the sender of the data.
- A digital certificate is used to verify the identity of its owner.
- Digital certificates are issued by recognised authorities, such as the government.
- Digital certificates allow their holder's identity to be verified because they include:
  - personal information to identify the owner
  - information which identifies the issuing authority
  - features which make them difficult to copy or forge
  - the ability to be withdrawn at any time by the authority
  - the ability to be checked for validity by contacting the authority
  - a definite time limit after which the certificate is invalid.
- Websites which do not have a current or valid digital certificate, should not be used for secure information.
- A valid digital certificate will be issued by a reputable organisation and not be out of date or expired.
- Web browsers will warn the user if they detect a problem with a certificate or if the website is not secure.

Glossary

& The symbol used for string concatenation in some languages; + is also used.

<!- -…- -> Used to add comments to the document which can help explain your code to others.

<a> The hypertext anchor tag.

<audio> Used to add audio to a web page.

<body> The web page content is placed inside these tags.

**
** Used to put a line break between pieces of text.

<div> Indicates a division or section within an HTML document.

<footer> Contains footer information to appear at the bottom of every web page such as copyright information, contact details, etc.

<form action="> Allows the web developer to create a page where the client can collect data from the user of the website.

<h1> … <h6> Heading tags. Decreasing in size from <h1> to <h6>.

<head> Shows the header, contains title and links to style sheets.

<header> Usually contains the header information for a web page to appear at the top of every web page.

<html> The html tag is used to show the beginning of mark-up.

<img> Used to display an image.

<input> A form element used for simple data entry into a form. Can be of several different types, e.g. text, number, radio, submit, etc.

<li> Indicates a list item in either an ordered or unordered list.

<link> Provides a link to an external stylesheet.

<main> Contains the content for each web page.

<nav> Contains the main navigation bar that generally appears on each web page. It does not have to contain all the hyperlinks that are present on each page, simply those that are part of the main structure of the website.

<ol> Ordered list/numbered list.

<option> Part of an HTML form which defines the contents of a drop-down list.

<p> Paragraph tag.

<section> Used to separate a web page into different parts for easy identification.

<select> A form element used to define a drop-down list.

<style> An HTML tag used to contain the styling for the page where each section to be styled is identified.

<title> Puts a title in the browser title bar.

<ul> Unordered list/bulleted list.

<video> Used to add video to a web page.

1D arrays See 'one-dimensional array'.

absolute addressing If the URL points to an external website with the full URL written, then the URL is said to be absolute.

acceptance testing The software is tested to see if it has met the original software specification. Tested by both beta testers and the original client.

accuracy of output To assess whether what has been produced is what was requested.

action Tells an HTML page where to send form data.

actual output The result the program actually produces.

actual parameters Parameters which are contained in a procedure or function call.

adaptive planning Agile methodology allows plans to be changed when what can be delivered differs from what was originally requested.

addition (+) See 'arithmetic(al) operations'.

address See 'memory address', 'web address'.

addressability The ability of the processor to identify each storage location.

address bar Part of a web browser which contains the URL of the page being loaded or displayed.

address bus Carries the address information from the processor to the main memory and any other devices attached to the bus. The address bus is unidirectional.

age-range (of users) The ages of the users of the information system, for instance: young child, teenager and adult.

aggregate functions A collection of functions that are used to perform calculations on a set of values across multiple rows in column. COUNT(), SUM(), MIN(), MAX() and AVG() produce one single value as an output.

Agile development methodology The process of designing a program to produce working software quickly so that the client can test it and then give feedback, at which point it can be altered and refined as required.

algorithm A series of steps to solve a problem.

alias Assigns a temporary name which is only displayed in that query.

alignment CSS term. Uses the <text-align> property to control how the text is positioned.

alphanumeric data Data consisting of text and numbers.

alt attribute Text description of image. The text is also displayed if the image cannot be found.

ALU See 'Arithmetic and logic unit'.

American Standard Code for Information Interchange (ASCII) A seven-bit code which can represent 128 characters.

analogue A signal which changes continuously rather than in steps, such as temperature and speed.

analysis The understanding of the problem and the conversion of a problem outline into a precise software specification which should include problem inputs, processes and outputs.

anchor HTML term, see '<a>'.

AND A logical operator used to combine two conditions where both must be True or False for a condition to succeed.

animation Data made up of moving graphics.

anti-virus software Anti-virus software protects a computer system against attack or infection by viruses and other types of malware.

application package (app) Software which performs a particular task.

architecture The structure of a computer system.

argument Parameter list in both the subprogram call and the subprogram itself. The order of arguments must be the same in both the subprogram call and the subprogram.

Arithmetic and logic unit (ALU) The part of the processor where all of the calculating and decision-making takes place.

arithmetic(al) operations Calculations involving numeric data. Arithmetical operators include add (+), subtract (-), multiply (*), divide (/) and exponent (^ or **).

array A list of data items of the same type grouped together using a single variable name.

array element One part of an array.

array of records Makes it possible to access a complete record's worth of data with a single reference.

ASC A standard SQL command to sort the data A–Z or 0–9 (ascending).

ASCII American Standard Code for Information Interchange.

assign values See 'assignment statement'.

assignment statement Used to give a value to a variable.

assumptions Where parts of the problem are not clear to the software developer, then assumptions should be made.

attribute An individual data element in an entity in a database.

attribute Some tags have attributes which provide additional information about an element in HTML. Attributes can contain values and are enclosed in quotes.

attribute In SVG, a file of data which stores the description of the object to be drawn.

attribute name The name given to describe a column of data.

attribute size The maximum number of characters in a text-type attribute.

attribute type Used to indicate the type of data associated with the attribute. Data types include: text, number, date, time and Boolean.

audio (media type / file format) A type of data made up of music or any sound produced by a computer.

audio HTML term, see '<audio>'.

audio quality See 'quality'.

Audio video interleave (AVI) The standard movie format for Windows®.

automate tasks One function of a program written in a scripting language, e.g. a macro, is to automate tasks for the user.

AVG() An SQL aggregate function that calculates the average value across a set of values in a column.

AVI See 'Audio video interleave'.

back button A button on a web browser which returns the user to a previously visited page.

background-color Specifies the colour of the background to be used in a particular area.

backing storage Used to store programs and data permanently.

backing storage capacity How much data may be held by the device.

backing storage device A device which allows data to be written to backing storage media.

backing storage medium An object which holds software and data, such as flash ROM.

bandwidth A measure of the quantity of data which may be carried by a communications channel at any one time.

bandwidth consumption A DOS attack which sends so many packets of data that the target organisation's service becomes overwhelmed.

base See 'number base'.

beta testing Testing the prerelease version of a program.

beta version A prerelease version of software given to selected outsiders or a version which is put on general release with users acknowledging the fact that they do not have a finished product.

binary (system) The binary number system uses two numbers: 0 and 1.

biometrics Using a person's physical characteristics in order to provide evidence of their identity.

bit A single unit in binary, either 1 or 0, is called a bit.

bit depth The number of bits used to represent a pixel in bit-mapped graphics.

bit-mapped graphics Bit-mapped packages paint pictures by changing the colour of the pixels which make up the screen display.

body HTML term, see '<body>'.

bookmark A method of recording a URL in a web browser.

Boolean (field / attribute type or variable) A Boolean variable contains only two values, e.g. true or false, 1 or 0, yes or no.

border A CSS property that sets the outside of an element's border.

bot-net A collection of computers under the control of a bot-net herder.

bot-net herder The person in control of a bot-net.

bottom-up design A design methodology which begins with writing procedures and blocks of code.

boundaries Help to clarify what the software should and should not do.

breadcrumbs A navigation method used in websites.

breakpoints A temporary halt in a program, used while debugging in order to take a snapshot of selected variables.

Brendan Eich The creator of the JavaScript® programming language.

broadband connection A high-speed connection to the internet, e.g. 50Mbps.

browser A program that allows the user to browse or surf through the World Wide Web.

browsing history A list of previously visited web pages.

brute force attack Using a fast computer to attempt to decrypt a message by trying a lot of possibilities.

buses A group of wires which connect the processor to the other parts of the computer, such as the memory.

byte A byte has eight bits.

cache memory Holds frequently accessed instructions and allows fast access to them.

capacity (of storage devices) The quantity of data that can be held on a backing storage medium.

carbon footprint The amount of greenhouse gases (including carbon dioxide and methane) produced by people or a particular activity.

cardinality One of three types of relationship: one-to-one (1:1), one-to-many (1:M) or many-to-many (M:N).

Cascading style sheet (CSS) A language used to describe the appearance of a web page.

central processing unit (CPU) The part of a mainframe computer which processes the information.

character Letter, number or symbol on the computer keyboard.

character set A list of all the characters, symbols and numbers which can be produced by a keyboard.

characters, storage of See 'ASCII' and 'Unicode'.

checksum Process performed on an uninfected program. Repeating the calculation on a suspect program allows the antivirus software to test if the program has been changed, and if so, it will issue a warning that the program may be infected with a virus.

chip A small piece of silicon used to make an integrated circuit.

circle SVG code for a circle.

class selector Allows the developer to pinpoint exactly where in the HTML document the style is to be applied and uses a full stop before the class selector name.

clear:both A CSS rule used to negate the impact of a float property.

client The person or organisation for which the software is being developed.

climate change When the temperature of the Earth's atmosphere increases, e.g. due to greenhouse gases.

clock The clock line carries a series of clock pulses at a constant rate in order to keep the processor and its related components in step with one another.

clock speed (Hz) See 'processor clock speed'.

coding Changing a program design into a program in a high-level language.

color CSS term which specifies the colour of the text to be used in a particular area.

colour depth The number of bits used to represent colours or shades of grey used in a graphic.

colour wheel A chart used to help choose complementary colours for a web page.

column Part of the structure of a relational database.

columns Part of an HTML form which dictates how many columns will be displayed in textarea input.

comma separated variable (CSV) file A type of text file that separates the values using a comma.

command-driven A type of human computer interface (HCI) in which the user must enter commands.

command language interpreter (CLI) The layer of the operating system with which the user interacts in order to give instructions to the computer; it interprets user commands.

compact flash A form of solid-state storage used in digital still cameras.

compatibility testing A type of testing based on device and browser type.

compilation error An error which is detected during the process of compilation (or translation) of the program into the object code before it is run. Compilation errors are usually syntax errors.

compiled language A computer language which is normally translated by using a compiler.

compiler A program that can translate a high-level language program into machine code in a single operation. Translates the source code into machine code, the object code.

complex conditional statement A condition consisting of two or more simple conditions, joined together by AND, OR or NOT.

complex search Searches on multiple fields or using multiple conditions.

compound key In a compound key the attributes used to uniquely identify the occurrence must consist of foreign keys.

comprehensive testing Means that all your programs should be tested as thoroughly as possible.

compression See 'data compression'.

computational constructs The parts of a programming language which are used to create a computer program.

computational thinking Thinking of a problem in such a way that makes it possible to solve it by using a computer system.

computer architecture See 'architecture'.

Computer Misuse Act 1990 This Act covers illegal activities relating to computers.

computer program The set of instructions that control how a computer works.

concatenation Joining of two or more strings.

conditional loop There are two types of conditional loop: test at start and test at end. Test at start may never be run if the condition is not met. Test at end is always run at least once.

conditional statement: IF See 'IF (conditional statement)'.

consistency A website is consistent if each page looks similar.

constructs See 'computational constructs'.

content filtering Controlling a user's access to certain web pages, normally by using a web proxy server.

context-sensitive help system A system which provides a different type of help depending on what it assumes the user is trying to do.

context-sensitive navigation Hiding those navigation features which are not needed and only displaying those required at a particular time.

control bus Made up of a number of separate wires or lines, each with its own function.

control characters These control certain operations of the computer system.

control line One of the wires which makes up the control bus, for example, address, data, reset, interrupt, clock.

control structure The three basic control structures used in procedural languages are sequence, selection and repetition/iteration.

control unit Controls all the other parts of the processor and makes sure that the program instructions of the computer are carried out in the correct order.

convert floating-point numbers to integers Removes the decimal part from a number and stores it as an integer.

convert from character to ASCII and ASCII to character Takes in a character and converts it its ASCII equivalent and vice versa.

cookies Used to identify and track visitors to web pages by storing data on the user's computer.

co-ordinates An SVG attribute to state where the object should be drawn on screen, e.g. x='50' y='50'.

copyright The right to prevent others from copying someone else's work.

Copyright, Designs and Patents Act 1988 (plagiarism) The Act covers breaches of copyright, such as illegal copying of software, music and movies.

COUNT() An SQL aggregate function that counts the number of rows in a column.

counting occurrences Used to count how many times a value appears in a list.

crash When a program abruptly stops executing due to an error.

CSS See 'Cascading Style Sheets'.

cx and cy Sets the centre point for an ellipse in SVG.

data A general term for numbers, characters, symbols, graphics and sound which are accepted and processed by a computer system.

data breach Where a company's security has been compromised and personal data has been accessed.

data bus Carries data to and from the processor, main memory and any other devices attached to the data bus. The data bus is bi-directional.

data compression This means reducing the size of a file in order to save backing storage space. There are two types of data compression, lossy and lossless.

data controller The person who determines the purposes for which and the manner in which the personal data are to be processed.

data dictionary A table which contains all the elements to be present in the database once it is implemented.

data duplication error Where two entries are the same; data in a relational database should only be entered and stored once.

data file A file containing data on backing storage or in memory. May be organised as a set of records.

data flow The movement of data (or the data flow) between subprograms is implemented by using parameters.

data integrity Data integrity rules include entity integrity and referential integrity.

data model Describes how a database should look and allows developers to check that their database design will work before it is implemented.

data modification error An error in a database caused by inserting the wrong information.

data representation How text, numbers and graphics are stored in a computer system.

data structures A way of storing and manipulating data in a program. An array is a type of data structure.

data subject An individual whose personal data is being held.

data types Include numbers, strings and arrays.

database management information system See 'database package'.

database package Software for creating and managing a database.

date (field / attribute type) Can only contain dates.

debugging The process of finding and correcting errors in a program.

declare (a variable) To assign a type and a value to a variable at the start of a program.

declare (an array) To assign a type and a size to an array at the start of a program.

decrypt To remove encryption and return to plain text.

delete A modification error caused by removing data from a database.

DELETE (FROM) A standard SQL command to remove records from a table.

denary The base ten number system.

denial of service (DOS) attack A procedure which tries to interrupt or suspend the services of a host computer connected to the internet.

DESC A standard SQL command to sort data Z–A or 9–0 (descending).

descendant selector Used to specifically identify one part of a web page to style it separately from the rest.

design Involves the careful planning of a solution to a problem using a recognised design methodology, e.g. top-down design using an appropriate design notation, such as structure diagrams or pseudocode.

design notation The way of representing the program design or algorithm.

design technique (graphical) Using diagrams to describe the design of a program, e.g. structure diagrams.

design technique (pseudocode) Using normal or everyday language to describe the design of a program.

desktop computer Used while sitting at a desk and is mains operated.

device A single item of computer hardware.

digital A signal which changes in steps and not continuously like an analogue signal.

digital (still) camera A digital camera mainly used for taking still photographs.

digital (video) camera A digital camera mainly used for taking video.

digital certificate Used is used to verify the identity of the owner of data being sent across a network.

digital signature A method of ensuring that a message or software or a digital document is valid and has not been tampered with. Calculated from the hash value of the data transmitted over a network.

directory An area on backing storage where files may be stored (also called a folder on some systems).

display A CSS property used to control the layout of a web page. Values used are block, inline and none.

distributed denial of service (DDOS) attack This takes place when many different computers carry out a DOS attack on a single host computer.

div HTML term, see '<div>'.

division (/) See 'arithmetic(al) operations'.

division by zero An execution or run-time error.

DNS See 'domain name service'.

DNS flood attack An attack that overwhelms a single DNS with a large number of valid lookup requests, making it difficult for the server to distinguish between the attack and normal heavy workload.

document object model (DOM) Contains a specific set of events that can trigger JavaScript.

document.getElementById Used to identify an element in an HTML document.

documentation A description of what each part of the program does.

documenting solutions Documentation is a description of what each part of the program does. May include a user guide and a technical guide.

DOM See 'Document object model'.

domain name Part of a URL.

domain name service (DNS) This acts like an address book for the internet.

dot notation This consists of the table name and the field required with a dot in the centre.

dots per inch (dpi) The number of dots or pixels that can be placed in an inch-long line.

draw package (vector) Vector packages work by drawing objects on the screen.

dry run The process of going through the program code manually either on paper or on screen, in order to find mistakes (usually logic errors).

efficient (solutions) Software should not use excessive resources in order for it to run properly, such as taking up a large quantity of memory or backing storage space and should make the best use of the processing power available.

efficient (use of code constructs) Use of appropriate structure in programming code, e.g. using loops rather than multiple, individual statements.

electronic communications Email messages and files that are sent over a network.

electronic mailing service (email) Sending messages from one computer to another over a network.

element Each part of an array is called an element.

elements of computer memory These are registers, cache, main memory and backing storage.

ellipse SVG code for an ellipse.

email Sending messages from one computer to another over a network.

empty (null) field A field which has no content.

encryption Putting data into a code to prevent it being seen by unauthorised users.

end-user requirements For a database, a planning document that details what the client wants to be able to do with the completed database.

end-user requirements For a website, a planning document that details what users would like to see in the website.

end-user The person, people or business that is going to be using the database.

energy use All computers use energy when they are switched on. The total amount of energy used will depend on how long the equipment is switched on and the task that is being carried out.

engine control unit (ECU) Provides precise control over the amount of fuel used in order to improve the performance of the engine and minimise the emission of harmful exhaust gases.

engine management system See 'engine control unit (ECU)'.

entity Any object we would like to model and store information about in a relational database.

entity integrity Exists if the table has a primary key which is unique and contains a value.

entity name The name given to describe a table in a database.

entity occurrence diagram Shows the relationship between entities using the occurrences within each entity.

entity relationship diagram Shows the relationship between two or more entities.

environmental impact What can happen to the environment as a result of the manufacture, use and disposal of computers.

equi-join Allows data from linked tables in the database to be queried. There must be a matching primary and foreign key in each table for this to be performed successfully.

error reporting The communication and explanation of errors in the software to the user.

evaluation An evaluation is when the software solution is reviewed against suitable criteria, such as comparing the solution with the original software specification.

exceptional test data Data which is invalid and should be rejected by the program under test.

execution (run-time) error Errors which show up during program execution. Include overflow, rounding, truncation and division by zero.

execution of lines of code in sequence The order in which things are done.

exhaustive testing Testing which involves all of the possible sets of test data and all of the program pathways.

expected output The result the program should provide.

expert user An experienced user of a website.

exponent Part of a floating point number which contains the power to which the base must be raised.

exponentiation See 'exponent'.

expressions A programming statement which will produce a value when executed.

extended ASCII code An eight-bit code which can represent 256 characters.

external (linked) styling Created as a separate file and linked using the rel attribute.

external hyperlink Takes the user to a different website, either on the same server or on a different server.

extreme test data Data which is at the ends of the acceptable range of data, on the limit(s) or boundaries of the problem. Also called boundary data.

favourites See 'bookmark'.

fetch–execute cycle The processor sets up the address bus with the required address; the processor activates the read line; the instruction is transferred from memory to processor by using the data bus (fetch); the instruction is decoded; the instruction is executed.

field A single item of data stored in a record.

field (database structure) An area on a record in a database which contains an individual piece of data.

field length (validation) Ensures the correct number of numbers or characters have been entered.

field testing Allowing users (other than the people who wrote the program) to test the program.

field type The type of data which is to be stored in a field. Field types include text, number, date, time and Boolean. You set up the field types when you create a new database.

field type (Boolean) See 'Boolean (field type or variable)'.

field type (date) See 'date (field / attribute type)'.

field type (number) See 'number (field / attribute type)'.

field type (text) See 'text (field / attribute type)'.

field type (time) See 'time (field/ attribute type)'.

field type check (validation) Ensures the correct type of data is entered.

file In a database, a collection of structured data on a particular topic.

file (external) Information held on backing storage or in memory. Files may hold data or programs.

file formats See 'standard file format'.

file operations File operations include open, create, read, write and close.

file quality See 'resolution', 'colour depth', and 'sampling rate'.

file server Provides central disk storage for users' programs and data on a network.

file size The amount of space taken up by a file when it is being held on a backing storage medium such as a hard disk or flash ROM. The factors which affect file size and quality are resolution, colour depth and sampling rate.

file transfer (attachment) Sending a file over the internet alongside an email message.

file virus Virus which attaches itself to files. It either replaces or inserts malicious code into the files. The types of files that are usually infected are those with the extensions .COM and .EXE.

fill Sets the colour of the object in SVG.

fill colour See 'fill'.

find minimum and maximum Finds the highest and lowest value in a list.

firewall A system (hardware or software) designed to prevent unauthorised access to or from a private network. Contains rules and conditions which specify what is and is not allowed to pass through.

first-party cookie Allows a website to recognise a user by remembering their log-in data and applies any settings required, such as language, shopping basket content or recent search terms.

fitness for purpose Measure of how well the software, website or database fulfils the original purpose and functional requirements which were agreed by both client and software developer.

fixed loop The purpose of a fixed loop is to repeat a set of program statements a predetermined number of times.

flash ROM A solid-state storage medium used in flash cards.

flat file A database which is contained in a single table.

float A CSS property used for positioning and layout of elements in a web page.

floating point representation A method of representing real numbers using a mantissa and an exponent.

flow chart A diagram made up of differently shaped boxes connected with arrows to show each step in a program.

font-family Specifies the font to be used in CSS.

font-size Specifies the font size of text to be used in CSS. Measured in points (pt) or pixels (px).

foreign key A field in a table which links to the primary key in a related table.

formal parameters Parameters which are contained in a procedure or subprogram definition.

formatting of input/output Arranging the position or appearance of the data on the screen when input or output is taking place.

forms dialogue interface A type of HCI in which data is entered into boxes.

forward button A button on a web browser which takes the user to the next page. Only works as intended if the user has first selected the backward button.

FROM A standard SQL command to select a table to be queried.

function Similar to a procedure and returns one or more values to a program.

function (predefined) A calculation which is built in to, or part of, a programming language.

functional requirements In database design, used to describe what the database system will do and should contain the types of operations the database should be able to perform.

functional requirements In software design, this should define inputs, processes and outputs to the program.

functional requirements In website design, the functional requirements are used to specify which pages are to be created and the function of each.

Gb See 'Gigabyte'.

GDN See 'graphical design notation'.

GDPR See 'General Data Protection Regulation'.

General Data Protection Regulation (GDPR) Covers how personal information may be held and for what purposes.

GIF See 'Graphics Interchange Format'.

gigabyte (Gb) 1024 Megabytes (1024 × 1024 × 1024 bytes).

gigahertz (GHz) A processor's clock speed is measured in Gigahertz (GHz).

global variables May be used anywhere in a program.

graphic (media type / file format) Includes diagrams, photographs and any other images.

graphical design notation (GDN) A design notation which uses lines and boxes to show the structure of a program, e.g. a structure diagram.

graphical object An image which is displayed on the screen as part of a computer program. Also known as a sprite.

Graphics Interchange Format (GIF) A standard file format for storing images, with a maximum of 256 colours.

graphics package A piece of software used for the production of, or editing, graphics.

graphics resolution The quality of the picture is determined by the resolution of the graphics available.

greenhouse gases Gases that have an environmental impact because they absorb heat and can cause climate change.

GROUP BY A standard SQL command to group together rows. Must appear before the sort order.

grouping selector Groups of HTML elements have the same CSS styles applied to them. It increases the efficiency of reading the styles rather than having the same ones repeated over and over.

guided navigation See 'faceted navigation'.

hacking The process of gaining entry to a computer system or file, usually illegally.

hand testing This is the process of going through the program code manually, in order to find mistakes.

hard copy A printed copy of your work, usually on paper.

hard disk A circular metal disk coated with magnetic material.

hard disk drive A storage device which holds a magnetic hard disk.

hardware The physical parts or devices which make up a computer system.

hardware firewall An electronic circuit in a router which prevents unauthorised access to a network from the outside.

hardware platform A particular combination of processor and operating system.

HCI See 'Human computer interface'.

head HTML term, see '<head>'.

headphones A personal sound output device.

height Sets the height of an image or video to be displayed in HTML.

hertz (Hz) Clock speed. A measure of processor speed.

hexadecimal A number system which uses base 16.

hibernate Stores the programs and data on the computer's hard drive before powering down. Hibernate consumes next-to-no power.

hierarchical A method of web page navigation.

hierarchical navigation A method of web page navigation.

high-fidelity (hi-fi) prototype A highly interactive version of the website which has a large amount of functionality.

high-level computer language A computer language that uses normal or everyday language.

high-level program code See 'high-level computer language'.

high-level (textual) language See 'high-level computer language'.

hit The results of a successful search, e.g. using a database program or a search engine.

home button A button on a browser which loads the home page.

home page The first page on a website or the URL which is loaded when a browser application is first opened.

hotspot A special area on a web page which is normally invisible when viewed in a browser; the mouse pointer changes shape when it is moved over a hotspot.

hover A CSS selector used to interact with an element when the mouse is moved over the element.

href Used with <a> to indicate the URL in HTML. The text in between the tags provides a hyperlink.

HTML See 'HyperText Mark-up Language'.

HTML events How HTML uses JavaScript® to run code when the user or browser does something in a web page.

HTML selector A way of identifying styles in internal and external stylesheets.

HTTP HyperText Transfer Protocol.

HTTPS HyperText Transfer Protocol Secure.

human computer interface (HCI) The way in which the computer and the user communicate.

hyperlink Link between World Wide Web pages, documents or files. Activated by clicking on text which acts as a button, or on a particular area of the screen like a graphic.

HyperText Mark-up Language (HTML) Used to create web pages which may be viewed by using a web browser.

Hz Clock speed. See 'hertz'.

ICO Information Commissioner's Office.

icon Symbol or picture on a screen; part of a graphical user interface.

id Part of an HTML form used to identify each of the options in radio buttons.

ID selector Used to identify and style one element in an HTML document and uses the hash or octothorpe (#) character to identify each element to be styled. Can only be used once in an HTML document.

identifiers The name of something in a program, e.g. the name of a variable, like counter.

identity theft When someone pretends to be someone else in order to carry out fraud.

IF (conditional statement) Suitable for use when a single selection (or a limited number of selections) is to be made.

img HTML term, see '<img>'.

implementation Changing the program design into instructions that the computer can understand and the production of internal documentation.

in parameters Data structures (such as variables) which are only passed into subprograms to be used.

inconsistent A database which contains data duplication or other errors.

indentation A structured listing is a program listing which uses indentations (formatting) to show some of the structure of the program.

independent test group A group which tests software independently of the company which wrote the software and is able to provide an unbiased opinion.

index/element number A number which identifies a single element of an array.

individual's rights GDPR gives data subjects a right of access to their personal data and to have it amended if it is incorrect.

infinite loop A loop which never stops and may cause the computer system to 'hang'.

information Data with structure.

inline styling Used within HTML tags. The style attribute is included in the line of code you wish to style.

innerHTML Inserts the content of the quotation marks in the web page in place of the text that is already present.

input To enter data into a computer system.

input device A device which allows data to be entered into a computer system.

input–process–output The sequence of operations carried out in a computer system.

input validation An algorithm used to check that data input is within a certain (acceptable) range.

inputs (software) These should clearly state what data must be provided for the software to function.

INSERT (INTO) A standard SQL command to add new records to a SQL database.

insert A modification error in a database caused by inserting the wrong information.

integer data A subset of real data which includes only whole numbers, either positive or negative.

integer variable A variable which can only hold either positive or negative whole numbers, without a fractional part.

intelligent system A computer system which is programmed in such a manner that it can emulate and automate some intelligent aspects of human behaviour.

interactivity The 'feel' of a web page, e.g. the feedback that is received from selection.

internal commentary So-called because it is contained inside the program itself, as part of the language statements. It has no effect on the running of a program. Helps to explain what the code is doing throughout the program.

internal (embedded) styling Defined in the <head> tag of a website and used to apply to the whole page.

internal hyperlink Takes the user to another page within the same website.

internet A wide area network (WAN) spanning the globe. It can be thought of as many different, smaller networks connected together.

internet service provider (ISP) A company that provides a host computer to which the user can connect in order to access the internet.

interpreted language A language which is translated and run one instruction at a time.

interpreter Changes one line of a high-level language program into machine code and then executes it before moving on to the next line, each time the program is run.

ISP See 'internet service provider'.

iteration Repeating a section of code contained in a loop.

iterative Any of the steps can be revisited at any point in the life-cycle of the development process if new information becomes available and changes need to be made.

iterative development process A series of stages for the development of software: analysis, design, implementation, testing, documentation and evaluation.

Joint Photographic Expert Group (JPEG) A standard file format for the storage of graphic images. 24-bit graphic format which allows 16.7 million colours and uses lossy compression.

JPEG See 'Joint Photographic Expert Group'.

KB See 'Kilobyte'.

key Made up of a long string of random bits which allows the sender to encrypt a message and the receiver to decrypt a message.

key field Used to uniquely identify a record in a database.

keyword A word which is used to search for an item in a database or on the World Wide Web.

keywords (software) Reserved words in programming languages to perform specific tasks.

kilobyte (Kb) One Kilobyte has 1024 bytes.

least significant bit (LSB) The right-most and smallest value bit in a binary number.

length A predefined function that returns the number of characters in a string.

li HTML term, see '<li>'.

LIKE Allows SQL to use wildcard characters % and _.

line SVG code for a line.

line colour See 'stroke'.

line width See 'stroke-width'.

linear A method of web page navigation.

linear search Used to find an item of data (the target value) in a list.

link HTML term, see '<link>'.

linked tables Tables in a relational database may be linked by using key fields.

linker Used to join a module from a software library to a program.

linking error When a program is incorrectly linked to a subroutine or module library.

lists HTML term, see '<li>', '<ol>', '<ul>'.

list-style-type A CSS property used to style the elements in a list, e.g. circle, bullet, none, etc.

local variable Defined only for use in one subprogram.

logic error Mistakes in the design of the program. They only show up when you run the program because the program does not do what it is supposed to do, e.g. it produces the wrong results.

logical data See 'Boolean (field attribute type / variable)'.

logical operators The set of logical operators includes AND, OR and NOT. They are used to link two or more conditions to create a complex condition.

loop counter Part of a loop which determines how many times it will repeat.

loop/iteration/repetition A programming construct used to allow a process to take place over and over again.

lossless compression Compression which does not lose any data from the original.

lossy compression Compression which removes some of the original data.

loudspeaker A sound output device.

low-fidelity (lo-fi) prototype Translates basic ideas from a wireframe into a basic testable product. It can be created using pen and paper but can also be produced electronically using either specialist prototyping software (with templates) or presentation software.

machine code The computer's own language. It is written in binary (1 and 0).

main memory Consists of a number of storage locations, each with a unique address. Made up of Random Access Memory (RAM) and Read Only Memory (ROM).

main steps In an algorithm, these become the main program and the refinements of each sub-problem become the code in the procedures.

maintainability How easy it is to correct or update the software in future.

maintenance Involves making changes in the form of corrections or updates to the program at some time in the future and is made easier by good practice in software development.

malware Software that has been deliberately created to disrupt the operation of a computer system or to gain illegal access to it in order to gather information.

mantissa In a floating point number, the mantissa holds the digits of a number, and the size of the mantissa determines the precision of the number.

manual testing Testing a program by hand without using a computer system.

many-to-many (cardinality) A relationship where many records in a table relate to many records in another, joined table (denoted by M:N).

margin A CSS property used to specify the space around an element.

mark-up language A programming language used for describing how text and other media are presented to the user.

MAX() An SQL aggregate function that returns the highest value in a column.

maxlength Part of an HTML form which defines the number of characters that can be entered.

MB See 'Megabyte'.

meaningful identifier A name used for any part of a program, such as the name of a subprogram or subroutine (procedure or function) and not just limited to variable names.

meaningful variable name Contains one or more words which describe it. Using meaningful variable names is a good way of improving the readability of a program.

media types Include graphics, sound, text and video.

media types (sound) See 'sound (media type)'.

media types (text) See 'text (media type)'.

media types (video) See 'video (media type)'.

megabyte (Mb) One Megabyte has 1024 Kilobytes.

megapixel 1024×1024 pixels (approximately 1 million).

memory address A binary number used to identify a storage location in main memory.

memory address register A register in the processor which is connected to the address bus.

memory capacity The amount of data that may be held.

memory data register A register in the processor which is connected to the data bus.

memory location See 'storage location'.

memory (RAM) The part of a computer where the data is held while it is being processed and the programs are held while they are being run.

memory read operation The steps involved are: the processor sets up the address bus with the required memory address; the control unit of the processor activates the read line on the control bus; the contents of the particular storage location in memory are released onto the data bus and are copied into one of the processor's registers. If it is an instruction, it is decoded and executed (carried out).

memory write operation The steps involved are: the processor sets up the address bus with the required memory address; the processor sets up the data bus with the value to be written to memory; the control unit of the processor activates the write line on the control bus; the value on the data bus is transferred to the required storage location in the computer's memory.

menu A list on screen from which choices may be made by the user.

menu-driven See 'menu selection interface'.

menu selection interface A type of HCI in which choices may be made from menus.

metadata Data about the data that is to be stored.

microprocessor The processor of a microcomputer.

MIN() An SQL aggregate function that returns the lowest value in a column.

min=…max= Part of an HTML form used to perform a range check.

MIPS (Millions of Instructions Per Second) A measure of the performance of a computer system.

modification errors Include insert, delete and update.

modular design A method of organising a large computer program into self-contained parts called modules. Top-down and bottom-up design are both forms of modular design.

modularity When a program is designed and written, it is divided into smaller sections called subprograms or subroutines.

module High-level procedural languages use two types of modules or subprograms. These are procedures and functions.

module libraries Predefined routines which support and speed up the software development process. Using a module library speeds up the whole software development process because time is saved in design, implementation testing and documentation.

modulus The remainder after integer division.

monitor An output device which accepts a video signal directly from a computer and displays the output on a screen.

most significant bit (MSB) The left-most and largest value bit in a binary number.

Motion Picture Expert Group (MPEG) Video file format. MPEG-1, MPEG-2 and MPEG-4 (MP4) are all standards used to store video.

mouse events See 'onmouseout', 'onmouseover' and 'onclick'.

MP3 (MPEG-1 Audio Layer-3) File format which is compressed to around one tenth of the size of the original file, yet preserves the quality.

MPEG See 'Motion Picture Expert Group'.

MPEG-4 (MP4) A compressed video format.

multi-core processor A computer containing more than one processor core.

multimedia pages Pages that contain text, images and video.

multiple Part of an HTML form used to allow selection of more than one item from a drop-down list.

multiple tables More than one table in a database file.

multiplication (x) See 'arithmetic(al) operations'.

name Part of an HTML form which identifies this part of the form when it is sent to be processed.

nanosecond 10^{-9} seconds.

navigation How the user finds their way around a website.

navigation methods Include browser features, menus, searching, hyperlinks, context-sensitive navigation, breadcrumbs, guided navigation, tag clouds and site maps.

navigation structure The way in which the pages or screens in a website are arranged.

navigational links Links to other pages both in the website and to other pages.

nested IF IF statement that is contained inside other IF statements.

nested loop Loop which is contained inside other loops.

network A linked set of computer systems that are capable of sharing programs and data and sending messages between them.

normal test data Data within the limits that a program should be able to deal with.

NOT Used to negate a condition.

novice user A beginner.

number (field / attribute type) Only stores numbers.

number base The number of different digits which may be used at each place value, including 0. Base 2 has two digits, 1 and 0. Base 10 has ten digits, 0 to 9.

numeric (float) See 'numeric (real)'.

numeric (integer) Whole positive or negative numbers.

numeric (real) All numbers both whole and fractional.

numeric variable A variable which can hold a number that may have a fractional part.

object The item of data which is involved in a process.

object attributes Numbers used to define the features of a vector graphic image.

object code A machine code program produced as the result of translation by a compiler.

offline Not connected to a remote computer system or a network.

ol HTML term, see '<ol>'.

onclick A JavaScript event.

one-dimensional (1D) array An array with only one subscript.

one-to-many (cardinality) A relationship where one record in a table relates to many records in another, joined table (denoted by 1:M).

one-to-one (cardinality) A relationship where one record in a table directly relates to one record in another, joined table (denoted by 1:1).

online Connected to a remote computer system or a network.

online help Help which is available in the form of information screens when using a computer program.

onmouseout A JavaScript event.

onmouseover A JavaScript event.

operating system A program that controls the entire operation of the computer and any devices which are attached to it.

operation A process which is carried out on an item of data.

operators See 'logical operators' and 'arithmetic(al) operators'.

OR (logical operator) Used to combine two conditions where one must be True or False for a condition to succeed.

ORDER BY A standard SQL command to determine the order in which the data should be sorted and displayed.

orphan page One which is not linked to any other pages in a website.

out parameters Variables which are passed out of subprograms are known as out parameters.

output Data passed out of a computer system.

output device A device which allows data to be displayed or passed out of a computer system.

outputs (software) The display of the result of a program.

overflow error When a number is too large to fit in a storage location.

padding A CSS property used to specify the space around the content of an element.

page See 'web page'.

paint package Bit-mapped packages paint pictures by changing the colour of the pixels which make up the screen display.

paragraph HTML term, see '<p>'.

parallel 1D array Two or more separate one-dimensional arrays that are used to store a set of related data by using the same element number or index.

parameter Information about a data item being supplied to a subprogram when it is called into use.

parameter passing (in, out) When a subprogram is used, the calling program must pass parameters to it.

partial transparency Not completely transparent. PNG images may be partially transparent.

pathname A name used to identify a file or a web page in a hierarchical directory structure or URL.

PB See 'Petabyte'.

permanent memory Another name for ROM (Read Only Memory).

personas Fictitious users which are created to accurately represent the individuals or audience who are likely to be using the website and can be related to the age and experience of the user.

petabyte (PB) One Petabyte has 1024 Terabytes.

PHP A general purpose scripting language for web development. Can be used in conjunction with SQL for form validation.

picture element Pixel. A tiny dot used to make up a picture on a screen.

pixel Picture element. A tiny dot used to make up a picture on a screen.

pixellation When an image is enlarged so that the pixels become visible.

platform A particular combination of processor and operating system.

PNG See 'Portable Network Graphic'.

points Sets the points for drawing a polygon in SVG.

polygon SVG code for a polygon.

portable devices Laptop computers and smartphones that may be operated while on the move.

Portable Network Graphic (PNG) Incorporates the advantages of GIF files, without the limitations, i.e. more than 256 colours may be represented.

positive integer A non-negative whole number.

positive real number A non-negative number with a fractional part.

precision of floating point numbers Increasing the number of bytes used for the mantissa will increase the precision of the number being stored.

predefined function A function that has already been created and is part of or built in to a programming language. See 'parameters'.

prepopulated database A database which already contains data.

presence check (validation) Checks to make sure that a field has not been left empty.

primary key A field used to uniquely identify a record in a database.

printer An output device used to produce a printout or a hard copy of the output from a computer.

private key A key used to decrypt data encrypted by a public key to which it is mathematically related.

problem description The problem you are given to solve, described in your own words.

procedure Produces an effect in a program.

procedure call Using a procedure in a program.

process This should determine what has to be done with the data entered.

processor The main part of the computer. It is made up of the control unit, the arithmetic and logic unit (ALU) and the registers. The processor is the part of the computer where all the sorting, searching, calculating and decision-making goes on.

processor clock Produces a series of electronic pulses at a very high rate.

processor clock speed Measured in Gigahertz (GHz).

program See 'computer program'.

program design The process of planning the solution.

program listing A printout or hard copy of the program code.

program maintenance Changing or updating a program, often some time after it has been written.

program or structure syntax error Happens when you have made a mistake in the structure of your program, such as incorrect use of a control structure.

programmer A person who writes computer programs.

project manager The person in charge of the software development process for a particular program.

properties Elements assigned to a CSS object. Include changing font size, family, colour and alignment and changing background colours.

protocol A set of rules that determines how something is to be done.

prototype (software) A working version of (parts of) a program with limited functionality.

prototype (website) Allows designer to demonstrate to the client how their website will look and feel before it has been created.

pseudocode Uses normal or everyday language to describe the design of a program.

public key A key mathematically related to the private key in public key encryption.

public key encryption A way of encrypting data to be sent over a network using private and public keys.

purpose What the software should do when it is being used by the client.

quality How closely a file matches when compared to the original.

query Used to search database tables for specified information but can also be used to sort the data contained in the tables into either ascending or descending order.

RAM See 'Random Access Memory'.

random A predefined function that generates a random number

between two numbers that are specified.

Random Access Memory (RAM) A set of microchips that stores data temporarily. The data is lost when the computer is switched off.

range check (validation) Keeps the data within given limits.

read line Part of the control bus. The read line is used in the memory read operation and in the fetch–execute cycle.

Read Only Memory (ROM) One or more microchips that stores data permanently. The data is not lost when the computer is switched off.

readability (web) A website is readable when it is easy to read and understand. May be tested by looking at the level of difficulty of the language used.

readability (of code) How easy it is for another person to understand your program code. See 'internal commentary'.

real (float) data Real data includes ALL numbers, both whole and fractional.

real (float) numbers, storage of See 'floating point representation'.

real (float) variable A variable which can hold a number that may have a fractional part.

record (database structure) A collection of structured data in a database on a particular person or thing, containing one or more fields.

record (program) Related data in a program stored together in one entity regardless of data type.

rect SVG code for a rectangle.

referential integrity Ensures that a value in one table references an existing value in another table.

refinements The main steps in the algorithm become the main program and the refinements of each sub-problem become the code in the procedures.

registers Used to hold data being processed, program instructions being run and memory addresses to be accessed.

rel Specifies the type of file being linked in CSS.

relational database When a database contains links between tables, it is referred to as a relational database.

relational operation Use relational operators to compare data and produce an answer of true or false. Relational operators include equals (=), compared to (==), greater than (>), less than (<), greater than or equal to (>=), less than or equal to (<=) and not equal to (≠, <> or !=).

relationship A link between the primary key in one table and the foreign key in another table.

relative addressing If the URL points to a page within the same website (i.e. internal), then it is known as a relative URL (relative addressing).

relative vertical positioning Where objects are placed relative to each other in web design.

reliability How well software operates without stopping due to design faults.

repetition Doing something over again, e.g. in a loop, either conditional or fixed.

report Formatted result of a database query.

required Part of an HTML form which is a presence check.

requirements specification See 'software specification'.

resolution The quality of the picture is determined by the resolution of the graphics available. The smaller the size of the pixels, the finer the detail that can be displayed on the screen.

resolution dependence When the resolution of an image is fixed in a bit-mapped package and cannot be scaled up without losing quality. See 'pixellation'.

resolution independence In a vector graphics package, the resolution of the screen has no effect on the resolution of the printout.

resource starvation Resource starvation attacks prevent availability by consuming services or processing power of the victim that are required by legitimate users.

restricted choice Gives users a list of options to choose from and so limits the input to pre-approved answers.

return values See 'functions'.

RGB (red green blue) colour system Used in HTML for the colours on a web page. Represents colour by using pixels in groups of three, one each for red, green and blue.

robustness A robust program should be able to cope with errors during execution without failing.

ROM See 'Read Only Memory'.

round A predefined function that returns a real or float number to the number of decimal places stated after the decimal point.

ROUND A standard SQL command to select the number of places after a decimal point.

rounding error An error caused by incorrectly rounding up or down.

row Part of the structure of a relational database.

rows Part of an HTML form which dictates how many rows will be displayed in textarea input.

running total within a loop The process of adding a sequence of numbers to a 'total' variable as a loop progresses.

run-time error See 'execution (run-time) error'.

rx and ry Sets the radii for an ellipse in SVG.

sample data Consists of digitally recorded sound data (e.g. MP3) and video data (e.g. a video clip – MPEG)

sampling depth The number of bits that are used for each measurement.

sampling rate The number of times in one second that measurements of the sound are taken.

scalable vector graphics (SVG) A method of representing vector graphics on a computer system.

scenarios Open-ended tasks in which the user has to perform a series of tasks based on a situation.

scope (project) The scope of a project should state clearly and concisely what the software must do, i.e. specific project goals. It should also state: start and end dates; deliverables, the design of the software, the software itself, results of testing and test plan.

scope (variable) The scope of a variable is the range of statements for which a variable is valid. The scope of a global variable is the whole program. The scope of a local variable is a subprogram.

screen The part of a monitor which displays the output.

script A program written in a scripting language.

scripting language A programming language that allows the user to carry out or automate tasks. Examples include JavaScript, VBScript® and AppleScript®.

scroll Moving the display on the screen using the cursor keys, mouse or track pad.

search Allows you to look for specific information in a database or on the World Wide Web.

search (complex) A complex search searching on multiple fields or using multiple conditions.

search (simple) A simple search performed on only one field with a single condition.

search criteria The condition(s) used when a search is performed.

searching Looking for an item using a database program or a search engine and perhaps one or more keywords.

secure A computer system is secure if it is unable to be accessed by an unauthorised person, and is not affected by malware.

security A method of making sure that data is private or that only authorised people can see the data, e.g. using passwords, encryption and physical security.

security precautions Include encryption and firewalls.

security risks Include hacking, malware and loss of data.

SELECT A standard SQL command to select fields to be displayed.

selected Part of an HTML form used to define a preselected option in a drop-down list.

selection Making a choice or deciding something. Based on one or more conditions, used together with a control structure such as IF.

selection construct An IF statement in a high-level programming language is an example of a selection construct.

selector (descendant) Used to specifically identify one part of a web page to style it separately from the rest.

selector (grouping) Groups of html elements have the same CSS styles applied to them. It increases the efficiency of reading the styles rather than having the same ones repeated over and over.

semantic element An HTML tag which clearly describes the area of the web page in a way that is easy to understand.

sentinel (terminating) value Often used to end a conditional loop.

sequence The order in which things are done.

sequential navigation (linear) Useful for processes that may be followed in a set order, like reading a story or making a purchase.

server A computer that handles requests for data, email, file transfers, and other network services from other computers.

simple condition A condition made using only one relational operator, for example age=18, average_temperature < 15.

simple search Searches on only one field with a single condition.

simple statement A condition made using only one relational operator, for example age=18, average_temperature < 15.

single stepping Going through a program one line at a time, usually in order to find mistakes. A feature of a trace facility.

site map One navigation method for a website.

size Part of an HTML form which defines the size of a text element.

sleep Stores the programs and data you are currently working with in RAM. Sleep mode reduces how much power is consumed but RAM requires some power so that it can maintain its contents.

smart motorway A motorway which uses traffic management methods to increase capacity and reduce congestion in busy areas.

smart thermostat Uses sensors and intelligent programming to learn how your home heats up and your preferred temperature in particular rooms at different times throughout the day.

smart traffic lights Incorporate sensors which can identify different road users and adapt the traffic management system to their needs.

software The programs run by the hardware of the computer.

software developer Any person involved in the software development process, such as the programmer.

software development process A series of stages for the development of software: analysis, design, implementation, testing, documentation and evaluation.

software firewall Contains rules and conditions which specify what is and is not allowed to pass through.

software library Made up of a number of subprograms, called library modules, which are held on backing storage.

software requirements See 'system requirements'.

software specification A precise description of the problem.

solution The answer to a problem.

sort on more than one field A complex sort.

sort on one field A simple sort.

sort order See 'sorting'.

sorting Allows the user to arrange the records in a database into a certain alphabetic or numeric order, such as: ascending order (A to Z or 0 to 9) or descending order (Z to A or 9 to 0).

sound (media type) Includes music or any other noise produced by a computer.

source code The original high-level language program.

sprint A short, fixed time period (typically two weeks) after which a prototype is ready to be tested by the client.

sprite See 'graphical objects'.

SQL See 'Structured query language'.

SRAM (Static Random Access Memory) SRAM is faster to access than DRAM, and does not need to be constantly refreshed.

src Filename of image in HTML. This can be a pathname or URL.

standard algorithms These include input validation, linear search, counting occurrences and finding minimum and maximum.

standard file format A way of storing data so that it can be understood by and transferred between different application packages.

start-stop (stop-start) systems A (petrol or diesel-powered) car is stationary and out of gear and cuts the engine in order to reduce fuel consumption and emissions.

statement syntax error A misspelling of a keyword, like typing rpint instead of print or reapeat instead of repeat.

stepwise refinement Taking each step and breaking it down as far as possible, until each step can be turned into a single line of program code.

storage location An item of data is stored in memory in a storage location. Each storage location has its own unique address in the computer's main memory.

storyboard A series of still drawings that map out a proposed story over a number of separate panels.

string A list of characters.

string operations Include joining strings, known as concatenation, and selecting parts of strings, known as substrings.

string variables A structured variable which holds one or more characters.

stroke Sets the colour of the line to be drawn in SVG.

stroke-width Sets the thickness of the line to be drawn in SVG.

structure diagram A diagram made up of different-shaped boxes containing text and linked by lines. Usually used to explain the structure of a computer program.

structure syntax error Happens when you have made a mistake in the structure of your program, such as incorrect use of a control structure. May be detected by examining or proofreading a structured listing.

structured listing A formatted display or printout of the program code.

Structured query language (SQL) A programming language intended for the creation and manipulation of relational databases.

style A CSS attribute included in the line of code to be styled.

subject rights GDPR gives data subjects a right of access to their personal data and to have it amended if it is incorrect.

sub-problem Part of a problem identified in the top-down design process and produced as a result of stepwise refinement, e.g. a procedure or a function.

subprogram See 'sub-problem'.

subscript Each element in an array is identified by the variable name and a subscript.

substrings Involves selecting parts of strings.

subtraction (-) See 'arithmetic(al) operations'.

SUM() An SQL aggregate function that sums/adds all the values in a column.

SVG See 'scalable vector graphics'.

syntax The way in which you give instructions to the computer.

syntax error Occurs when the syntax, or rules of the programming language, are broken. A mistake in a programming instruction, e.g. PTRIN instead of PRINT.

system error Occurs when the computer system (rather than just the program that you are working on) stops working properly. Windows™ users will no doubt be familiar with the so-called 'blue screen of death'.

system requirements To find out which platform a particular item of software requires, it is necessary to consult the system requirements.

systematic testing Systematic testing involves using a test plan.

tabbed browsing A method of opening several web pages in a single window.

table (database) A set of data items in a database organised in rows and columns like a spreadsheet.

table (test data) Test data is used to test a program

tablet computer A flat computer with a large touch-sensitive LCD screen as the main input and output device. It is powered from batteries and may be operated while travelling.

tag Each part of an HTML document is separated by a tag. Each tag has a start like this <> and an end tag like this </>.

tag cloud A list of terms, either displayed with numbers or in

differently sized typefaces to show popularity.

target audience The people who will use a website.

TB See 'Terabyte'.

TDN See 'textual design notation'.

template A ready-made blank document, with placeholders for items like text and graphics. Using a template can speed up the creation of a document, because much of the page layout has already been done for you.

terabyte (TB) One Terabyte has 1024 Gigabytes.

terminating (sentinel) value Often used to end a conditional loop.

test cases Used when specific features of the website need to be tested and a series of instructions need to be followed to complete the task. These test cases would be created from the initial user requirements.

test data Used to test that a program works. There are three different types of test data: normal, extreme and exceptional.

test plan Outlines what you are trying to test and how you are going to do it, e.g. what program (or module) is being tested; what the program (or module) should do; list suitable test data; expected results from the test data.

test report Summarises the results of testing a program.

test table A table containing test data.

testing Ensures that: a database does not contain any mistakes and produces the correct results when queried; a computer program does not contain any mistakes and that it works as intended; and a website displays correctly and navigation works as intended.

testing (database) Ensures that a database does not contain any mistakes and produces the correct results when queried.

testing (software) Ensures that a computer program does not contain any mistakes and that it works as intended.

testing (web) Ensures that a website displays correctly and navigation works as intended.

text Any character which appears on a computer keyboard is text. The most common file format used for storing text is ASCII.

text-align Controls how the text is aligned in CSS: center, left, right or justify.

text editor Allows source code to be entered and edited.

text (field / attribute type) Used to hold letters, numbers and symbols.

textual design notation (TDN) Pseudocode is an example of a textual design notation.

third-party cookie See 'tracking cookies'.

this A JavaScript event which refers to the object being handled.

time (field / attribute type) Can hold hours, minutes and seconds.

title HTML term, see '<title>'.

title attribute Required in addition to alt in some browsers when an image cannot be displayed.

top-down design Involves looking at the overall problem and breaking it down into a series of steps.

touch-sensitive screen / touchscreen Useful when it is not appropriate to use a mouse. A screen is an output device, so a touch-sensitive screen is both an input and an output device.

trace facility Allows the programmer to follow the path through a program at the same time as it is being run. A trace facility also allows the user to go through the program one line at a time. This is called single 'stepping'.

trace table A list of all the variables in the part of a program under examination one line at a time.

trace tool Allows the user to go through the program one line at a time.

track pad / touchpad A flat touch-sensitive area used instead of a mouse to control a pointer. Movements of the user's finger over the plate control the movement of the pointer on the screen.

tracking cookies Collect information about the user that may be used in marketing, such as age, origin, gender and user behaviour on the web.

translation See 'translation of high-level program code'.

translation of high-level program code Converting a computer program from one language to another, e.g. from a high-level language to machine code.

translator Converts a computer program from one language to another (for example, from a high-level language to a low-level language), e.g. compiler, interpreter.

translator programs Compilers and interpreters are types of translator programs.

transparency The degree to which a graphic may be seen through.

traversing a 1D array Inputting or outputting data to and from an array.

trojan (horse) A program that appears to be safe, but hidden inside is usually something harmful, like a worm or a virus.

true colour Represented on a computer system using 24 bits per pixel, giving a total range of 16,777,216 different colours.

truncation error Truncation means shortening a number to a given number of decimal places. A truncation error is the difference between the original number and the truncated number.

two's complement A method of representing integer numbers in binary. To change a binary number

into its negative counterpart, change all the ones to zeros, all the zeros to ones, and add one.

two-state machine A computer system is known as a two-state machine because the processing and storage devices in a computer system have one feature in common: they have two states only. These two states are 'on' and 'off' and are represented using the digits 1 for 'on' and 0 for 'off'.

txt file Contain only plain, unformatted text.

type Part of an HTML form which identifies the type of input. This can be text, number, textarea, radio and submit.

ul HTML term, see '<ul>'.

UML Unified Modelling Language.

Unicode (Universal Character Set) Designed to represent the writing schemes of all of the world's major languages.

Uniform Resource Locator (URL) A unique address for a specific file available on the internet (web address).

unique value A primary key has a unique value which identifies individual records in a database.

units of storage A quantity of data. The smallest unit of storage is a bit (1 or 0). Other units include: byte, KB, MB, GB, TB, PB.

UPDATE (… SET) A standard SQL command to change parts or all of a record.

update (modification error) An error caused by updating data in a database.

URL See 'Uniform Resource Locator'.

usability When evaluating the usability in your solution, you should consider the nature of the HCI, help screens, instruction screens, visual appeal, screen layout and prompts for the user.

usability testing How easy the website is to use and achieve specific goals with actual users or

the clients who have commissioned the website.

USB flash memory The media contained within a USB flash ROM drive.

USB flash ROM drive A solid-state storage device containing flash ROM. It connects to the computer via the USB interface.

use energy See 'energy use'.

user-defined function A function which is created within a program rather than being already present or predefined as part of the normal syntax of a programming language.

user friendly Programs that are easy to learn to use and help you understand as you are using them are called user-friendly programs.

user interface The nature of the HCI, help screens, instruction screens, visual appeal, screen layout and prompts for the user.

user interface design The way in which the layout of the screen is designed.

user interface requirements Visual layout, navigational links, consistency, interactivity and readability.

user story How a project is broken down into what the client requires.

validation A check to make sure that an item of data is sensible and allowable. A range check is one way of validating data.

value Part of an HTML form which identifies which radio button was selected when it is sent to be processed.

VALUES A standard SQL command to identify both the field names and values to be inserted into a table.

variable The name that a software developer uses to identify the contents of a storage location.

variable type error When a value of the wrong type is assigned to a variable, for example, a numeric variable cannot hold a character.

vector graphic (object-oriented) Vector packages work by drawing objects on the screen. Vector graphics are stored as list of attributes, rather than as a bit map.

video Data made up of a sequence of moving or 'live' action images.

video (media type/file format) HTML term, see '<video>'.

virus A program which can destroy or cause damage to data stored on a computer system. A virus infects other host files and is distributed along with them.

virus checker An anti-virus program.

visual layout The way a program or website looks on a monitor/screen.

volatile memory Memory whose contents are erased when the power is switched off, for example, RAM.

walled garden A closed system where the service provider has total control over content, e.g. phone apps.

watchpoint A watchpoint is used for following the value of one particular variable. This pauses execution when a particular value is reached or if a value is changed in a variable.

Waterfall life-cycle A series of stages for the development of software: analysis, design, implementation, testing, documentation and evaluation.

Waterfall model See 'Waterfall life-cycle'.

WAV WAVeform audio file format is the native sound format for Windows.

web address See 'Uniform Resource Locator (URL)'.

web browser A program that allows the user to browse or surf through the World Wide Web.

web content See copyright'.

web navigation A type of navigation through a website.

web page A single page of information on a website.

web proxy A server used to access web pages requested by other computers on a network.

web safe colours A set of colours for web pages which will show up correctly in a web browser.

website A collection of related web pages that may be accessed from a single home page.

website structure The way in which the pages in a website are arranged.

What You See Is What You Get (WYSIWYG) What you see on a screen is exactly the same as the way it will be printed.

WHERE A standard SQL command which identifies a condition to be met.

white space (programming) In programming, adding white space improves the readability of a program because it makes it easier to see where one section of code ends and another begins.

white space (visual layout) The part of the screen that does not contain any content. It helps to focus the reader's attention on what is important in the page.

Wide Area Network (WAN) Covers a large geographical area, such as a country or a continent.

width Sets the width of an image or video to be displayed in HTML.

wi-fi The Wireless Fidelity Alliance standard for wireless networking.

wildcard (character) The wildcard operator * represents

any information. This allows users to search for results with similar information, such as names beginning with Jo*.

wildcard (SQL) Used in SQL to find a specific pattern in a column: % is for a string of any length; _ is for a match on a single character (* and ? respectively in MS Access).

WIMP environment A type of human computer interface which uses Windows, Icons, Menus and Pointers.

windows Areas of the screen set aside for a particular purpose, such as displaying files or documents.

wireframe (software) A diagram or sketch of the input and output screens in a software with which the user will interact.

wireframe (website) A design method for websites which uses labelled blocks to show the layout of the content of each page on the website without any of the actual content of the page being present.

wire-framing See 'wireframe'.

word The number of bits that can be processed by the processor in a single operation. Each storage location can hold a quantity of data called a word.

World Wide Web (WWW) A collection of information held in multimedia form on the internet.

worm Malware that can replicate itself from computer to computer usually across a network.

write line Part of the control bus, used to send a signal from the control unit to the main memory.

WWW See 'World Wide Web'.

WYSIWYG See 'What You See Is What You Get'.

zombie army See 'bot-net'.